Information and Communication Technologies

Visions and Realities

Information and Communication Technologies

Visions and Realities

Edited by William H. Dutton

with the assistance of Malcolm Peltu

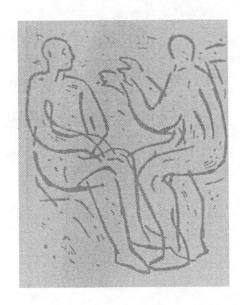

Oxford University Press

This book has been printed digitally and produced in a standard specification in order to ensure its continuing availability

OXFORD
UNIVERSITY PRESS

Great Clarendon Street, Oxford OX2 6DP

Oxford University Press is a department of the University of Oxford.
It furthers the University's objective of excellence in research, scholarship,
and education by publishing worldwide in

Oxford New York

Auckland Bangkok Buenos Aires Cape Town Chennai
Dar es Salaam Delhi Hong Kong Istanbul Karachi Kolkata
Kuala Lumpur Madrid Melbourne Mexico City Mumbai Nairobi
São Paulo Shanghai Singapore Taipei Tokyo Toronto
with an associated company in Berlin

Oxford is a registered trade mark of Oxford University Press
in the UK and in certain other countries

Published in the United States
by Oxford University Press Inc., New York

ISBN 0-19-877459-1
ISBN 0-19-877496-6 (pbk)

Preface

Major advances in information and communication technologies (ICTs) have been among the most exciting and far-reaching developments in science and technology in the late twentieth century. Personal computers, the Internet, video games, cellular phones, electronic banking, and satellite television are just a few of the ICT innovations that have become an intrinsic part of modern life. The rapid pace of ICT innovation and diffusion will be maintained well into the twenty-first century as computing, telecommunications, and broadcast and print media continue to converge on common digital-based techniques.

This technical revolution has generated vigorous debate around a number of 'hot button' issues, such as concerns over employment, privacy, and the growing gaps between information 'haves' and 'have nots'. However, it has also generated many visions which have been focused on concepts like the *information society*, *information superhighway*, *virtual organizations*, and *post-Fordist industrial processes*. These visions have driven government policies, the opening of new product and services markets, and the development of new ways of living, working, and doing business.

About This Book

Most books about ICT-related visions look primarily to future technological breakthroughs and what they will mean to business and society. This book critically examines the visions and realities that have already shaped technological change in order to provide practical insights into how the long-term social and economic implications of ICTs can be addressed. In doing so, it provides much evidence to help readers understand the ways individuals, households, schools, organizations, governments, and regions are shaping technologies—as well as being shaped by them. Most importantly, this journey into the social and economic complexities surrounding ICTs not only challenges prevailing wisdom about the effects of ICTs, it also provides direction for policy and practice to achieve the opportunities presented by the profusion of ICT innovations.

Fruits of a Decade of Research

This book is derived from the ten-year Programme on Information and Communication Technologies (PICT), a major initiative launched in 1985 by the UK Economic and Social Research Council (ESRC) to study the long-term social and economic implications of ICTs. PICT brought together sociologists, geographers, economists, political scientists, technologists, communication specialists, and other scholars in collaborative multidisciplinary teams. It involved over a hundred researchers in six university centres, who worked on more than sixty projects that encompassed research on the production, utilization, consumption, and governance dimensions of ICTs.

As well as contributing to the development of better theoretical perspectives and empirical understandings of the many issues encompassed by its brief, PICT also aimed to engage practitioners and policy makers in its research. This ambitious attempt to broaden the audience for social science research was supported by targeted activities that disseminated PICT research beyond the bounds of academic disciplines (see Appendix 1).

This book brings together some of the most significant PICT work in a form designed to be of value to students as well as this broad community—government and corporate policy makers; information technology and telecommunications professionals; managers; researchers; and anyone who takes seriously the social and economic significance of the important technologies explored by PICT. Each chapter originated as a PICT working paper, lecture, or other research activity. These have been substantially reworked and extended by authors to provide a fresh and authoritative overview of the major findings from PICT's decade of research. They have then been edited into an easily accessible style to assist a wide variety of readers to appreciate the practical and theoretical insights which emerged from the research programme.

Many of the issues which faced PICT researchers when the programme was launched have been clarified by their subsequent work. However, debates about the social and economic implications of technological advances remain because of the complexity of the forces which shape the outcomes of applying such a rapidly evolving technology. This book and its companion volume, *Society on the Line* (Dutton forthcoming), seek to take forward PICT's work to help provide a more informed basis for future policy decisions, practical innovations, and related research activities.

Acknowledgements

When I became its Director in 1993, my prime objectives were to develop a synthesis of the body of work built up by all those who contributed to PICT—and to extend this knowledge to help shape policy and practice in the future. This book is a key element in achieving that goal. I am therefore indebted to all the contributors, who have worked hard to make the book valuable to a broad audience.

In addition to co-authoring several chapters, Malcolm Peltu collaborated with me and the authors on all phases of the editorial process. I thank Malcolm for helping us in our efforts to reach new audiences for the social sciences. His craftsmanship, genuine interest in academic research, and sound judgement provided a friendly interface between the social sciences and the wider communities which the book aims to reach.

Antony Mason also helped to make chapters more accessible. Steve Russell, whose work is incorporated in the design of the book's cover, has brought PICT to life in his drawings depicting the relationships between technology and people. David Musson and his editorial team at Oxford University Press have provided valuable support and advice in shaping the book. My students at Brunel University and the University of Southern California provided feedback on PICT papers and draft chapters. This also helped in the selection and presentation of material in the book.

The UK's Economic and Social Research Council (ESRC) supported the preparation of the book as part of its overall sponsorship of PICT. I thank all those at the ESRC for their contributions to PICT and would like to express my particular appreciation to Sir Douglas Hague, Howard Newby, Bruce Smith, Ron Amann, Chris Caswill, Peter Linthwaite, Adrian Alsop, Tim Whitaker, Iain Jones, and Ros Goldstraw for the help provided during my period as Director of PICT. I am also grateful to the Annenberg School for Communication, University of Southern California for granting me the sabbatical leave required to allow me to direct the last years of PICT.

The idea of a synthesis of PICT research, which eventually led to this book, was derived from the initiative and leadership of the distinguished scholars, practitioners, and policy makers on the PICT Steering Committee. This was chaired by David Stout and included Brian Allison, Jay G. Blumler, Arthur Francis, and Brian Oakley. I value their support and advice in developing and editing this book.

Acknowledgements

One upshot of the way ICTs can enable work processes to be transformed is that I have no one to thank for typing the many versions of manuscripts, except the authors themselves. However, the management of correspondence, electronic files, and budgets associated with this project owe a big debt not only to the Internet, but also to the people who helped me to manage the PICT national office based at Brunel University, especially Helen Foster, Denise McShane, and Marjorie Bunn.

There are also many other people who participated in the work of PICT as researchers, advisors, administrators, and users and critics of the research. These many hundreds of people have all contributed in some way to the ideas and insights which are represented by this book. Ultimately, it is to the concept which inspired PICT that the book is dedicated—social science research committed to helping shape policy and practice.

W. D.

Contents

Contents

Contributors

Walter S. Baer directs information infrastructure studies for the Centre for Information-Revolution Analysis at The RAND Corporation in Santa Monica, California and its European–American Centre for Policy Analysis in Delft, the Netherlands.

Christine Bellamy is a Professor and Head of Politics and Public Administration at Nottingham Trent University.

Jay Blumler is Emeritus Professor at the University of Leeds and at the University of Maryland.

Peter Cochrane is head of the BT Advanced Research Department, which has a staff of over 600 who are investigating a wide range of future technologies, applications, and services. He is also a Visiting Professor to University College London and the Universities of Essex and Kent.

Richard Collins is a Lecturer in the Department of Social Psychology at the London School of Economics and Political Science and was a member of the PICT research team at Westminster University's Centre for Communication and Information Studies (CCIS).

Rod Coombs is a Professor in the Manchester School of Management at the University of Manchester Institute of Science and Technology (UMIST) and Director of the Centre for Research on Organisations, Management and Technical Change (CROMTEC), which was one of the PICT Centres.

James Cornford is a researcher into geographical implications of ICTs at Newcastle University's Centre for Urban and Regional Development Studies (CURDS).

Jason Dedrick is Senior Research Fellow at the Center for Research on Information Technology and Organizations (CRITO) at the University of California, Irvine.

William Dutton is a Professor at the Annenberg School for Communication, University of Southern California. He was the Director of PICT and a Visiting Professor at Brunel University during PICT's last phase.

David Edge founded the Science Studies Unit at Edinburgh University and was its Director until his retirement. He was a principal investigator for the PICT Centre at Edinburgh's Research Centre for Social Sciences (RCSS).

Christopher Freeman is Professor Emeritus at Sussex University's Science Policy Research Unit (SPRU), of which he was a former Director. He is also a Professor at the Maastricht Economic Research Institute on Innovation and Technology, University of Limburg. He played a key role in formulating the initial PICT proposal.

Nicholas Garnham is Professor of Media Studies and Director of the Centre for Communication and Information Studies (CCIS) at the University of Westminster, from where he co-ordinated Westminster's PICT research.

Michael Gell runs Multi Business Zones (MBZ) Research, a company devoted to the study, promotion, and creation of virtual enterprises. He previously set up BT's research unit investigating future communication and business systems.

Andrew Gillespie is a Senior Lecturer in the Department of Geography at the University of Newcastle and has been Deputy Director of the Centre for Urban and Regional Development Studies (CURDS) at the university.

John Goddard is Professor of Regional Development Studies at the Centre for Urban and Regional Development Studies (CURDS) at the University of Newcastle, which was one of the PICT Centres. He preceded William Dutton as Director of PICT.

Richard Hull is a Research Fellow in the Centre for Research on Organisations, Management and Technical Change (CROMTEC) at the University of Manchester Institute of Science and Technology (UMIST).

Kenneth L. Kraemer is Professor of Management and Computer Science at the University of California, Irvine and Director of the Center for Research and Information Technology and Organizations (CRITO), a joint centre of the University's Graduate School of Management and the Department of Information and Computer Science.

Donald MacKenzie is a professor in the Sociology Department at Edinburgh University and was a principal investigator on projects at the Edinburgh PICT Centre.

Robin Mansell is Director of Graduate Studies and Director of the Centre for Information and Communication Technologies (CICT) within Sussex University's Science Policy Research Unit, where she is a Professor. CICT was a PICT Centre.

Contributors

William H. Melody is Professor and Chairman of the International Advisory Board, Centre for Tele-Information, Technical University of Denmark, Lyngby. He was the founding Director of PICT in London and the Centre for International Research on Communication and Information Technologies (CIRCIT) in Melbourne.

Ian Miles is Director of the Policy Research on Engineering, Science and Technology (PREST) centre at the University of Manchester. He was formerly a Senior Fellow at the Sussex University PICT Centre.

Malcolm Peltu is an editorial consultant and IT journalist who has edited many research-based publications aimed at a non-academic audience, including PICT Policy Research Papers.

Charles Raab is Reader in Politics at the University of Edinburgh, where he has conducted research on privacy and data protection.

Ranald Richardson is a Research Associate at Newcastle University's Centre for Urban and Regional Development Studies (CURDS).

Stuart Shapiro is a Research Fellow at the Open University and was a researcher at Brunel University's Centre for Research into Innovation, Culture, and Technology (CRICT).

Roger Silverstone is Professor of Media Studies at the University of Sussex and Director of the Graduate Research Centre in Culture and Communication. He was the first Director of the Centre for Research into Innovation, Culture and Technology (CRICT) at Brunel University, which was one of the PICT Centres.

John Taylor is a Professor and Director of Research in the Business Faculty, Department of Management, Glasgow Caledonian University. He was a Research Fellow at the Newcastle PICT Centre.

Juliet Webster is a Senior Lecturer in the Department of Innovation Studies at the University of East London. She was a Research Fellow at the Edinburgh PICT Centre.

Robin Williams is a Senior Lecturer in the Research Centre for Social Sciences (RCSS) and co-ordinator of PICT and other socio-economic research on technology at Edinburgh University.

Steve Woolgar is Professor of Sociology in the Department of Human Sciences at Brunel University and Director of the Centre for Research into Innovation, Culture, and Technology (CRICT).

Figures

Tables

Boxes

Abbreviations and Acronyms

AI	Artificial Intelligence
ARPA	Advanced Research Projects Agency
ATM	Asynchronous Transfer Mode or Automatic Teller Machine
BBS	Bulletin Board System
BPR	Business Process Re-engineering
bps	bits per second
BT	British Telecommunications
CAD	Computer-Aided Design
CAM	Computer-Aided Manufacture
CASE	Computer-Aided Software Engineering
CCIS	Centre for Communication and Information Studies (University of Westminster PICT Centre)
CCITT	Consultative Committee on International Telegraphy and Telephony
CCTA	the UK Government Centre for Information Systems
CD	Compact Disc
CEPT	Conference of European Postal and Telecommunications Administrations
CICT	Centre for Information and Communication Technologies (University of Sussex PICT Centre)
CIM	Computer-Integrated Manufacture
CNC	Computer Numerically Controlled machine
CRICT	Centre for Research into Innovation, Culture, and Technology (Brunel University PICT Centre)
CRITO	Center for Research on Information Technology and Organizations (University of California, Irvine)
CROMTEC	Centre for Research on Organisations, Management, and Technical Change (PICT Centre at UMIST)
CSCW	Computer-Supported Co-operative Working
CTA	Constructive Technology Assessment
CURDS	Centre for Urban and Regional Development Studies (Newcastle University PICT Centre)
DAE	Dynamic Asian Economy
DBS	Direct Broadcasting by Satellite
DTI	Department of Trade and Industry (UK)
EBU	European Broadcasting Union
EC	European Community (earlier name for the EU)
ECU	European Currency Unit
EDI	Electronic Data Interchange
EFTPoS	Electronic Fund Transfer at Point of Sale

ESD	Electronic Service Delivery
ESPRIT	European Strategic Programme for R&D in Information Technology
ETSI	European Telecommunication Standards Institute
EU	European Union
EVH	Electronic Village Hall
FCC	Federal Communications Commission (USA)
FMS	Flexible Manufacturing Systems
FTP	File Transfer Protocol
GATS	General Agreement on Trade and Services
GATT	General Agreement on Tariffs and Trade
GDP	Gross Domestic Product
GNP	Gross National Product
GUI	Graphical User Interface
HCI	Human–Computer Interaction (or Interface)
HDTV	High-Definition Television
HMSO	Her Majesty's Stationery Office
ICT	Information and Communication Technology
IITF	Information Infrastructure Task Force (USA)
ILO	International Labour Organization
IPR	Intellectual Property Rights
ISDN	Integrated Services Digital Network
IT	Information Technology
JIT	Just-In-Time system
K	1,000 in general terms, 1,024 for measurements specific to computing
LAN	Local Area Network
MIT	Massachusetts Institute of Technology
NC	Numerical Control machine
NHS	National Health Service (UK)
NIC	Newly Industrializing Country
NIE	Newly Industrializing Economy
NII	National Information Infrastructure (USA)
NPM	New Public Management
OECD	Organization of Economic Co-operation and Development
Oftel	Office of Telecommunications (UK)
ONA	Open Network Architecture
OSI	Open Systems Interconnection
OTA	former Office of Technology Assessment (USA)
PABX	Private Automatic Branch exchange
PC	Personal Computer
PEN	Public Electronic Network (Santa Monica, California)
PICT	Programme on Information and Communication Technologies
POTS	Plain Old Telephone Service
PoS	Point of Sale

Abbreviations and Acronyms

PRP	Policy Research Paper (PICT)
PSTN	Public Switched Telephone Network
PTO	Public Telecommunication Operator
PTT	Post, Telegraph, and Telephone authority
QA	Quality Assurance
RBOC	Regional Bell Operating Company
R&D	Research and Development
SCOT	Social Construction of Technology
SISP	Strategic Information Systems Planning
SPRU	Science Policy Research Unit (University of Sussex)
SSK	Sociology of Scientific Knowledge
SST	Social Shaping of Technology
STAR	Special Telecommunications Action for Regional development programme (within EU)
STN	Swedish National Telecommunication Council
TCP/IP	Transmission Control Protocol/Internet Protocol
Telco	Telecommunication company
TQM	Total Quality Management
UMIST	University of Manchester Institute of Science and Technology
VAN	Value-Added Network
V-chip	Violence-chip
VLSI	Very Large Scale Integration
VR	Virtual Reality
WAN	Wide Area Network
WTO	World Trade Organization
WWW	World Wide Web

Introduction
William H. Dutton

At the end of the twentieth century, the depth and significance of the revolution in information and communication technologies (ICTs) is broadly acknowledged, although vigorous debates continue about its driving forces and social implications. The widespread consensus over the increasing centrality of computers and telecommunications across all levels and sectors of society and the economy has been reinforced by the way the mass media have discussed these major technological and business advances.

Much media attention has been paid to leading-edge technologies of the day, whether it be cable and satellite systems in the 1970s, the personal computer in the 1980s, or the Internet in the 1990s. A great deal of coverage by the mass media is also motivated by a desire to bring a human dimension into what is often portrayed as the inevitable march of technological advance. For example, considerable efforts are being made to tie the ICT revolution to a person, just as Henry Ford has become identified with the revolution in automotive technology and mass-production processes. However, although it is possible to pick out a few dozen individuals who have had an exceptionally important role in ICT developments, the search for the Henry Ford of the information age has a major flaw. It underestimates the role of the millions of people who consume, apply, and often change the technology in organizations and households; who produce the products and services which users can exploit; and who manage and regulate the burgeoning industries supplying the innovations.

The contributors to this book explore beyond this focus on technology and personalities. They provide detailed arguments which demonstrate that the revolution in ICTs and its social and economic implications are products of countless numbers of both strategic and everyday decisions by a multitude of entrepreneurs, managers, workers, teachers, households, and policy makers around the world. Our future is therefore not simply discovered or invented by the few: it will unfold as the outcome of open-ended and interrelated social processes involving a myriad of individuals, communities, and organizations. Understanding the social dynamics of these players is central to developing policies and practices that will realize the potential of this technological revolution.

In illuminating the processes shaping the use and impacts of ICTs, this book seeks to challenge many taken-for-granted assumptions about the development of ICTs and to further public understanding of the implications of ICTs for social and economic development. The book grew out of an effort to synthesize the results of a decade of research undertaken through Britain's Programme on Information and Communication Technologies (PICT), launched in the mid-1980s as a means of generating high-quality research to inform policy and practice related to ICTs.

PICT researchers placed an emphasis on detailed case studies and qualitative analyses. As a result, this book really can put a human face on the social shaping and implications of the revolution in ICTs. The authors avoid overly abstract discussions of disembodied social and economic forces. They convey the significance of social theory and practice in terms linked to concrete decisions made by real entities—software developers, managers, manufacturing firms, households, schools, and governments. In doing this, the book shows how social research can support policy and practice by illuminating the ways in which social, cultural, political, and economic processes shape the development, use, and implications of advances in ICTs.

Social Research on the Revolution in ICTs

Since the 1950s, a diverse array of practitioners and scholars has addressed the social and economic implications of ICTs. Nevertheless, the development of a cumulative body of knowledge based on this work has been hampered by two main obstacles. First, social research on ICTs has been splintered by disciplinary boundaries and specialized areas of application. For example, computer scientists and engineers have dominated discussions of technological innovation, while economists, politicians, and lawyers have had the most influential roles in regulation and public policy. Secondly, the rapid pace of innovation has made it difficult to consolidate knowledge before new capabilities have radically changed the prevailing technological context.

2

When PICT was launched in 1985, there was already a strong view that research on the social and economic aspects of ICTs could be of greater benefit to the business and policy communities. At that time, many practitioners and policy makers were fully aware of the many related 'hot button' issues, such as concerns about the implications for unemployment, privacy, and the need to 'make a business of information'.[1] The founders of PICT also recognized a need for better information on which to base policy and practice, which they felt required a more cumulative and interdisciplinary understanding of the many dimensions to the ICT revolution. The UK Economic and Social Research Council (ESRC), which supported the programme, therefore created a federal structure, with six PICT Centres encompassing more than a hundred researchers (see Appendix 1). This encouraged centres and individuals within them to pursue studies that built on their own strengths, within a co-ordinated national framework.

The benefits of this strategy became evident in the last years of PICT, when the focus of the programme shifted from field studies to the synthesis of research across the centres. This aimed to overcome the fragmentation in this field and to yield more general and practical insights. As this volume makes clear, PICT researchers came from diverse disciplinary backgrounds and pursued a wide range of topics. Nevertheless, some key themes and concepts proved to be important to research across PICT.

These revolved around four main areas (see Table I.1), which also characterize social research on ICTs in general. As shown in Table I.1,

Table I.1. Social Research on Information and Communication Technologies

	Information Economy: Making a Business of Information	Information Society: Balancing Competing Values and Interests
Visions	Social dimensions of the technical: social, cultural, and political processes shaping technological development and innovation	Public policy and regulation: actors, goals and strategies
	Production I	IV Governance
	Utilization II	III Consumption
Realities	ICTs in organizations, management, and work: reinforcing and transforming the structure, processes, and geography of the firm	Living in an information society: ICTs in the home, education, and democratic processes

this research can be categorized along two main dimensions, depending on the focus of individual studies:

1. *'Visions' of the future of ICTs versus the 'realities' of their use and impacts in different social and organizational settings.* The visions of scientists, technical experts, business entrepreneurs, economists, and politicians are important because they help to set the goals to which technology and public policies seek to give concrete meaning. However, it is in the realities of organizational and social life that technologies and policies are diffused, implemented, and reinvented. These realities defy prediction based on the capabilities of the technology or the designs of the policy makers.

2. *The 'information economy' versus 'information society'.* These terms are broad and overlapping, but they signal distinctive criteria for assessing the visions and realities of ICTs. For example, studies of the information economy concentrate on the development or utilization of new ICT-based capabilities, such as in exploring the impact of computers on productivity in different sectors of the economy. In contrast, studies of the information society grapple more directly with the social, cultural, and political issues raised by advances in ICTs, such as concern over the cohesion and quality of social relations in a more ICT-mediated society.

The four quadrants of Table I.1 help clarify the distinctions between various categories of research in this field. These are focused on:

I. *production:* the wide range of social, cultural, and political processes that shape innovations in products, services, and industries;

II. *utilization:* the ways in which ICTs are used in organizations, management, and work to reinforce or transform the structure, geography, and processes of the firm;

III. *consumption:* the many ways households, citizens, consumers, and the public at large actively consume and otherwise adapt ICTs to fit into their everyday lives;

IV. *governance:* the criteria and processes by which public policy and regulation balances competing values and interests.

PICT research has drawn many connections across these areas, such as the degree to which users are also involved in production as they reinvent and reconfigure technologies in the workplace and the household. These links are among the major themes of PICT research.

Cross-Cutting Concepts and Themes

Social research on ICTs is anchored in studies of different actors and contexts, ranging from software developers to IT managers to politicians to lone-parent households. Within this broad spectrum, many cross-cutting themes arise across the four areas of PICT research. The main themes and their relationships to the four sectors defined in Table I.1 are summarized in Table I.2. The following sections describe each of these themes.

Limits of Technological Determinism

Many prominent accounts of trends in technology imply a known path toward a particular future predetermined by properties of the technology (see for example Negroponte 1995). This book highlights social dimensions of technological development and innovation which challenge perspectives on the development of ICTs based on views that change is determined primarily by either technological or social forces. It is a combination of the processes of both social and technological innovation which influences the course of change, often in unpredictable ways.

For instance, social processes shape the design of technologies (Chapter 3) and science and engineering know-how is itself socially shaped (Chapter 4). ICTs tend to be implemented in ways that follow and 're-inforce' prevailing structures of power and influence within organizations, rather than systematically supporting specific configurations of control, whether centralized or decentralized (Danziger *et al.* 1982). An example of this is the way social processes affecting the design of ICT systems can reinforce the role of women in the workforce (Chapter 8). At the same time, ICTs can facilitate the transformation of organizational structures and work practices (Chapter 7). ICTs therefore cannot be seen as systematically empowering any particular group or privileging any particular structural arrangement.

The impacts of government policies and national and international regulation in stimulating or constraining technological developments is also a vital consideration (Part IV, Chapters 17 to 22). In different social and political contexts, ICTs could become 'technologies of freedom' (de Sola Pool 1983*a*) or a means of great control and surveillance over citizens.

Table 1.2. Illustrations of Themes Cross-Cutting Major Areas of Social Research into ICTs and their Implications

Cross-Cutting Themes	Research Areas			
	Production: Social Dimensions of the Technical	Utilization: Organizations, Management, and Work	Consumption: Living in an Information Society	Governance: Public Policy and Regulation
Limits of Technological Determinism	Social shaping of technical choices	Reinvention of ICTs by users	Uncertainty of consumer response	Effects of shifts in policy and regulation
Centrality of the User	Conceptions of the user; producer–user relationships	Rising priority for the end-user and end-user services	The active viewer; domestication of ICTs	Increasing reliance on marketplace competition
Cultures of Technology	Advantages of language, e.g., multi-lingual skills; technology as text	Acceptance of new business processes; 'innovation' v. 'safety-first' cultures	Attitudes to technology; interest in communication and information	Support for policies promoting both the production and use of ICTs
The Power of Ideas	The 'chip' and 'networking'	ICTs and new management paradigms	'The Internet'; electronic democracy	The 'information superhighway'
The Bias of Emerging Technologies	Software becoming 'electronic concrete'; changing cost structures	Payoffs of exploiting speed, efficiency, connectivity	More options, opportunities, and threats	National policy in a global village; rethinking regulations
Interactions of Local–Global Dimensions	Concentrations of skills; regional economies	Space bias; relocation of jobs and functions; telework	Virtual communities; cultural sovereignty; distance learning	ICT industrial policies; global networks for local development
Access to the Information Society	Concentration of ownership; cost of R&D	Facilitating organizational change, e.g. networked enterprises	Information 'haves' and 'have nots'	Redefining 'universal service'

Centrality of the User

Technologically deterministic perspectives often fail to recognize the central role that users play in technological change. In all areas, PICT research has found that the user takes a more active role in shaping and, in the household, 'domesticating' ICTs than a deterministic perspective would allow (Chapter 12). This book provides many concrete examples of how users shape the design and impacts of technological change.

For instance, in organizational settings, hardware and software are redesigned and reinvented by users in ways that defy linear models of system development (Chapter 9). In business services as well as in the public sector, greater resources are being focused on the electronic delivery of services directly to consumers and citizens as 'end-users' (Chapter 15). The convergence of information and communication industries, such as between print publishing and television companies, has been constrained by the history of investments made by various companies and industries to protect and serve distinct markets with specialized products and services (Chapter 6). Similarly, computing and telecommunication disasters, which can cost lives, often result from a failure to recognize the realities of the organizational settings in which systems are built and the human limits governing their use (Chapter 10).

In the household, consumer responses to innovations in ICTs diverge repeatedly from technical forecasts, which have been based simply on new capabilities of ICTs (Chapters 12 and 13). For example, the market failures of many new technologies, like the video telephone in the early 1970s, demonstrate the weakness of forecasts based on what technology can supply consumers, rather than on what the marketplace wants from suppliers at any given point in time. Reasons for these failures can often be traced back to the producers of ICTs and their limited stereotypes of the user, suggesting the need also to rearrange the processes of designing and manufacturing ICTs in ways that better incorporate user requirements.

The ways in which producers and users choose to design and employ products and services are influenced by the perceived advantages and existing properties of ICTs. Nevertheless, ICTs remain malleable and more open to interpretation than technologically deterministic perspectives suggest (Chapter 5). Political and economic debate about the balance that should be struck between market forces and public-led policies is also an important factor in determining the relations between producers and users (Chapters 15, 21, and 22).

Cultures of Technology

Attitudes, values, and habits surrounding ICTs, such as prevailing mass-media conventions, are culturally patterned and influence the behaviour of users, producers, and regulators in critical ways. Cross-national research in PICT brought cultural variations to the forefront of analyses, such as the differential receptivity of governments to ICT-led industrial policies (Chapter 22) or the public's acceptance of technological innovations, for instance in electronic service delivery in the public sector (Chapter 15) and the receptivity of audiences in different countries to pan-European satellite television (Chapter 13).

In some areas, however, technological developments seem to be converging around common models, overriding cross-national cultural variations. For example, the development of cable and satellite networks, the diffusion of the Internet, and interest in the 'information superhighway' seem to be on converging paths rather than on unique national trajectories (Chapter 22). This indicates that cultural and other social factors can influence outcomes. Nevertheless, there is no single determinant of technological change.

In the organizational context, cultural constraints on change emerged in research on the 'productivity paradox' which suggested that many firms fail to take advantage of ICTs unless they also introduce changes in organizational design and processes that take advantage of ICTs (Chapters 7 and 9). Organizational culture has many other effects, such as in the way the 'masculine' ethos that dominates some areas of the information and communication industries can place constraints on women's role within the workplace (Chapter 8). Similarly, the way a company treats safety and reliability aspects of ICT systems will be very different in firms characterized by an 'innovation-driven' versus a 'safety-first' culture (Chapter 10). In addition, public policies that derive from national and regional cultures strike very different balances between the production and use of ICTs. In such ways, cultures can advantage some individuals, firms, and nations and constrain others in responding to new technological opportunities or threats.

The Power of Ideas

Technologically deterministic perspectives fail to recognize the influence of ideas in shaping the course of technological and policy change. The 'power of ideas' has been most often credited in the area of regulation and public policy (Derthick and Quirk 1985). For example, economists were able to convince the larger policy community of the value of competition versus regulated monopolies in the provision of major services like telecommunications well before evidence began to accumulate on the value of this policy change (Chapters 1 and 20). Likewise, the idea of an information superhighway proved pivotal not only in policy debate, but also in fostering greater public interest in new media like the Internet (Chapter 22).

Outside the public policy arena, shifts in the way people think about technology have been equally powerful. The idea of the 'chip' as a major enabling technology has buttressed industries focused on the production of microelectronics (Chapters 2 and 18). New ways of thinking about the design of organizational and manufacturing processes—new 'techno-economic' (Chapters 1 and 7) and management (Chapter 9) paradigms—have been an important element in achieving the productivity gains expected from ICTs. For example, visions of community-based idyllic electronic town halls and counter-models of electronically policed 'surveillance societies' can give direction to policy, ignite public interest, and create the political will to address issues of major social importance (Chapter 16).

The Bias of Emerging Technologies

While this book underscores some of these major limitations on technologically deterministic views on the information society, it does not underestimate the importance of technological change. Contributors recognize that technologies can bias social choices by making some options more economically, culturally, or socially rational than others (Chapters 2 and 5). Technologies can open, close, and otherwise shape social choices, although not always in the ways expected on the basis of rationally extrapolating from the perceived properties of technology. For example, in theory software is extremely flexible. However, programs become very complex and difficult to change once software is tailored to particular systems and embedded within the routine operations of organizations. This means software turns effectively into what PICT researcher Paul Quintas (forthcoming) calls 'electronic concrete'.

As for organizations, this book reinforces the significant degree to which economies are becoming increasingly dependent on the effective production and utilization of ICTs (Chapters 1, 7, 18, and 20). The application of ICTs can make production more efficient, enhance existing products and services, and create new ones. It can reduce the cost to business of obtaining and processing information on markets, suppliers, and competition, thus facilitating organizational efficiency and responsiveness (Chapter 9). In addition, the IT industry itself can be a source of economic growth and jobs (Chapters 1, 18, and 20).

In the creation of an information society, ICTs can be used to enhance democratic participation (Chapter 16), improve learning and education (Chapter 14), and provide more choices for consumers to be entertained and informed (Chapter 13). Yet the same technologies can be used to undermine genuine participation in politics (Chapters 2, 16, and 22). In addition, the availability of ever growing numbers of television channels and information pages on the World Wide Web, combined with the use of multimedia personal computers, might actually diminish the quality of news, educational, and entertainment services and products. The explosion in new electronic media forms and communication channels could also swamp the voice of responsible citizens in a cacophony of electronic chatter and banality; reduce the diversity of television programming; undermine the cohesion of communities; and differentially advantage those with particular skills, values, or cultural backgrounds. The policies chosen to regulate media innovations and other emerging ICT innovations is again a critical factor in shaping outcomes (Part IV, Chapters 17 to 22).

Interactions of Local–Global Dimensions

One of the most prominent biases attributed to ICTs has been the relative ease with which the new electronic media can overcome the constraints of time and distance (Innis 1951; McLuhan 1964; de Sola Pool 1990). PICT researchers found important connections between technological change, the geography of organizations, and the geography of the economy as a whole that refine conventional evaluations of the degree to which new ICTs undermine the importance of space and place. This research has concluded that geography might well matter more rather than less in the information economy.

ICTs are connected to changes in the location of employment and shifts in which particular functions are performed within increasingly decentralized and networked organizations (Chapter 11). Locally unique historical and geographical circumstances can create competitive advantages within a global marketplace for capital and labour. Public policies and programmes need to address the opportunities and threats posed to particular localities (Chapters 11 and 19).

Access to the Information Society

This impact of emerging ICTs on local employment opportunities under-scores the significance of electronic access to information, people, work, health care, technology, leisure, entertainment, and other services in an information society.[2] In fact, the major long-range social and economic consequences of ICTs derive from their increasingly central role in open-ing, closing, filtering, and otherwise shaping such access. This emerges vividly in research on ICTs in the household (Chapter 13), education (Chapter 14), electronic service delivery (Chapter 15), and regional dis-parities (Chapters 11 and 19).

By facilitating organizational change, such as in the form of networked organizations, ICTs create an important new dimension to the access issue. In the policy arena, concerns over access to new ICTs have gen-erated debate over ways to redefine 'universal service'. This concept has been applied to telecommunications for decades, but needs substantial updating before it can be translated into effective guidelines for the multimedia services delivered by new information highways (Chapters 19 and 21). Mechanisms will be needed to ensure that some minimal levels of access to information infrastructures and to services that go beyond the plain old telephone are available to everyone. For example, broader universal service requirements might be needed to cover tele-communications provision to households in distressed areas of cities and rural areas that are well off the information superhighway.

Implications for Decision Makers, Practitioners, and Researchers

PICT research has taken issue with many claims surrounding the infor-mation society and the revolution in ICTs.[3] For example, it has chal-lenged and jettisoned the arguments put forward by those who see society progressing along an inevitable course towards new stages of develop-ment, such as a 'post-capitalist society' (Drucker 1993), as well as those who advocate utopian treatments of ICTs as instruments of freedom and community (for example Kelly 1994 and Rheingold 1994). At the same time, PICT research does not add to the growing set of critics, like Burstein and Kline (1995) and Slouka (1995), who perceive advances in ICTs primarily as part of an 'assault' on civilization. Such dystopian accounts of the information society can be as deterministic as the utopian positions they contest (Chapter 2).

In challenging such claims, social research can refine understanding of the complex roles that social, organizational, and cultural processes play in the development, management, and use of ICTs in various sectors of society. Yet the complexity and interdependencies of technological, organizational, and social change make prescriptions for policy and practice problematic and highly contingent on the specific historical and social context.

The implications of technology and policy are seldom straightforward. Nevertheless, the thrust of PICT research, as conveyed by the contributions to this book, provides a coherent overview of the social and economic implications of ICTs. These suggest some very general guidelines for policy and practice.

Guidelines for Policy and Practice

ICTs have been used to the advantage of some managers and professionals, students, consumers, organizations, nations, and regions. Many, however, remain disadvantaged in a global information economy (Chapter 14). ICTs do not represent a quick fix to deep and historically rooted problems of social, economic, and political systems. The economic payoffs of ICTs are not automatic. In order to reap these rewards, managers, users, and politicians need to make informed policy choices—backed by the vision and will to see through a successful implementation of the strategy. Moreover, as the contributions to this book make clear, many social and economic objectives can be at odds, necessitating wise trade-offs between competing values and interests.

That said, a recognition of the role that social choice plays in shaping the information society places added responsibility on researchers to provide insights of value to policy and practice. Such insights are amply provided in the remainder of this book. My interpretation of the body of research on which these are based leads me to highlight the following seven main points.

1. Leaders within business, industry, labour, government, and not-for-profit sectors need to position ICT strategies at the centre of their socio-economic policies and set clear targets in all relevant areas. This will require most governments and agencies to raise the priority given to ICTs by top managers and policy makers. At all levels, leaders need to

seek novel and effective means of encouraging the social and organizational innovation necessary to make full use of the potential of advances in technology.

2. Politicians should move beyond dichotomous views on the superiority of public-led versus *market-led* ICT developments to craft complementary roles for both the market and the public sector that fit the political and administrative traditions and climates of each nation. The public sector is often a more appropriate forum for developing a vision of what to do, rather than for determining how to do it—a role best left to business and industry in a competitive market. The public sector is also able to create a co-ordinated focal point for debate, policy formulation, and follow-up actions related to ICTs.

3. Regions should encourage the development of manufacturing and other businesses associated with the production of ICT hardware, software, and services. New businesses created around ICTs account for a substantial number of new jobs and can promote the greater utilization of ICTs by developing a skill base and a greater sense of ownership of the technology. The development of ICTs can also be facilitated by breaking down barriers separating ICT producers and users, helping the developers of hardware and software gain more realistic conceptions of the users of their work and the products they design.

4. Nations, regions, and localities should identify and focus on local advantages that can be exploited in a more global arena. The unique historical and geographical advantages and disadvantages of locales are likely to become more rather than less important in a global information economy.

5. Governments at all levels should promote investment and training in the use of information and communication technologies. This might require nations to pull down barriers, like trade restrictions, to the import and use of ICT hardware and software. It should also lead nations and regions to promote competition in the provision of ICT infrastructures, such as telecommunications facilities, as well as in information and communication services. All sectors of the economy remain essential to nations and regions—agriculture and manufacturing as well as the new information and service industries—and they can all benefit from the effective use of ICTs in organizations that design work to take full advantage of their capabilities.

6. Regulators should recognize that technological innovation and effective competition in ICT services may be critical—but so is the need for

regulatory and public supervision to avoid abuses by information and communication industries and in the way ICTs are applied in the business marketplace and by public agencies. Ensuring competition, protecting privacy, regulating content, and providing for choice and diversity of information and entertainment services are likely to require innovative policy responses and continued public vigilance. The public sector needs to establish effective processes to develop and enact relevant regulations, legislation, and standards which promote innovation and consumer choice while protecting the rights of individuals, groups, and enterprises. The public should ensure that government has the authority and resources to assert and monitor protection of the public interest in applications and developments. Governments need to work with the private and non-profit sectors to find suitable mechanisms to support 'public interest' facilities and applications. For example, the concept of a 'public library' needs to be reinvented for the information age.

7. The general public must see education as crucial to the social and economic development of an information society. The role of education in an information economy is not limited to the training of scientists and engineers vital to high-technology industries, nor to providing consumers with a basic level of technological proficiency. Education must also promote basic literacy, enabling individuals to learn the skills necessary to gain access to information and communication services, fostering both the creativity necessary to devise imaginative multimedia content and a culture that respects the rights and responsibilities of individuals to privacy and expression in an electronic community. ICTs also open many opportunities to deliver high-quality educational services to all sections of the population, in all locations (Chapter 14).

Social Research and Choices Shaping the Future

The revolution in ICTs is not over. Its implications will continue to spread and evolve. ICTs will therefore remain at the centre of developments across most sectors of the economy. This has been recognized both at government levels, such as in the UK's ambitious 'technology foresight' initiative (OST 1995*a*), and by leading ICT entrepreneurs and inventors, like Microsoft's Bill Gates (1995) and Nicholas Negroponte (1995) of the leading-edge Media Lab at the Massachusetts Institute of Technology.

PICT research, as revealed in subsequent chapters of the book, argues that the validity of these expectations and the actual course of change over the coming decades will be determined by choices made by a countless number of consumers, users, and producers of information and communication products and services. Social research can provide a better understanding of the critical options facing individuals and societies, which offers a sound basis on which to make informed judgements on the implications for policy and practice.

Three decades ago, as chair of a Commission on the Year 2000 for the American Academy of Arts and Sciences, Daniel Bell wrote (1967: 639):

> Time, said St Augustine, is a three-fold present: the present as we experience it, the past as a present memory, and the future as a present expectation. By that criterion, the world of the year 2000 has already arrived, for in the decisions we make now, in the way we design our environment and thus sketch the lines of constraints, the future is committed. Just as the gridiron pattern of city streets in the nineteenth century shaped the linear growth of cities in the twentieth, so the new networks of radial highways, the location of new towns, the reordering of graduate-school curricula, the decision to create or not to create a computer utility as a single system, and the like will frame the tectonics of the twenty-first century. The future is not an overarching leap into the distance; it begins in the present.

With the arrival of the twenty-first century, we are already living in information societies, but are still searching for concepts to describe the new age we are creating. Although current information societies differ in many ways from that which Bell had imagined in 1967, he made a crucial point then which is still valid now: the future is not on a predetermined technological path. Instead, present choices about the design, development, and use of emerging ICTs are shaping future outcomes.

Visions play an important role in setting public and corporate policy agenda. This is illustrated by the way seminal works by Bell (1973; 1980) on the post-industrial or information society helped to create perceptions that came to underpin policy initiatives ranging from information superhighway developments in the USA to strategic plans for building a 'European information society' (Chapter 22). Such visions provide maps which guide practitioners and policy makers on where to go. They seldom provide instructions on how to get there. The social sciences, however, can offer guidance on how to arrive at different social, political, and economic destinations. It is in this sense that the kind of social research undertaken by PICT—anchored in the visions and realities of ICT policy and practice—can be critical to realizing the potential of ICTs.

Notes

1. 'Making a Business of Information' was the title of a report by the British government's Information Technology Advisory Committee (ITAP 1983). Charles Read and other members of ITAP were instrumental in the launch of PICT.
2. This theme is broadened to pull together and synthesize the major findings of PICT research in a companion volume (Dutton forthcoming).
3. Examples of critical perspectives on the information society within the PICT programme include those provided by Robins (1992) and Garnham (1994). In this book, Ian Miles (Chapter 2) provides an overview of some of the key issues in debates over the information society.

Part I

Social Dimensions of the Technical: Social, Cultural, and Political Processes Shaping Technological Development and Innovation

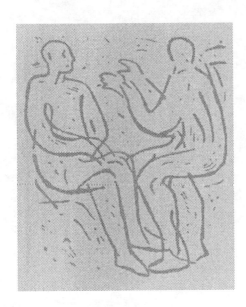

1 The Two-Edged Nature of Technological Change: Employment and Unemployment

Christopher Freeman

This first chapter provides a vivid illustration of the main theme examined throughout this book—the long-range social and economic significance of the revolution in ICTs. In the chapter, Christopher Freeman assesses alternative perspectives on the relationships between technical innovation and changes in the levels and patterns of employment.[1]

He explores the insights that can be gained by viewing the changes from an historical perspective, including an analysis of the successes in the late twentieth century of the most dynamic East Asian countries. He argues that a new way of thinking about information and communication technologies—which he describes as a 'paradigm shift'—is critical to realizing the full advantages of their widespread diffusion.

Employment Patterns and Technical Change

Interest in the role played by ICTs in shaping employment patterns grew during the 1980s and 1990s because the dramatic spread of ICTs coincided with rising underlying levels of unemployment in developed economies. An important context for understanding this role is provided by economic analyses of general long-term techno-economic forces and a number of approaches specific to ICTs developed since the 1950s.

Christopher Freeman

Techno-Economic Waves

Economists have long recognized that technical change both destroys old jobs and creates new ones. This duality raises a number of crucial questions about the balance between job creation and destruction, as well as the precise nature of the shifts that take place in employment characteristics.

Sir James Steuart (1966 edn.) was one of the first to advocate measures to alleviate unemployment brought about by the introduction of machinery. His proposals, which could now probably be described as Keynesian, were published in 1767 in an essay on political economy—nine years before the more famous classic *Wealth of Nations* by Adam Smith, which stressed the benign equilibrium that could be established by the 'invisible hand' of the market. The main controversy about the dual-edged nature of technical change was triggered in 1821 by David Ricardo. He wrote to much surprise at the time (Ricardo 1821):

> **The opinion entertained by the labouring class that the introduction of machinery is frequently detrimental to their interests is not founded on prejudice or error but conforms to the correct principles of political economy.**

This appeared to contradict what had by then become the conventional wisdom of classical economics on equilibrium. Ricardo was referring to what has become known as 'structural adjustment' to the rise of new technologies. This can be prolonged and difficult, mainly because new jobs may not match the old ones in terms of either skills or location. The 'compensation' involved in making such adjustments would not be painless, instantaneous, or automatic. Economists have subsequently argued that the job-creation effects of technical change have outstripped the job-destruction impacts in the long run, albeit accompanied by a steady reduction in working hours throughout the nineteenth and twentieth centuries. Where the mismatch is severe and/or prolonged, economists have come to refer to 'structural' unemployment, in contrast to the more usual notion of 'frictional' unemployment, which covers everyday employment changes. Schumpeter (1939) gave a new twist to the debate with his conception of 'long waves' of successive industrial revolutions. In each cycle, new technologies could give rise to major waves of new investment and employment in new industries and services.[2]

The Growth of Structural Unemployment

The exact borderline between structural and frictional unemployment is not always easy to define precisely. However, there is now a universal recognition that some fairly severe problems of structural unemployment have existed since the 1970s. This has become obvious from the rapid increase in recorded unemployment in the EU, which averaged about 12 per cent during 1994. Although this level fluctuates, there are many reasons for continuing concern with the unemployment problem. For example, the OECD (1993) has warned that there are disturbing and potentially alarming aspects of employment prospects in many Western European countries approaching the twenty-first century. Similar problems are also likely to apply to the USA and other industrialized economies. These include:

- hardly any job growth in the private sector;

- job losses in services as well as manufacturing;

- youth unemployment remaining 'stubbornly high';

- social tensions and conflicts with immigrants associated with high unemployment;

- many new jobs that are part-time, of which a significant and growing percentage are for 'involuntary' part-time workers who would be in full-time work if they had the chance (see for example Kettle 1993).

A correct measure of the 'unused' labour potential in an economy is also generally much higher than the officially recorded figures because many people not in employment do not register for a variety of reasons, for example because they have retired early, do not receive unemployment benefit, are dependent on their families, or are operating in the informal 'black economy'. Some estimates suggest this 'non-employment' could be two or three times higher than recorded figures. For instance, among males aged 25 to 64 in the UK in 1991, the official total of 9.0 per cent unemployment has been contrasted with an estimated 20.9 per cent non-employment, with equivalent US rates of 5.8 per cent and 16.3 per cent (Nickell and Bell 1994). Rates are also likely to be much higher for specific groups, such as the young, unskilled, long-term unemployed, and ethnic minorities.

All this means that even a level of 7 per cent recorded unemployment could still be uncomfortably high, with feelings of insecurity still widespread.

Direct and Indirect Employment Effects of ICTs

Whether or not they accept Schumpeter's long-wave ideas, few economists or engineers would now deny the enormous worldwide socio-economic impact of ICTs. In fact, many commentators go even further and suggest that ICTs are ushering in an entirely new era, which Daniel Bell (1973) called the 'post-industrial' society.

Everyone would today accept that the extraordinarily rapid and continuing reduction in costs and improvements in performance of microelectronics is having substantial effects on almost every branch of the economy. This comes from the way these gains have been applied in successive generations of integrated circuits, telecommunications, and electronic computers (see for example Freeman and Soete 1994). Previous new technology systems, such as steam power or electricity, had similar pervasive effects—but ICTs are unique in touching every function within the firm, as well as every industry and service. Scientific research, design, development, marketing, processing plant, production systems, marketing, distribution, general administration, and many other activities are deeply affected by these revolutionary technologies. Moreover, the counter-inflationary effects of falling costs and prices in ICTs are being carried through into a widening range of products and services.

In attempting to assess the overall employment impacts of ICTs, it is important to distinguish 'direct' from 'indirect' effects. The direct effects relate to the new jobs generated in creating and delivering new products and services and the old jobs which are lost. Indirect effects are the consequences felt throughout the economy as a result of the impetus of a new wave of investment and market opportunities.

Examples of direct effects are the major ICT industries that barely existed before 1950 but each of which now employ more than a million people around the world. These include manufacturers of computers, software, microelectronics, televisions, and videocassette recorders. However, it is not always clear whether the applications of computers are displacing workers or adding additional new services and employment. For instance, the computer industry itself provided machines which displaced earlier types of electro-mechanical office equipment and the microelectronics industry largely displaced the old valve (tube) industry.

In telecommunications, new digital telephone exchanges require far less labour to manufacture and maintain than old electro-mechanical ones, so the number of people working in the telephone switch industry has fallen in most industrial countries. Competitive restructuring of the old monopolistic telecommunications networks has also resulted in a reduction of the number of employees, even though the number of firms and the number of lines and calls has increased. In the USA, for example, employment in telecommunications industries fell from a total of 982,000 in 1984 to 895,000 in 1992 (see Chapter 20, Table 20.2). At the same time, the new telecommunications infrastructure provides the basis for numerous new information service industries and equipment, such as electronic mail, fax, data banks, and the innovative multimedia services of the future.

To compare the balance of gains and losses in such a complex environment is a difficult undertaking. This is indicated by the different approaches to analysing these impacts which have emerged since the 1950s.

Techno-Economic Approaches to ICTs

The various ways in which the techno-economic impacts of ICTs have been viewed are summarized in Table 1.1. Any sophisticated attempt to assess the employment effects must take into account both job destruction and job creation. The approach which encompasses Bell's post-industrial society conception ('Information Society' column in Table 1.1) recognizes the job-creation effects but has little to say about the technology. The naïve view of ICT applications as simply a process of job destruction (the 'Automation' column in the Table) has its counterpart in the equally naïve view of information technologies as a purely positive source of new employment ('IT Sector' column).

The cybernetics pioneer Norbert Wiener (1949) was one of the first to promote the view that mass computerization would inevitably lead to mass unemployment. His pessimism was also emphasized by many trade unions in the 1970s and 1980s when the broad impacts of information technologies first became evident (see for example Jenkins and Sherman 1979). The more optimistic job-creation perspective was typified by technologically inspired visions of many new 'sunrise' industries (see for example Mackintosh 1986).

The 'creative destruction approach' adopted in this chapter ('ICT Paradigm Change' column) is a specific instance of more general ideas about what occurs when there is a change of techno-economic paradigm in moving between long-wave cycles. Its emphasis on ICTs and their pervasive effects throughout the economic and social system in both job creation and job destruction was first articulated in the early 1950s by the computer pioneer and consultant John Diebold (1952), whose predictions have proved to be much more accurate than those of Wiener. The

Table 1.1. Various Ways of Looking at ICT

Approach to Information Technology	Information Society	Automation (Job Destruction)	IT Sector (Job Creation)	ICT Paradigm Change (Creative Destruction)
Main Focus of Approach	Knowledge occupations White collar displaces blue collar	Process Innovations Robotics	Microelectronics Computers Telecommunications	Pervasive technology and changing institutions
Major Economic Consequences	Informatization in post-industrial society	Unemployment and de-skilling as main problems	Rise of electronics industry	New occupations, new industries, new services, and transformation of old
Representative Strategies and Policy Proposals	Education for white-collar work	Shorter hours Job sharing	Support for IT sector	Diffusion strategies in all sectors Re-skilling
Approach to Software	Software as just another occupation	Software neglected	Emphasis on software industry and hardware suppliers	Emphasis on users for all computer applications
Implications for Technology Policy	No special implications for technology policy	Slow down technical change	Support for electronic industry R&D	Generic technology programmes linked to diffusion networks

'ICT paradigm change' points to the direct effects of the rise of entirely new ICT industries in the second half of this century. Even more, however, it stresses the indirect effects of the ICT revolution, following Schumpeter's analysis of the bandwagon effects generated by the opening of new markets and numerous new opportunities for profitable investment. This conception of new technology as the most potent stimulus to waves of new investment, subject only to the willing compliance of the monetary authorities, was accepted unreservedly by John Maynard Keynes (1930), even though his main concern was with the shorter business cycles.

The effects of a major new pervasive technology such as ICTs must be recognized as including job destruction and creation. Whether the net balance is positive or negative in a given national economy cannot be assessed by simply counting the direct effects in new jobs gained and old jobs destroyed. It has to be recognized that the expansionary effects on any national economy, or the world economy as a whole, paradoxically depend on rapid increases in labour productivity that can stimulate waves of new investment throughout the economy.

A revolutionary new technology can create the basis for a virtuous circle of growth in which investment is high, labour productivity grows fast—and output even faster. The result is a net growth of employment. Whether this virtuous circle can be sustained depends on macroeconomic, employment, and trade policies as well as on the new technologies. Prolonged periods of full employment can result if there is a good match between technologies, policies, and institutions.

This was the happy situation in Europe, Japan, and North America in the 1950s and 1960s, when there were considerable increases in employment and very low unemployment. That was based on cheap oil and very rapid expansion in the production of automobiles and other consumer durables, in the steel and plastics industries, and in many related services.

The Role of ICTs in the 'East Asian Miracle'

Figure 1.1 demonstrates that the virtuous circle achieved in the 1950s and 1960s in most OECD countries was also attained in the 1980s and 1990s with the aid of new technologies. The difference is that in the later period the beneficiaries have been in Dynamic Asian Economies (DAEs), most notably the 'Four Tigers' of East Asia: Hong Kong, Singapore, Taiwan, and South Korea. The DAEs achieved such remarkably high

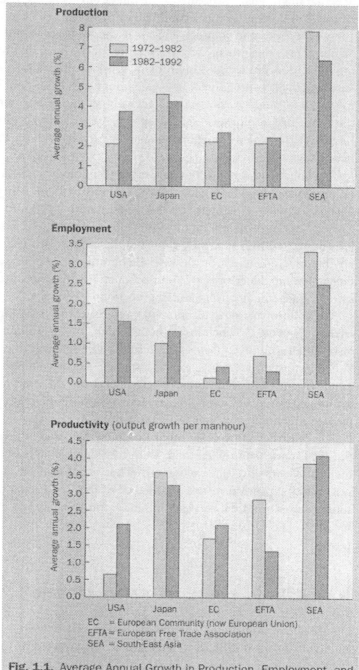

Fig. 1.1. Average Annual Growth in Production, Employment, and Productivity, 1972–1992

Source: Freeman and Soete (1994).

output, productivity, and employment growth that the World Bank described them as participating in the 'East Asian Miracle'. Like many other commentators, the Bank has pointed to the role of exports, education, and training in achieving this success but has not discussed the role of ICTs (World Bank 1993).

Kenneth Kraemer in Chapter 18 examines ICTs in the economic development of East Asian economies. However, few others have analysed the changing commodity composition of East Asian exports or the role of new technologies. That is the purpose of this section, which analyses the extraordinarily high rate of diffusion of ICTs in East Asia and the crucial role this has played in their export success, in their output and productivity growth, and in their related success in generating new employment through virtuous-circle effects.

Success of the 'South'

It has become a commonplace to suggest that the countries of the 'South' are overtaking the 'North' in total output, in manufacturing production, and in shares of manufacturing exports. For example, *The Economist* of October 1994 had a supplement entitled 'The War of the Worlds'. This presented numerous graphs and tables to illustrate its predictions that the 'South' could account for nearly two-thirds of world output by 2020. Although these forecasts might possibly be accurate in the aggregate sense, most do not take account of the extreme differentiation between various regions and countries of the 'South'.

The reason such predictions are made at all is due almost entirely to the success in the 1980s and 1990s of DAEs, especially the Four Tigers. The experience of Africa and Latin America was quite different. Their per capita incomes fell in the 1980s, while they rose by a record amount in East Asia (World Bank 1991). The share of East Asian exports in total world exports of manufactures rose by six or seven times from 1965 to 1990, while that of African countries fell (GATT 1990). The huge success of East Asian countries in industrialization, output, and export growth can certainly not be explained by an earlier start with industrialization than Latin America. The DAEs were actually far behind the main Latin American countries in levels of industrialization as late as the 1950s (Maizels 1962). The progress of DAEs has been based on a remarkable structural transformation, on high levels of infrastructural investment, and increasingly in the 1980s and 1990s, on the scale and efficiency of their ICT industries, services, and exports.

Importance of the Telecommunications Infrastructure

A vital condition for export success in today's world economy is an efficient telecommunications infrastructure. This can be seen in the priority given throughout the world to modernizing networks, including major initiatives in Eastern Europe and China. The infrastructure is not only an essential foundation for conducting routine business everywhere in the economy; it is also of much importance as the basis for a rapidly expanding network of new services which can be traded internationally, and in greatly enhancing the efficiency of many other services, especially education and health. That explains the political and industrial importance attached to 'information superhighway' policies around the world (see Chapter 22).

It is therefore significant that world telecommunications statistics demonstrate very clearly the great success of the DAEs in rapidly catching up and overtaking Europe in the diffusion of telecommunications networks and services. In terms of number of main lines per 100 inhabitants, by the mid-1990s Hong Kong was ahead of advanced European countries like the UK, Germany, and Italy, while Singapore, South Korea, and Taiwan were ahead of countries like Spain. Another feature of Asian development in the early 1990s was the growth rate of new networks such as cellular mobile phones, which reached about 40 per cent in Hong Kong and Singapore at the start of 1993 (Siemens 1994).

The DAEs were very far behind Europe in the 1970s. By 1995, countries like Hong Kong and Singapore had come to depend very heavily on their telecommunications infrastructures as the foundation for their entrepreneurial economies and their roles as major manufacturing centres and providers of trading services. These countries have taken extraordinary measures to accelerate investment, to link traders with the network through computerization, and to provide new services to business and academic communities (Mansell and Jenkins 1992).

Some other countries in the 'South', such as Brazil or Chile, have achieved moderately high rates of growth in their networks in the 1990s (Siemens 1994). Yet they still lag well behind DAEs, although they were once ahead of them.

ICTs and Export Growth

Even more impressive than the DAEs' ICT infrastructure development, but closely related to it, has been their export success. The enormous increase in their share of world manufacturing exports has been universally acclaimed, but the change in the commodity composition has gone relatively unnoticed.

There are very wide differences in the relative rates of growth of various commodity groups in world trade, ranging from 2 per cent for all primary commodities, including fuel, food, and raw minerals, to 8 per cent for all manufacturing, and 13 per cent for ICT goods. The Four Tigers have been particularly successful in the most rapidly increasing sectors of the world market—ICT activities like office machinery and telecommunications equipment (GATT 1990: vol. 2). This gives them a built-in expansionary advantage compared with those countries of the 'South' which remain geared to low-value-added primary commodities. For instance, ICT exports account for more than a quarter of all exports from South Korea, Singapore, and Taiwan.

The Four Tigers were followed by Thailand, Malaysia, and mainland China in the pattern of increasing output and exports of ICT goods and services. In 1992, for example, electronic products accounted for nearly 20 per cent of Thailand's exports. Imports of ICT goods into the Four Tigers, China, and the countries in the region were also very high, illustrating the point that the whole of East Asia had become a zone of highly interdependent production and trade in electronic components and the ICT industries.

Japan was the main source of technology imports and, especially when the yen appreciated so much on the foreign exchange markets in the 1990s, it also became the main source of new investment. However, the Four Tigers also became major suppliers of new capital for other countries in the region, increasingly in China and South-East Asia. This can be illustrated at the micro-level by the example of Samsung Electronics. Until the late 1960s, Samsung Trading was not in the electronics industry at all. Then pressure from the South Korean government induced it to enter this market. It was so successful that Samsung was itself investing in new plants by the 1980s, not only in Asia but also in the USA, Canada, Mexico, the European Community, and Eastern Europe.

The stimulating effects of rapidly growing exports in the most dynamic sectors of world trade have themselves generated much new employment, both directly in the export industries and indirectly by multiplier effects throughout the economy. This phenomenon was identified by Alfred Maizels in his classic book *Industrial Growth and World Trade*, which studied world production and trade between 1899 and 1959. In it, Maizels (1962: 17) concluded:

> Since exports are also an important part of total demand for final output in most industrial countries, a change in competitive

power—which implies a change in export sales—will itself affect the rate of growth in industrial production. Thus, exports interact in a dynamic way with the growth of the whole economy. There has in fact been a remarkably close relationship over the past sixty years in the relative growth rates of the main industrial countries and their shares of the world export market in manufactures.

The Four Asian Tigers in a Virtuous Circle

The virtuous-circle effects of rapidly increasing output, not-quite-so-rapid increases in labour productivity, rising employment, and steeply rising exports have been most clearly seen in Singapore. By 1993 employment in electronic products and components had risen to 121,336, over a third of total employment in manufacturing, compared to 65,837 or about 24 per cent of manufacturing employment ten years earlier. The total output of manufacturing in Singapore almost doubled between 1986 and 1993, but that of electronics nearly trebled (Singapore Government 1994). The slower increases in output, employment, and productivity in traditional electrical machinery and equipment are noteworthy since many countries have grouped these two industries together in their industrial statistics.

South Korea has also experienced extraordinary dynamism in its ICT industries. For instance, its output of office machinery and of television and communications equipment increased at more than double the rate of total manufacturing or traditional electrical equipment between 1987 and 1993.

The position in Hong Kong and Taiwan is more complex. In these cases there has been a big shift of investment and employment to other Asian countries because of lower labour costs, especially to mainland China. Therefore, whereas the total output of manufacturing continued to increase, the rise slowed down dramatically in Hong Kong towards the mid-1990s, including the output of electronics. There was also a substantial fall in employment in electrical equipment and electronics in Hong Kong. Although employment in the electronics industries increased from 49,000 to 114,000 between 1970 and 1980, it fell from 114,000 to 84,000 between 1989 and 1993.

In Taiwan, manufacturing employment also began declining in 1987. However, in both Taiwan and Hong Kong the decline in industrial employment was more than compensated by the rise of employment in services. Unemployment rates remained low in the mid-1990s, at 2.1 per cent in Hong Kong in 1992 and 2.4 per cent in Taiwan. This meant services were becoming the main source of jobs, as has already occurred in advanced industrialized countries of the 'North'.

Within the overall expansion of employment in the services sector, business services and software employment have been especially dynamic. Business services employment in Taiwan, excluding financial services, rose from 79,000 in 1983 to 205,000 in 1993. In Hong Kong, it increased from 79,000 in 1987 to 125,000 in 1993. Financial services in both countries increased employment even more rapidly.

Employment Impacts of ICTs in East Asia

In considering the overall stimulus to output and employment in the Four Tigers over the last twenty years, it is important to consider both the direct employment effects in all industries and services and the indirect effects on the competitive performance of the total economies. Indeed, the entire region must be taken into account, including China and countries like Thailand and Malaysia, where the direct employment generating effects are still strong. In the Four Tigers themselves, the direct effects in the ICT industries were greatest from the 1960s to the early 1980s. During this time, their share in total manufacturing employment grew to nearly 15 per cent in Hong Kong; about 20 per cent in Taiwan and South Korea; and even more in Singapore. The share of ICT equipment in total manufacturing exports rose to even higher levels (GATT 1990: vol. ii, table IV.40).

In the late 1980s and 1990s the direct employment effects remained important. However, they were felt primarily in the areas of financial services and telecommunication-based activities. The indirect effects on the competitive performance of the entire region became even more important. The high labour productivity and falling costs of the ICT producers themselves facilitated diffusion of ICT throughout the region. Labour productivity increases in the ICT manufacturing sector were extremely large because of the microelectronics-inspired technical changes which have dramatically enhanced the cost-performance characteristics of ICTs (Freeman and Soete 1994).

Policies for Employment Growth

The key policy questions arising from the above analysis relate to finding ways of ensuring the job creation–destruction equation does not tip over drastically to the negative side. This requires an understanding of a country or region's special strengths and weaknesses, rather than just trying to adopt practices that have worked for some, like the Four Tigers (see Chapter 11).

Given the intense business pressures to reduce costs, it might seem sensible even in developed economies to compete by reducing the wages of the unskilled. Such policies are mirages. They are likely to exacerbate social tensions between groups when income and quality-of-life differentials between them grow wider, as they have been doing since the 1980s in many countries. Trying to compete through low wages could also create resistance to change by giving credence to fears that technology is being used to de-skill certain jobs. Such anxieties about this kind of de-skilling have often motivated protests against technical change. Low-wage policies are a bottomless pit because there are so many countries able to supply even cheaper labour costs.

A more effective approach for most industrial countries of the 'North' is to create a strong movement towards employment growth in higher-wage, higher-skilled, higher-technology, and more science-based rather than labour-intensive sectors (see for example OECD 1991). The positive employment-generating effects of this shift, however, have not been sufficient to offset the loss of jobs in the lower-skill and lower-tech sectors, or the job-destruction effects of ICT in some higher-skill sectors. Moreover, the intensity of international trade competition means it is unlikely that there will be much employment growth in manufacturing in the OECD countries in the 1990s. This implies that strategies for full employment in the older industrial countries will have to rely on a combination of two main sectors:

1. high-skill, internationally competitive industries and services based increasingly on ICTs;

2. a second-tier 'sheltered' non-traded sector, also using ICTs, which needs to provide community and personal services on a sufficient scale to absorb many of the currently unemployed and the unskilled and low-skill part-time and full-time workers.

Winning in Competitive Markets

Much employment can be created directly through the development and use of ICTs. Building the physical infrastructure for new telecommunications 'superhighways' can itself generate employment. In addition, further new ICT-based industries will continue to be developed, as they have since the 1950s. Some job creation will also continue to come from the transformation of old industries by the application of ICTs, as has been occurring in financial-service enterprises.

However, the most important sector for new job creation in many OECD countries will probably come from education, training, publishing, and software services. The improvement of skills will be a central issue in enabling developed countries to compete with the rest of the world, as encapsulated by the slogan: 'Get Smarter or Get Poorer.' ICTs should play a central role in creating a new educational and training infrastructure that could cope with this growing demand. Multimedia techniques can be used to provide new ways of learning in every discipline and subdiscipline (as discussed further in Chapter 14). Teachers and software and animation specialists could participate in a major effort to design and develop new educational materials, including CD-ROMs and videos.

Home education cannot be substituted for schools, although it will certainly grow. On the contrary, teachers will be needed more than ever to provide personal support, counselling, and guidance on a large scale. Nevertheless, if the potential for ICTs to bring better education and training to more people is to be realized, it is vital that teachers be on the side of change. Experience everywhere shows that ICTs cannot be successfully applied without the active support and involvement of users.

Teachers must therefore be encouraged to acquire software and other ICT skills. There is a great deal of work involved in reworking a syllabus and creating textbooks, encyclopedias, and other educational aids to take advantage of advanced multimedia features. These new capabilities—like personal computers, the Internet, and CD-ROMs—can be especially valuable for children who have difficulties in learning with older methods. Effective multimedia educational aids will be developed successfully only through a close partnership between educational and ICT specialists. This could be achieved through initiatives such as allowing more teachers to take sabbatical leave to develop educational software. That would also create more employment within education.

Software development is one of the most important ICT employment sectors. It is also an arena that is increasingly being competed in by newly industrialized countries in Asia and elsewhere, who can offer high skills at relatively low costs. In order to remain competitive in software, developers from traditional software sources, like the USA and Europe, will need to concentrate on areas where they can add most value. In addition to education and training, this should include:

1. **Organization and technical change.** Much creativity is needed in applying new ICT capabilities and software development techniques innovatively to meet the challenges posed by changing business requirements.

2. **Wired and wireless networks.** Demands for much new infrastructure development and applications software come from the attractions of new networked services.

3. **Middleware.** The spread of networks increases the need for intermediate 'middleware' layers of software to overcome incompatibilities between different systems and devices.

4. **New information technologies.** Innovative software development techniques and products are required to provide successful applications of technological advances like parallel processing, virtual reality, and multimedia. The skills involved in multimedia often extend beyond traditional notions of software into what has traditionally been regarded as publishing, film, or television production expertise.

5. **'Green' objectives.** Software can be imaginatively used to meet energy-saving and environmental goals, including developments in telecommuting and transport systems.

A Thriving Non-Traded Economy

The intense pressures of international trade competition combined with the effects of technical change are reducing the demand for unskilled labour. It is also therefore essential to create jobs in a more sheltered 'non-traded' area of the economy. Predictions of future occupational trends indicate that a realistic strategy can be based on seeking to match job-creation needs by satisfying the growing demand for more personal and community services. For example the US Bureau of Labor Statistics forecasts that many of the occupations likely to grow fastest to 2005 include such services as, for example, home health aides and child-care workers (see Figure 1.2).

In order to meet this demand, public sector initiatives at local and central government levels will probably be more important in Europe than in the USA. The issue of fair employment practices will also be vital.

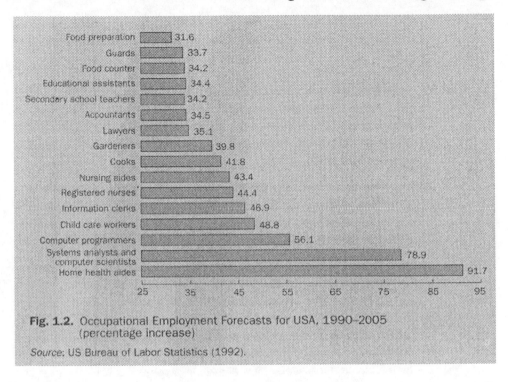

Fig. 1.2. Occupational Employment Forecasts for USA, 1990–2005 (percentage increase)

Source: US Bureau of Labor Statistics (1992).

Policy Conclusions

Schumpeter's long-wave theory of techno-economic waves has been confirmed in the post-war period by the shift from oil-based mass production to ICTs. These effects highlight why it is necessary to take account of both job destruction and creation. The success of the DAEs in the 1980s and 1990s demonstrated that national investments in new technological infrastructure and the fostering of higher skills can pay major dividends in economic growth and international competitiveness. It also indicated that ICTs can be the major engine of economic and export growth, a role which is likely to remain dominant well into the twenty-first century.

Given their very different social and economic backgrounds, it would be wrong for the developed 'North' to try to mimic the environment in the more newly industrialized countries, say by competing through low labour costs. Instead, economic growth should be encouraged by focusing on high-skill, high-wage business operations and using ICT investments imaginatively to support a large expansion of employment in the non-traded economy and in education, training, publishing, and entertainment.

35

The important roles government can play in trying to ensure that the two-edged nature of technical change has an overall positive effect include:

1. **Improvement of the telecommunications infrastructure.** This should include the information byways and ramps for small firms, educational establishments, and others—as well as the main superhighways. This has been described as the most important commitment of governments (Gore 1991).

2. **Creation of centres of excellence for educational technology to promote new multimedia.** These could bring together academics and government experts with suppliers and users. Such a blend can have an extraordinary effect, provided it is given sufficient priority and resources.

3. **Co-ordinated exploitation of educational resources for wider community services.** ICTs give the potential to move educational and training activities away from traditional shared public facilities, like schools and universities, to home-based and commercial environments. Nevertheless, there are sound economic and social arguments for maintaining shared public educational facilities. These can offer major savings through the economies of scale they allow for purchasing ICT services and products. Many schools have found that the most intensive use of technological resources like computers comes after school hours. This can be usefully extended to bring in more people, at more times, by opening out educational resources to wider community needs.

4. **Emphasizing social needs in ICT-related policies.** For instance, it would be a social and educational disaster if the trend to home-based teaching goes too far, as it will be the lowest achievers who get the worst deals in equipment and other support.

Notes

1. This chapter is an expanded and updated version of Freeman's PICT lecture, given on 14 Dec. 1994 at the Policy Studies Institute in London and originally reported in Freeman (1995).
2. I discuss Schumpeter's analysis and its implications for current ICT diffusion in more detail in Chapter 7.

2 The Information Society: Competing Perspectives on the Social and Economic Implications of Information and Communication Technologies

Ian Miles

Advances in ICTs have been a major driving force in the move towards an information society. In practice, however, there will be many possible information societies, just as there have been different post-war industrial societies. For instance, the ability of ICT to permit increased transnationalization in many activities, such as the trade in services and the diffusion of popular culture, may combine with other forces promoting globalization to erode some national differences—or offer equal scope for fragmentation and diversity within and between countries.

This chapter by Ian Miles draws on much PICT research to provide an overview of the main alternative viewpoints on the social and economic implications of ICT-based innovation.[1] He argues that the outcome of social and political choices will result from a synthesis among these polar views. He calls this scenario 'structuralism'—a term which highlights the significant roles played by different actors within various organizational and group contexts in constraining and otherwise 'structuring' the ways in which the information society will actually develop. The issues he outlines are explored in detail throughout this book.

Compass Points to the Information Society

Information processing is an integral feature of human activities. Innate human capabilities have been augmented by various technologies since ancient times—writing to store information, drums and flags to transmit and display it, the abacus to process it. But current social and technological developments are distinctive. Information storage, processing, and communication have become increasingly visible and important in economic, social, and political life. New ICTs that help to perform these activities are a substantial advance on earlier technologies and offer tremendous scope for transforming the ways in which we produce and use information.

Developments in ICTs are at the heart of the processes shaping the 'information society' and the many important unanswered questions about it.[2] For example, some people believe that the widening of political support for public services is the result of developments and improvements stemming from the application of ICTs. They regard the likely alternatives to be new forms of social inequity and continuing decay of the welfare state. However, the choices offered are not open-ended, nor are the individuals and groups concerned anything like equal players. Inequalities between the information-rich and information-poor may grow if commercial interests gain undue precedence over citizens' groups and voluntary associations as new services proliferate.

There are two dimensions underlying much of the debate on the social implications of ICTs.[3] As summarized in Table 2.1, these are:

1. **Depth.** These perspectives are concerned with issues surrounding the speed and extent of change. At one extreme, 'continuism' has a 'more of the same' view which stresses the limited extent of ICT-related change and social and economic innovation in an information society. (The concept of an information society is not even accepted by some continuists.) In contrast, 'transformism' takes a 'something different' stance which stresses that the information society is fundamentally new and that ICT has an all-pervasive revolutionary potential. 'Structuralism' seeks a synthesis of these views.

2. **Width.** This dimension reflects debates between, on the one hand, 'concordists', who see ICT and the information society as being characterized by greater democracy, decentralization, self-expression, and personal choice—and, on the other, 'anatagonists', who stress the threat of greater surveillance and control on political and personal activities by a centralized state. Again, structuralism aims for a synthesis.

Table 2.1. Views of the Depth and Width Dimensions of the Information Society

DEPTH: The 'change' dimension

Continuism	Transformism	Structuralism
Claims about the information society, ICTs, and the predicted rate of diffusion of the technology are regarded as overstated. Main features of society and basic power structures are thought unlikely to alter, although social and political initiatives may lead to change. Forecasting mainly for short- and medium-term, based on extrapolating past experience.	Information society is viewed as representing a major historical shift, changing the bases of political power and social classes with a growing role for information workers and knowledge class. ICT seen as revolutionary technology with practical benefits which will promote repaid diffusion. Long-term forecasting based typically on generalizations of leading-edge experiences.	Recognizes both barriers to change and openings for far-ranging innovation. Outcomes expected to depend on actors and interests shaping ICT applications, with an uneven diffusion of the technology. Social change seen coming mainly in new organizational structures, styles, and skills. Forecasts draw on other approaches, usually in areas like industrial organization, employment.

WIDTH: The 'control' dimension

Concordism	Antagonism	Structuralism
Access to information regarded as liberating; communication systems as promoting decentralization and democratization. ICT seen as aid to abolishing tedious and dangerous work and improving quality of working life. Options opened for: new forms of community; meeting growing education and training needs; dissolving distinctions between regions and social groups.	Information linked to great increases in social and political control. Existing inequalities expected to be widened by gaps between information-rich and poor. ICT seen as increasing de-skilling and degradation of work and separation between mental and manual labour. Likely acceleration of tendencies to withdraw into private, often highly stressful worlds in everyday life.	Information society treated as a shift between different regimes of social actors with unequal opportunities to intervene, but all of whose actions have consequences. Some de-skilling is likely but new skills and job types will be created. Evolution to new cultural forms; new resources and interests; and new areas of co-operation and contestation.

The Importance of Structuralism: The Search for Synthesis

These viewpoints reflect the 'consensus versus conflict' debates which have long been apparent in social science research and literature about ICT and the information society.[4] These initially found expression in disputes between 'post-industrial' (Bell 1973) and 'de-skilling' (Braverman

1974) analyses of changing work relations. More recently, the theme of expanding information opportunities versus growing information inequalities has been prominent.[5]

The polarized attitudes at the extremes of the dimensions (continuism–transformism and concordism–antagonism) are limited ones. A synthesis is required which draws on the contributions of all positions and overcomes the limits of each extreme. 'Structuralism' is one such synthesis which recognizes that a diversity of actors and interests—embodied in the different social structures of different countries, organizations, and groups—confront a multiplicity of choices which lead to many possible outcomes. It importantly emphasizes that trends breed counter-trends as actors seek to offset the costs of change. Forecasts about the impacts of social and technological change rarely recognize the complexity of this process.

The structuralist analysis implies that there is not simply one future outcome. Rather, there are many possible information societies—just as there have been many different post-war advanced industrial capitalist societies, as reflected, for example, in the differences between the economic approaches of the USA, Sweden, and Japan.[6] Figure 2.1 distinguishes four visions of how future alternative information societies may differ in terms of four quadrants defined by the intersections between depth and width dimensions. The significance of the structuralist perspective as a focal point encompassing both dimensions comes from the way that it seeks to find a synthesis of these competing views, rather than the middle ground.

Key Factors Shaping Information Societies

The Special Characteristics of ICT

The specificities and revolutionary potential of ICT are vital factors in the debates about the nature of the information society. Advances that have led to the convergence of digitized forms of computing and telecommunication technologies that can process, store, communicate, display, and manage all kinds of information have made it possible for all ICTs to benefit from the increased power and reduced cost of using microelectronics and related information-processing technologies, like optical fibre telecommunications. These developments have dramatically increased the range of ICT applications.

This has led to much exaggerated talk of its wondrous potential.

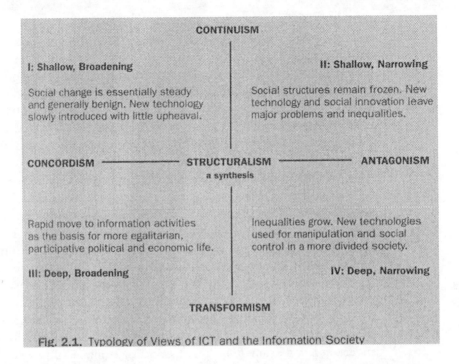

Fig. 2.1. Typology of Views of ICT and the Information Society

Nevertheless, a strong case exists for viewing ICT as forming the basis for a technological revolution because it enables numerous activities to be done in many new ways—using tools perceived as advantageous—and thus widely adopted (Miles *et al.* 1990). In terms of the economics of innovation (Dosi *et al.* 1988), a technological revolution involves upheaval in the structure of costs and opportunities, implying changes in our 'common-sense' notions of how to organize production. According to Perez (1983: 361; 1985), a new key factor of production emerges when there are

> a clearly perceived low—and descending—relative cost; unlimited supply for all practical purposes; potential all-pervasiveness; and a capacity to reduce the costs of capital, labour and products as well as to change them qualitatively.

ICT certainly fits this description. For instance, there has been an exponential rate of improvement in the performance of features such as the density of circuits and amount of memory on a microchip. This has contributed to the smaller size, reduced cost, and increased reliability of hardware. As a result, the technology can be incorporated unobtrusively and at increasing cost-effectiveness into an expanding range of devices and environments, from portable computers and telephones to cruise missiles and oil rigs. It has also enabled computer-based information systems to be run as distributed networks rather than through centralized data processing facilities. ICT systems are also extremely flexible, as their capabilities can be altered by changing the software. Overall, the costs of all forms of information processing have been lowered while the quality, speed, user-friendliness, and range of capabilities have increased dramatically. And these improvements are ongoing.

Older computing and telecommunication technologies were restricted to large-scale and expensive operations because of their higher cost and size. Modern ICTs have become a personalized commodity, as well as being a powerful aid to global transactions for transnational corporations. Their rapidly improving cost-effectiveness encourages innovative applications of many kinds and offers ever-widening scope for supporting organizations, such as making it possible to engage in more detailed control of process operations and product design. The application of ICT does not merely substitute for human labour or for earlier generations of technology—it also enables previously unthinkable activities to be undertaken, for example in interconnecting millions of people through the Internet. ICT is therefore not just a new product, or even a radical transformation of a particular economic sector. It is a revolutionary heartland technology whose applicability across all sectors is continuing to grow.

Bounded Social Choices

ICT poses substantial challenges to economic analysis and organizational decision making. The peculiar properties of information and the difficulties in cost-justifying many new services and facilities also mean there is a proliferation of claims and counter-claims about the role of ICT in public policies and corporate strategies. New ICT-based products, production processes, and linkages between formal and informal economic activities and sectors will emerge. New opportunities are opened up for changes in work organization and ways of life, in patterns of demand and institutional relations, and in organizing production and consumption. Many of these possibilities will be desirable, at least for some leading actors.

As a result, not only does information work *per se* become more crucial, as many transformist/concordist accounts of the information society would have it; in addition, the information processing inherent in all work has become a candidate for technological intervention through what has been inelegantly called 'informatization'. However, cultural and cognitive factors may facilitate or inhibit recognition of different opportunities. The diverse interests of groups and individuals may also lead to particular applications being pursued and others left unexplored; for example certain 'trajectories' of ICT application have been emphasized because of perceptions about technical possibilities developed in laboratories and boardrooms, rather than in response to research into consumer demand (Cawson *et al.* 1995; Miles and Thomas 1995).

These developments have resulted in a new ICT-related techno-economic paradigm, as explained by Christopher Freeman in Chapter 7. In this, the patterns of development that emerge from seemingly unlimited technological innovation involve social choices which are still bounded. For instance, ICTs make many new options available but cannot fulfil every wish on demand. However, the boundaries and consequences of choice are uncertain because software makes ICT so malleable, and the technology is associated with a greater internationalization of economic activities, which may erode national economies and cultures. All actors are making decisions under conditions of considerable uncertainty—even those with the best understanding of one technical aspect may be ignorant of associated developments. And the choice of any one actor or set of actors is strongly conditioned by the choices of others, as are the results of these choices.

The future will result from the interaction of many choices and revisions of choices. This suggests that policies and strategies should be flexible, with technical prototyping and social experiments playing a substantial role in guiding them. Seeing ICT as a revolutionary technology suggests a specific perception of an information society as a complex of new and restructured social and economic practices (re)constituted around the potential of ICT. Although some common themes may emerge because the structures of dominant actors are similar, ICT is only one of the elements in flux in the restructuring of political and economic life. Different cultures, countries, and regions are as capable as ever of having radically different responses to apparently similar challenges.

Three main aspects of social change are particularly affected by ICTs: the 'formal economy' of paid work and officially organized production and services; the 'informal economy' of unpaid domestic activities and voluntary work; and the boundaries between public and private services. These are examined in the following sections.

ICT and the Formal Economy

Changing Employment Patterns

ICTs enable major innovations in practically every aspect of production and service processes, in almost all economic sectors. One of the most active and controversial areas of analysis of this widespread innovation has been in forecasting the employment impacts of ICT (see for example Daniels 1986; Kortteinen *et al.* 1987; Ducatel 1994; and Chapters 1, 7, and 18 in this book). This has led to general agreement that three trends will persist in advanced industrial societies:

- employment will continue to shift from the primary (agricultural, fishing, and mining) and secondary (industrial) sectors to the tertiary (services) sector;

- ancillary, administrative, and professional occupations will increase relative to traditional manual and production jobs; and

- average lifetime working hours will decline, although there may be either an intensification of work within working hours or an increase in working hours for some groups of workers.

Continuism projects slow and steady development of these trends, whereas transformism forecasts major shifts in employment. The deep, broadening vision summarized in Quadrant III of Figure 2.1 would involve a rapid rise in employment in ICT-related services, changes in working conditions (such as more self-employment, employment in decentralized and small enterprises, and telework), and in changing working hours (for example much more retraining, sabbaticals, and shorter working weeks). The Quadrant IV scenario would mean greater polarization between skilled and de-skilled employees and between the employed and unemployed.

It is dangerous to extrapolate from past experience with ICT systems to new generations, especially given the differing characteristics of network-based activities compared to earlier stand-alone systems. However, the available evidence suggests the unemployment problems of industrial societies are related more to political and economic changes than to the use of new technology. The trend in skills changes has been to upgrade expertise required for some jobs and to increase demand for new technical skills and skill combinations. Alongside this, there has been the degradation of a smaller proportion of jobs, the creation of new low-skill work, and a shift to much more unstable 'flexible' work conditions for 'peripheral workers', like part-time employees. Some polarization of the workforce has ensued—and even more so the polarization between employed and unemployed.

Structuralism suggests these developments are not so much products of ICT *per se*, but stem from the interplay of social actors and the resultant managerial and public policies. Workers and managers have the opportunity to influence the outcome of choices about the redesign of jobs and reductions in the volume of formal work, which will determine whether there is an increased 'dualism' in society between those in skilled and well-paid jobs and those who are unemployed or working in less skilled and less rewarding jobs. Changes in working time and conditions have repercussions in other areas of life—notably the money and time available for leisure activities, for consumption, for production using domestic equipment in the informal economy, and for the knowledge, attitudes, and interests brought to everyday life.

Attitudes and values typified by Quadrant III in Figure 2.1 indicate a growing interest in 'self-actualization', in freedom from bureaucratic and other constraints, and in social participation. But Quadrant IV accurately portrays the threat that there might be a growing dualistic experience of working life, with many people excluded from employment, which will also be reflected in greater dualism in leisure interests and political concerns. A structuralist perspective accepts that growing technical competence at the formal workplace could lead to a more sophisticated understanding of the potential of system design, thereby making people better equipped to challenge claims that work organization and the administration of public agencies are dictated by technical necessities, rather than by design choices. However, it also recognizes that dualism is a real danger that must be addressed.

Interorganizational Changes

Change in the formal economy is not just a matter of individual work experience. There are important movements under way in the structure of, and interrelationships between, organizations. In Quadrant III, this involves a shift to smaller-scale and/or decentralized organizations because ICT can be used to change the calculus of organizational costs. The Quadrant IV view, however, is one of growing transnational corporations moving into sectors previously organized on a local basis, including many services.

From a structuralist perspective, it is possible to identify several plausible outcomes depending on how various actors behave. For instance, telecommunication's much-vaunted ability to offset existing spatial in-equalities in the distribution of technical and managerial roles will be fulfilled only when there is an act of political will to provide incentives to relocate head office activities in peripheral areas (see also Chapters 11 and 19). In addition, many kinds of organizations could use ICT to create options like:

- closer linkage between production and remote markets and head-quarters;

- decentralization of many production operations and decisions, within a framework of greater co-ordination and strategic control, resulting in growing competitive advantage for effective users of such systems;

- increased use by organizations, groups, and individuals of sophistic-ated modelling techniques to analyse the impacts of decision and policy options as a means of challenging or seeking to influence the opinions or actions of others;

- growing treatment of information as a commodity and increasing at-tention to information facilities and telecommunication networks as strategic resources.

The Informal Economy: Household Production and Consumption

Substantial changes in domestic production and consumption are likely to accelerate the processes which have displaced domestic consumer services whose poor innovation performance resulted in little improve-ment in quality and a relative increase in prices. In the past, this process led to consumers undertaking 'self-servicing' in many domestic activities, for example in the displacement of laundries by washing machines (Gershuny and Miles 1983; Gershuny 1987). ICT innovations could ex-tend this trend to encompass most domestic activities, including im-provements to the cost-effectiveness of service organizations, as well as to the consumer goods and new services associated with them (Barras 1990; Miles 1993).

The household innovations provided by ICT will include improve-ments in the capabilities and quality of existing products—such as adding interactivity to CDs—and the introduction of entirely new ones, like monitoring aids for 'do-it-yourself' health care. There will also be many innovations in home-based services, such as electronic mail and computer conferencing through the Internet and video-on-demand, telebanking, and games on interactive TV services. Many previously separate functions will be integrated within one piece of equipment—like an integrated personal computer (PC) and TV—or through the co-ordination of functions using computer-communication links, such as the ability to integrate emergency alarms with databases to ensure appropriate experts can respond rapidly to medical and other crises in the home (Miles 1988*b*).

However, the continuist perspective expects innovation in home entertainment devices to carry on through relatively marginal improvements in familiar products, such as PCs, wide-screen TV, and new satellite and cable channels. Continuists are also sceptical about the value of innovations like interactive-CD encyclopaedias and networked educational aids. In contrast, transformism emphasizes the potential for such capabilities to be of practical benefit in activities which go beyond just entertainment and game playing.

Changing Relationships between Formal and Informal Economies

A structuralist perspective suggests that the diffusion of ICT-based goods and services and the development of new living patterns using them will be considerable. How these developments take place will be shaped by social action—and, indeed, often opposition.[7] Such developments are likely to benefit the population unevenly, with those not having the new technologies often disadvantaged by the subsequent decline of traditional services. In the past, the state has played an important role in promoting new innovations—for example by building roads and supporting the installation of electric power supplies to private households. It may need to do so again to stimulate demand, or at least to regulate private enterprise to ensure market forces do not produce gross inequities.

The implications of consumer innovations can be substantial. The automobile was a vehicle for economic growth and cultural change. Its diffusion facilitated new living patterns, such as suburbanization and associated designs for housing, neighbourhoods, and shopping centres. This gave a boost to construction industries, affected public transport, and changed the context for social mores. Future developments in consumer products and services are likely to be equally multi-faceted—especially if they are related to developments in the formal economy like telework.

Tracing the determinants of broad changes in ways of life is not easy, as indicated by the tortuous debate on the effects of TV (Comstock *et al.* 1978) and the Internet on children (Shields 1995). Changes in ways of life defy easy summary. Simplistic assertions about growing isolation versus renewal of community do not capture the complexity and active nature of social change. This involves people with different interests interacting together, including some who are likely to react in creative ways against undesirable developments in their own lives. For instance, TV and the Internet may have led to a decline in some forms of socializing. But home-based leisure has meant families spend more time together and the growth in active leisure has parallelled the consumption of broadcast media (Bessant *et al.* 1985; Cawson *et al.* 1995). The Internet has also created opportunities for creating new forms of 'virtual' communities and social interactions.

There is little reason to believe fully either in the view that ICT will permit communities to reverse spontaneously the underlying causes of society's ills, such as drug addiction and violence, or that the galloping 'privatism' will cause households and small groups to draw in on themselves and communicate with the outside world only through highly selective electronic media. A less sensational but still radical set of developments is more likely, reflecting the structuralist analysis rather than those of the polarized extremes. These developments will involve changes in the relation between household activities and formal services, rather than questions like whether new demand will create new jobs or how changing working patterns like telework will affect demand and lifestyles.

For instance, just as earlier generations of domestic equipment substituted for many traditional consumer services—as washing machines did for laundries—new consumer goods might stimulate service operators to look to ICTs to help them maintain a competitive edge. In particular, new combinations of products, software, and telecommunication capabilities could be applied to information-intensive services that need to be tailored to individual characteristics and circumstances, like self-tutoring educational services and automated expert advice on a variety of business, health, or leisure topics.[8]

Shifting Boundaries between Public and Private Domains

Distinctions between private and public activities and goods are challenged by the applications of ICT which facilitate new private modes of provision in areas that were traditionally the preserve of public authorities.

This potential is not just a product of ICT. It reflects a number of inter-related trends affecting public services.

For instance, critics of collective provision of welfare services argue that they are too bureaucratic, sometimes inhumanely and inefficiently managed, foster dependency, and encourage waste and fraud. ICTs could help to manage these services more efficiently and effectively (see Chapters 15 and 16). Similarly, traditional approaches to health and education are being questioned by alternatives, such as innovations in preventive medicine and patterns of care that allow for greater degrees of self-management. ICTs can help this process by supporting facilities like electronic fitness-monitoring devices.

Developments like these are creating markets for private services offering packages combining traditional and ICT-based elements of provision, ranging from the privatization of major areas of education, healthcare, and many other conventional public services. New modes of ICT provision may also undermine public services by draining off to the new services many of the more articulate and innovation-promoting clients, as well as skilled staff. On the other hand, real and perceived inequities in public service resourcing, delivery, and outcomes could be increased by the greater use of the traditional services by those who are also using the new services, such as patients with printouts of health trends from 'self-help' ICT medical aids. Some traditional services might then be perceived as second-rate because they do not display quality improvements visible in other sectors of the economy. This would undermine the willingness to invest the high levels of expenditure required to maintain and improve public services.

These trends are blurring distinctions between public and private areas of responsibility for information, commodities, services, telecommunication infrastructure, and other activities.[9] The redefinition of these boundaries will be affected by general government orientations, agency-specific missions, and staff and client interests. For instance, the data-security interests of professional workers like teachers, doctors, and police may often diverge from those of the general public. The outcome will depend on the mobilization of popular feeling against intrusions into privacy.

Public agencies are likely to rely increasingly on ICT and other technological innovations to tailor services to satisfy the changing individual requirements of clients and to mobilize support for public investment. However, many services will continue to rely on personal contact rather than automated aids, say in the provision of child care and in meeting the needs of a growing elderly population. Restrictions on public expenditure are the main threat to the ability to provide these human services. There are also financial and other barriers that could constrain the benefits achieved by applying ICTs to augmenting public services, as explained in Chapter 15.

In the face of these continuist-type obstacles to the flowering of transformist-type potentials, change is bound to be uneven and characterized by false starts and partial solutions to evolving problems. The alternative to improving and expanding services is likely to be new forms of social inequity and a decaying welfare state. Competitive service provision with increased privatized consumption will pit individual choice against bureaucracy. This could help to reduce some inefficiencies and encourage the introduction of new services to improve quality. However, the choices offered are not in practice open-ended—inequalities and divisions in society could increase if particular types of ideological and commercial interests become dominant.

Critical Issues Facing Information Societies

ICT suppliers and users have developed strategies based on the expectation that there will be continuing trends towards an expansion of the power available from the telecommunication infrastructure and the computing power that end-users can apply in conjunction with it. Planning also continues to be based on the assumption of substantial growth in the volume, range of channels, and multimedia capabilities of networked, interpersonal, and mass-communication information flows between producers and their consumers, clients, and citizens. An increased willingness to pay for ICT-based security and surveillance measures is also considered likely by those who believe in the dualistic antagonism scenario.

The concrete form these developments will take is open and their social and economic implications will depend on the answers found to important questions posed by the contrasting views summarized in Table 2.1. Key questions are summarized in Box 2.1.

Some of these questions will be the centre of fierce political debate while others will be resolved by default or through behind-the-scenes manœuvres—and many answers will be determined by the relative power of social actors pursuing different strategies. However, despite the difficulty of predicting specific outcomes, some general characteristics of ICT-related innovation are likely to emerge.

For instance, new demands will be stimulated for information about,

---

Box 2.1. Critical Issues Facing the Information Society

....

- Will developments be driven by the growth of private markets or by the activities of public service agencies who have some redistributive intent, for instance in using ICT to improve the lives of physically disadvantaged people?

- To what extent will new communities of interest emerge spontaneously from the public—or be the product of organizations with the financial power and professional skill to define and package issues in particular ways?

- Will a more technically literate population emerge, capable of marshalling counter-expertise to tackle civil liberties issues (Burnham 1983)?

- Will the expansion of computing and telecommunication power within the home lead to new forms of privatization of family and personal life and the strengthening of boundaries between individuals and groups—or to the encouragement of more interpersonal contact involving mutual reliance, problem-solving, and understanding?

- How will ICTs be deployed in reconciling conflicting pressures of centralization and decentralization? And what political action, if any, will be taken to deploy ICT to alter regional disparities?

....

---

and participation in, an ever-widening range of social issues. New social movements and new forms of interest-group and organizational lobbying and mobilization are also likely to emerge. Complex regulatory problems are being posed by new information and communication channels, particularly in terms of access conditions, media content, competition rules, and technical standards. And if social dualism increases, so will tension between groups and alienation from many public institutions, and—to counter these—demands will grow for new strategies and redistributive action.

The future is therefore indeterminate in many important ways. Policies to influence future directions need to recognize that ICTs allow for new rules of the game in all areas of economic activity and that organizations of all types need to innovate and redefine their objectives in this context. Not all developments will involve the new technologies, but often they will be central. Standing still is rarely an option. Although beleaguered services and individuals may resent being told about the need to adapt, a sea change is taking place—hence the importance of elucidating and understanding competing views of the information society.

Notes

1. The chapter is an updating and further development of a paper prepared by Miles when working for the PICT centre at the University of Sussex, where he conducted research on mapping and measuring the information economy with colleagues at a number of PICT centres (Miles 1988*a*). He draws on studies by Bessant *et al.* (1985), Miles (1988*b*), and Miles *et al.* (1988), together with empirical data on the growth of the 'information economy' from Miles *et al.* (1990).

2. The work of Daniel Bell (1973) has been seminal to discussions of the idea of an 'information society'. Interesting critiques and elaborations of this concept have been provided by Webster and Robins (1985), Beniger (1986), Lyon (1986; 1987), Gershuny (1987), Castells (1989), and Robins (1992).

3. These dimensions emerged from the PICT-sponsored literature review and survey research on which this chapter is based. Surveys of expert opinion which yielded two similar dimensions are reported in Bessant *et al.* (1985) and Rush and Miles (1989). These reflect more general debates between different world-views in social science (Chambliss 1973).

4. See for example the debates between 'benign utopian' (Toffler 1980; 1990; NEDO 1987) and 'malign dystopian' (Burnham 1983; Webster and Robins 1985) viewpoints. Lyon (1986; 1987) and Fincham (1987) provide valuable sociological analyses of these issues. Robins (1992) offers a set of distinctive perspectives associated with various lines of PICT research.

5. Helpful collections of articles dealing with different facets of the debate include Finnegan *et al.* (1987), Forester (1989), and Heap *et al.* (1995).

6. Berger and Piore (1980) discuss one important feature of the differences among industrial capitalist countries: the (re)structuring of labour markets.

7. Public resistance to, or acceptance of, technological change is discussed in more detail in Miles and Thomas (1995).

8. For more on ICT and services in general, see Miles (1987; 1993). Petit (1986) examines differences in the shape of the 'services economy'. Ideas of 'flexible specialization' in manufacturing which could be applied to ICT-based services are most notably expounded by Sable and Piore (1984).

9. In this context, it is interesting to note that private sector activities dominated the fifteen 'Technology Foresight' Panels established in 1994 by the UK Government's Office of Science and Technology (OST). These aimed to bring together industrialists and scientists to identify opportunities and markets in technologies likely to emerge in the next ten to twenty years (see for example OST 1995*b*; 1995*c*; 1995*d*).

3 The Social Shaping of Technology

Robin Williams and David Edge

The way organizational, political, economic, and cultural factors influence the process of technological change has been investigated through a growing body of research on what has become known as 'the social shaping of technology'. Researchers in this field are as concerned with the content of technologies and the social factors which explain technical innovations as they are with the social and economic outcomes.

PICT contributed substantially to this area. Two leading PICT researchers into social shaping, Robin Williams and David Edge, provide an overview of the subject in this chapter. They explore its origins and contributions to policy, practice, and theoretical understandings, as well as explaining its relationships to views of science and technology derived from other disciplines. The subsequent chapters in this part provide examples of research that investigate the ways in which social factors shape technological development and innovation.

Understanding Social and Technical Choices

Studies of the Social Shaping of Technology (SST) emerged in the 1980s through a critique of the prevailing 'technological determinism' tradition, which had limited its scope of enquiry to monitoring the social adjustments required by technological progress.[1] In contrast, SST researchers 'problematized' technological change by showing that it is patterned by the conditions of its creation and use, rather than developing solely according to an inner technical logic.

The variety of scholars with differing concerns and intellectual traditions who have found a meeting point in SST are united by an insistence that the 'black box' of technology must be opened. They aim to expose and analyse the socio-economic patterns embedded in two key factors—the content of technologies and the processes of innovation (MacKenzie and Wajcman 1985; Bijker and Law 1992). However, an awareness that technologies are 'socially shaped' leaves unresolved many important questions about the character and influence of the forces involved in that shaping. In seeking to grasp the complexity of these socio-economic processes, SST researchers have gone beyond a simplistic notion of 'social determinism' which sees technology as reflecting a single rationality, such as an economic imperative.

By no longer viewing technology as emerging from a single social determinant, or through the unfolding of a predetermined technical logic, innovation can be understood as a 'garden of forking paths'. Every stage in the design and implementation of a technology involves choices between different technical options, although these are not necessarily conscious choices. The actual options selected depend on 'social' as well as simple 'technical' factors. These choices shape the content of artefacts and the direction (or 'trajectory') of innovation programmes, resulting in many potential technological outcomes with differing implications for society as a whole and particular groups within it (see Chapter 2).

The SST perspective has important policy implications. Its proponents argue that it makes possible a broader and more pro-active policy agenda. For example, the Constructive Technology Assessment (CTA) model developed mainly in the Netherlands (Rip *et al.* 1995) provides an alternative to conventional technology assessments that were concerned primarily with the retrospective evaluations of the costs and benefits of technologies already designed and developed. In contrast, CTA holds out the prospect of strategic intervention from the early stages of innovation because it highlights the different technological routes available, their possible societal consequences, and the problems and opportunities of influencing the paths taken to meet societal goals. PICT studies have helped move towards the development of policies which emphasize the role of the user, as well as the supplier, and the need to study linkages between them, as discussed later in the chapter.

SST thinking was influenced from the outset by a desire to democratize technological decision making or, at least, to subject it to forms of social accountability and control (Winner 1977; 1985). This view of science and technology as areas of social activity, subject to social forces and amenable to social analysis, has sought to overturn the view that science and technology hold a privileged 'neutral' standing 'above' society.

Roots of the Social Shaping Perspective

A Critique of Technological Determinism

The social shaping perspective seeks to counter the notion of a 'technological imperative'—the idea, particularly prevalent in the public rhetoric of government and industry, that paths of technological change are inevitable and necessitate particular social changes (Edge 1994). This has involved two kinds of technological-determinist argument, which claim that:

1. the nature of technologies and the direction of change are unproblematic or predetermined by factors like 'inner technical logic' or 'economic imperative';

2. technology has necessary and determinate 'impacts' upon work, upon economic life, and upon society as a whole.

Technological change is thereby seen as both requiring and producing social and organizational change. Moreover, many social scientists have treated technology as a given, merely assessing its positive or negative 'social impacts'. In failing to address the content of technology, they have also frequently regarded diverse technologies—such as robotics and computer-controlled machine tools—as if they were a homogeneous class of objects, uniform in their characteristics and stable over time (Fleck *et al.* 1990). Apparently accepting the rhetoric of suppliers and promoters, they assume that these technologies are effective and reliable vehicles for achieving organizational change. However, this overlooks often protracted difficulties in their implementation and frequent failures to deliver predicted and desired outcomes (Senker 1987).

In challenging this view, many PICT researchers have sought to investigate the ways in which social, institutional, economic, and cultural factors shape the direction and rate of innovation and the overall form of technology. The following subsections summarize the main disciplines which have been drawn on in developing SST concepts.

The Sociology of Scientific Knowledge and Technological Artefacts

The development of scientific fields has been widely examined in the Sociology of Scientific Knowledge (SSK) in order to identify crucial decision points and to explain why scientists decided to take the chosen course rather than one of the alternatives. This approach has also been extended to Social Construction of Technology (SCOT) studies, which investigate technological artefacts to identify the key influences that determine why one design approach generally triumphs (Pinch and Bijker 1984). These studies highlight 'interpretative flexibility'—the potentially divergent meanings and responses to technical artefacts by different social groups (see Chapter 4 for further discussion of these issues).

The Sociology of Industrial Organizations

In contrast to SCOT's focus on particular technologies, an approach has been developed that concentrates on the specific organizational and social contexts in which technical change takes place. Much of the research was stimulated by Braverman (1974), who argued that technology was designed to displace the need for workforce skills and, therefore, to enhance the control of capital over the production process. Subsequent work following up this analysis created a more detailed understanding of the complex web of interests within organizations which shape the adoption and implementation of technology.

For example, Noble (1979) showed how Numerical Control (NC) machine tools were designed with the explicit objective—shared by the tool suppliers, users in the aerospace industry, and the US Air Force sponsors—of increasing managerial control by reducing reliance on craft machinists. These machines were to be programmed by technicians; an alternative technology which left control over the production process in the hands of the skilled machinist was rejected. However, it proved difficult to eliminate the need for metal-cutting skills in preparing NC programs and new products were eventually developed to allow shop-floor programming, partly subverting the original development goals.[2]

Critical Studies of Technology Policy

Research into the political, economic, and social forces underlying the developments of technology policy have also been influential in 'social shaping' work. For example, Alfonso Molina (1989) at Edinburgh University has shown how the creation of a new technology often involves the building of a 'socio-technical constituency'. This refers to the alliances of individuals and organizations directly involved—such as supplier firms, technologists, and potential users—with their technical knowledge and other resources. The values and interests of participants in its constituency underpin the shaping of a new technology.

The broader institutional and societal context is also important, including factors like market dynamics, cultural influences, legislation, and public policy. Cross-national comparisons can help to reveal the influence of particular social formations on both specific instances of technology and 'the general characteristics of a society's technological ensemble' (Russell and Williams 1988: 11). For example, compatibility problems in the development of Automatic Teller Machines (ATMs) convinced UK bankers to design their Electronic Fund Transfer at Point of Sale (EFTPoS) system as a level playing-field for all banks. With the shift towards a more competitive environment in which banks compete more vigorously for retail customers, the initial EFTPoS system—including its £150 million development costs—was abandoned in favour of competing systems (Howells and Hine 1993). In Germany and Denmark, on the other hand, a more heterogeneous structure of banking meant that EFTPoS developed later. Moreover, the greater importance attached to questions of privacy in these two countries led to the selection of different technical configurations, whereby the individual customer could remain anonymous when paying electronically.

Much of the initial research into technology policy highlighted the role of the state, for example in regulation and in the promotion of specific innovations. The analysis of technological convergence by Nicholas Garnham (Chapter 6) fits this tradition, with its focus on how the wider social system can limit choice and technological change. Such studies share a common problem with the 'industrial sociology' tradition—an emphasis on explaining an apparent absence of choice, rather than revealing the available choices and analysing the forces that determine which options are eventually adopted.

Economic Analyses of Technological Change

Economists differ widely in their treatment of technology as an explanatory variable (David 1975). For example, the 'instrumental' approach of some 'neo-classical' economists assumes that technologies will just 'appear to order' in response to the demands of the market at any one time (Coombs *et al.* 1992). However, a 'post-Schumpeterian' viewpoint (an approach taken in Chapters 1 and 7) emphasizes the unevenness, discontinuities, and qualitative shifts involved in the process of industrial and technological development. This analysis has been of value in understanding the social shaping of technology because it emphasizes the interaction between 'supply-push' from the technology and 'demand-pull' from users, rather than imputing a deterministic triumph to one over the other. Yet this approach has failings from the SST perspective: tendencies to overgeneralize and see technological innovation as the deterministic 'motor' of socio-economic change.

A closely related approach (Saviotti and Metcalfe 1991) is based on the 'evolutionary' model of innovation inspired by Nelson and Winter (1982) in the USA. For instance, Dosi (1982) suggests that particular economic and social contexts create 'selection environments'. The patterns of innovation established in these environments result in periods of broad stability (described as 'technological trajectories') during which the design of technological artefacts changes in an incremental, evolutionary manner according to characteristics of that particular techno-economic paradigm.

The 'technological trajectory' concept has been explored widely in empirical studies investigating the dynamics of social shaping. For example Fleck *et al.* (1990) studied the development of workplace technologies. They showed how the trajectory towards displacement of shop-floor skills by NC machine tools was undermined with the arrival of Computer Numerical Control (CNC) systems. By attaching a computer to the machine tool, shop-floor programming was possible. This made the technology more flexible to use and more attractive to the larger market of smaller engineering shops.

Many people who find it hard to accept the idea that technology is 'socially shaped' have little difficulty with the idea that technology is economically shaped (Weingart 1984). However, as MacKenzie (1992: 25) has noted:

> In studies of technology, the gap between economic and sociological explanation is pervasive. Economic analysis is often based upon assumptions sociologists regard as absurd, while sociological writing often almost ignores the dimensions of cost and profit . . .

Attempts have been made from an SST perspective to close this gap (MacKenzie 1992). Nevertheless, the main emphasis of social shaping research has remained on innovation within localized contexts—for example within the laboratory or firm, where the most obvious influences are the 'political' struggles and actions of individuals—rather than on the adoption of these technologies in a broader context, where market dynamics and economic factors are salient (Miles 1988*c*; Mackay and Gillespie 1992). Ultimately, 'economic' and 'social' are merely different ways of describing the behaviour of networks of actors—the 'economic' being geared to describing the cumulative outcomes of regularized patterns of action and the 'social' to specific local actions.

A Model of Social Shaping

The many approaches to technology discussed above have contributed to the development of a model of the social shaping of technology which highlights the importance of the form and content of technology and the reasons why they can and should be subject to social analysis. The model regards innovation as contradictory and uncertain, not just as a rational-technical process of 'solving problems' in which success is dependent on the political, economic, and social processes involved in building an effective socio-technical constituency. This helps to explain why the excellence of a particular technological solution or the availability of sufficient finance to fund a development will not, as such, guarantee its success.

Factors Affecting the Innovation Process

The shaping process begins at the earliest stages of research and development. Although the 'invention' process is at least partially unpredictable, systematic patterns have been identified within it. SST researchers have explored how technologies develop within the specific local contexts of industrial and academic laboratories. They have also examined how innovations must later be transformed as they move to commercial production and widespread use. This contrasts with conventional ideas about technological diffusion, which treat technical products largely as fixed entities.

The SST approach is illustrated by the investigations of Molina (1990) into the development of the Inmos 'transputer' microprocessor for parallel-processing applications. Success in the microprocessor industry has generally depended on the ability of manufacturers to open up their technology to broader markets, for example by agreeing standards with other producers and consumers (Molina 1992). However, Molina found that the development of the transputer reflected the designers' concern for the technical elegance of their solution, but it neglected users' needs. This led to it being launched in 1985 with a technically sophisticated special programming language (called OCCAM), which proved to be an unintended marketing barrier because it delayed commercial exploitation until support software became available for more widely used languages.

Developing an Alternative to the Linear Model of Innovation

The diffusion of a technology may sometimes occur simply through transferring particular instruments and techniques (known as 'instrumentalities'). For instance, in the commercial exploitation of Artificial Intelligence (AI) since the 1980s, the systems which have actually been implemented are very restricted compared to the broad range of developments and claims of AI. The most widely diffused AI products are relatively simple 'expert system shells' that can be applied to a wide variety of applications and are barely distinguishable from conventional computer tools and techniques.

However, SST analyses have rendered the social processes of innovation problematic by showing that oversimplified views of the technological imperative behind innovation processes do not adequately explain what actually occurs. For example, more than an awareness of instrumentalities is needed to understand why complex technological systems often need to be reconfigured, 'translated', and redesigned to meet new requirements during the diffusion process.

This SST perspective has evolved as part of a developing critique of the traditional linear model of innovation, which treats the cycle of invention–innovation–diffusion as separate 'stages' in a one-way technologically determined process (Edge 1994). In the linear model, technologies are regarded essentially as appearing 'fixed' or 'black-boxed' at the early invention stage. During diffusion, these established artefacts are seen as having 'impacts' upon society, work organization, production systems, skills, and other activities. SST researchers propose an alternative, 'interactive' model of technological development as a 'spiralling' rather than a linear process. This suggests that crucial innovations take place in the implementation and use of technology as well as at its design stage, providing important feedback that helps shape future rounds of technological change.

James Fleck and others at Edinburgh University have highlighted the importance of implementation as a site of substantive innovation. They coined the term 'innofusion' to describe the way users' requirements are discovered and incorporated into the system 'in the course of the struggle to get the technology to work in useful ways, at the point of application' (Fleck 1988: 3). Such a focus on implementation highlights the role in innovation of the 'users' of technology as well as the suppliers.

Implementation is a particularly important arena with ICTs because software-based information-processing techniques are capable of flexible customization that draws on the contingent local knowledge of various user groups. ICT implementations are therefore often a 'test ground'—a site for learning about the usefulness and problems of the technology and the users' requirements. This knowledge is fed back. to the suppliers, and can inform subsequent innovations. The significance of such supplier–user interactions has been demonstrated in a range of ICT applications, including robotics (Fleck 1988), financial services (Brady *et al.* 1992; Fincham *et al.* 1995), and manufacturing management systems (Webster and Williams 1993).

Research on the Social Shaping of ICTs

The Inseparability of Social and Technical Factors

Several chapters in this book highlight empirical research which has contributed to this model of the social shaping of technology, for example in relation to ICTs in household environments (Chapter 12); the implications of gender for the use and development of ICTs (Chapter 8); and the role of economic, social, and policy factors in the convergence of ICTs (Chapter 6). These and other SST studies have established that social settings shape technologies as much as technologies affect organizations and society (MacKenzie and Wajcman 1985).

Technological development proceeds by the interaction of various social and technical elements. They cannot be separated from one another as they are in constant mutual tension. Thus, workplace technologies are in part prefigured by existing forms of work organization in that they embody elements of earlier divisions of labour and expertise, as described by Juliet Webster (Chapter 8) in her discussion of the 'office of the future'. In addition, technical change is frequently motivated by particular ideas about the organization and how it should develop, for instance in the kinds of Business Process Re-engineering (BPR) initiatives discussed in Chapters 9 and 15. Once developed and implemented, technologies react back upon their environments to generate new forms of technology and new environments (Fleck *et al.* 1990). Analyses of the development of technology and of work organization must therefore proceed in tandem.

Configurational Technologies

The vital need for a co-ordinated view incorporating SST understanding is illustrated in the increasing development of complex production and administration systems which integrate automated and non-automated activities. Such systems have facilitated the move from ICT-based 'islands of automation' to more integrated systems which cross traditional boundaries within and between organizations (see Chapter 9). These systems cover a diverse range of activities that can rarely be supported in the form of standard solutions. Instead, firms must customize solutions to fit their particular organizational structure, working methods, and functional requirements.

This may require the linking together of a variety of standard components from different suppliers into a configuration consisting of a complex array of standard and customized elements, such as computer-integrated manufacturing (CIM). Fleck refers to this kind of development as a 'configurational technology' (Fleck *et al.* 1990). He argues that this involves the need to look beyond the emergence of complex IT systems in order to address 'information integration' in the firm, which is concerned with the way in which automatic and conventional information-processing elements and activities are combined. As configurational technologies are highly specific to the individual firms in which they are adopted, local knowledge of factors like the firm's markets, business processes, and information practice should be seen to be at least as important as knowledge about the technological aspects of a system.

The potential significance of innofusion is not just of local relevance. Suppliers may discover opportunities to develop more or less generic technological applications that can be sold to a range of other companies. Indeed, some important new technologies, such as robotics, have evolved and become technically viable and commercially successful through the development of particular applications in close collaboration between the supplier and a user (Fleck 1988).

We thus see the development of industrial technologies in terms of a double dynamic. On the one hand, there are processes that lead certain technical artefacts to become stabilized and standardized—'black box' solutions which can be marketed as commodities. On the other, we see the innovatory dynamics arising from continuously evolving user requirements and new technical opportunities which may open up new application possibilities and undermine existing solutions. The resultant increases in complexity and uncertainties in system development may reverse the trend to stabilization (Brady *et al.* 1992). Understanding the complex interactions between these processes requires detailed considerations of the relationships between specific technologies and the organizational contexts within which they are applied.

Future Directions for SST Research

Although there is much consensus about the underlying elements in the social shaping model described above, there remains much debate among SST researchers about which issues need to be given most prominence and the levels of analysis that are most appropriate.[3]

Consumption and the Role of Markets

One of the areas where SST researchers need to engage more strongly is the study of how technological innovation is influenced by the creative tension between supply and consumption. This involves social interactions across a network of actors within and between firms, including technologists, managers, marketing and sales staff, and direct users of systems (Webb 1992). Marketplace characteristics are also crucial. For instance, the selling of a technology to an existing market as incremental change—like a new version of an operating system for an existing personal computer (PC) range—generally requires a different marketing approach to selling a radical innovation, which might even involve creating an entirely new market (Green 1992).

This perspective draws attention to the very different forms of 'coupling' (Freeman 1984) that may exist between suppliers and users of technology. In areas where products and markets are emerging and developing rapidly, with high levels of uncertainty, close forms of coupling are likely, including collaborative development. 'Vertical' collaboration between supplier and user allows an exchange of information about technological opportunities and user needs, for example in the development of strategic IT systems in financial services (Fincham *et al.* 1995). 'Horizontal' collaboration allows players to share the risks in development, as typified by the strategic alliances entered into by Japanese microelectronics firms, whose collaboration in research and development for new products is co-ordinated by the Japanese government (see Fransman 1992; 1995).

Complex patterns of stabilization and destabilization are evident in other ICT sectors. For instance, the emergence of industry-standard products 'creates' markets which bring users lower-cost products, a wider choice of suppliers, and some degree of confidence that a product will not become obsolete (Swann 1990). Suppliers may collaborate to create such stable markets or they may evolve in a competitive environment, for example the proliferation of vendors of IBM PC 'clones'. Some dominant suppliers may also seek to tie in users through various forms of proprietary capabilities, such as the incorporation by Microsoft of its own networking system into its Windows 95 PC operating system.

With mass consumer products and services, the consumer may be represented 'by proxy', for example through market research using panels of representative potential customers. However, suppliers also take a major role in defining the customer or user and the market. For example, Thomas and Miles (1990) draw on evidence from electronic mail, videotex, and fax capabilities to show that the success of new telematics services depends on more than just a system's functionality and price. The extent to which systems are compatible with the skills and traditional practices of potential users are also key success factors.

Consumption is an active process. For example, consumers can appropriate novel artefacts into domestic routines in different ways (Berg and Aune 1994; Miles *et al.* forthcoming; Chapter 12). Markets are also shaped by legal, political, cultural, knowledge, and other social processes (Green 1992; Walsh 1993). The market should therefore be seen as a form of socially constructed organization—a particular type of network between actors.

Dealing with SST Dilemmas

One of the main characteristics of different approaches to empirical research within SST lies in the way instances of innovation are selected. For example, the 'macro-theorists', such as Noble (1979), started by analysing relationships between technologies and established large-scale economic and political interests. They then moved towards seeking finer-grained accounts of the influence of local processes. Conversely, 'micro-theorists', like those interested in actor-network theory (Callon 1980; Latour 1986; 1988), began from the level of interactions amongst individuals and groups and have then 'scaled up' these processes to obtain broader explanations.

Although these two groups seem to have moved towards similar positions from different starting-points, trying to meld their distinct approaches into a unified form of explanation is fraught with difficulties. These go beyond the varying research foci and methodological strengths to deeper objections from different schools. For instance, actor-network theorists like Callon and Latour are highly sceptical about the nature and influence of pre-existing, large-scale social structures such as classes and markets. They, in turn, have been criticized for ceding too much power and autonomy to individual actors and eschewing existing social theory, leaving them poorly equipped to explain particular developments and beset by a tendency to offer mainly descriptions and post-hoc explanations (Russell and Williams 1988).

A second major area of debate within SST concerns how to handle the interplay between 'the technical' and 'the social', which early work emphasized as a closely knit 'seamless web' (Hughes 1983). Some scholars insist that we can never directly 'know' the 'reality' of 'the technical', as the performance of technologies is always socially mediated (Chapters 4 and 5). Callon and Latour have taken a different approach to dealing with 'the technical' by extending their analyses of social networks of innovatory actors to include non-human actors, such as microbes and integrated circuits and their physical properties—a formulation criticized by Collins and Yearley (1992) for reintroducing empiricist concepts of the natural world which the sociology of science had sought to eradicate.

Others, particularly those concerned with policy issues, have argued that a useful theory of the relationship between technology and society needs to address more directly the characteristics of the material world. For example, Miles (1988c) acknowledges that technology does not 'cause' particular social changes, while pointing out that it can change the parameters with which humans interact. Questions concerning 'how we know about technologies' underpin another area of debate surrounding relativism, typified by the concept of 'technology as text', which suggests any account or knowledge-claim is provisional, even where there appears to be some consensus as to its correctness (see Chapter 5).

Debates within the SST community have generally taken place at a high level of abstraction. However, these have not immobilized empirical research, which has also highlighted the problems of particular approaches and identified possible synergies between different frameworks. This suggests that the development of SST approaches might most usefully be pursued in the context of specific empirical studies. PICT played an important role, together with other researchers, in this process of bringing together scholars from a variety of backgrounds to provide a critique of traditional conceptions of technological determinism. The intellectual cross-fertilization this generated has developed into the distinctive 'social shaping of technology' perspective described in this chapter. However, this remains a 'broad church' which is unlikely to converge into a unitary or permanent 'orthodoxy'.

The Influence of SST on Policy and Practice

SST research has contributed to a growing understanding among some policy makers in government and industry of the limitations of traditional approaches. These are now widely acknowledged as having given too much emphasis to the supply side of technologies and overestimated the contribution of technical specialists and their know-how to innovation—while giving insufficient attention to the 'non-technical' knowledge of users and consumers of technology. As Sir John Fairclough (1992: 17), an experienced science advisor to the UK government, has declared: 'I have come to appreciate that the widespread belief in the "linear model" has not helped but positively hindered the development of effective policies.'

An important general implication of SST analyses is that many of the traditional disciplinary boundaries have been unhelpful, particularly as they have narrowed the search for social explanations of complex phenomena. For example, we have highlighted the need to integrate sociological and economic accounts of innovation. Many SST researchers also seek to overcome the gulf between the 'social' and the 'technical'—and thus between the social sciences and the natural sciences and engineering. Some scholars have interpreted this lack of boundaries as pointing to the need for SST to maintain an intellectual distance from all its social or technical objects of study and to treat them all with a similar analytical scepticism (see for example Woolgar 1991a). Others have argued that SST should not limit itself to critical sociological interpretations, but should explore and foster links with other disciplines—especially in science and engineering (see for example Sørensen and Levold 1992 and Hamlin 1992).

SST research has contributed to the understanding and management of innovation, thereby helping to address a growing concern about the failure of technological development to take into account the requirements of the 'market' of potential users. For instance, some SST researchers have articulated their role as actors in shaping technological development, alongside technical and other specialists. As Law (1988) noted, those concerned with developing new technologies do not play a narrow technical role, but are engaged in 'heterogeneous engineering', deploying various sources of knowledge to create and grapple with the behaviour of complex socio-technical systems.

This role is possible because SST research seeks to go beyond traditional concerns with the 'social impacts' of technology by getting 'inside' science and technology. This enables the SST approach to examine what factors shape the technology which has the 'impacts', thereby opening opportunities to influence technological change and its social consequences by identifying at early stages where effective control could be exercised. The social shaping model thus offers the prospect of moving beyond defensive and reactive responses to technology towards a more pro-active role.

Notes

1. We thank Wendy Faulkner and Donald MacKenzie for their detailed comments on this chapter, as well as our many colleagues at Edinburgh who assisted us in preparing it.
2. Other SST studies on the choices surrounding the selection and design of new technology and the influence of aspects like managerial and workforce strategies and organizational culture include Wood (1982) and Jones (1988). See also Chapters 8 and 9.
3. For a full discussion of some of the major dilemmas and controversies surrounding SST research, see Williams and Edge (forthcoming).

4 Computers, 'Bugs', and the Sociology of Mathematical Proof

Donald MacKenzie

When we think of technology, what usually comes to mind are things: objects, artefacts, machines—the physical 'hardware'. Yet *The Oxford English Dictionary* reminds us of the central role of knowledge in the original meaning of technology: 'a discourse or treatise on an art or arts; the scientific study of the practical or industrial arts.' Social science research on technology therefore needs to encompass not just machines, but also our beliefs about those machines.

In this chapter, Donald MacKenzie aims to demonstrate that specialist knowledge of the behaviour of computer systems is not an entirely technical matter, about which social science would have nothing useful to say. He does this by showing how a sociological perspective on mathematical proof can yield useful practical insights into what we 'know' about the properties of computer-based systems. Implicit in the chapter is also a more general argument that social science research on technology is broader than the 'obviously social' questions, such as the effects of ICTs on employment and organizational structures, or policy questions like the regulation of telecommunications.

A Sociology of Technical Knowledge

By getting 'inside technology', social science can greatly improve understanding about the social shaping of both technical artefacts and of technical knowledge.[1] This helps to raise policy issues that merit more public attention, like the validation of safety-critical systems whose failure could endanger lives. The development of such a 'sociology of technical knowledge' can draw on work in the sociology of scientific knowledge dating back to the early 1970s. Until then, sociologists had largely been concerned with the analysis of political, religious, and philosophical belief systems.

The 'strong programme' of the sociology of knowledge formulated in the early 1970s recommended a 'symmetrical' approach to the sociological investigation of scientific knowledge (Bloor 1973). This was not restricted to examining inferior or superseded science. It also sought to analyse sociologically the generation and reception of well-established, well-regarded scientific knowledge. This programme remains controversial, largely because it is assumed that the intention is to debunk scientific knowledge or to denigrate science. However, the best work of this kind (such as Harwood 1993 and Shapin 1994) clearly reveals that this is not true. In the specific area discussed in this chapter, my approach is based on a respect for the effort to subject computer systems to mathematical reasoning and a belief that this work deserves greater attention and support than it has traditionally enjoyed.

Nevertheless, it is true that the approach I have taken focuses mainly on actual and potential disagreement between technical specialists, rather than on what they agree upon.[2] The intention is not to criticize. My focus arises in part because sociology-of-knowledge analyses are more straightforward when there is disagreement amongst specialists. It is usually easier empirically to identify the social bases of disagreement than to understand the social grounds of consensus, although the sociology of mathematical proof must also do the latter.[3]

Non-specialists often have a particular need to know about areas of disagreement among experts. In science and technology, 'distance lends enchantment' (Collins 1985: 145) in the sense that those at one remove from research often attribute greater certainty to its results than do front-line researchers. For example, managers and policy makers are rarely involved in front-line research and so lack direct access to its uncertainties, which can lead to a false sense of certainty. At the same time, uncertainty about the products of science and technology typically seems to rise again among people—like the general public with little knowledge of a subject—who are at greater 'social distances' from research. This creates an overall pattern I call the 'certainty trough' (MacKenzie 1990; forthcoming).

Computers, Testing, and Proof

Before turning to a sociological analysis of the effort to apply mathematical proof to the design of computer systems, it is necessary to explain why many computer scientists believe this effort is needed. A key aspect of knowledge of computer systems is the knowledge that computers will perform as the relevant technical specialists, users, managers, regulatory authorities, and, in some contexts, the public expect them to. This is becoming increasingly important as ICTs become so pervasive that failures of crucial computer systems may place many lives, much money, and public and private security at risk (see for example MacKenzie 1994 and Neumann 1995).

Empirical Exhaustive Testing

One obvious response to the desire to know the properties of computer systems which we rely on is to test those systems empirically. For example, sets of input data can be selected and a check made to ensure the corresponding output is correct. To yield certainty, such testing would, at a minimum, have to be exhaustive—otherwise, errors could lurk in the untested aspects of computer systems.[4] However, computer scientists do not agree on whether or not it is possible to test the hardware or software of a computer system exhaustively.

Not surprisingly, the answer given tends to depend upon what 'exhaustive' is taken to mean. If it is seen as covering all possible sets of inputs, exhaustive testing will often be out of the question because the number of possible inputs is infinite. Even in the cases where there are only a finite number of valid inputs—say because integers are restricted to a certain size—it can still be argued, as was done in the standard textbook of program testing by Myers (1979: 8), that 'to be sure of finding all . . . errors, one has to test using not only all valid inputs, but all possible inputs'. In other situations, the number of valid inputs will be effectively infinite. This is the case, for instance, with a 'compiler', a computer program which translates software from a programming language used by software developers into the binary code understood by the hardware. The valid inputs to a compiler could be considered to be all the possible executable programs written in the corresponding language, which are effectively infinite in number.

On the other hand, 'exhaustive' can have more restrictive meanings—say, that the 'test cases' which have been tried out have exercised all possible execution paths through a program. In this narrow meaning of exhaustive, Myers (1979: 10) puts it rather equivocally: 'possibly the program can be said to be completely tested.' Unfortunately, even in the more restrictive meanings, the practicalities of exhaustive testing are typically daunting. For example, Myers (1979) shows that the number of possible execution paths through even simple programs of just ten to twenty lines of code can be enormously large, of the order of 100 trillion (10^{14}). It therefore takes only modest complexity in the system being tested to render exhaustive testing infeasible in practice.

There are two broad responses to this practical limitation. On the one hand, proponents of testing point out that it can be a very powerful way to discover errors provided certain conditions are fulfilled, like: enough resources are devoted to testing; the system under investigation is designed to facilitate testing; testing is carried out systematically; and the tests are conducted by suitably skilled and motivated people not directly involved in the development of the system in question. On the other hand, many computer scientists agree with Dijkstra (1972: 864) in seeing that the implication of the impossibility of exhaustive testing is that 'program testing can be a very effective way of showing the presence of "bugs" [errors], but it is hopelessly inadequate for showing their absence'.

Verification by Mathematical Proof

In 1994 the world's leading microprocessor firm, Intel, had to set aside $475 million to cover the costs of an error in the implementation of the division function in its Pentium chip, although tests had not detected it prior to its release (Sharangpani and Barton 1994). Despite occasional disasters like this and a general acknowledgement that testing is imperfect, there is a general feeling in the commercial and business world that testing is still the best practical means of gaining knowledge of the properties of computer systems in advance of their use. This view is reinforced by the growing competitive need to control development costs and move products to the market quickly.

Since the late 1960s, however, a significant strand of thought has begun to take a different approach. This originated with academic computer scientists like Dijkstra, but has also been influential in government and certain sectors of industry. Practitioners of this approach seek to verify programs and hardware designs mathematically, rather than just by empirical testing. One appeal of this is that a deductive, mathematical analysis can cover all cases, not merely the finite number which can be subject to empirical testing. A mathematician who wants to demonstrate the truth, say, of a theorem about triangles does not embark on the endless task of drawing and checking all possible triangles. He or she looks for a mathematical 'proof'—a compelling argument that the result must be true for every triangle.

To verify mathematically the properties of a computer system requires the drawing up of an exact specification of its intended behaviour. Natural languages such as English are not considered adequate because of their many ambiguities. So the requirement specification has to be expressed in a mathematical formalism, from which an attempt can be made to derive deductively a detailed design that would implement it. More commonly, a program is written or a hardware design produced by more traditional methods—and then a mathematical proof is constructed to show that the program or design is a correct implementation of the specification.

In the first academic works on this topic (such as Floyd 1967), computer scientists used the traditional mathematician's tools of pencil and paper to prove that some simple examples of computer programs corresponded to their specifications. However, specialists in this field typically believe that hand-proof is of limited use as the reasoning involved is too tedious, intricate, and error-prone—especially for real-world systems rather than 'toy' examples. From the 1970s, therefore, they have turned to specially written computer programs for assistance in proof construction. These take two main forms:

1. **proof checkers**: 'book-keeping' programs, intended to store proofs and to detect errors in them; or

2. **automated theorem provers**: programs with a limited capacity to find proofs for themselves (MacKenzie 1995).

Mathematical Proof and the Sociology of Knowledge

Mathematical proof is a hard case for the sociology of scientific knowledge, a field in which nearly all the empirical studies have concerned the natural sciences, rather than mathematics or logic. Yet it is proof that gives mathematics its special status. For example, our knowledge that $2 + 2 = 4$ is usually taken to be absolute—and therefore excluded from the sphere of the sociology of knowledge—because we have a proof of that statement which seems to compel acceptance of it in a stronger sense than that achieved by the arguments of the natural sciences.[5]

The history of mathematics, however, reveals variation in the kinds of argument that have been taken as constituting mathematical proof. Work in calculus in the eighteenth century, for instance, often relied on manipulating infinitesimally small quantities or infinite series in ways that became unacceptable in the nineteenth century (Grabiner 1974). Early twentieth-century mathematics was riven by a dispute over the acceptability in proofs involving infinite sets of the 'law of the excluded middle'—the principle that necessarily, if a proposition is meaningful, either it or its negation is true (Kline 1982: 216–44). To the sociologist of knowledge, these are clues that mathematical proof is a less straightforward, absolute matter than it is ordinarily taken to be.

The effort to apply mathematical proof to computer systems was widely pursued by the late 1980s. This began to move mathematical proof into a commercial and regulatory arena. It seemed likely that the pressures of that arena would force potential variation in the meaning of 'proof' out into the open. Disputes about proof would then no longer simply be academic controversies but, it was predicted (Pelaez *et al.* 1987: 5), would probably come before a court of law to be settled. That nearly occurred in 1991, when litigation broke out in Britain over the application of mathematical proof to the microprocessor chip called VIPER (Verifiable Integrated Processor for Enhanced Reliability) developed by computer scientists working for the UK Ministry of Defence.

Legal action was taken by Charter Technologies Ltd. against the Ministry, from whom the company had licenced aspects of VIPER technology. Among other things, Charter claimed that VIPER's design had not been proved to be a correct implementation of its specification (MacKenzie 1991). A key question in the litigation was therefore whether the chain of mathematical reasoning connecting the detailed design of the microprocessor to its specification was strong enough and complete enough to be deemed a proof. Some members of the computer-system verification community denied that it was and, largely for unconnected reasons, sales of VIPER were disappointing (Cohn 1989; Brock and Hunt 1990).

No bug had been found in the VIPER chips. Indeed, their design had been subjected to an unprecedented amount of testing, simulation, checking, and mathematical analysis. At issue was whether or not this process, as it stood immediately prior to the litigation, amounted to a mathematical proof. Matters of fact about what had or had not been done were not central; the key questions which had been raised by critics were about the status, adequacy, and completeness—from the viewpoint of mathematical proof—of particular kinds of argument. With the Ministry of Defence vigorously contesting Charter's allegations, the case failed to come to court only because Charter became bankrupt before the High Court heard it.

Mathematical Proof, Intentions, and Physical Reality

Although the VIPER lawsuit indicates the potential practical importance of different meanings of 'proof', the attempt to apply mathematical proof to computer systems raises wider issues than those encapsulated in any one incident. One of the most important of these highlights a potential gap between what specialists and lay people might mean by 'proof'. Experts in the mathematical verification of computer systems agree that human intentions, as psychological entities, and computer systems, as physical artefacts, cannot be the objects of mathematical proof. They believe that 'proof' or 'formal verification' applied to a computer program or hardware can only be proof of correspondence between two mathematical models. One model is the formal specification, which is a model of the intended behaviour of the program or hardware. The other is a model of the program itself or of the detailed design of the hardware.

This specialist's view of 'proof' does not refer to the relationship between these models and either psychological or physical reality. For example, translating a natural-language military command—like 'Shoot down all enemy missiles!'—into a logic-based specification introduces a gulf which is not verifiable in any formal system (Jones 1990: 279–80). This immediately opens up a potential discrepancy between specialist and lay views of the assurance conveyed by terms such as 'proved' or 'verified'. Unlike a specialist, a layperson might infer that systems to which these terms are applied are correctly designed or cannot fail. The specialist would mean merely that a mathematical model of their detailed design corresponds to their formal specification (Cohn 1989).

This potential discrepancy matters. Laypeople's views of the trustworthiness of computer systems can be of considerable importance, as the safety of many systems depends on the interaction between computers and human users. Computer-related fatal accidents seem to be caused much more commonly by problems in this human–computer interaction (HCI) than by failures of the computer system itself. An analysis of reports of computer-related accidental deaths (MacKenzie 1994) suggests that HCI problems accounted for about 92 per cent of a total of around 1,100 such fatalities worldwide to the end of 1992. Software errors accounted for just 3 per cent and physical causes like electromagnetic interference for only 4 per cent.[6] Users' undue trust in computer systems appears to play a significant role in these HCI difficulties (see Chapter 10). This reinforces the importance of trying to avoid using terms to describe the results of applying mathematical proof to computer systems that encourage uncritical reliance on computer-based ICTs.

Applying Mathematical Proof to Computer Systems

The potential discrepancy between lay and specialist views of 'proof' is substantively important. However, it is not of central concern to the sociology of scientific knowledge. A more interesting issue in this area, deriving from the application of mathematical proof to computer systems, is the variation among specialists in their interpretation of what 'proof' means. This is raised not so much by the fact that 'proof' is applied to computer systems, but more by conducting that proof using computer systems. It also goes beyond the latter.

Formal Proof and Rigorous Argument

When we examine proofs within the disciplines where deductive proof is central—notably mathematics, logic, and computer science—we find a large variety of types of argument. Of course, much of this variety is to be explained simply by variation in the subject-matter being reasoned about, rather than by phenomena of direct interest to the sociologist. Nevertheless, it is also possible to classify proofs into two more over-arching categories:

1. **Formal proof.** This consists of a finite sequence of formulae, in which each formula is either an axiom or derived from previous formulae by the application of rules of logical inference (Boyer and Moore 1984). The steps in such a proof are 'mechanical' applications of the inference rules: they depend on the pattern of symbols in formulae, rather than on what these symbols mean. The correctness of the proof can therefore be checked without understanding the meaning of the formulae involved.

2. **Rigorous argument.** This broader category includes all those arguments which mathematicians or other relevant specialists accept as constituting mathematical proofs, but that are not formal proofs as defined above. The proofs of ordinary Euclidean geometry, for example, are rigorous arguments. Although some of these involve deducing a theorem

from axioms, the steps involved in these deductions are typically not simply applications of rules of logical inference, as would be the case in a formal proof.

This distinction is widely recognized by specialists, although there is no entirely standard terminology for describing it. Thus, many mathematicians would call deductions from axiomatic set theory 'formal proofs', even if these deductions are not simply applications of rules of logical inference. What I call 'rigorous argument' (a term I draw from Ministry of Defence 1991: pt. 2, p. 28) is sometimes called 'informal proof'—a phrase I avoid because it carries the connotation of inferiority *vis-à-vis* formal proof.

The distinction between formal proof and rigorous argument bears a close, though not one-to-one, relation to the computerization of proof. Formal proof has been relatively easy to automate. The application of rules of inference to formulae, considered simply as strings of symbols, can be implemented on a computer using pattern-matching programs.

The automation of rigorous argument, on the other hand, has been a far more difficult problem. There are some parts of specific rigorous arguments that can be reduced to calculation or algorithmic checking. The potential for automation is high in these cases. In addition, there are also widely used commercial programs which automate symbol manipulation in fields like algebra and calculus (see Stoutemyer 1991 for a critical discussion of their soundness). However, as yet it has not been possible to create 'artificial mathematicians', in the sense of automated systems capable of handling the spectrum of rigorous arguments used in different fields of mathematics. The proof checkers and theorem provers employed in computer system verification generally automate formal proof, not rigorous argument.

Debates about Different Approaches to Proof

Formal proof and rigorous argument are not necessarily inherently opposed. It is widely believed, for example, that rigorous arguments are 'sketches' or 'outlines' of formal proofs which present arguments with gaps that could, in principle, usually be filled by sequences of applications of rules of logical inference. There is, however, general acceptance of the 'incompleteness theorem' derived by Gödel (1931). He concluded that any finite formal system rich enough to encompass arithmetic must contain true statements for which there is no formal proof within the system (Gödel 1931). This means that it cannot be proved consistent without using a more powerful system, the consistency of which in turn would have to be proved, so beginning an endless regress.

Yet formal proof and rigorous argument can also be counterposed, for there is a sense in which they have complementary virtues. The steps in formal proof do not depend, at least directly, on the meaning of the formulae being manipulated. They therefore avoid appeals, often implicit, to intuitions of meaning, appeals that can contain subtle, deep pitfalls. The ability to check formal proofs mechanically is a great advantage in a field like computer system verification, where proofs are typically not 'deep' (in the mathematicians' sense of involving profound concepts) but are large and intricate—and where it is particularly desirable to have a corrective to human wishful thinking.

Rigorous arguments, on the other hand, typically have the virtue of surveyability. They are nearly always very much shorter than corresponding formal proofs, and are thus easier for human beings to read and to understand. By virtue of their appeal to the meaning of formulae, rigorous-argument proofs can produce a psychological sense of conviction ('it must be so') that is hard to achieve with formal proof. Rigorous arguments also have a certain robustness. For example, although typographical mistakes in them are commonplace, what carries conviction is the overall structure of the argument—which is more than an aggregate of individual steps. This overall structure can be grasped mentally; others can check it, use it in other contexts, and reject or improve it as necessary.

At their most extreme, defenders of one variety of proof can deny the label 'proof' to the other. That was the basis, for example, of an attack on program verification (proof of the correspondence of programs to their specifications) mounted in the late 1970s by the American computer scientists DeMillo, Lipton, and Perlis. They argued (DeMillo *et al.* 1979: 273) that program verifications were mere formal manipulations, incapable of being read, understood, and assessed like 'real' mathematical proofs. A proof, they said, is not an abstract object with an existence independent of these 'social processes'. They claimed that program verifications should not be seen as proofs because they could not be subject to these social processes.

A similar, albeit less sweeping, contrast between formal proof and rigorous argument also underpinned the most explicit defence of the VIPER proof, which was mounted by Martyn Thomas (1991, e-mail communication), head of the software house Praxis and a leading figure in the UK software industry:

We must beware of having the term 'proof' restricted to one, extremely formal, approach to verification. If proof can only mean axiomatic verification with theorem provers, most of mathematics is unproven and unprovable. The 'social' processes of proof are good enough for engineers in other disciplines, good enough for mathematicians, and good enough for me . . . If we reserve the word 'proof' for the activities of the followers of Hilbert [David Hilbert, the leading formalist mathematician of the early twentieth century], we waste a useful word, and we are in danger of overselling the results of their activities.

Proof and Disciplinary Authority

There is a general divide between the disciplines of logic and mathematics which relates to more than just the contexts in which formal proof and rigorous argument are counterposed. Although these disciplines are often thought of as similar enterprises, and in a general sense there is a considerable overlap between their subject-matter, they are, to a degree, socially distinct. The origins of logic as a discipline are closer to philosophy than to mathematics. Logicians still distinguish between mathematical logic and philosophical logic. Some university mathematics departments do not see either of these as a genuine part of their province, resulting in some mathematics undergraduates learning no more than the most elementary formal logic. 'I was going to be a mathematician, so I didn't learn any logic,' said one computer scientist with a special interest in mathematical proof who was interviewed as part of the research on which this chapter is based.[7]

The distinction between 'formal proof' and 'rigorous argument' is, to an extent, underpinned by this social divide. Logic has provided the notation and conceptual apparatus that make formal proof possible and provides a viewpoint from which proof as conducted by mathematicians can be seen as unsatisfactory. One logician (Nidditch 1957: v) wrote that: 'in the whole literature of mathematics there is not a single valid proof in the logical sense.' An interviewee in our study reported that even as an undergraduate: 'I knew, from the point of view of formal logic, what a proof was . . . [and was] already annoyed by the vagueness of what constitutes a mathematics proof.' Mathematics, on the other hand, provides the exemplars of proof as rigorous argument and, as we have seen, the main practical resource for criticism of formal proof.

However, attitudes to proof are not in any simple sense determined by disciplinary background. Disciplines are not homogeneous, specialists' backgrounds are complex, and other factors are involved. Many of those who work in the formal aspects of computer science have training in both mathematics and logic, so have three disciplinary identities potentially open to them. Those who have wished to computerize proof have generally had little alternative but to automate formal proof, whatever their disciplinary background. The connection between discipline and proof is more a matter of having the disciplinary authorities of mathematics and logic available to those who, for whatever reason, want to defend rigorous argument and attack formal proof—or vice versa.

Logics, Bugs, and Certainty

Those who perform computer system verifications are nearly all adherents of formal proof in practice.[8] For example, by the mid-1990s the only regulatory standard in this area that distinguishes formal proof from rigorous argument—the safety-critical software standard of the UK Ministry of Defence (1991)—came down in favour of formal proofs. The way a defence procurement standard is forced onto philosophical terrain such as this is one reason why this area is so fascinating.

Areas of Consensus

Within the field of computer system verification, but not more widely, there is therefore a potential consensus that 'proof' should mean formal, mechanized proof. But does such consensus lead to a version of proof beyond sociological analysis, or remove the possibility for future dispute and litigation? Agreement on the formal notion of proof still leaves open the question of the precise nature of the logical system to be used to manipulate formulae. There are different formal logics, including a continuing divide between 'classical' logic—which allows one to prove that a mathematical object exists by showing that its non-existence would imply a contradiction—and 'constructive' logic, which requires the actual construction of the object in question.

Computer science has also been an important spur to work on 'non-standard' logics. For instance, 'relevance logic' excludes the elementary theorem of standard logic that a contradiction implies any proposition whatsoever (Bloor 1983: 123–32) and has long been thought of as a philosophers' plaything. Now it is being automated with a view to helping sensible inferences to be made in the presence of contradictory items of information in computer databases (Thistlewaite *et al.* 1988). In the 1990s there has also been much interest in, and several practical applications of, 'fuzzy logic', which permits simultaneous adherence to both a proposition and its negation. This violates what some critics of the sociology of scientific knowledge have felt to be a cultural invariant (Archer 1987).

This zoo of diverse, sometimes exotic, formal logics has been a less potent source of dispute than might be imagined. Not all of the logics are regarded as suitable for mathematical reasoning or computer system verification. Furthermore, there has been a subtle shift in attitudes to formal logic away from a unitary view of logic in which there is only one true logic and all else is error. A more pluralist, pragmatic attitude in which different logics are seen as technical tools appropriate in different circumstances has become much more common, especially in computer science. Direct clashes between the proponents of different logical systems are far less common than might be expected by extrapolation from, for example, the bitter earlier disputes between classical and constructive logics (Kline 1982).

Nevertheless, the possibility remains that the pluralist, pragmatic attitude to different logics is a product of the early, exploratory, academic phase of the application of formal logic to computer systems. This cannot be guaranteed to remain intact in a situation where there are major financial or political interests in the validity or invalidity of a particular chain of formal reasoning. Specialists who are called upon to justify their formal logic under courtroom cross-examination by a well-briefed lawyer may face difficulties, such as the way that the process of justification is fraught with philosophical problems. The best known of these problems is Gödel's incompleteness theorem (1931), discussed above, with its conclusion that attempts to prove the truth of a rich formal system will lead to an endless regress.[9]

Proving the Provers

Another source of potential dispute, at least equal in importance to the diversity of formal logics, is the simple fact that the tools of mechanized formal proof, such as proof checkers and automated theorem provers, are themselves computer programs. As such, they may contain errors—especially the automated theorem provers, which are usually quite complicated programs. The designers of automated theorem provers whom we interviewed often reported experiences of bugs in their systems that could have allowed theorems to be proved although they were known to be false. Such bugs were not large in number; they were corrected whenever they were discovered; and no interviewee reported such a bug causing a false result whose falsity had not been detected readily. Nevertheless, no designer seemed able to give an unequivocal guarantee that no such bugs remained.

By the mid-1990s, no automated theorem prover had itself been subject in its entirety to formal verification, although an attempt was then being made to re-engineer a leading US system, the Boyer–Moore prover, to try to use it to verify its own correctness. But even if a prover is verified—or if results of an unverified prover are checked by an independent proof-checking program (something several interviewees advocated, but which is rare in practice)—many specialists in the field would still not regard this as guaranteeing complete certainty. The reasons given by them range from 'Gödelian' concerns about the consistency of formal systems to the possibility of coincident errors in different automated theorem provers or proof checkers.

Reactions to the difficulty of achieving certainty with automated theorem provers varied among the computer scientists we interviewed. One, who was not a program and hardware verification 'insider', suggested that it indicates the overall enterprise of formal verification is flawed, perhaps because of what he felt to be its impoverished notion of proof:

> You've got to prove the theorem-proving program correct. You're in a regression, aren't you? . . . That's what people don't seem to realize when they get into verification. They have a hairy great thing they're in doubt about, so they produce another hairy great thing which is the proof that this one's OK. Now what about this one which you've just [used to perform the proof]?

Verification 'insiders' would generally have a very different response because—although they pay considerable attention to soundness—they feel that theorem-prover bugs are not important practical worries compared to ensuring that the specification of a system expresses what, intuitively, is intended. One such insider commented:

> If you . . . ask where the risks are, and what are the magnitudes of the risks, the soundness of the logic is a tiny bit, a really tiny bit, and the correctness of the proof tool implementing the logic is slightly larger [but] actually . . . quite a small risk.

Almost all insiders share this perception that the risk is small of a serious mistake in computer system verification being caused by a bug in an automated prover. However, they are also wary of claiming that the risk can ever be shown to be zero. Their judgements differ as to what measures are necessary to allow claims of proof to be made safely. Some would not be happy without a full formal proof checked by an independent proof checking program; others feel that this would be a waste of effort, compared to the need for attention to more likely dangers, notably deficient specifications.

One potentially contentious issue is the use of 'decision procedures', which can decide in a wholly deterministic, algorithmic way whether or not mathematical statements in particular domains are true. Typically, decision procedures return simply the judgement 'true' or 'false', not a formal proof of truth or falsity. To some experts, decision procedures are a necessary and harmless part of the 'real world' of computer system verification. To others, decision procedures must themselves be verified formally, which has traditionally been far from universal. Otherwise, in the words of one interviewee, using them 'is like selling your soul to the Devil—you get this enormous power, but what have you lost? You've lost proof, in some sense.'

The Sociology of Mathematical Proof: Future Prospects

It is worth re-emphasizing that the goal of applying the sociology of knowledge to this field is not to debunk or to denigrate the work of those attempting to subject computer systems to mathematical reasoning. Variation in what constitutes proof, and the way in which insiders do not believe absolute certainty is achievable, are not arguments against seeking to apply mathematical proof to computer systems. The effort to do so has shown its practical worth in finding errors not found by conventional methods (Glanz 1995). Furthermore, this is a dynamic field and some of the issues raised in this chapter are active research topics, like the verification of decision procedures. Even the overall divide between formal proof and rigorous argument is not necessarily unbridgeable, with many insiders believing it to be possible to construct proofs that are formal in their detailed steps but which still have a humanly surveyable overall structure.

The risk of errors in computer systems, and the doubtful status of empirical testing as a means of eliminating them entirely, remain among the deepest problems faced as growing aspects of our lives—and often our very lives themselves—become increasingly dependent on computer-based ICTs. The application of mathematics to computer system design is therefore a potentially crucial activity. Once it is mature, it will offer substantial strategic advantages to firms and countries that are proficient in it.

However, government support for the field suffered from cutbacks to defence budgets caused by the end of the Cold War. In particular, interest has slackened considerably in applying mathematical proof to computer systems critical to national security, which in the late 1970s and 1980s was the largest single sphere of application in countries like the US and UK. While activity in other sectors has grown, there are structural factors which are inhibiting promotion of the field by market forces alone, such as the discrepancy between industrial needs and the academic reward system within which many in this field work. Government encouragement needs to change its form, but it remains crucial.[10]

The main practical implication of the sociological analysis of mathematical proof offered in this chapter concerns the hazards that will be faced as computer system verification grows in practical importance. Those involved should avoid strong claims of certainty for the results they obtain, despite the incentives to make such claims which are offered unwittingly by a commercial or regulatory context. This is not meant as a criticism of the field; indeed, it is a position that many specialists in the area would share.

Unqualified claims of proof potentially mislead laypeople about the scope of the assurance being claimed and open the way to attack from fellow insiders who, as explained earlier, have access to a repertoire of reasons why absolute certainty is an impossibility. With modest claims—perhaps even avoiding the charged word 'proof' (Rushby 1993)—and with a good understanding from policy makers of the field's potential and of its uncertainties, the very considerable benefits of applying mathematical reasoning to computer systems can be reaped without the costs of false confidence and damaging dispute.

Notes

1. MIT Press gave the name 'inside technology' to a series of books devoted to this area of study (see for example Bijker *et al.* 1987, the first title in the series).

2. The chapter is based on research by myself and colleagues which was supported by the ESRC through the PICT programme and two research projects (R000290008 and R000234301). Other support came from the UK Safety Critical Systems Research Programme for the Engineering and Physical Sciences Research Council (Grant J58619). Our research included extensive interviewing of computer specialists, especially those involved in using mathematical proof as a means of increasing confidence in such life-critical systems.

3. Important clues about how to analyse the social grounds of consensus are given in Bloor (1973), one of the earliest sociology-of-knowledge discussions of mathematics.

4. There are other issues here too, for example concerning what it means for output to be correct and the possibility of physical failure of a computer system or its components.

5. For a sociological discussion of the proof of $2 + 2 = 4$, see Bloor (1994).

6. These figures must be treated as indicative only. They are based on reports in *Software Engineering Notes*, published by the US Association for Computing Machinery (ACM), and other data. Coverage of computer-related deaths in these sources is unlikely to be comprehensive and some of the cases are controversial.

7. The interviews referred to in the remainder of this chapter were conducted by Tony Dale, research fellow on the ESRC-funded 'Studies in the Sociology of Proof' (project R000234301).

8. The main exception to this generalization concerns decision procedures, which are discussed later in the subsection 'Proving the Provers'.

9. See Haack (1976) on more general problems of circularity and regress in the justification of deduction.

10. A detailed diagnosis and policy proposals regarding appropriate government roles is provided in Cleland and MacKenzie (1994).

5 Technologies as Cultural Artefacts

Steve Woolgar

The commitment by many social scientists to understanding the social dimensions of technical developments, as highlighted in this book, reflects a growing interest in the need to take account of the 'human and social' aspects of science and technology. As argued in Chapter 3, generalized expressions of the importance of social dimensions admit a variety of interpretations, disciplinary standpoints, and research perspectives. The different interpretations arising from these variations can result in significantly different prescriptions for policy and practice. Hence, an important task is to clarify the nature and consequences of the different approaches.

This chapter by Steve Woolgar briefly surveys some important interpretations in recent social analyses of technology.[1] He explains how attempts to expose the social dimensions of ICTs encourage a focus on 'the user'. The metaphor of 'technology as a text' is introduced and evaluated to illustrate the pivotal role of social relations between producers and users in determining the success of ICTs. Woolgar also discusses how the approach derives from, and contributes to, a more general argument about the nature of cultural artefacts and the conduct of social science research.

The 'Social Dimensions' of Technology

What does it mean to say that technology has 'social dimensions'? Answers to this question vary widely. One view—typified by the general injunction to 'take the human element into account'—supports the idea that the design, development, and use of ICTs are driven, on the whole, by the 'actual' characteristics of the technology. It admits the involvement of 'humans', for example through their participation in economic and political decisions affecting the adoption and implementation of ICTs. But this involvement is generally regarded as having no bearing upon the hardware and software which make up the core of the technology. Such a restricted conception of 'the social' also supports a version of 'technological determinism'—the belief that new technology emerges as an extrapolation of previous technologies, with the characteristics of a technology having a direct impact on social arrangements.

By contrast, much other social research on technology sets itself in opposition to technological determinism. Thus, for example, proponents of the 'social shaping' and 'social construction' of technology approaches (see Chapter 3) have argued that social factors are not merely incidental to the nature and direction of technology development, they are intimately tied to it. In some versions of this argument, social factors are cited as causing shifts in the direction of development. One implication of this view is that the actual characteristics of the technology itself become problematic. As illustrated in debates over the information superhighway (see Chapter 22), actors will understand, view, experience, and describe technical characteristics by drawing on various expectations, conventions, and metaphors. These descriptions may differ, especially in situations of controversy; they may change over time; they may or may not reach consensus. The social researcher has no 'neutral' (that is, free of the social milieu) description of the technology around which to build a picture of 'social influences'. Instead, the 'technical character' of the technology—like what it can do and how it does it—becomes part of the phenomenon to be explained by reference to social and political factors.

The Technographic Approach

While social shapers and constructivists are generally united in their condemnation of technological determinism, it is far more difficult in practice to achieve and maintain the level of scepticism about descriptions of technology just alluded to. A common approach is to contain variations in technical description within a defined historical framework. Thus, a typical social constructivist account will focus upon periods of time during which descriptions of a technology were contentious and end the discussion at the point where a consensus forms on the 'agreed character' of a technology, known as the point of 'closure' (Bijker 1995).

Unfortunately, this focus on controversy underemphasizes the fact that changes in the understanding, interpretation, and description of a technology go on long after 'closure'. Think of how technologies like the personal computer or electronic banking are constantly being redefined.

A key difficulty in maintaining the necessary level of scepticism is that most people have become part of a culture which depends on accounts of the way technology works and of what it can and cannot do. I myself want the latest information technology! Thus, many of the programmatic attacks on technological determinism give way to a form of technological determinism in practice. There is still some distance between many social constructivist accounts and a fully fledged account of technology as being 'constitutively social', a view that prioritizes the social dimensions of technology by suggesting that we can no longer innocently accept that what a technology can do is ever just a technical matter (Grint and Woolgar 1995). Attempts to develop the constitutively-social perspective through empirical studies of ICT development can be subsumed under the rubric 'technography' (see for example Cooper and Woolgar forthcoming; Hine 1994; Rachel and Woolgar 1995).

Technography is the social-scientific study of technical settings. It adopts certain features of the 'ethnographic' method, which draws on anthropologists' approaches to observing and describing social behaviour. For instance, social scientists involved in ethnographic studies join the technical setting as participant observers who work with 'the natives', but who remain wary of straightforwardly accepting the language, beliefs, and expectations that characterize the setting in which they are carrying out the study. This approach emphasizes the need to resist taking for granted the various categories and characterizations used by the people being observed, such as the distinctions made between 'producer', 'consumer', and 'user'. A main focus of technography is to determine how these distinctions are created and sustained, as well as determining what effect they have on design and development.

Focusing on the User

One version of the argument about the importance of 'social dimensions' construes technology as embodying the various social factors involved in its design and development. Technologies are socially shaped or constructed such that their resulting material form reflects the social circumstances of development. In this way of thinking, technology can be regarded as 'congealed social relations'—a frozen assemblage of the practices, assumptions, beliefs, language, and other factors involved in its design and manufacture. This version of the 'social dimensions' perspective offers significant new understandings of the impact of technology, as it suggests that the social relations which are built into the technology have consequences for subsequent usage, which differs from the way much traditional sociology of technology has concentrated on the production rather than consumption of technology.

Technography sees technology as re-presenting a kind of 'social order' represented by the linking together of sets of social relations (Latour 1991). It regards technology as a cultural artefact or system of artefacts which provides for certain, often new, ways of acting and interrelating. Technography can therefore be summarized by the slogan 'technology is society made durable' because it argues that a particular fixed version of social relations as the basis for action is 'frozen in material form' by the use of a specific technology.

From this perspective, users of a technology confront and respond to the social relations embodied within it. They experience the effects of the material artefact as far more immediately compelling than any mere interpretation or description. Ways of using the software other than those the designers had in mind are possible, but they turn out to be prohibitively costly (since alternative sets of material resources will be needed to counter or offset the effects of the technology) and/or heavily socially sanctioned. The social relations confronting the user of technology are therefore relatively durable because they are not easily disrupted and repackaged. If we are to understand the effects of ICTs and the conditions for their success and failure, we must obviously give a central role to considerations of the user (see for example Friedman and Cornford 1989). We need to ask what generates and sustains users' expectations and what influences their responses to ICT systems.

The Importance of Social Relations between ICT Producers and Consumers

One aspect of the social relations built into new technology is the preconceptions about the user by producers, such as system designers and manufacturers, which include the user's supposed requirements and levels of skill and experience. These preconceptions may be explicit, for example as elicited from market analysis and market research. They may also be implicit within the producers' organizational culture and affected, in part, by the dynamics of relations between different groups within both the producer's and user's organizations.

It is not uncommon, for example, for the engineering design and technical writing sections of an ICT company to hold quite different and contested views about 'the user'. The process of development of an ICT product, stretching from inception to after-sales support, can be construed as a struggle between competing company sections over the 'true character' of the user of the end-product. This process of 'configuring the user' involves the identification and definition of 'users', and a series of decisions—in design, manufacturing, and sales—which both enable and constrain the actions of users (Woolgar 1991*b*). Dominant producer preconceptions of the user thereby become embodied in the final product. In the ensuing deployment of the technology, actual users are effectively confronted by, and asked to engage with, 'configured users'—the concretized preconceptions of themselves (Woolgar 1993*b*).

Technography's emphasis on the social relations between producers and consumers provides a way of understanding the 'impact' of technology which goes beyond what can be offered by social research that pays more attention to production rather than consumption. It enables the 'impact', 'success', 'value', and other outcomes from the use of a technology to be understood, at least partially, in terms of the extent to which users are willing or able to conform to—and in terms of the costs involved in challenging—the configured preconceptions embodied in the technology.

One drawback of this model is uncertainty over exactly how the social relations embedded in the technology are to be recognized. While the notion of embodiment can work well as a social researcher's shorthand overview of the social dynamics involved, it does not explain how and why users react in the way they do. Although many analyses (such as Winner 1985) indicate that users respond without being aware of the configured preconceptions built into the systems, there is a danger that social scientists will assume that the embodied social relations are clearly available on inspection. This would lead to a form of social analysis which portrays the actions of the user as being straightforwardly determined by these embodied relations, such as those resulting from the gender, racial or product bias of the producer. For example, the desire by a computer manufacturer to sell particular auxiliary software products could be manifested in the incorporation of information about them in its own support package. In this kind of account, the technological determinism which originally provided the critical target in social research on technology is supplanted by a social determinism.[2] It leaves unclear how, and within what constraints upon interpretation, embodied social relations can be discerned by either analysts or users.

Technology as Text

In order to stress the interpretive flexibility of technology, the wide variety of possible designs and uses, it has been useful to refer to technology as a 'text' (Woolgar 1991a). This version of 'taking social dimensions into account' offers the opportunity for giving a new focus to analyses of the problem of the user. When construed as a text, technology is to be understood as a manufactured entity, designed and produced within a particular social and organizational context. Significantly, this is often done with particular readers or sets of possible readers in mind—it is fabricated with the intention that it should be used in particular ways. On the consumption side, the technology is taken up and used in contexts other than, and broadly separate from, its production.

Of course, the actual situation is much more complicated than this. For example, there are many intermediaries, such as marketing specialists, corporate ICT purchasers, consultants, and journalists, who occupy strategic positions between the producer and final user of an ICT product. They intervene in the interpretation ('reading') of the technology by the user through their comments on the product's nature, capacity, use, and value. Nonetheless, the central idea of the metaphor—that the software is designed (authored), on the one hand, and used (read), on the other—brings to centre stage the question of the extent to which the character of the technology influences its use.

In the scholarship which deals with the general question of relations between texts and their readers, there is a diversity of positions which mirrors the range of views about the relationship between technologies and their users.[3] At one extreme, there is the 'essentialist' position that texts possess intrinsic characteristics (Wimsatt and Beardsley 1954); at the other extreme is the view that the character and capacity of texts are nothing but the attributes given them by their readers (Fish 1980).

A New Perspective on Technological Determinism

The metaphor of technology as a text shows that the position of technological determinism is a particular case of a much broader problem in the humanities and the social sciences. This more general position can be called 'textual determinism', the view that the reading and interpretation or use of entities arises from the inherent characteristics of the text or product itself. One extreme form of this view is typified by the religious groups which refer to a 'divine text' that is seen as revealing its actual character and identity directly to mere mortals. To these groups, it is blasphemous even to suggest that the meaning is unclear or requires articulation, because it would imply that ordinary people can detect and iron out imperfections in the divine author's text.

Treating technology as a text indicates that a critique of technological determinism has implications for the more general questions surrounding textual determinism. But it is also instructive to reverse the metaphor and consider texts as a form of technology.[4] From this perspective, text is one of a number of examples of technology, like writing, computer software, and electronic media. These have had particular, and sometimes profound, effects on life and thought. Thus, as Ong (1982) has suggested, literacy should be understood as a particular means of 'technologising the word'.

How then should social scientists understand the interpretation and use of technologies? The 'social shaping' and 'social constructivist' attempts to understand the direction of technological development, for example, regard externally originating factors such as social interests as becoming embedded in the technology during development, thereby giving the technology its character and capacity—typically through social and historical processes of closure and consensus (Molina 1989; MacKenzie 1990). By contrast, the technology-as-text metaphor goes beyond this, for example by suggesting that technology texts 'perform communities' by creating and making available a preferred moral order in which appropriate interpretations can be made.

The technology-as-text approach indicates an irremediable ambiguity about what the technology is and can do, which is overlaid by sets of preferences for its interpretation and use. It begins by construing the text as embodying these preferences in the form of sets of social relationships which informed its construction. However, this is itself subject to irremediable ambiguity and instability because the possibility of stable preferred readings would imply that knowledge of the conditions of production, of the author's intention, or of the social interests of relevant parties would enable a correct reading. It follows that the idea of a text 'performing community' needs to stress the contingency and ambiguity of the process of construing preferred readings (Cooper and Woolgar 1994a).[5]

How Preferred Readings are Established

In order to elaborate on, and make more specific, the ways in which the software text attempts to establish preferred readings, I posit a process which includes the following features:[6]

Steve Woolgar

1. Confronted with a stream of words, the reader will draw upon any available resources to ease the task of making sense of the text.

2. The form of the organization of the text is a key resource available to assist the reader in making sense. For example, Sacks (1972) suggests that readers use collections of identities and activities, known as Member Categorization Devices (MCDs), to ascertain the meaning of different items in the text. An example of an MCD given by Sacks is the mutual resolution of the sense of 'baby' and 'mummy' in the phrase: 'The baby cries. The mummy picks it up.' He suggests that readers can identify 'baby and 'mummy' as members of the same collection. They become the kind of baby and mummy they are in virtue of their co-location in an organizing device (the MCD) which we might refer to as the collection 'family'. The co-location of different terms within the same MCD category provides an easy and economical way for the reader to make sense of the passage. The reader's rule of thumb is that if an MCD can be identified such that two terms can be subsumed within it, then they are heard or read as belonging to that MCD—which provides a minimal means of resolving meaning by reference to a local context provided by the organization of the text.

3. Smith (1978) elaborates this in a detailed analysis of a report about an individual (known as 'K') who is said to have been behaving oddly. The reading that 'K is mentally ill' can be achieved, says Smith, by readers attending to the relations, attributes, and distributed characteristics of individuals and groups named in and throughout the account. For example, the reader is offered a contrast between the activities carried out by a group of people who can be said to be friends, and the quite different activity carried out by K. The text is organized in terms of the population of its human characters using 'semiotic' signs and symbols which define the characters by assigning attributes to individuals and collectivities, granting some features while withholding others, and sketching their relationships with each other. The described community offers a resource for making sense of the reported behaviour of any one individual. Smith notes that the text she analyses can be read in terms of social exclusion or as an account of mental illness, but that neither is prescribed.

4. The community thus created can extend beyond the cast of semiotic characters explicitly mentioned in the text. In particular, this happens through the implicit enrolment of the reader. Thus, sets of characterizations made available in the text offer the reader a way of identifying with and making sense of the text. This can be illustrated by an acceptance

speech for a Nobel prize which includes the words 'we are all familiar with the twinkling of ordinary stars'. When you read or hear this, you are being offered the choice of enrolment in the text or being debarred on grounds of ignorance. The royal 'we' is the unidentified and un-mentioned number of persons colluding with the speaker's knowledge. If you are not familiar with the 'twinkling' not only does this make you different from 'us' but, the suggestion is, it also undermines (or at least makes immensely difficult) your continued legitimate presence in the unfolding story. In effect, this usage of 'we' specifies a condition for membership of the community of legitimate readers (Woolgar 1980).

5. Clearly, the community which the text performs is usually more complex than this example suggests. Instead of straightforward alignment with the author's community ('we'), the reader may be offered a position in conflict or contrast with the author, or perhaps a position tied to a more specific notion of professional community (McHoul 1986). Typically, we might expect a range of identities and positions to be implicated both within and beyond the text, so that the reader is faced with choices of alignment.

6. Crucially, the choice of alignment also implies the kinds of appropriate responses, interpretations, or uses. For example, when seeking assist-ance on a technical-support telephone line, a user (reader) may need to choose between certain positions, such as between 'novice' and 'experienced' user. Certain prescribed actions defined through the form and nature of questions and responses encountered by the user may then be deemed appropriate to the adequate enactment of the chosen position (Woolgar 1993*b*).

Implications of Having a 'Preferred' Reading for Users

The process described in the previous section reveals that a text or tech-nology can configure its readers or users to present themselves and react in an 'ideal' predetermined way. This does not, however, imply textual determinism. As Smith points out in relation to the 'K' narrative, differ-ent readings can exist with none being prohibited. Even in less ostensibly ambiguous texts, the reader is not absolutely forced to act in a particular way. Maverick and deviant readings are always possible. But in a text which successfully performs community, such readers will be castigated as just that: deviants and mavericks. Thus, when the text performs com-munity, it offers readers a normatively sanctioned moral order into which their 'correct' preferred response can be readily accepted and against which non-preferred responses are discouraged and/or made prohibitively costly. To say that the 'text performs community' or that it 'offers a moral order' simply provides shorthand descriptions of the temporary upshot of reading practices.

The version of 'social dimensions of technology' analysis which treats technology as 'congealed social relations' suggests that, at some point, features of the social relations involved in the production of the text become frozen through their embodiment in the technology. From the perspective of the technology-as-text approach, however, this point offers a summary description of possible readings. Similarly, it is to be considered as a comment on the ways in which a text might be read to say that preferences are embodied in the text or a technology in the form of sets of social relationships which informed its construction.

The Example of the Software Text

Computer software offers an important example of how a technology can be considered as a textual process involving intertextual relations between its producers and consumers. This can be illustrated by a fictitious case study based on a composite of findings from technographic studies undertaken by our research team (see for example Hine 1994; Shapiro 1994; Cooper *et al.* 1995; Rachel and Woolgar 1995; Shapiro and Woolgar 1995). The example concerns the development of a word processing or operating system program for personal computers, which we call 'Access '98'.

The development of Access '98 involves much discussion between different sections within the producing company about how users set up their particular printer requirements. The Technical Support and User Support sections feel strongly that they will be besieged by calls and queries if the icon for printer setup is 'buried' within several nested menus, rather than being presented to the user as a control item on its own. Their experience of the reaction to the company's previous products told them that one of the first things users wanted to know was how to set up a new printer—so the icon to do that is needed up front. Otherwise, they argue, countless hours of effort will be expended explaining to users where to find the damn thing. By contrast, members of the Marketing section claim that the printer-setup function should be part of a general 'control item', in a way similar to functions like setting the date or the colour and founts for Access '98 screen displays.

The Marketing section therefore pushes the view that 'it is logical' to put printer setup within 'Printers', alongside other control items. However, members of the software design team cannot see what all the fuss is about. They reckon that users will be happy with being able to move the Printers icon easily to whichever location suits them best. As long as they are not expected to provide extra code to make it happen, the software designers say they are willing to place the printer-setup icon anywhere. This is seen by Marketing as the opportunity for a rare alliance with Software Design, whose argument is essentially about the need for flexibility. And this, according to Marketing, is the very thing that users want most: flexibility and a logical design—which is a major selling point! Users, they say, want to be able to move the icon between different program groups, as well as to have the freedom to create their own new groups, such as 'All About Printers'. Further protests from User Support, for example about the positioning of printer-management functions in relation to control items, are to no avail.

In simple terms, the upshot of this debate is that the configured user becomes an individual requiring flexibility and valuing 'logic' over immediate access. When Access '98 is released, this is one characteristic of users which becomes 'fixed' in the software. This explanation reports no more than a highly contingent outcome of reading practices: what counts as being 'found' and 'fixed' is achieved through 'reading the text'. The particular concatenation of relationships which were frozen in bringing the Access '98 cultural artefact to fruition are now those which make available its preferred (that is, its socially sanctioned) reading or use.

The user's determination of the preferred reading takes place within the community 'performed' by the text. In our example, the performed community might be said to include the various icons, their corresponding programs and functions, and the Help routines. The definite and indefinite identities expressed in instructions and dialogue boxes are also important parts of the performed community, for example, the 'you' in statements like 'You can access control items by selecting . . .' in the 'Help' or 'Coach' routines. More important is the organization of the text and thence of the performed community, which the reader is offered as a resource in arriving at preferred interpretations. The reader will learn that icons are arranged in a nested fashion, such that access to one group of icons and their functions is necessary before other functions can be revealed. In seeking help in setting up the printer, the reader will encounter the 'you' of the help routines and, with due persistence, the 'you' of 'in case of further difficulties consult your manual or phone Technical Support'. This organization of the text maps out a preferred route for the reader in solving the 'how do I set up my damn printer' problem. The preferred reader is the one who telephones Technical Support only when the other guided efforts have been exhausted. As a corollary, the Technical Support person receiving calls is entitled to feel exasperated when a user has phoned without first trying to get an answer through Help, the Access '98 tutorial, or the manual.

In the process of design and development, different representations of the user come into conflict. In this case, Marketing's view of what typical users want wins out, thereby providing the basis for establishing some uses (readings) as more preferred than others. It remains possible to behave in quite different ways than intended by the producers—but non-preferred readings, such as trying to use a spreadsheet program for word processing, are more costly and difficult to sustain. This makes it easiest to proceed in the preferred fashion. Departing from the producer's embedded consensual version often requires recourse to other allies, such as a nearby friendly colleague who is an experienced user of Access '98 and evidently knows how get a printer to work.

The embodiments of the social relations of production are, of course, decidable only during or after the text's appropriation by the reader. It is in this sense that the effects of the congealed social relations amount to a specific and important form of power relation embedded in the software. And that lends itself to the slogan 'technology is politics by other means'.

Wider Conceptions of User

The metaphor of technology as a text highlights the social contingency of the processes of both designing (producing, writing) and using (consuming, interpreting, reading) technology. It draws attention to the complex social relations between producers and consumers and points to the importance of preconceptions of the user embodied in the technology text, which mean users can only 'adequately' apply the technology if they conform to the community of social relations which the technology makes available. Any reading is possible in principle, but only certain readings are acceptable in the context of the performed community.

The value of this perspective is that it sets technology in the more theoretical framework of studying how cultural artefacts in general are created and used, which can be understood as occurring in virtue of the reorganization and realignment of sets of social relations. However, by comparison with other cultural artefacts, technology and science are experienced as particularly 'hard' because the social relations seem especially costly to challenge. Cultural artefacts such as the mass media, on the other hand, comprise social relations which are seen as relatively easy to interpret in alternative ways.[7]

In this broad framework, software lies somewhere between the two poles of the apparently robust texts of hardware technology and the apparently flexible texts of popular culture. It is a cultural artefact which, like other technologies, comprises congealed social relations but which, like popular-culture texts, sometimes invites and allows modification by users due, for example, to its commodity-like mobility over a wide range of social arenas. Whereas technology in general is society made durable and social science texts are society in the making, software is society made malleable.

This conception of software emphasizes that the production of all cultural artefacts involves a continual struggle, on the one hand to freeze and embody social relations and, on the other, to render sets of social relations manipulable and manageable. To the extent that this back-and-forth process characterizes the production and consumption of all cultural artefacts, it is productive to extend the metaphor of 'software' to encompass a conception of 'hardware', 'software', and 'textware' as all particular instances of software in the more generic sense. Some forms of software come to seem harder than others.

This leads to wider questions. If all cultural artefacts are social texts which afford, define, and prohibit certain usages, why do some come to be regarded as harder or softer than others? Why do some texts seem more robust in that they afford the same interpretation regardless of the particular use to which they are put? And why do some acquire a wide currency and pervasiveness whereas others enjoy little or no circulation at all? A key task for social science is to explain the different fate of these social texts. By asking why it seems more costly to unpack the social relations of technology texts than of other cultural artefacts, we are asking fundamental questions about the nature of social order.

New Ways of Understanding New Technologies

The idea that technology is a text which performs community opens up new ways of understanding the complex range of responses to, and interpretations of, new technology—without falling back on assumptions of a linear dependency between the 'actual character' of a technology and its users. The style of analysis described in this chapter has several important theoretical and practical implications.

1. By drawing on the theories of textual analysis undertaken in realms quite removed from technology, it is possible to inform our thinking about technical change by illuminating new features of the social dimensions involved in the development and use of technology.

2. Conversely, by working through the problem of producer–user relations in the case of technology we are able to build a platform for tackling a range of more general problems. Technology offers an arena of social action which, at first sight, might seem unwelcoming to the efforts of social science research. But it is for just this reason that the demonstration of the applicability of social science analysis to the very character of technical capacity tests the robustness of the theory. If we can demonstrate the viability of textual analysis applied to the user's determination of what a computer can do, then we may have established a case for textual analysis more generally.[8]

3. It follows that the idea of texts performing community can be applied to a range of cultural artefacts. One particularly interesting example concerns changes in the status of the cultural artefacts which are the output of academic research. In the UK, for example, there were a series of institutional and political injunctions to traverse the divide between academic social science and its potential 'users and beneficiaries'.[9] The notion of technology as text provides a handle for understanding the difficulties and uncertainties of communicating across social and organizational boundaries.

4. The style of analysis pursued here suggests that changes in the success or failure of new technology in practice will come about only through the realignment of producer–user relations. This means, in particular, that the success of technology cannot depend on technology-driven development strategies, whereby more technically advanced products are thought to guarantee their own market. Instead, the realignment of producer–user relations will involve nothing short of institutional change. ICT suppliers will need to reorganize in ways that enable them to perform user communities more in tune with the ways in which users identify themselves. For example, they might introduce better mechanisms for helping producers to gain more informed conceptions of their users.

5. For software, this implies a design strategy which is much more sensitive to users. The idea of 'user involvement' and initiatives that argue for ICT systems design to be 'user centred' (Norman and Draper 1986; Norman 1994), 'human centred' (Cooley 1987; Rosenbrock 1989; 1990), and 'participatory' (Bjerknes et al. 1987; Ehn 1989; Greenbaum and King 1991) have been advocated for many years. These movements

have championed the figure of the user, mainly in the interests of a more humanist and democratic technological development (Agre 1995). Rules of thumb such as 'get the users on board early' have also become popular. However, it is not yet sufficiently clear how the appropriation of the rhetoric of 'the user' can be effectively embedded in design practice. For example, in their study of the social dynamics involved in the course of a major initiative to promote software quality, Cooper and Woolgar (1994b) note that the idea of 'user involvement' is often invoked quite cynically in the expectation that the inclusion of such rhetoric would increase the chances of success of a research proposal (see also Cooper and Bowers 1995).

6. Finally, we need to continue to examine in detail the important, but often unnoticed, effects of producers' preconceptions of users. To what extent do these preconceptions permeate the language and activities of producers of cultural artefacts? How can relations between producers and users be improved (Curtis 1993)? How can rhetorical distinctions be sustained between the 'real work' and its 'mere' presentation and dissemination, when the social implications of any text or technology hinge on whether and how users are enrolled by the producer?

Notes

1. This chapter is an extension and development of arguments worked out in collaboration with Geoff Cooper and colleagues at CRICT, the PICT Centre at Brunel University. It draws in particular on Cooper and Woolgar (1993; 1994a), Cooper et al. (1995), and Woolgar (1991a; 1991b; 1993b).
2. See Grint and Woolgar (1995) and Woolgar (1991a) for an exploration of the argument that this analysis misses the importance of questioning the concept of determinism per se—a concept which arguably finds its most developed form in discussions of technology.
3. For an overview of these different positions in literary theory see, for example, Suleiman and Crosman (1980), Jefferson and Robey (1986), and Newton (1990). For the particular focus on reader-response criticism, see Tompkins (1980), which has a useful annotated bibliography.
4. For many years, this problem of whether effects derive from the essence of things or from their antecedent circumstances was debated in terms of the essences of 'texts'. From this point of view, texts are the general problem and technology the particular example. More recently, the ascendance of the notion of 'technology' makes it seem more natural that technology is the general phenomenon and texts the particular example.
5. In the terms associated with the important French philosopher Jacques Derrida (1992: 21), if a text attempts to prescribe a reading, and thereby an implied

set of social relations, the interpretation of the text works against and with the limits of this reading. The interpretation can attempt to construct other 'models of community'.

6. This list draws on the textual analysis of Anderson (1978), as well as the other authors cited.

7. But see Woolgar (1993*b*) for a discussion of the factors affecting our perception of the relative strengths of different cultural artefacts.

8. See Collins (1982) and Woolgar (1991*a*) on the notion of scientific knowledge as the 'hardest possible case' for certain types of sociological explanation.

9. This phrase recurs in UK government policy statements such as OPSS (1993) and policy statements from research councils on the criteria by which research proposals are to be evaluated (such as ESRC 1994).

6 Constraints on Multimedia Convergence

Nicholas Garnham

A process of technological convergence within ICTs has enabled text, graphics, still pictures, moving images, and sounds to be stored, manipulated, displayed, and transmitted in an integrated way by computer-based systems. This has unleashed an enormous potential, but its realization will be determined by economic, social, political, and cultural processes and structures. In this chapter, Nicholas Garnham explains why these outcomes are likely to differ markedly across different fields of application. He emphasizes the dangers which arise when the use of terms like 'convergence' and 'multimedia' give an illusion of technical change overcoming distinct processes, firms, markets, and patterns of development. Garnham also highlights the many real constraints on multimedia convergence that are often left out of discussions of new ICTs, focusing particularly on the regulatory problems which could arise.

Evolution of the Media Sector

A pervasive, technological determinist perspective has dominated much popular and scholarly discussion on ICT innovations and related policy debates and initiatives. Proponents of this view have argued that developments leading to a digitally based convergence of ICTs are fundamentally restructuring communications and the communication industries as part of the process of ushering in the information society. They claim the challenge for policy makers is to ensure that outdated regulatory structures are not a barrier to economically and socially beneficent change (Bell 1973, 1980; Toffler 1980; de Sola Pool 1990; Negroponte 1995).

However, a historical perspective on such developments strongly indicates that no technological or economic changes are so revolutionary that they completely overturn an established regime. There is huge inertia built into the system stemming from the accumulated financial, social, cultural, political, and psychic investments made in the past. Changes therefore work by accretion, by the establishment of new forms in niches which may, over the long term, lead to the slow undermining and transformation of an economic and social ecology. In order to understand how the technological potential of convergent digital ICTs might be exploited and, more importantly, the nature of its economic, social, and cultural impacts, it is therefore necessary to understand how media industries developed in the way they have.

The media sector actually evolved in a quasi-geological process which involved successive layers of distinct production and distribution technologies being laid one on top of the other—first based on print, then photography, then electronics (Garnham 1990). These technologies still shape the way we think about related industries, for instance in the way they are named on the basis of their distinct underlying technologies, such as press, records, radio, television, and telecommunications. Each industry aimed to exploit the unique cost structures and benefits of its technology. They therefore developed distinct ranges of products and services, systems of distribution, relations with their users, cultures of usage, organizational forms and cultures, and—last but not least—distinct regulatory regimes (see Table 6.1).

Some forms declined in the face of competition from new forms. In general, however, that decline was slow and rarely absolute. The old forms survived and the new media lived to some extent off the older media they were partially replacing, adding a further layer to the media mix. For instance the cinema partially lives off the theatre and television off the cinema. The same is true for the post and written communication *vis-à-vis* telecommunication, where the often-prophesied death of the postal service has been endlessly postponed.

Moving to a Digital Era

The potential impact of digital convergence on the inherited, largely pre-digital media system is to break down the technical barriers between these industries. This has effects at all levels of the system illustrated in Table 6.1.

Production technology becomes computer-based, creating new media

Table 6.1. Structure of the Pre-Digital Media Industry Sector

	Print	Film	Record	Radio/TV	Telecoms
Production technology	Printing press	Film, Camera	Recording apparatus	Video, Microphone	Telephone
Carrier material	Paper	Film	Vinyl tape	Radio waves	Wire, Switches
Production system	Publishing company	Film company	Record company	Broadcaster	PTO
Distribution technology	Road, Rail	Projector, Cinema	Road, Rail	Transmitter, Receiver	Network
Distribution system	Wholesale, Retail	Cinema	Wholesale, Retail	Broadcaster	PTO
Regulation	Competition	Licence	None	Regulator	Regulator
Ideology	Free press	National culture	Artistic freedom	Public service	Universal service

forms. The carrier material is increasingly based on digital techniques, including broadband, which allow a more effective exploitation of the radio spectrum. These offer new economies of scope in the production system and—by providing capabilities for new modes of consumption and markets—potential new entrants are produced in each traditional sector. There is also competition for markets between sectors, leading to cross-ownership initiatives and the building up of transnational conglomerates. At the same time, digital networks provide the means to transform distribution technology and systems.

These raise important regulatory issues and conflicts because regulatory regimes in many areas have a technological basis or bias. For example, cross-media ownership rules designed to promote information diversity obviously depend on an ability to distinguish clearly between media and their respective markets, which has a purely technological foundation. Overall, these changes have ideological impacts by questioning traditional concepts of the demarcation between public-service and market-driven approaches.[2]

Pre-digital media industries clustered around two key distinctions—between products and services and between one-way and interactive. Industries like print publishing and sound recordings created physical products which they sold to consumers through wholesale and retail distribution networks similar in structure and operation to that of other

> **Box 6.1.** Different Forms of Digital Convergence
>
> - The convergence of technical distribution channels onto a common digital, broadband, and switched system.
>
> - The convergence of media forms through the computer-controlled storage, manipulation, and display of combinations of text, moving images, still pictures, and sound.
>
> - The convergence of modes of media consumption—between one-way and interactive, switched (like the telephone system) and non-switched (like satellite broadcasting).
>
> - The convergence of modes of payment towards systems based on charging for individual products or services, for example using a 'conditional-access' device like a television signal decoder to unscramble pay-per-view cable, or satellite TV channels and programmes addressed to a particular household.
>
> - The convergence of the residential and business markets.

consumer-goods manufacturing industries. The key to the chain of activities that added economic value to their business (the 'value chain') was the ownership and sale of rights, which allowed charges to be made for access to a specific form of content. On the other hand, broadcasting and telecommunications are typical of other industries which were based on networks that delivered services. The key to their value chain was monopoly or oligopoly control over scarce distribution channels—and their prime commodity was contentless interconnectivity itself. All were one-way, except telecommunications.

The Implications of Digital Convergence

Digitization is blurring such previously clear demarcations. Yet the use of all-embracing terms like 'multimedia' and 'convergence' disguises important distinctions that should still be drawn between a number of separate but interrelated processes which affect the potential impact of digitization (see Box 6.1).

The Importance of Different Contexts

Each of these processes has a distinctive set of technological and economic drivers and social, economic, and cultural impacts. The policy concerns, players, and stakes will therefore also all be different, depending upon the process we are discussing. For instance, if we are concerned with network convergence then we will be primarily interested in the clash between the telecommunication and computing models of network design and control, as well as in the competition between telecommunication companies, cable firms, and broadcasters for control over access to homes and businesses. If we are concerned with the development of multimedia products, the central focus will then be issues of print and audio-visual industry convergence, of copyright, and the development and use of new media forms. If we are concerned with the convergence of payment modes, then issues of control over conditional-access systems, of the future of advertising and public funding, and of control over customer data will loom large. If convergence of markets is our concern, then personal computer (PC) penetration may be the technological driver, the Internet the model of the future, the impact of teleworking the problem, and IT companies like Microsoft or IBM the main global players.

Each of these processes must be kept distinct because, for example, it is clearly possible to have the development of a major market for multimedia products and services delivered on competing, non-converged networks or, alternatively, a monopoly-based converged network delivering a range of non-converged media forms. During the 1980s and early 1990s, however, the main focus of policy attention was network convergence. This was because telecommunications networks have played such a large economic role in developed economies and because most media regulation has focused on the control and use of distribution networks.

Broadcasting and Telecommunications

The technological determinist argument is that developments like the digitization of broadcasting and provision of switched broadband networks are driving together broadcasting and telecommunication industries. However, while technological developments undoubtedly provide the necessary conditions and the potential for forms of convergence, they are far from sufficient to break down traditional barriers to such convergence.

When radio was first conceived, some forecasters saw it as a form of person-to-person communication and the telephone as a form of broadcasting.[3] They soon took opposite and divergent paths. Broadcasting used over-air transmission and exploited its economies of scale to provide low-cost, one-way entertainment and information services to relatively undifferentiated mass publics in their homes. It was free at the point of use, financed by a licence fee, state subsidy, or advertising. The content was highly regulated. On the other hand, telecommunications used wire transmission to deliver two-way narrowband telephony and, later, data services to business and residential subscribers. Telecommunications usage was overwhelmingly business-oriented and was charged on a usage basis. The transmission was regulated, but not the content.

The dream of integration between these sectors is not a new one. The thinking of telecommunication network planners has been dominated for most of the industry's history by the search for ways of exploiting economies of scale and scope in the utilization of their very capital-intensive fixed networks. For example, AT&T was only removed from broadcast station ownership by the government in the 1920s, although—as has happened with public telecommunication operators (PTOs) in many other countries—it continued to distribute broadcast signals between stations and transmitters. The development and implementation of the Integrated Services Digital Network (ISDN) approach from the 1960s has also sought to maximize the use of telecommunications networks for a wide variety of services. In spite of their desire for economies of scale, telecommunications companies also developed their telephone networks by means of a series of distinct overlay networks—such as for the packet switching used for interconnections between computers as in the Internet—rather than by network integration.

When Convergence Failed

Talk of convergence started in the 1970s with a focus on telephony and computing. This became one of the motivations for deregulation in the USA in the 1980s and led to much serious speculation that computer giant IBM would take over the telecommunications industry—or that PTOs like AT&T would move strongly into the computer market. Many companies lost a great deal of money trying to achieve this. Eventually, a form of convergence did actually take place, in the sense that telecommunication networks have become very large distributed computing systems.

Yet, contrary to forecasts and despite rapid data-traffic growth, voice telephone traffic continued to dominate network usage and has remained the economic driver of the system during the 1990s. In fact, much of the network and service planning undertaken by the PTOs and organizations like the European Commission since the early 1980s has been based on the unfounded assumption of the saturation of the voice telephone market.

The rapid growth of the Internet in the 1990s is another good example that counters some widely held beliefs about convergence. Earlier electronic mail services offered by PTOs largely failed. The Internet uses telephone network facilities, but it is based mainly on installed computing capacity. This is beyond the control of PTOs and has grown out of a computing culture. It is thus an example of hybridity, rather than network or industry convergence.

A Realistic Appraisal of Convergence

Discussions about broadcasting and telecommunications convergence often assume a scenario including some or all of the following elements:

1. A switched broadband network will be rapidly provided to the majority of homes, either through adding bandwidth to the installed switched telecommunications network or by adding switching to the established cable TV network. Whichever path is chosen, the end result will be a single pipe delivering all electronic services to homes and business premises.

2. In some versions, all these services will then be received by the user on a converged multimedia computer terminal.

3. The existence of such a physical infrastructure will mean more than just distributing existing telecommunications and broadcasting services over the same network. In addition, a range of new interactive entertainment and information services—such as video games and teleshopping—will become possible and will eventually supplant more traditional one-way services.

4. All of this will be paid for directly by consumers through some form of usage-based payment system.

The optimistic version of this scenario argues that it will increase information and entertainment diversity and will enhance individual choice and freedom (de Sola Pool 1990; Bangemann Group 1994; Negroponte 1995). The pessimistic version stresses the dangers of monopoly control, of social isolation and fragmentation, and the further decline of the public sphere (Schiller 1989; Garnham 1993). But what is the realistic scenario?

At a technical level, it is clear that PTOs will roll out capacity in their networks to deliver video to the home, where the regulatory system allows. At the same time, cable TV operators will build in capacity to provide switched telephone and data services to their customers. Since provision of a fixed-link local loop is likely to retain natural monopoly characteristics, there will probably be severe competition between PTOs and cable companies to control that link. How it works out in practice will depend largely on regulatory intervention.

Regulators could impose on the industry the economic costs of maintaining local fixed-link network competition, which raises questions about how these costs fall on users. Alternatively, regulators might accept the logic of natural monopoly and have tight common-carriage regulation to make such monopoly acceptable and keep network operators out of the programme-content service business. In the absence of regulatory intervention, the sheer financial muscle of the PTOs is likely to lead to their victory and dominance (*Telecommunications Policy* 1994).

There also remain major technological barriers to smooth convergence. It does not obviously make sense to merge networks designed for largely one-way delivery of broadband services with networks designed to optimize the delivery of switched two-way narrowband services (Elton 1991). By the mid-1990s most examples of convergence were of shared ducting because civil engineering—not transmission and switching facilities—remained the largest cost element in network building. There is also uncertainty as to whether the path to video-service delivery is via the provision of more bandwidth, for example with fibre-optic networks, or greater digital data compression that can allow greater use of traditional wired networks.

In the longer term, there are important broadband switching problems to be faced. One of the models for the converged 'information superhighway' is the Internet. However, scaling up the Internet's usage in the mid-1990s to that possible on a broadband network points to a potentially unmanageable demand for network services, even if the Internet's enormous growth rate falls when more users have to pay for access.[4] It will be especially difficult to build the complex switching software necessary to provide the reliability required by a public telecommunications service.

Economic and Cultural Barriers

Even if technological problems are surmountable, economic and cultural barriers to convergence will remain significant. For instance, any possible cost advantages gained from the improved technical efficiency of a converged network are unlikely to be the main determinant of market structure. Alternative delivery mechanisms will continue to exist and economic power is likely to shift from control over scarce distribution channels to control over scarce intellectual property. The owners of that property—such as broadcasters, film companies, video game makers, and teleshopping retailers—are unlikely to allow any single distribution channel to dominate the market.

The fact that PTOs have owned and operated transmitter networks has not given them any power over broadcasting. In the extensively cabled US market, for example, the major television networks regained a steady 60 per cent market share of the audience in the mid-1990s, after an initial loss of audiences in the face of this new competition. Moreover, digital broadcasting makes over-air transmission less scarce and therefore relatively cheaper. Conventional over-air broadcasting is thus likely to remain the most cost-effective approach for many years, whether financed by advertising or subscription.

The main problem for the PTOs is to find services which will generate enough revenues to justify the costs of upgrading their networks to cover broadband residential connections. Video-on-demand has been much touted as the PTOs' entry point into the audio-visual programme market. But in the mature US market of the early 1990s, the average home with a video recorder consumed one video per week at an average cost of about $2.30, while pay-per-view consumption in subscribing homes was just one film per year (Veronis, Suhler and Associates 1993). This confirms other evidence that, despite its added convenience, the video-on-demand market is highly constrained by available disposable income and is very price-sensitive.[5] Even if the whole traditional home video market were to migrate totally to the PTOs' networks, it would be entirely marginal in comparison with telephone revenues—and only a fraction of revenues would go to the network operator, with most continuing to go to the rights holders of the content. PTOs would also be competing with both video shops and other subscription film channels for the market.

The way these concerns do not seem to have entered the initial planning calculations made by PTOs illustrates another major barrier to convergence: the huge gulf between the cultures of telecommunication operators and of the audio-visual programme business. PTOs are accustomed to dealing with the sale of a small set of standardized services, largely to business customers. This is a market which is not highly 'price-elastic'. It is not primarily price that determines how many phone calls are made by users, particularly business customers; reliability can be as important as price in choosing between competing network and service suppliers. PTOs have also been accustomed to a business in which the primary focus is the management of the smooth, rapid, and reliable flow of large quantities of undifferentiated bits through networks, using probability calculations of variable traffic flow to maximize economies of scale in the network and ensure that peak demand can be met, and then billing customers for that service.

The audio-visual market is quite different. It involves constantly creating new prototypes and selling them into a very uncertain residential market. The problems are ones of co-ordinating creative labour, controlling rights, and marketing. These cultural differences are reinforced by differences between the corporate market, on which telecommunications has largely depended, and the domestic entertainment and information market, particularly in terms of buyer–seller relationships, patterns of investment, and skills required. All the signs are that it is difficult, if not impossible, to serve both with equal efficiency by combining the very different skill sets and associated reward structures within one corporate organizational structure.

This may well prove to be the major barrier to the effective exploitation of the technical potential for converged products and services. As a result, we are likely to see new multimedia products and services developing out of the computer software and specialist publishing industries, based on the technical infrastructure of the installed base of PCs and on professional and telework markets. They will probably have minimal impact on either the existing telecommunications or audio-visual programming industries.

The Regulatory Policy Dilemma

The way the communications sector actually develops in response to the technological potential of convergence will in part depend on regulatory responses to strong opposing arguments. On the one hand, the participating industries claim that traditional regulations in telecommunications and broadcasting are built on obsolete technological foundations, such as spectrum scarcity, and thus act as a barrier to desirable development—so should be swept away as soon as possible. However, many public interest and consumer advocates argue that these developments might not be socially beneficial and that they threaten to abolish necessary existing regulatory defences of the public interest, such as universal service in telecommunications and public service in broadcasting.

The policy dilemma is that the regulatory philosophies and regimes governing the converging industries of telecommunications, broadcasting, and print are very different. In particular, telecommunications regulation has been based on the presumption of natural monopoly in the provision of fixed networks, the separation of carriage and content, and the regulation of access but not of content. In broadcasting, regulation was based on spectrum scarcity and the strict regulation of content. Print remained largely unregulated and governed by the philosophy of a 'free press'. In addition, the content-based audio-visual and print industries' reliance on legal regimes governing the ownership and control of rights—which was founded on definitions of publication, performance, and territory—has been threatened because they are increasingly difficult to define or police in global digital networks.

Short of total deregulation, it will not be easy to meld these different regulatory approaches into a unified regime for a converged sector. Cross-ownership rules designed to ensure media pluralism have been based upon easily understood, but increasingly obsolete, technological distinctions between print, television, radio, and telecommunications. Yet it is not easy politically to sacrifice pluralism to those transnational corporate players eager to construct global multimedia oligopolies.

There are two responses to this regulatory dilemma. One is to base media ownership rules on a proportion of total media consumption (so-called 'share of voice') rather than on technologically defined markets. In share-of-voice calculations, for example, the newspaper circulation and radio and television audiences controlled by one company would be aggregated into a common system of measurement and no company would be allowed to control more than a set percentage of the total media market thus defined. The problem is to define the share-of-voice concept sufficiently tightly for legal purposes.

The second response is to move to a strict separation of carriage and content. The problem here is that many of the corporate players involved, and their regulatory allies, argue that such separation will itself act as a barrier to development. For example, they say it will no longer be possible to subsidize new services in their early days from network revenues or to justify investments in network upgrading without access to substantial service revenue streams. This argument lies at the heart of regulatory battles involving telecommunications operators and cable companies against content providers and the controllers of broadcasting programme channels. In my view, fears over monopoly control of the future broadband network are likely to lead to the extension of traditional common-carriage principles to include conditional-access systems and 'system navigators'—the software needed to find your way around in cyberspace.

Even a strict separation of carriage and content is unlikely to leave content as unregulated as many content providers would wish on the basis of 'freedom of speech' arguments. Concern over issues like screen violence, pornography on the Internet, video game addiction, and invasions of privacy all lead to calls for more, not less, regulation of content. In addition, as economic power shifts from those who control network access to those who control rights to scarce quality content, competition authorities have to pay greater attention to ways in which control over rights and TV-channel packaging can be used anti-competitively.

The New Media Markets

The many historical cultural, market, economic, technical, and other differences discussed above clearly indicate that the mere potential convergence of transmission technologies will not be sufficient to converge the industries themselves. Wire and over-air transmission systems, for instance, are therefore likely to continue to compete with each other and the development of one dominant 'superhighway' digital pipeline is unlikely. The big problem for network operators will probably be to cope with bandwidth overcapacity and a trend towards PTOs' networking operations becoming a competitive commodity business in which transmission is an ever-decreasing proportion of the total costs of any service.

The need to fill bandwidth has stimulated the search for 'killer applications' which will open lucrative new markets. Video-on-demand, home shopping, and teleworking have been among those proposed for this role. But whether or not a killer application is found, the balance of economic power will tend to swing towards the rights holders who control content rather than channel capacity. This is why PTOs, ICT companies, and terminal manufacturers are buying—or trying to forge alliances with—film, music, and other companies controlling rights.

Terminal and Software Markets

You can transmit as much digital information as you like down a broadband link, but it doesn't become a saleable good or service without a decoder and display terminal. Moreover, potential users are going to require some way of finding what they want among the plethora of rival offerings. This is not only a large market in its own right. It also gives strategic control over content design and billing systems. In a way similar to Microsoft's dominance of the PC software market with its DOS and Windows proprietary operating systems, such control over a key access point gives a strong strategic position in the value chain. The control of conditional-access systems for satellite broadcasting by firms such as News International and Canal Plus has therefore been a contentious regulatory issue.

As a result, a crucial market battle will be the one to control the multimedia operating and decoding system in the 'set top box' which manages the interactions between a TV and the digital communication link(s) coming into the home. It involves a battle of the giants from many sectors, including computing, microelectronics, consumer electronics, mass media, and video games. For instance, video game enterprises like Nintendo and Sega were the first companies which could be said to have created a successful and global multimedia product market. 'Multimedia' in this context refers essentially to the efforts of the computer industry and the manufacturers of other electronic hardware, particularly television sets, to find a new generation of hardware to sell and for each to expand into the other's market. This is illustrated by efforts in the 1990s to introduce high-definition television and digital broadcasting.

Multimedia Forms and Interactivity

Multimedia productions are not new. For example, Wagner conceived his operas as 'Gesamtkunstwerke' which melded spoken and sung text with music and visuals. Similarly, films and newspapers can be montages of different symbolic forms. Nonetheless, the impact of digitization does make it possible to have new forms of media and, thus, new products or services and new markets. Sometimes, these forms will be a development of old ones. The 'electronic newspaper', for instance, could be said to provide more timely access to a wider range of text-based news and the 'electronic encyclopedia' to amplify the speed and range of referencing, as well as adding sound and moving pictures. The establishment of a strong market niche for any new media form depends on how users judge its costs and benefits compared with existing substitutes and the relationships established between traditional book and newspaper publishers and the audio-visual and computer industries.

The most significant potential impact of digitization on content comes through interactivity, which takes two distinct forms—person-to-machine or person-to-person. Person–machine interactivity provides multimedia capabilities by allowing users to interact via a computer with stored digital information. At one end of the spectrum, this could offer new video games; at the other, access to sophisticated electronic databases. The electronic newspaper lies somewhere in between. If the right formula can be found, as video games have shown, such interactivity can be a great attraction to users. This provides suppliers with two key challenges. One is whether the necessary intelligence and databases will be sold as stand-alone terminals and software (the PC model) or embedded in networks (the telecommunications model). The other is whether the aim is to create a product or service and what appropriate charging mechanism should be chosen—a very difficult problem upon whose solution depends the ability to venture beyond very specialized niche markets.

Person-to-person interactivity is based on the telecommunications model of information distribution, typified by the telephone, rather than a broadcasting model. The key characteristic of both the telephone and the Internet is that users create their own content. The service has a collective value to its users, with no single participant able to claim ownership or authorship. This is not a promising basis for a new market, which is another reason why the Internet is probably not a good model for the multimedia broadband superhighway. Indeed, the two outstanding successes in this field are great advertisements for socialism, as they have both been highly subsidized by the public sector—the Internet, which received funding from the US Department of Defense, and the Teletel, the French videotex service, which was subsidized by the provision of free Minitel terminals by France Télécom.

The Convergence of Markets

Convergence has an important impact on market structure. Broadly speaking, the traditional communication industry created two models of market development. One was that of the publishing, film, music, and broadcasting industries, where companies focused on developing and serving mass consumer markets. Their size and buoyancy depended upon the availability of discretionary consumer spending, which is relatively constrained—in the USA, for instance, personal consumer expenditure on recreation as a percentage of total disposable income remained in a band between 4.0 per cent and 6.5 per cent for sixty years from 1929 (Vogel 1995: 18). The other model is that of the telecommunications industry. As explained earlier, this has served primarily a business market and allowed the service to trickle down slowly to the residential market, which remains marginally, if at all, profitable for a PTO. The growth in information industry revenues, fuelled by the ICT revolution, has been overwhelmingly driven by the business market.

A major challenge facing those trying to forge a new converged multimedia industry is the clash between these two very different markets. One view is that multimedia products and services will be developed first to serve the business market using versions of desktop videoconferencing controlled through a broadband Windows-type operating system giving access to a range of business services—and designed and priced accordingly.[6] This market will then slowly spread into the home largely as an extension of the work environment, as PCs have done. Domestic innovations will also often be driven by the strategies and economies of business, such as the retailing forces which shape multimedia home-shopping services.

The major media companies, on the other hand, see multimedia as a way of expanding the stagnant markets for newspapers and television by adding interactivity and choice, thereby capturing a major share of consumers' discretionary leisure expenditure. Whichever view is taken, the winners and losers and the regulatory problems will be very different.

Policies for Convergence

The above analysis indicates that developments to which the term 'convergence' point are therefore both fragmentary and evolutionary. So, policy makers do not need to be rushed into ill-thought-out policy initiatives by the supposed need to keep up in a race that does not exist towards a goal that is illusory. The future policy challenges facing governments in the fields of telecommunication and the audio-visual are the same as they have long been.

For instance, there is the need to construct a regulatory environment which optimizes both network development and network access. Even if a single network is unlikely to be the ultimate outcome, there is little doubt that ICT developments tend to reinforce the natural monopoly characteristics of fixed-network provision. In particular, the local-loop bottleneck is likely to be reinforced. Network competition is thus unlikely to reach a level sufficient to do away with the need for strong regulation.

Given the desirability of ensuring maximum plurality of both business and residential information services, this points to the need to move towards a strict separation of carriage and content—which will be strongly resisted by network operators. This separation will also have to be designed to ensure that network navigation and conditional-access systems cannot be used anti-competitively to control access to switched network services. As such access becomes increasingly essential as the gateway to participation in an ever-wider range of economic and other social activities, this regulation must be accompanied by a clear, economically sustainable, and enhanced universal-service policy.

However, ensuring access to networks will not ensure access to the desirable plurality of competing services, unless it is accompanied by enforceable powers to prevent the concentration of control over content, to which the industry will remain prone. Indeed, as economic power shifts from distributors to rights holders, such concentration will tend to increase rather than diminish in the absence of countervailing public powers. With the clear technological barriers between content industries disappearing, new methods of defining levels of concentration against the public interest will have to be defined. Until then, traditional, crude, technology-based media distinctions should remain in place. Nor should the claimed needs of European content providers to operate globally be allowed to muddy the issue. In fact, for most content and consumers the relevant market is national or even subnational. The same is true for networks that are in most cases inevitably territorially fixed and serve relatively territorially fixed users.

Maintaining a Public Service Commitment

It is important that the claims made for the information superhighway in terms of wider consumer choice in information and media services through the introduction of increased competition should not be allowed to undermine publicly funded support of public service media, as it has consistently tended to do within European policy making. Such support to ensure an optimally plural range of services is a policy tradition which we would discard at our peril, although it is a legitimate matter of public debate to question how this support is provided.

The need to harness the technological potential of ICTs to enhance social productivity and the quality of life will remain crucial. There has been much talk in the mid-1990s of the contributions that the information superhighway could make to education, healthcare, political participation, and the delivery of social services (see also Chapters 15 and 22). But many of these promised enhancements could have been delivered many years before—and indeed were promised before.[7] There is little in the technology *per se* this time around that makes their delivery more likely. The barriers are economic, social, and political—and they are deep-seated. They will not be overcome if development is left to the very market that in part created them. Therefore, focused efforts to break down the barriers using existing technologies and services, supported from public funds, should be given a high priority.

Notes

1. This chapter is a development from PICT-sponsored research on the convergence of media Garnham directed at the CCIS at the University of Westminster. Reports on the CCIS research include Garnham and Mulgan (1991).
2. The policy, regulatory, and ideological issues discussed in this chapter are also explored in Chapters 13, 17, 21, and 22.
3. Key figures in the early history of the telephone industry, such as Theodore Vail, developed business plans around the telephone system as a person-to-person medium, but many forecasters were wildly off the mark. For an overview of early forecasts of the telephone, for example, see de Sola Pool (1983*b*).
4. The Internet first grew in popularity among academic users to whom the service has been free, although universities support the costs of the networks. An increasing number of subscribers to online computer services are paying directly for access to the Internet as it is more widely used for commercial and business purposes—approaching 32 million users by the end of 1994 (IMO 1994).
5. The relative weakness of the video-on-demand market has been confirmed by disappointing results to the mid-1990s of broadband interactive service trials in a number of localities around the world, such as in Orlando, Florida.
6. Visions anchored in developments around multimedia PCs suggest this scenario (see for example Emmott 1995). The scenario has also been linked to the corporate strategies of companies like Microsoft and IBM (Cringley 1992).
7. For a comparison with the promises surrounding the development of interactive cable television systems, see for example Dutton *et al.* (1987).

Part II

Information and Communication Technologies in Organizations, Management, and Work: Reinforcing and Transforming the Structure, Processes, and Geography of the Firm

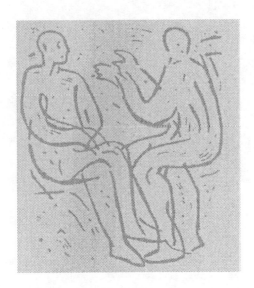

7 The Factory of the Future and the Productivity Paradox

Christopher Freeman

Many people in the 1980s became puzzled because economic growth rates slowed down throughout the industrialized countries, just when computers were being diffused widely in offices and factories. The possible reasons for this 'productivity paradox' are discussed in this chapter by Christopher Freeman, particularly in relation to the visions and realities of the so-called 'factory of the future'.[1] He explains the conditions required to realize the productivity potential which these new technologies offer and highlights some social and organizational implications of managing technological innovation successfully. He also further develops the background to the emergence of important new ways of thinking about the role of ICTs in organizations—the concept of the 'ICT techno-economic paradigm' which he introduced in Chapter 1.

Predictions about the Factory of the Future

In May 1987 *The Economist* published a special supplement entitled 'The Factory of the Future', which started with this statement:

> The factory is being reinvented from scratch. Traditional production lines are being ripped apart to make room for flexible 'make-anything' machinery . . . Long narrow production lines with men [*sic*] crawling all over them—a feature of manufacturing everywhere since the early days of the car-making dynasties—are

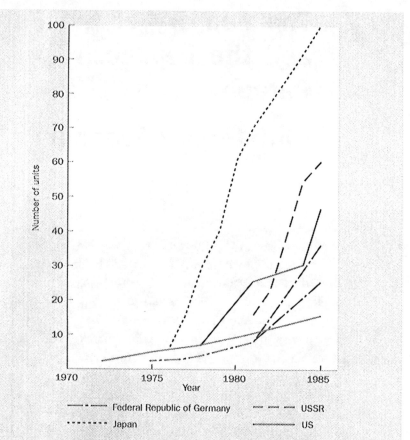

Note: The two lines for the USA apply, respectively, to a wider and stricter definition of FMS. For the Federal Republic of Germany, an interval estimate is given for the number of FMS installed at the end of 1984.

Fig. 7.1. Growth of Flexible Manufacturing Systems, 1970–1984
Source: UN/ECE (1986).

being . . . replaced with clusters of all-purpose machines huddled in cells run by computers and served by multi-fingered robots. The whole shape of the industrial landscape is changing.

Evidence of this change was indicated by what, at the time, were very imperfect statistics of diffusion of computer-numerically-controlled (CNC) manufacturing systems, flexible manufacturing systems (FMS), computer-aided design / computer-aided manufacture (CAD / CAM), and other intermediate forms of flexible and programmable automation for all industrial countries. Figure 7.1 illustrates this trend for four leading nations from

1970 to 1985, which clearly indicates that rapid diffusion of FMS started in the late 1970s.[2]

Although early pioneers of computerization foresaw the general trend towards the automated factory and office, they made huge forecasting errors about the patterns of diffusion. While the former head of IBM, T. J. Watson Sr, greatly underestimated the potential of electronic computers for business applications, errors of overestimation were more characteristic of the technological enthusiasts of the 1940s and 1950s. Many estimates then predicted big increases in labour productivity and widespread technological unemployment arising from computerized automation by the 1960s. These fears were so widespread that international organizations, such as the OECD and the International Labour Office (ILO), commissioned special studies and convened international conferences on the employment effects of automation. In the USA, a special national commission produced a massive five-volume report on the topic (USNCTAEP 1966).

In fact, the process of technical change in the early post-war period was of an incremental type concerned with the improvement of mass production systems and related mainly to speed and accuracy of machining, and using new and improved materials. Automation was often little more than advanced mechanization, rather than the use of telecommunication and computers. Productivity increases were high when economies of scale based on long production runs for standardized products could be attained. This was much more feasible with vehicles, consumer durables, and oil and plastics, for example, than with industries based on mechanical engineering. Unemployment remained low throughout the 1960s.

The Growth and Productivity Paradox

Despite this slight initial impact, a whole family of innovations relating to computerization was launched in the 1950s and began to diffuse in the 1960s. It was with the advent of the microprocessor in the 1970s that they rapidly became more important. Developments anticipated in the 1950s only became reality thirty years later—and continue to do so.

Yet in the 1980s, when computers were seen everywhere, not only in factories but in all kinds of office and service activities, the question remained: Where were the productivity gains from this large-scale application of electronic computers? High levels of unemployment are generally associated with *low* growth of labour productivity, despite widespread belief to the contrary. High productivity growth, as in the 1950s and 1960s, offers a 'virtuous circle' of high levels of investment, strong output growth, and low unemployment. A return to higher levels of employment is most likely to be attained when productivity growth and investment recover. Thus, it is important to try to understand the productivity paradox of the 1980s from the standpoint of employment policy as well as growth objectives.

All the main industrial countries show a fairly consistent pattern of economic and productivity growth in the twentieth century. For example, there was relatively slow growth or stagnation in the inter-war period followed by a quarter-century of very high growth after the Second World War, then another period of slower growth in the 1970s and 1980s. 'Total factor productivity' growth—which measures the part of economic growth which cannot be attributed to increases in the quantity of labour or capital—for six leading industrial countries averaged more than twice the rate from 1950 to 1973 than it did between 1973 and 1984.[3] Although there are problems with this concept of 'total factor productivity', the basic trend of a big reduction in the rate of growth is the same whether this measure is used or the more straightforward notions of labour or capital productivity. Yet this was the very period when it might have been expected that productivity gains would increase because of the advent of the microprocessor and many other cheap and reliable innovations based upon microelectronics, which are now finding application throughout the economy.

National Differences in Growth Trends

The trends of productivity increase across various countries and different industries during the 1970s and 1980s showed an extremely uneven pattern. There are some industries in which productivity increases continued at a very high level throughout this period, such as in the computer industry generally and in other parts of the electronics industry, such as components where particularly impressive gains were made in capital productivity. In an industry like steel, remarkable gains in labour productivity were widely achieved through a process of rationalization involving the closure of uneconomic plants.

There have been striking differences between countries in the pattern of productivity advance in the same industry, such as the manufacturing of automobiles and machine tools. In these cases and several others, there is a strong contrast between Japanese productivity performance and that of most other countries.[4] Greater productivity performance in Japan compared to most other countries led to much interest during the

1980s in Japanese management techniques and industrial relations, especially in Japanese policies towards investment in robotics and other types of automated machinery. It seems clear that in the automobile industry much of the Japanese superiority in productivity must be attributed to organization and managerial innovations rather than simply to greater investment in new equipment (Womack *et al.* 1990). Moreover, the performance of Japanese plants in the USA and UK, such as the General Motors/Toyota plant in the USA and the Nissan plant in the UK, has shown that these innovations are to a considerable extent transferrable.

A Japanese example of an organizational innovation in the 1980s was 'Just-In-Time' (JIT) systems. This is much more than the reduction of stocks of components held in assembly plants; it represented a new approach to the organization of work flow and quality control. Its most important characteristic is the devolution of greater responsibility to shop-floor workers for both quality and flow of work. It can also lead to substantial reductions in production down-time and improvements in quality. However, the introduction of this system involves an entire package of social innovations. The most important are multi-skilling of the workforce based on intensive training and retraining, reducing the number of middle-level managers, and organizing good 'horizontal' flows of information both within the firm and with component suppliers and distributors.

These interrelated organizational innovations did not arise directly from computer-based information systems, but were originally attempts to overcome some of the obvious defects of the assembly line, mass production system. However, JIT lends itself particularly well to computerization and complements other Japanese social innovations designed to take full advantage of computerization.

Lessons from Japan?

Studies in the 1980s of different sectors of industry and of the economy identified a number of characteristics of Japanese industrial and technological policy that confers major advantages in the adoption of new technology (see for example Gregory 1986; Bounine and Suzaki 1987; and Freeman 1987). These characteristics included:

1. **The horizontal integration of R&D, design, production engineering, and marketing.** In the electronics industry, this has been described as treating 'the factory as a laboratory' (Baba, unpub. diss. 1986). Many studies agreed that the integration of product and process design and

development was an outstanding strength of Japanese innovation management. For example, Aoki (1986) contrasts the horizontal information flow characteristic of Japanese large firms with the vertical information flow characteristic of the management style of US firms.

2. **Motivation of the workforce.** This was achieved through a variety of techniques, particularly high levels of education and training combined with greater delegation of responsibility.

3. **The development of a consensus in industry, government, and universities on the priorities for R&D and technical change.** This included the co-ordination of the necessary long-term R&D investment to meet those priorities ahead of the competition. The early identification of ICTs as the key technologies for Japanese efforts to overtake and outstrip the US economy was especially important.

These features of Japanese society explain, in part, the strength of the Japanese challenge to US and European industry since the 1980s. Nevertheless, there have been some industries, especially services, where the rate of Japanese productivity increase has been much lower than that achieved elsewhere.

To summarize, the 'leading-edge' industries—computers, electronic components, and other electronic products—maintained very high rates of productivity advance between 1960 and 1990. These advances were increasingly related to the introduction of computer-based automation. Elsewhere in the economy, the evidence was mixed. Productivity gains were made in various sectors by a variety of methods, such as organizational innovations and rationalization, as well as by the introduction of computer-controlled systems. At the same time, there was little advance in many areas, even where computers were widely diffused. To make sense of this uneven and varied picture, the next section examines in greater depth the types of technical innovations which have been introduced since the Second World War.

A Taxonomy of Innovations

There is a great deal of evidence showing that all sectors of developed economies underwent a change of paradigm from the capital-intensive, energy-intensive, inflexible, mass and assembly line production technology of the 1950s and 1960s to an information-intensive, flexible, computerized technology in the 1970s and 1980s (see for example Soete 1985 and Freeman and Soete 1987). In every industry, there was a great variety of incremental and radical innovations. The following subsections describe four categories into which innovations introduced to business and industry since the Second World War can be classified.

Incremental Innovations

Incremental changes occur more or less continuously in any industry or service activity, although at differing rates in different industries, depending on demand pressures and technological opportunities. Although many incremental innovations may result from formal R&D programmes, they are often the outcome of inventions and improvements suggested by engineers and others engaged in the production process, or of initiatives and proposals made by users.

Radical Innovations

There is a second group of innovations which cannot be construed as the cumulative addition of small modifications to existing products and processes. For example, nuclear reactors could not have emerged from incremental improvements to coal-fired electricity-generating stations, nor nylon from improvements in cotton. Radical innovations are discontinuous events, often resulting from deliberate R&D activity in enterprises and/or university and government laboratories.

These innovations are important as potential springboards for the growth of new markets and for big improvements in the cost and quality of existing products. They may often combine product, process, and organizational innovations. Their economic impact is relatively small and localized, however, unless radical innovations are linked together to give rise to new industries and services. Joseph Schumpeter (1939) argued that radical innovations, far from being introduced by 'rational' entrepreneurs on the basis of an accurate understanding of consumers' demands, are usually imposed on an initially unreceptive and unwilling market by rather unusual entrepreneurs, who differ from routine managers.

Changes of 'Technology System'

Far-reaching changes in technology affect one or more economic sectors and often give rise to entirely new sectors. They are based on a combination of radical and incremental innovations, together with organizational innovations affecting more than a few firms. The Schumpeterian theory of economic development has also been described in terms of 'constellations' (Keirstead 1948) to refer to technically and economically interrelated innovations. One example is the cluster of innovations involving synthetic materials—which include innovations in petrochemicals, injection moulding, and extrusion machinery—and innumerable application innovations for synthetics introduced from the 1930s to 1950s (Freeman *et al.* 1982).

Changes in 'Techno-Economic Paradigm'

Some changes in technology systems exert a major influence on the behaviour of the entire economy. These are what Schumpeter (1939) called the 'creative gales of destruction', which are at the heart of the theory of 'long-wave cycles' in economic development of successive 'industrial revolutions' as new technologies are diffused through the productive system. These waves stimulate expansion throughout the economy for a time, but are followed by a period of relative stagnation or depression until a new stimulus develops from a new set of technologies. Schumpeter called them 'Kondratieff cycles' after the Russian economist who, in the 1920s, documented past cycles of boom and depression which each lasted about fifty years.

Neo-Schumpeterian economists have developed these ideas in greater depth (see for example Freeman and Perez 1988; Grübler 1990; Berry 1991; and Tylecote 1992). They have stressed the role of new infrastructural investment and new abundant inputs with falling costs and reliable quality, such as cheap steel in the latter part of the nineteenth century, cheap oil in the twentieth century, or cheap microelectronics today.

Table 7.1 summarizes the main successive waves of technical change that have been identified and their dominant infrastructure characteristics. The first four waves occurred in roughly fifty-year Kondratieff cycles, starting in the late eighteenth century. The dating of the fifth and still more the sixth 'green' wave is of course speculative. A new 'techno-economic paradigm', such as that represented by steam power or microelectronics, emerges through a process of economic selection from a range of the technically feasible combinations of innovations (Perez 1983; 1985). It takes more than a decade for a new paradigm to crystallize and still longer for it to diffuse throughout the system. This diffusion involves a complex interplay between technological, economic, and political forces.

The development of a new techno-economic paradigm involves a new

Table 7.1. Successive Waves of Technical Change

Long waves or cycles (Kondratieff waves)	Key features of dominant infrastructure		
	Science, Technology, Education, Training	Transport, Communication	Energy systems
1st 'Industrial Revolution' Factory production	Apprenticeships, learning-by-doing, scientific societies	Canals Carriage roads	Water power
2nd Age of steam power and railways	Professional mechanical and civil engineers University Ph.D.s Technical *Hochschulen*	Railways (iron) Telegraph	Steam power
3rd Age of electricity	Industrial R&D, chemicals and electricals, national laboratories	Railways (steel) Telephone	Electricity
4th Age of mass production ('Fordism')	Large-scale industrial and government R&D Mass education	Motor highways Radio	Oil
5th Age of microelectronics and computer networks	Data networks, R&D global networks, software universal Lifetime educational training	Information highways Digital networks	Gas/oil
6th Green techno-economic paradigm	Humanities and arts reconnected with social and natural sciences	Telematics Teleworking	Renewable energy

'best practice' set of rules and customs for designers, engineers, entrepreneurs, and managers, which differs in crucial respects from the previously prevailing 'common sense'. The economic and technical advantages to be derived from the application of the new technology in product and process design become increasingly apparent and new 'rules of thumb' are gradually established. Such changes in paradigm make possible a 'quantum leap' in potential productivity which is initially realized only in a few leading sectors. In other sectors, such gains cannot usually be realized without fundamental organizational and social changes. This is the key to the productivity paradox and Japan's relative success.

The ICT Techno-Economic Paradigm

The 'ICT paradigm' is based on a constellation of industries which are among the fastest-growing in all leading industrial countries, such as computers, microelectronic components, and telecommunications. From the 1960s, it led to vastly improved technical performance, a drastic fall in costs, and a counter-inflationary trend in these sectors—a rare combination in the history of technology. The paradigm therefore clearly satisfies all the requirements for a Schumpeterian revolution in the economy. Factory and office automation are the extension and application of this paradigm to manufacturing production and service work generally, but the productivity gains depend on combining new fixed investment with institutional change.

Main Features of the Paradigm

Perez (1985) distinguishes three main features of this paradigm. First, she emphasizes the central importance of the shift towards products and processes which make intensive use of information rather than energy and materials. There were massive changes in relative costs in the 1970s brought about by more expensive energy prices and relatively cheaper information inputs. This favoured designs which economize on materials, energy, and moving parts—and which utilize electronics. This implies a major shift in product mix and in the relationship between manufacturing and services, as well as a transformation of the production process.

The second feature is the change from inflexible, dedicated, mass production systems towards more flexible systems, capable of manufacturing a diverse range of products as efficiently as a single product. This change has consequences for the rapid evolution of product design and the products themselves, as well as for economies of scale in many production lines. 'Economies of scope' will become more important than economies of scale, although these will continue to be significant.

Perez describes the third feature as 'systemation'. This creates new patterns of business organization by the integration of office and plant and of design, production, and marketing. In addition, it establishes much closer communication links between assembly plants and suppliers, and between manufacturers and distributors. These links permit more rapid design changes, as well as better stock control. They also permit a wider range of inputs into the design and development process from both internal and external sources.

Adapting to the Paradigm

It is sometimes difficult for companies and countries to adapt to a change of paradigm. Indeed, depressions are periods of mismatch between an emerging new paradigm and the existing institutional framework. Boom periods of expansion occur when there is a good match between a new techno-economic paradigm and the socio-institutional climate. The widespread generalization of a new paradigm across the economy is possible only after a period of change and adaptation by social institutions to the potential of the new technology. Whereas technological change is often very rapid, there is usually a great deal of inertia in social institutions, buttressed by the political power of established interest groups. Many individuals may also respond slowly. In this perspective, the structural crises of the 1980s can be seen as a prolonged period of social adaptation to the new paradigm.

This integration is reminiscent of Karl Marx's theory of tension between 'productive forces', which have a certain degree of autonomy based on technical change, and 'production relations', which tend to reinforce and preserve existing social arrangements. However, Perez does not suggest that socialism is the only possible outcome, although each successive structural crisis raises problems of institutional adaptation. On the contrary, socialist economies have also been confronted with the need for profound institutional changes, as has been recognized in China and the former Soviet Union. The very word 'perestroika' implies a recognition of the importance of and need for structural change.

There are various social and political solutions, many of which might offer a good match. The outcome of social and political searching for satisfactory solutions will depend on the lucidity, strength, and bargaining force of the conflicting social groups—and the experience of various countries as they strive for technological and economic leadership and attempt to foster a variety of institutional experiments and innovations. For example, the Swedish pattern, which involves close consultation between management and trade unions and greater mobility of labour, may prove more acceptable in Europe than a Japanese-style solution. However, all potential solutions are likely to be based on the widespread use of ICT.

The structural crisis of the 1980s involved the transition of the world economy to a new technology based on information-intensive products and processes. Similarly, the structural crisis of the 1930s involved the transition to a new energy-intensive mass and assembly line production system. The reason that such changes of paradigm give rise to periods of great instability is precisely because they affect almost all investment decision making and they intensify the uneven development of the world economy. This leads to the need for a new regulatory institutional framework, both at a national and international level.

The diffusion of ICT throughout the economic system is not just a matter of making incremental improvements, or of extending existing capacity in a few new industries. It involves a major upheaval in all sectors of the economy and changes in the skill profile and capital stock throughout the system. It is for this reason that periods like the 1930s and the 1980s must be regarded differently from the minor recessions of the 1950s and 1960s.

Difficulties in Realizing ICT Productivity Gains

Developments such as FMS and computer-integrated manufacture (CIM) are examples of the worldwide trial-and-error investigations that have sought to find the most effective forms of development and application of the new techno-economic paradigm. Insight into the reasons why it has been so difficult to implement innovations like FMS successfully and to realize productivity gains quickly was provided early on by John Diebold (1952) in a remarkably imaginative vision of the 'automatic factory'.

Diebold recognized that computers had to be widely and cheaply available. He also foresaw that their general application in factories and offices would necessitate the redesign of most of the existing stock of capital equipment. He pointed, for example, to the problem of materials-handling equipment in automated machining systems and was one of the first to recognize that inflexible, dedicated, mechanized production lines would have to be replaced with much more flexible machines. While he identified early examples of this redesign process, he recognized it would take a long time before attitudes changed and engineers would be able to change the layout of factories on a large scale. He also saw that the design and investment costs would be enormous and would have to be accompanied by the redesign of products as well as processes.

The continuing relevance of his perceptions is indicated by examples of product changes in the 1980s. The 1985 model of the IBM dot-matrix printer, for instance, had only sixty parts compared to 150 in the 1983 model. The entire product line of Black & Decker was similarly redesigned, reducing the need for both inspection and assembly line labour, which indicated a trend that could ultimately lead to the elimination of assembly line production (Ayres 1987).

Diebold (1952: 53) did not envisage such an elimination, but he did recognize the need to transform the entire organization of the firm:

> One of the impediments to re-thinking of products and processes has been that the traditional division of responsibilities has the effect of localizing the areas in which re-thinking is done. Almost by definition however, re-thinking must be done on an extremely broad basis—viewing the objectives of the entire organization as a whole. It cannot be confined to the product design engineering department. It must be an attitude, a state of mind, permeating the entire organization . . . An organization so structured as to maximize contact, interchange, and correlations between the product design personnel and the production, sales and other departments is of course desirable for reasons other than ease of automation but the extension of re-thinking to everything affecting the product and process is an essential step in making machines automatic.

This conception of rethinking throughout the organization led him to emphasize the new skills that would be needed and the new employment which could be generated. He stressed the unique abilities and qualities of human beings and the dehumanizing aspects of the assembly line and of work paced by a machine. He quoted with approval an observation of cybernetics specialist Norbert Wiener (1949: 163):

> It is a degradation to a human being to chain him [*sic*] to an oar and use him as a source of power: but it is an almost equal degradation to assign him purely repetitive tasks in a factory which

demand less than a millionth of his brain power. But it is simpler to organize a factory or a galley which uses individual human beings for a trivial fraction of their worth than it is to provide a world in which they can grow to their full stature.

The visions of Diebold and Wiener clearly recognized the full extent of the profound social transformation that would be needed in the shift from one type of techno-economic paradigm to another. This includes a huge scale of new investment; the redesign of machines, factories, and products; dramatic changes in the skill profile of the workforce; and, above all, changes in attitudes throughout business organizations.[5]

Success and Failure in the Management of Innovation

There are likely to be a considerable number of failures as well as successes in the development of new processes or products which set out with identical or similar objectives, as has happened with ICT. The factors affecting success and failure at the enterprise level with such innovations have now been widely studied.

Patterns of Success and Failure

An important and indicative early analysis was carried out by Rothwell *et al.* (1984) in the 1970s in the SAPPHO study, which made comparisons between projects involving such new product and process innovations in chemicals, instruments, and machinery. It identified a characteristic pattern of success and of failure, with only the following few factors being statistically significant and strongly interrelated:

1. Successful innovations were based on great efforts during the design and development process to understand the needs and circumstances of potential users of the new process or product. Unsuccessful innovators either did not make such efforts (in a surprisingly large number of cases) or made inadequate or belated efforts.

2. Information networks with external sources of scientific and technical expertise were almost equally important. Unsuccessful innovations were characterized by excessive secrecy and a reluctance to interact with external organizations.

3. Successful innovations depended on the power within the organization of a 'business innovator' and a 'technical innovator' (sometimes the same individual, but usually not). The power and experience of the business innovator (or 'product champion') were necessary to ensure that resources were available and the necessary links were made between user and innovator, and between the various departments or functions within the innovating firm—especially R&D, design, production, and marketing. Innovations which failed were characterized by inadequate (or non-existent) links between these functions and a lack of any adequate 'coupling' mechanisms. This coupling between R&D, design, production, and marketing depended on an effective, continuous interchange of information. Successful innovators were characterized by horizontal information flows at various levels in the innovating organizations, failures by excessive compartmentalization and rigid, hierarchical flows of information.

Other innovation research has been broadly consistent with these results. For example, a study by Lockett (1987) covering twenty-nine ICT-based projects in a major multinational manufacturing company also concluded that organizational issues were much more important than technological ones. The major factors he identified behind successful projects included:

- a project champion in a business function;
- late formalization of the project;
- a development team bridging the gap between the information systems function and users;
- prototyping in the early stages of a project; and
- transition from a development to an implementation phase with different management requirements.

These and many other studies have stressed the importance of the interface between the user and the developer of the innovation as well as the key role of the business innovator. Lockett also identified the importance to success of a discretionary phase, where would-be innovators could commit small-scale resources on an experimental basis for a month or two. On the other hand, rigid evaluation procedures were inimical to success.

Effective Management of ICT-Based Innovation

These findings could be regarded as typical of the management of innovation in any industry or technology. The user–producer interface must always be important; so too must be the initiative, enthusiasm, and power of the innovator and flexibility in decision making in situations of uncertainty. However, there are distinctive features of ICT innovations, which were shown by differences of emphasis between the SAPPHO study by Rothwell *et al.* and the more ICT-oriented Lockett studies. One of the most significant differences is the nature of the dialogue between user and developer.

In Lockett's projects, the developers did not understand the requirements of the managers for whom they were developing information systems. This was also often the case in SAPPHO's projects and, indeed, it was a major characteristic of failure that the innovators made an inadequate attempt to understand user needs. But whereas the potential users in Rothwell *et al.* were usually able to articulate their needs, this is a major difficulty in many ICT projects as managers and other users are often unable to conceptualize their requirements, much less articulate them to others.

This is a familiar problem for managers of information systems. It is compounded by the fact that the manager's role in the organization may itself be changing, so that the specification of today's requirements, even where it is successfully accomplished, may be a short-lived success. This highlights one of Lockett's main points: organizational flexibility and organizational issues in general are more important for success than technological issues.

It is tempting to conclude from this that organizational innovation is the main (or the only) problem in the diffusion of ICT and that problems of technical innovation have already been solved. This reflects Diebold's point that large-scale organizational innovation is indispensable in the development and diffusion of the automatic factory. It has also been the view of many management consultants who have been preoccupied with changing management attitudes and practices in innumerable companies unfamiliar with ICT and its potential.

However, it would be a profound mistake to ignore the importance of technical innovation and fixed capital investment in the further development and diffusion of ICT, especially in the development of the automatic factory. For instance, Lockett's study was concerned specifically with intrafirm diffusion of ICT using established off-the-shelf hardware. The problems of organizational change and adaptation encountered often related to making use of this hardware and to the establishment of effective management information systems in various areas of company activity. Software development should also itself be regarded as a form of innovative investment.

Organizational change is, of course, absolutely essential for the paradigm change. This applies not only to firms but also to social institutions of all kinds at the regional, national, and international level. However, the overall diffusion of a new techno-economic paradigm involves a complex interplay between technical, organizational, and social innovations. This interplay continues throughout the life of the paradigm. To put the stress exclusively on one or the other is to deny the true complexity of the process. The potential for continuing technical change within the ICT paradigm will continue into the twenty-first century. One has only to think of the rapid rate of innovations in microelectronics, intersystem networking, parallel processing, multimedia, virtual reality, and many other areas to realize the magnitude of the changes that show no sign of diminishing.

Conclusion: Realizing the Potential of the New Paradigm

As a techno-economic paradigm crystallizes and develops, the advantages become increasingly apparent and the logic of the new system appears self-evident. The combination of technical and organizational innovations helps to resolve the main problems and bottlenecks. But in the early stages, there are great difficulties and risks in adopting the new equipment because it is not yet an integrated system, and adoption involves a process of trial and error.

The ICT paradigm could be seen to be in its relatively early stages even by the mid-1990s. Despite the widespread use of CAD, CNC, and FMS in manufacturing and electronic information systems, and networks in services industries, there was still a long way to go to implementing fully integrated, computerized systems. The advent of the automatic factory and electronic office has also required the redesign of innumerable processes and products, which will take a long time to work through. For instance, not only does the configuration of the factory of the future leave behind the factory of the past in its layout and capabilities, but it will also create new generations of products.

The potential of the ICT paradigm will be realized only when there is a good match between the technology and the institutional framework—

when ICT has clearly become the dominant technological regime and when the organizational barriers and social rigidities have been transcended. Thus, it might be true to say that in the period of 'gestation' of a new techno-economic paradigm, the main emphasis is on 'technical innovation' rather than organizational innovation, although the two can never be entirely disassociated. As the technology matures and new key factors become universally and cheaply available, the main problems then become the 'diffusion' of the new paradigm from the leading-edge sectors to the economy as a whole. The emphasis then shifts to 'organizational and social innovation', although technical innovation continues to be important even during this phase of structural adaptation and adjustment. Finally, when the mismatch has been overcome and the socio-organizational problems have been largely resolved, then the institutional factors which once contained and limited diffusion may now encourage, stimulate, and reinforce a further wave of technical innovation.

It is from this perspective that we need to see the productivity slowdown and the relatively slow take-off of the automatic factory in the 1950s to 1980s. During this period, and beyond it, neither the supply side nor the demand side was organized to provide the capability to offer truly integrated systems. However competent the supply side may be, ultimately it is the users who will determine the future direction of innovations like the automated factory and productivity.

One of the main unresolved issues is the degree to which ICT leads to greater humanization of work or the opposite. Where machines pace workers or the external environment completely dominates the response, as in the case of air-traffic controllers, the stress on workers increases, however advanced the technology. If the new paradigm is to fulfil the dreams of people like Diebold and Wiener and avoid the degradation of human beings, JIT and other innovations must lead to small groups of workers or individuals taking full responsibility and determining the pace of work. This is often the case with professional workers, craftworkers, and maintenance workers. Whether the humanization of work becomes associated with the diffusion of ICTs will depend in large part on the social and political solutions which are attempted in various countries. Of course, as discussion of information superhighways and the Internet-inspired 'cyberculture' tend to suggest, a happy combination of work humanization and productivity advance is conceivable—and has become a goal for many actors, countries, and regions.

Notes

1. This chapter is based primarily on Freeman (1988).
2. Problems of definition and international comparability mean that the diagram should be taken as illustrative of trends and not as an accurate international comparison.
3. The countries were France, Germany, Japan, the Netherlands, the UK, and the USA (see Maddison 1987).
4. Between 1970 and 1981, the time spent on making a motor vehicle in Japan fell from about 250 person-hours per vehicle to 140. During the same period it rose from about 200 to 210 hours in the USA. In West Germany, equivalent rates averaged around 195 and 205 hours between 1977 and 1981 (Altshuler *et al.* 1985).
5. The kind of sweeping transformations identified here are discussed elsewhere in the book, such as changes in relation to organizations in general (Chapter 9) and education (Chapter 14).

8 Revolution in the Office? Implications for Women's Paid Work

Juliet Webster

Public debates about ICT and employment have generally been a mix of high hopes and profound fears about the forward march of automation. From the early 1980s, increasing attention in investigations of the realities behind the hopes and fears has been placed on the implications for women's work and the overall relationship to the division of labour between genders.

In this chapter, Juliet Webster explores the impact of technology on women's jobs and outlines some of the intellectual advances that have been made in our understanding of gendered work and the reasons why there have been relatively limited changes in the sexual division of labour as a result of the introduction of ICTs.[1] In addition, Webster examines how the male dominance of technological knowledge, practices, and institutions places ICTs into workplace cultures which are often alien to women. She emphasizes the importance of management policies that could help organizations better integrate women into positions of responsibility for the development and use of ICTs. The role of public policy in improving the quality of working life for women is also highlighted.

ICT, Women, and their Work

The growing use of large mainframe data processing systems in the 1950s and 1960s started public debates about the expected impact of computer-based technologies on levels of employment and patterns of work organization. Many of the themes of these early 'automation debates' have subsequently recurred. One side of the debate stresses the technology's potential to eliminate the repetitious tasks characteristic of many jobs, thereby freeing people to develop new skills and abilities. The other side highlights fears that computers could cause mass unemployment and an increasing intensification of work and enslavement to machines for those remaining in jobs.

With hindsight, it is clear these debates were cast in an overly simplistic way. One of the most important problems was an initial focus on stereotypical skilled manual work—metalwork, mechanical engineering, coal mining, and printing. Because they involved skills acquired through apprenticeships and access to them was carefully restricted, these jobs were male-dominated. In the late 1970s and early 1980s, studies of the impact of technologies on work therefore tended to deepen understanding of the implications for certain jobs done by men, while awareness of what was happening to women's work remained very poor. It was in this context that feminists and others began to address the impact of the new technologies on women's employment, especially through the automation of office work (see for example Mandon 1988 and Thompson 1989).

Some commentators (such as Barker and Downing 1980; Cooley 1981; and Huws 1982) predicted that office automation would fundamentally alter both the level and nature of office employment. Women were seen as being most vulnerable to the ill effects of automation since they did the bulk of the low-status, low-paid work which could be most easily automated (Wernecke 1983). There was also concern that this type of extreme sexual division of labour was leading to a similar 'occupational ghettoization of women' in many other sectors. This potential vulnerability went hand-in-hand with an exclusion of women from substantial areas of technical know-how and skill in the workplace. Women's relationship to technology was therefore particularly problematic as it had its own dynamics, which could not be simply read off from studies of men's work and technology.

The first studies of the impact of ICTs on women's jobs were concerned principally with office work because:

1. Women are very strongly represented in office work. In secretarial work, for instance, 99 per cent of workers in the mid-1990s were women.

2. The office was where ICTs were seen as having the most potentially decisive effect on job and skill levels. The low rate of productivity in the

office relative to the factory seemed to make it the most likely candidate for management's most searching attempts at rationalization through the integration of previously separate computing and telecommunications technologies.

Predictions about the Automated Office

Two major themes emerged at the end of the 1970s in discussions about a predicted 'automated office'. A 'post-industrial' vision was promoted by many government departments, consultancies, and business firms. This argued that jobs destroyed would be replaced by new occupations in new industries—and degraded and routine work would be consigned to machines, releasing human beings to 'cleaner', more creative, and more fulfilling work (Central Policy Review Staff 1978; Curran and Mitchell 1982).

The counter-argument viewed the development and implementation of new office technology as a radical innovation in the organization and management of work that would introduce techniques more traditionally associated with the assembly line—characterized by fragmentation, de-skilling, alienation, and the intensification and pacing of office work. It was said this was being done by employers as a deliberate mechanism to cut labour costs, achieve greater productivity, and maintain the rate of capital accumulation. This was often supported by evidence from the USA, as typified by this quote from a female word-processing operator in a bank in San Francisco (CSE Microelectronics Group 1980: 50):

> People felt that they were plugged into machines, that they were appendages to machines rather than people performing functions with other people . . . We used to have jokes about how we expected that they'd chain us to our desks and give us catheters, so we'd never have to go to the bathroom. And the thing is that once word processing is introduced, it's possible to keep track exactly of the amount of productivity each individual displays, and set rises and evaluations accordingly. People feel very pressurized to get their production out. When I first started at the bank, the standards were 8,000 keystrokes an hour and when I left five years later they were 12,000.

Although this approach has been extremely influential and ideologically powerful, it is now seen as being too simplistic.

145

Office Revolution or Old Regime Continued?

Both the negative and positive predictions of the employment implications in the 'office of the future' suffered from a technological determinism that saw dramatic organizational change as a consequence of the introduction of word processing and other new technologies. This ignored organizational patterns and changes which preceded, and set the scene for, the introduction of new technology into the office. It also did not allow for situations in which a wholesale restructuring of office work did not coincide with the automation of office tasks.

Predictions about the effects of information technologies on women's office work therefore failed to consider the ways in which office technology is implemented in practice. In particular, they neglected the differences that exist in the forms of office work and in the implementation of office automation. This led to a lack of sensitivity to the specific contexts within which new information technologies were introduced and to the requirements of individual employers.

The environment in which ICTs are introduced into the office varies considerably, depending on the kinds of typing-related work involved. For instance, word processing in a university department may be one of a range of activities performed by the office staff, who also deal with visitors and students, perform administrative tasks, and arrange meetings and placements. In a manufacturing company, by contrast, women might be confined to a small word-processing pool and have no tasks other than typing, giving them very little variety or stimulation in the course of their working day (see case studies in Webster 1990).

The distinctions between secretarial and typing work, and between various kinds of typing jobs, are crucial to the analysis of likely effects of ICTs in offices, as was emphasized by Arnold *et al.* (1982: 60):

> female typists—essentially machine operators—have existed as long as the machines themselves. As specialist machine operators, they can be managed like factory shopfloor workers; this may not be true for secretaries, who perform a range of other duties in addition to typing.

In much of the literature on office automation, these very different jobs were indiscriminately conflated into one. Predictions about the impact of word processing were generally based on a notion of all office jobs as containing variety and discretion and requiring 'craft skills'— characteristics in fact only of secretarial work. Significant differences between the work of secretaries and the 'office battalions' have crucial implications for the ways in which technologies are utilized and affect working patterns. These differences relate to the range of office tasks with which the two groups are concerned, the extent to which typing is the main aspect of their work, and the degree to which this task is itself fragmented.

These are issues of job design, division of labour, and the organization of work, rather than being outcomes of the application of new forms of office automation. Where office work has been technologically determined, the main impacts initially came from the application of mechanical technologies. For example, McNally (1979: 74) noted:

> Although a great deal of the secretary's day is spent over the keyboard, the great range of other non-mechanical tasks which she is expected to perform are held to distinguish her from the 'mere' shorthand-typist . . . In recent years, the division of labour has infiltrated much of the office, while leaving the secretary's job as yet intact. With the exception of certain categories of clerk, and supervisors, many of these office girls are defined in terms of the machine they operate in much the same way as many blue-collar workers.

The routinization of office work, then, is not a new state of affairs brought about by the application of ICTs. The typing pool dates back to at least the 1880s, when row upon row of women confined to the single activity of typing were overseen by a supervisor who sat facing them (Delgado 1979). Certain types of women's office work were therefore fragmented long before the introduction of any kind of computerized office technology.

Financial institutions, in particular, had highly standardized and routinized working patterns which created regimented typists' jobs based on an organizational system that presaged that introduced for word processing. Correspondence had been routinized and simplified; there was extensive use of pads of pre-printed letters with tick boxes; and clerical staff and the typing pool were divided to handle different categories of work. Automatic typewriters generated additional standard documents by printing them out and then pausing while the operator filled in the variable information. In some offices each worker specialized in one detailed operation, such as putting letters into envelopes or typing details into standard letters (Webster 1990).

A company's ICT-based office system can therefore often be seen as 'an accumulation of what had gone on before'. The organizational rationalization of work has taken place over a long period, beginning considerably before the introduction of systems like word processors. In the pre-ICT era, the division of labour was sometimes so tight and work routines so monotonous that it led to high rates of labour turnover. This combined with the separation of typists from the source and destiny of their work to cause great inefficiencies in organizations.

Office Work and Technological Change

It has therefore become clear that when ICTs like word processing are applied to established women's office jobs, they seem to extend and reinforce the patterns of work organization already set in motion by management design. This is reflected in findings on three issues where word processing was predicted to have significant effects—de-skilling, work intensification, and management control.

De-skilling

The introduction of word-processing technologies in the 1980s brought little change in the extent of the skills deployed in particular jobs, where 'skill' can be taken to mean both the use of manual dexterity and control over working pace and method (see the case studies in Webster 1996, for example). The most significant differences were not found between automated and non-automated jobs, but between different grades of office job which were subject to differing degrees of task fragmentation.

The office workers with the more varied jobs—mainly secretaries—continued to apply the skills they had previously exercised, including the ability to take decisions in the course of their work. However, word processing altered the manner in which they carried out their typing tasks. Instead of manipulating a typewriter's carriage and levers to lay out work, they could give the machine instructions to do what was needed.

The mental labour and component of choice was a function of the complexity of the typing task, not of the machine used. Software-based systems like word processors are far more complex and offer more choices about how to achieve a particular objective than their manual counterparts. Whether the operator is able to exercise that choice depends crucially upon the complexity of the work itself. Given a complex item of work, the operator can indeed use initiative and judgement in tackling it. Yet when systems are programmed for largely standardized work, operators have no choice other than to fill in the spaces in forms presented to them.

Work Intensification

Another popular early misconception of office automation was the idea that word-processing and computing systems would remove the control which enables office workers to regulate their working patterns. Increasing automation of work pacing and the elimination of natural breaks in a working day were expected to mark a move away from previous regimes of work, constituting a radical new mechanism for the heightened intensification of work.

Work intensification is, however, a far more well-established and complex phenomenon than this argument suggests. One of the two crucial determinants of the level of effort exercised by secretaries and typists is structural—the degree to which work is fragmented. The other is the normative managerial pressures on office workers to exert themselves, which are often exercised through typing supervisors. Neither of these are primarily functions of the technology. Stand-alone ICT devices like word processors seem to play a marginal role in the intensification of office work.

A number of studies have drawn attention to the pacing inherent in certain machines. For example, Baldamus (1961: 60) noted that lathes impel operatives to keep going even when fatigued, so that effort can be controlled by 'methods of machine-paced production, including the whole apparatus of flow production which requires that the speed of work is stabilized through the interdependence of co-ordinated activities'. Yet this cannot be claimed of the word-processor or computer operator. Her work station, when switched on, has no fixed and unvarying rhythm to which she is subordinated. In that sense she still makes use of it, rather than it making use of her. As McNally (1979: 80) found:

> The degree to which work output is measured varies from the situation where the supervisor merely checks that the girls remain anchored to their machines all day, to the situation where a supervisor actually counts the number of invoices, index cards or whatever, that each girl produces. Even the typing pools which have certain minimum standards set in terms of productivity, however, are unable to set a fixed pace to the work, in the same way that many factory floor machines can dictate the pace of

their operatives. It is this factor which permits the occasional daydream, or an aside to one's neighbour, which may help to pass the time between breaks.

Office jobs with few natural breaks, such as those composed of single monotonous activities like typing, are much more susceptible to attempts to speed up work than are those which consist of a variety of different tasks involving planning, thought, and movement around the office. For example, many years before the advent of word processors, office managements used work flow techniques comparable to the assembly line— such as centralized dictating systems and work allocation to fix typists to their positions to increase the degree of effort expended on the core activity of typing. In this way, office work can be intensified. However, the principle behind it is one of work organization which is by no means 'new' or specific to the automated office.

Managerial Control of Office Workers

The introduction of ICTs into offices was seen by technological pessimists as a means for shifting control over the labour process from office workers into the hands of management, on the lines of the scientific management techniques originally proposed by Frederick Taylor (Glenn and Feldberg 1979; Barker and Downing 1980). A clear link was made to the concept of a 'technical control' that is 'embedded' in the technology itself (Edwards 1979: 112).

Nevertheless, control practices with the new technology have evolved from the particular requirements and traditions of work organization which, as we have seen, generally pre-dated their utilization of IT devices (see for example Webster 1990). Moreover, these practices could not be uniformly characterized as 'Taylorism'. In those organizations where the technical division of labour was strongest and Taylorist control practices were most clearly in evidence, say in typing pools, these techniques operated quite independently of office automation. For instance, in the early 1970s, before the introduction of any office automation, a typist in a financial-services company commented (Webster 1990: 18):

We weren't allowed to go and make a cup of tea . . . So you couldn't eat at your desk or drink. You couldn't smoke. You had to go into this, like a common room, like at school . . . You could stop and talk if there was nobody watching, but you had this partition, so it was a bit hard really. If you really wanted to get involved in a conversation you had to lean over your partition, so somebody would soon see. But me and this other girl who I was next to, we had this little hole in ours, so it was alright. If anybody saw you, you would get into trouble. It was very strict.

When information technologies were introduced, such tight methods of control over staff were perpetuated by management and there was no consequent work restructuring. In fact, word processors were often bought to function simply as sophisticated typewriters which could also produce neater documentation more rapidly. From this perspective, increased productivity provided by the new machinery was seen by managers to be sufficient cost saving without any work rationalization scheme. Of course, word processing is a far more versatile technology that need not have such limited implications for the work of typists.

The particular method of managerial control to be found in a specific office is therefore best understood in terms of the imperatives of the organization in question. These tend to be geared to the long-term conditions within which companies operate and therefore are not suddenly transformable overnight. The degree and type of control exercised over an office labour process is mediated by management's profit-making requirements and its historical use of control strategies; the position of female office workers in the labour market in particular industries and geographical areas; and the state of the economy in general.

ICTs and Women's Work

The impacts of ICTs on office work outlined above have broader implications for other areas of women's work. The discussion illustrates why the direct effects of the technology are so difficult to gauge, as they are influenced by so many non-technological factors. Unemployment arising from ICTs, for example, proved hard to separate from wider economic forces, such as the severe recessions of the 1980s. Clearly identifiable redundancies merged with job loss through natural wastage, so that job opportunities disappeared much more imperceptibly than had been expected. Attempts to quantify the employment effects of technology alone must always keep these limitations in mind.

Although it was easier to assess the effects on women office workers, the results, as already discussed, did not support either optimistic or pessimistic predictions about the introduction of ICTs. Detailed studies of women's office jobs and women's experiences of the introduction of ICTs confirmed the low status of women in the workplace. They also highlighted a particular system of patriarchal control over these women which was a result of the peculiarly gendered character of office roles and relationships, as typified by the term 'office wife' (Benet 1972), which depicts the role of female secretarial workers in their relationship to generally male superiors.

Research also indicated that the sexual division of labour has proved to be remarkably durable. No unambiguous patterns of change caused by the application of ICTs were found, because the impact of technologies on women's jobs proved to hinge on three key factors which were independent of technology (see Box 8.1).

These various modifying factors mean that definitive statements about the impact of ICTs on women's jobs are impossible to sustain. Awareness of the criticality of the context of technological change forces us to focus attention on management strategies, economic imperatives, company and organizational practices, and sexual divisions of labour. This view shows that technology, far from being somehow neutral, free-floating, or separate from its social context, is intimately bound up with that human, social, and political context.

This is a salutary lesson. Women's work in general has undergone profound changes since the mid-1980s, but these are less the product of technological change than the result of the restructuring of Western economies. For example, in Europe and North America in the 1990s there has been an increasing reliance by employers on casual forms of work— more part-time jobs, more temporary contracts, more self-employment. These are particularly marked in certain sectors of the economy, such as retailing. This casualization of women's work has been supported by the introduction of ICTs, but is the product of concerted restructuring programmes in which management deploy a panoply of different techniques to try to address the contemporary competitive environment.

Shifting Spatial Divisions of Labour

On a global scale, profound changes in the location of women's jobs have been much more decisively brought about by the introduction of ICTs. These changes have facilitated the process of relocating corporate activities away from the more expensive regions in the so-called 'First World' to less favoured regions within the same country or to entirely different countries in the 'Third World'. This globalization of production

> **Box 8.1.** Key Factors Affecting the Impact of ICTs on Women's Jobs
>
> - The specific work context is crucial—the nature of the work performed and the distinctions between different kinds of work. It is therefore not possible to draw the same conclusions about the effects of ICTs on all women's jobs. Understanding how jobs were constructed in the first place is an important element in analysing these differentiated effects.
>
> - The objectives of the employers who introduce new techniques can profoundly shape the impact of the technologies on women's jobs. For example, in the finance sector new technology was used primarily to rationalize and so cheapen the processing of information and was often introduced into offices that were long-standing white-collar factories. Company managements also typically use male and female labour differently because they are differently priced and continue to work in markedly different areas and conditions. So the automation of men's work proceeds differently from the automation of women's work, and for different reasons. This is an important point to bear in mind when considering equal-opportunities or positive-action programmes.
>
> - The broader economic environment and labour market conditions in particular places and at particular periods are essential considerations in drawing conclusions about the impact of new technology on women's jobs. For example, enterprises in many countries embarked on a profound reappraisal of their international competitive position in the 1990s. This has included re-evaluating all aspects of management strategy in relation to the use of technology and labour in the structuring and restructuring of organizations. Companies are looking to reduce operational costs; the labour market is tight; and countervailing power is comparatively weak. In this context, the opportunities for using technology to advance the position of women in the workplace seem much fewer than they did during the 1980s when there was a period of so-called 'skills shortages'.

has been prominent in electronics and ICT assembly and software production; in the garment and textile industries; and, increasingly, in the clerical industries. The infamous use of young, 'docile', non-unionized South-East Asian women for microelectronics manufacture has been extended by the use of ICTs to relocate data-entry and clerical jobs into low-wage, low-overhead regions including the Caribbean, Latin America, South-East Asia, India, and China. Such developments have done nothing to alter the sexual division of labour or the low status of women's work—they have simply altered the location of work and added race to the gender divisions within labour forces.

ICTs have also assisted work relocation through developments in teleworking. Here again, the change in location brings little change in the low-grade status of women's work. For example, in Britain the majority of clerical teleworkers are married women in their mid-thirties. Many are performing routine and intense work, and are low-paid, isolated, non-unionized, and uncertain about the status of their employment (Huws 1984; Wajcman and Probert 1988).

There are also marked differences between the types and work conditions of teleworking jobs that men and women do. An Australian study, for example, found that teleworking men were mainly in professional occupations, such as management and computer systems analysis. Teleworking women, however, were largely in clerical occupations and were married with young children. Like female homeworkers in the traditional sweated industries, they were typically paid at piece rates and earned substantially less than comparably skilled workers in offices, while also meeting their own overhead costs such as heating, lighting, and power for machines (Wajcman and Probert 1988).

It has been found that men often become self-employed teleworkers after having been made redundant from their jobs. On the other hand, women generally take up teleworking in order to combine child care with work, although they end up working extremely diverse and unpredictable hours as they seize opportunities to work without interruptions when their children are at school or in bed (Fothergill 1994). Furthermore, women are increasingly debarred from using teleworking to combine work with child care (Huws 1993).

Even though teleworking is very much facilitated by ICTs, the decisive factor in influencing employers' telework strategies has again not been technology so much as social and economic factors, such as the need to reduce building overheads or to restructure companies. Teleworking is accorded enormous importance in corporate and public policy—as when its significance was reaffirmed at the EU's political summit in Corfu in 1994. However, teleworking is more likely to replicate workplace divisions of labour and relocate them into the home, rather than deliver the promised beneficial flexibility for women workers.

The Social Shaping of Technology and the Role of Gender

Technologies in the workplace have largely been appropriated by men at the expense of women—a process which dates back to the mechanized technologies of the Industrial Revolution and has continued despite the most enthusiastic campaigns to get women into technology and to broaden the scope of technical and computing education. In order to understand the impact of technology on women's jobs, we therefore have to understand this relationship.

The creation and consumption of technologies, including ICTs, are subject to an extreme sexual division of labour. Technologies themselves can also be heavily imbued with masculinity in its various guises, through the institutions and processes which generate and perpetuate the technologies and in the values and culture which underlie them. This creates a variety of barriers to women's access to technology—from social attitudes, to girls' education, to the teaching of engineering and technology in post-school education, to the employment policies of firms (see for example Faulkner and Arnold 1985; Kirkup and Keller 1992; and Murray 1993). Equally, technology has come to be perceived as an activity appropriate for men and as part of the definition of masculinity.

Women are usually notably absent from the design of technologies and from decision making concerning their implementation. Within the IT profession, for example, men are much more strongly represented in senior jobs. In terms of IT qualifications, only 10 per cent of the professional membership of the British Computer Society was female in 1994 and the proportion of women entering computer science degrees and further education courses was dropping (Committee on Women in Science, Engineering and Technology 1994). Those women who do enter the IT profession often find their qualifications count for less than adherence to a set of informal 'rules of the game' for which their male counterparts are culturally far better prepared.

Women in IT are on alien territory. The culture and practice of the computing profession is redolent with myriad forms of masculinity, as was graphically depicted by Cringley (1992: 22) in his book on the IT personalities in Silicon Valley:

> Hippie programmers have long hair and deliberately, even pridefully, ignore the seasons in their choice of clothing. They wear shorts and sandals in the winter and T-shirts all the time. Nerds are neat little anal-retentive men with penchants for short-sleeved shirts and pocket protectors. Nerds carry calculators; hippies borrow calculators. Nerds use decongestant nasal sprays; hippies snort cocaine. Nerds typically know forty-six different ways to make love but don't know any women . . .

Although this is a humorous account, it is derived from a valid analysis that has important implications. Successful membership of the computing profession could be said to be based on an almost obsessional techno-philia—which has indeed been linked with masculine inadequacy in personal relationships. In much systems-development work, intensity of experience is also achieved through the 'project mentality', which involves working long and odd hours under stress in a hermetically sealed world, urgently chasing milestones, deliverables, and objectives in almost siegelike conditions—and revelling in doing so. This is a culture which is not only alienating to many women, but incompatible with their lives.

A Woman-Friendly Technology Policy

The structural and cultural processes working to the exclusion of women from technology can be challenged only through policies that address the serious lack of regard for women's needs and priorities in technological innovation and design. This requires confronting a host of related organizational, political, and economic challenges at several levels.

First, we need to understand the mechanisms which cause women to opt out of technological activity in large numbers. Girls' lack of awareness and motivation have conventionally been regarded as the source of the 'problem' of their lack of participation in science and technology, although they perform at least as well as boys in these subjects at school. As it seems that science and technology themselves can alienate women, education and training in these areas should therefore be made more appropriate and relevant to women and their needs. This will involve rethinking science and technology courses in school and post-school education, as well as the emphasis of 'women in technology' campaigns. Such initiatives might see the problem as simply being women's exclusion from technological work and promote solutions based on increased information and encouragement to women to participate (Henwood 1993).

Secondly, the processes and practices of some professions and occupations need to be addressed. For example, ICT systems-development projects could draw women users into the design process or closely elicit their particular detailed knowledge of the work processes to be automated (see for example Greenbaum and Kyng 1991; Green et al. 1993; and Probert and Wilson 1993). Such projects can demonstrate that women need not merely be passive recipients of the IT systems they use, but also knowledgeable agents who can directly help to construct the systems they will work with. The projects can employ a powerful set of systems-development tools that facilitate a new approach which is more sensitive to the needs of female users, such as 'study circles' and the greater use of 'shared' rather than 'authoritarian' knowledge (see for example Suchman and Jordan 1989 and Vehvilaïnen 1991).

Thirdly, as already noted, changes in women's jobs—for better or worse—are wrought essentially by managements rather than determined simply by technologies. If the automation of their jobs is to improve the quality of working life for women, conscious decisions must therefore be taken by employers about the organization of work and technology.[2] That involves a concerted programme which recognizes women's existing skills; creates conditions for building new skills; develops clear equal-opportunities policies and promotion paths for women; and pays serious attention to child-care provision by employers, the state, and men.

Finally, the state itself must be a key player. It must help in:

- providing ICT awareness, education, and training;
- enacting and enforcing legislation which safeguards the interests of women employees;
- co-ordinating different levels and types of policy initiative to ensure they cohere with one another so that there is a firm commitment—articulated throughout various economic, organizational, educational, and cultural spheres—to using the opportunity of technological change to improve the quality of women's working lives.

Notes

1. Juliet Webster drew on two PICT Policy Research Papers (Webster 1991; 1995) in developing this chapter.
2. For a discussion on the interplay between organizational and technical change, particularly through business process re-engineering initiatives, see Chapter 9.

9 The Politics of IT Strategy and Development in Organizations

Rod Coombs and Richard Hull

Management theorists since the 1950s have linked ICTs to power shifts in organizations, such as the growing influence of individuals with expertise in ICTs. More generally, the adoption and implementation of ICTs have become bound up not only with how an organization accomplishes its tasks, but also with the nature of the products and services it provides. Technological innovation is inseparable from organizational change and, therefore, from the political interplay among actors within an organization. To deny or neglect the role of organizational politics in the adoption, implementation, and routinization of ICTs is to court failure and possible disaster.

Rod Coombs and Richard Hull explore this political conception of ICTs in this chapter.[1] In discussing a growing awareness of the close-knit relationships between the technology and organizational strategy and structure, they focus on techniques for 're-engineering' organizations which have been widely adopted in the 1990s. However, they emphasize that this has not always been accompanied by an adequate appreciation of the role of organizational politics as a vital factor in the successful development of ICT applications in different organizational contexts.

ICT and Business Strategy

ICT is one of a small number of 'generic' technologies—like steam power and electricity—which have caused what the Austrian economist Schumpeter (1939) called 'gales of creative destruction' in market economies by fuelling economic growth. However, the forms of diffusion of the technology have been neither smooth nor simple (see Chapters 1 and 2). The complex nature of the diffusion process has contributed to uncertainty over its implications for organizations. It took decades of using the technology before there was widespread recognition that ICT-based systems did not simply change the way business is done—they changed the business itself and the structures of organizations involved in it.

A significant catalyst in building this new perception was the 'Management in the 1990s' research project at the Massachusetts Institute of Technology (MIT), which ran for five years from 1984 (Scott Morton 1991; Allen and Scott Morton 1994). Its investigation of the impacts of IT on organizations highlighted the potential of the technology for transforming some organizational arrangements, in addition to being capable of automating those arrangements to help reduce costs.[2]

Such transformations could take the form of innovative cross-functional linkages within companies to create new ways of processing work and defining job roles. For example, the processing of a customer's order for a product or for a service like an insurance policy might traditionally have involved the passing of information between many departments, such as sales, credit checking, accounts processing, and various production and delivery units. Each unit handling the order would be part of a separate department with its own hierarchical reporting and responsibility structure. The MIT researchers suggested that the whole process could be transformed by making a single person or team responsible for all stages of satisfying an order, with the roles of people changing from ones of departmental responsibility to those of ensuring a particular company-wide process is completed satisfactorily. Many processes and roles which had been based on the existence of separate departments and the transfer of work between them could be eliminated in this way, particularly through the use of ICTs to share and process information in new ways.

New patterns of relationships could also be developed between firms, for instance through electronic ordering and funds transfer services provided through interlinked networks, so that, for instance, manufacturers and retailers are linked electronically with their suppliers. IT could also be used effectively not just in the support and auxiliary functions to which it was applied traditionally, but also as major features of actual products, services, or delivery systems—like allowing customers to buy goods or interact with their bank account from interactive TV sets in their homes.

The increasing awareness among senior managers from the late 1980s that IT should be a key ingredient in strategic business decisions was accompanied by the identification of the following three key issues in debates about the role of the technology within organizations:

1. **the 'Alignment Problem'** caused by the difficulty in aligning IT and corporate strategies because IT policies had previously been developed in relative isolation;

2. **the 'Culture Gap'** between IT professionals and top business management, which was an increasing source of resentment and mistrust as the technology became more central to business functions and IT managers began to rise to the upper echelons of senior management (Grindley 1991); and

3. **the 'Productivity Paradox'**, which arose when traditional accounting analyses of returns on investment suggested that the rapidly increased expenditure on IT was not generally resulting in corresponding increases in productivity (see Chapters 7 and 18).

Many IT practitioners and researchers responded to these problems by developing complex procedures and methods, with the intention of enabling senior IT managers to identify, develop, and evaluate the key applications of information systems for their organizations.[3] An alternative, non-traditional accounting treatment was also developed. This views investment in ICTs as part of a broader attempt—with associated risks—to transform major features of an organization's structures and goals, such as in rethinking the products or services offered and how they can be delivered (Porter 1985). However, the new accounting approach was difficult to sell to management because the idea of clearly demonstrating a quick financial return is so deeply rooted in business culture. What is more, the Culture Gap resulted in an unwillingness to let IT managers be excused the rigours of cost-justifying their investment proposals, especially when other groups had to do this.

With the movement of ICTs into the 'core' strategic organizational agenda, other important issues arose in organizations over the diverse understandings of ICTs and their effects on the organization. Our research has identified, in particular, the way in which this move has led to a heightened degree of political manœuvring around ICT strategy and development as information systems have contributed more strongly to the formation of 'new understandings of reality among organisational members' (Bloomfield *et al.* 1994: 146).

Frameworks of Computing

These issues and problems reflect the extent to which managers use different 'frameworks' for thinking about the role of ICTs in organizations. We have labelled them 'frameworks of computing' as they have evolved from computer-oriented innovations, although they can also relate to other technologies (Hull 1994; Coombs and Hull 1995*a*).

A 'Technical' framework totally dominated the early years of computing. It is a mechanistic perspective on optimizing organizations by building them around the power and accuracy of computing hardware. Although dated, the framework has continued to permeate most areas of computing. However, since the late 1950s, it has been gradually supplemented by two additional ways of understanding and working with computers.

The 'Partnership' framework emerged strongly in the late 1970s. It emphasized the view that there are fundamental incompatibilities between humans and computers and that IT systems have to be designed and 'configured' to the needs of individual users. It emphasized the view that the computer should be designed as a tool and an adjunct, rather than designing systems around the computer as a master. Aspects of this framework are evident in work on Human-Computer Interaction (HCI), like developments with 'windows'-type graphical user interfaces.

The third, 'Benevolent', framework became visible in the early 1980s. It focuses on improving communication and decision making within organizations and society, in contrast to the Partnership Framework's emphasis on the human-computer relationship. Communication and knowledge are seen within this framework to be 'social' as well as 'technical' issues, which promotes approaches which treat organizations and their IT systems as integrated entities (Zuboff 1988). These are represented in developments like 'groupware' software, such as Lotus Notes, for team-based activities and Computer Supported Co-operative Work (CSCW) disciplines, which were founded on the belief that computer networks radically alter the working patterns and relations of groups of users.[4] Initiatives to re-engineer business processes and—at a broader level—the 'information superhighway' debates also reflect the perceptions which characterize the Benevolent framework.

This framework is of value, in part, because it 'problematizes' the relationship between 'the organizational' and 'the technical' by high-lighting the negotiations that need to take place between technologists and non-technologists about how to use IT adequately (Bloomfield and Vurdubakis 1994). However, many expressions of the Benevolent frame-work fail to grapple adequately with the difficulties of organizational change, resulting in an underdeveloped appreciation of organizational politics and the dynamics between IT and organizational change.

Later frameworks do not automatically displace earlier ones. The three frameworks are therefore layered and folded into each other in contra-dictory ways, especially in discussions of IT strategy. The Technical frame-work can still burst through from time to time, especially where powerful economic forces appear to demand radical and rapid cost savings rather than more gradual long-term progress.

Technical Perspectives on Systems Development: The Waterfall Method

Frameworks of computing affect broader organizational issues. For ex-ample, linear models of systems development were supported for dec-ades by the Technical framework, which strongly influenced management methods for dealing with the relationship between IT innovation and organizational change. Linear models—extrapolated from the linear way a program is written—described the development of larger information systems as a series of logical sequential steps. They also characterized the decision making process within such developments as a linear sequence of straightforwardly rational, logical activities.[5]

In response to the increasingly wide-ranging impacts of the time and cost overruns which were becoming commonplace on computer projects from the late 1960s, examinations of the intricate details of programming and systems development began to be regarded as being of more impor-tance. Terms such as 'structured programming' and 'software engineer-ing' were employed both to describe and prescribe systems-development practice in this linear manner and to achieve greater direct management control over development projects (Friedman and Cornford 1989). For instance, the 'waterfall' model of the life cycle of a development project describes the sequence shown in Figure 9.1. Starting from the top, each step in this has to be concluded satisfactorily—in theory at least—before proceeding to the next.

Strong objections to such models were raised from a number of per-spectives within the IT community (see Chapter 10 for a discussion of

Initial objectives

Requirements specification

Systems specification

Systems design (often in the form of modules)

Program/module coding and debugging

Implementation (first successful use)

Operation

Maintenance/enhancement

Fig. 9.1. The Waterfall Method

related systems-development issues). For instance, although each stage of the waterfall was always understood to include a number of iterations or feedback loops before achieving the 'correct' conclusion of that stage, there was no such provision for iteration over the whole life cycle. Some critics suggested that actual practice was far more iterative and non-linear over the whole life cycle, while others pointed to the way such linear methods discourage user involvement or participation, except in the early requirements specification phase.[6]

Nevertheless, the waterfall and similar models remained the prevalent form of understanding and organizing ICT development until the early 1990s. Furthermore, they became institutionalized through the designation of specific roles, such as the constantly contested distinction between 'systems analyst' and 'programmer', and by the widespread use of a variety of Computer-Aided Software Engineering (CASE) 'tools' which have inbuilt models of how development projects should be routinized (Quintas 1993).

Organizational Politics and ICT Developments

As IT policies migrated towards the core strategic agenda of more organizations, the inadequacies of linear models of systems developments and other prevailing Technical framework approaches became more visible and significant. The responsibility for solving the problems that arise from these inadequacies has often been the subject of argument and attribution of blame for perceived failures. However, there has been a growing realization that IT will be hotly contested and intrinsically political as it becomes more intertwined with strategic organizational decision making, which seldom follows a linear model. Strategic decision processes are better represented in the way that a novelist describes the ebb and flow of fortunes and ideas, unexpected accidents, interference of events from other spheres, and strongly held personal beliefs. This may seem to be a more difficult form of description than the simpler 'truths' of formal decision making models. Yet it provides a more realistic, and therefore more effective, approach to decision making because it does not sanitize and obscure key practical issues arising from organizational politics (Knights and Morgan 1991).

IT and organizational strategy have become so intertwined that it is not surprising that vehement disputes about 'best practice' have taken place (see Chapter 10). These disputes have been heightened by the difficulties involved in trying to align organizational change with the increasingly complex options for new information and communication systems created by rapid technological innovation. It is therefore important for the development of ICT-based systems to be conducted in ways that recognize and accept the political character of organizations. If common sense tells us that organizations are political, it is necessary to explore and explain that insight seriously—not to work around it with schemes which try to ignore or squeeze out the politics. The following case study illustrates the importance of this view.

Case Study: Health-Care Resource Management

In the late 1980s, a major area of IT investment in the UK National Health Service (NHS) was in 'resource management' information systems (Coombs and Cooper 1990; Bloomfield and Coombs 1992; Bloomfield *et al.* 1992). These systems aimed at building databases containing information like a patient's diagnoses, treatments, and periods spent in hospital. Management information about the patterns of care for different patient groups and different doctors were to be generated from the databases by applying standard costs for each activity. The reports would highlight differences in practices and costs between medical staff and between hospitals, thereby raising the visibility of 'efficiency and effectiveness' issues in dialogues between doctors and managers.

The resource management systems offered the potential for new levels of managerial surveillance and intervention in areas which were previously the exclusive domain of doctors. Indeed, NHS senior management explicitly argued that a major aim of the system was to change the position of doctors with respect to the management process by encouraging medical staff to take more responsibility for working within budgets using the new management information to assist them.

This was an important reason why many doctors were initially hostile to becoming involved in the teams developing the new resource management systems. Although they deployed arguments about the possible 'wasting' of money on administration rather than direct patient services, the doctors' underlying concern was the political anxiety that the system threatened their received principles of clinical freedom and autonomy. According to these, a doctor's prime responsibility is to give patients the treatment they see as appropriate—not to get directly involved in making choices between patient treatments based on efficiency criteria.

These political concerns soon emerged in meetings of the resource management teams, which had the task in individual hospitals of designing and implementing the systems. The teams used information systems management approaches regarded as 'received wisdom' from the IT community. So they began by discussing organizational goals, then progressed to data requirements, performance measures, and reporting arrangements. But the meetings quickly ran up against fundamental political conflicts deriving from the different cultures and values of doctors and managers as reflected in discussions on goals, performance, and reporting. Doctors emphasized the subtlety, complexity, and ultimately judgemental character of medical work; managers stressed the possibility of systematizing and analysing data on groups of patients with similar conditions. On the surface, the confrontation was about effectiveness versus efficiency; underneath, the conflict was also about responsibility, surveillance, and control.

Surprisingly, given the entrenched power positions of the participants, these situations began to shift gradually as one hospital got to hear about what another was doing and doctors began to talk in their professional bodies. Eventually, some doctors began to accept the view that measures of relative efficiency were useful and even compatible with their notions of clinical freedom—which created a division from others who retained their original hostility to the idea. The 'conversion' of some doctors was facilitated by IT systems which went beyond cost-accounting functions to generate interesting clinical data for research and medical audit procedures, for instance in monitoring treatment patterns and results for cancer patients. Some IT professionals built on the appeal of such capabilities to design systems whose HCI attracted doctors precisely towards this 'clinical relevance' benefit.

At the same time as the resource management systems were being developed, the NHS was undergoing far-reaching and radical change in moving to an 'internal market'. This introduced more business-oriented management and accounting procedures, while keeping the NHS in public ownership and generally free at the point of treatment. Over a period of about five years, these upheavals resulted in changing cultural attitudes towards the balance between management and medicine. As a result, resource management at national and local levels began to be more accepted by the medical profession. Many processes contributed to this cultural change. One of the most critical was the encounter with designing a strategic IT system like the NHS resource management application. The organizational politics and ICT systems mark each other in such encounters to the extent that they become 'joint products'. For example, some NHS managers began to argue that the IT systems had succeeded by contributing to this recasting of the managerial agenda and the tighter integration of doctors into it, irrespective of how well they worked in purely technical terms.

The Realities of Organizational Decision Making

This NHS example demonstrates an underlying principle of the relationships between organizational politics, strategy, and ICTs—the choices made depend on much more than the issues raised in traditional computer system development, like data structures and rational evaluations of business policy. In addition, political 'readings' of the situation in the organization and of the interests which people have in reshaping corporate goals and structures are crucial factors in determining the actual decisions made.

For example, the conversion of some doctors to a positive view of resource management was encouraged by technical aspects of the ICT system, such as the clinical-support features—a conversion that led to divisions between doctors as well as between management and medical professionals. This shows how initial intentions, goals, and the perceived usefulness of the system change during the course of development, often resulting in new sources of conflict that impinge on ICT plans (Bloomfield and Vurdubakis 1994). Another lesson from this experience is that the capture and portrayal of organizational data through a computer-based information system put into play some vital features of the organization itself.

These illustrations of the inseparability of ICT systems and organizational politics also highlight the importance of the varying understandings which different employees may have during this joint production (Knights and Murray 1994). People in organizations decide on their actions—and make sense of them—through a process of replicating some existing organizational practices and sometimes developing or importing new practices. In this way, they regularly re-create their identity in terms of an idea of their place and role within and beyond the organization. People define who and what they are not according to some absolute external yardstick. They do that through a complex network of understandings and practices that are the lenses through which people actually perceive and calculate their interests and seek to display their competence. These networks are therefore the very territory which is in play as part of the 'real stuff of organizational politics' whenever strategic issues are under discussion.[7]

From this view of organizational behaviour, it is not surprising that the clear statement of goals 'necessary' for ICT plans is in fact a moving target. Nor is it surprising that both business and ICT strategies have a covert content—to secure new, or to sustain existing, relations of understanding and practice with respect to other members of organizational networks.[8] This was illustrated by the relationships between managers and medical professionals in the changing NHS resource management processes. Seen in this light, the foundering of overly rationalistic IT strategies on the rock of organizational politics is not a technical failure or some shortcoming in the rationality of the parties involved. It is simply 'how the world is'.

Responses to Organizational Politics: 'Soft' Methods and Consultants

Among the strategies used by IT professionals to deal with this political reality has been the adoption of methodologies generally called 'soft' to distinguish them from 'harder' structured engineering approaches. Such 'soft methods' and 'socio-technical' approaches emphasize the human and social contexts of technical systems design and encourage user participation and 'stakeholder involvement' (see for example Checkland and Scholes 1990; Mumford 1995). Nevertheless, when conflicts involving the IT system arise between individuals and groups, IT professionals may still treat the disputes as 'irrational' and the result of 'personality clashes' or ingrained routines. These views are based on an implicit model of human behaviour in which calculative interests and preoccupations with competence predominate. By contrast, our research recognizes the importance of interests and competencies (as in the conflicts between NHS managers and doctors)—but suggests it is necessary to complement this with a perception of the dynamic context in which people understand their own day-to-day actions (like the doctors' growing appreciation of the clinical support offered by resource management systems).

Some organizations attempt to 'handle' organizational politics by employing outside consultants. Although this offers the potential for genuine novelty and competence transfer, even successful interventions by consultants should not be seen as 'organizationally neutral'. The relationship between consultant and client is actually yet another set of networks—and intersections of existing networks—governed by the same principles as 'internal' organizational politics. In this case, the conflicts and struggles reflect the consultant's concerns about achieving a construction of 'the problem' which accords with that of key functionaries in the client organization—and is also consistent with the consultant's ability to implement a recognized solution to that problem. The role played by consultants in attempting to solve problems therefore also has an intrinsic political dimension. This indicates why using outsiders does not change the fundamental need for IT systems to be reconciled with shifting perceptions of the organization's objectives and how people understand the role of IT in achieving them (Bloomfield and Best 1992).

Structural Organizational Change and the Pace of ICT Diffusion

Until the 1990s, the organizational arena described above seemed to be consistent with a slow, painful, and conflictual pattern of ICT diffusion rather than one of radical change. In practice, ICTs have subsequently been adopted and developed, particularly in the private sector, at an increased rate and many previously perceived problems have faded.

For example, the Productivity Paradox has been replaced by an understanding that ICT is now an intrinsic part of the way organizations work and can achieve substantial and uncontested efficiency gains. Investment in ICT is therefore no longer generally seen as problematic. Instead, attention has turned to achieving cost reductions through major organizational restructuring that takes full advantage of the opportunities presented by ICTs. In a similar way, management has given less priority to the Alignment and Culture Gap problems while placing more emphasis on issues like 'change management', ICT infrastructures, and the problems and opportunities associated with buying in software and ICT services (including the 'outsourcing' of IT functions to be run by 'facilities management' service providers).[9]

This dramatic turnaround is characterized by three main types of structural change:

1. **Within organizations**. Managers have given higher priority to horizontal, customer oriented operational processes over vertical, functionally-oriented management control—for example by focusing on optimizing the processes involved in receiving and fulfilling an order even when changes have to be made to the departmental boundaries through which an order previously passed.

2. **Within an increasingly global competitive environment**. The cost-base of many companies has been exposed to powerful pressures from foreign competitors.

3. **In the broad patterns of ICT development and deployment**. ICT infrastructures have become more embedded in organizational processes than was the case in earlier periods when 'islands' of ICT capabilities existed in different parts of a company to meet the needs of local management.

Business Process Re-engineering

A key element in these structural changes has been Business Process Re-engineering (BPR) concepts. These have been underpinned by the principles summarized in Box 9.1, which have led to some important

Box 9.1. Main Principles of Business Process Re-engineering

- Organizations are understood within a 'process' perspective focused on the horizontal chain of activities that add value to the final product or service delivered to the customer. These 'business processes' cut across traditional functional boundaries. BPR projects involve identifying the processes, analysing them in terms of activities, then redesigning them for greater efficiency.

- BPR generally relies on two ICT developments. One is the increasing flexibility and efficiency in sharing databases and systems between user departments, overcoming the constraints caused by the traditional focus on building systems based on isolated functional 'islands'. The other is the creation of networked computer-based communications infrastructures, which many organizations had achieved by the early 1990s.

- Despite its origins in computing, BPR is always presented as an overall strategy for global competitiveness that utilizes the potential of IT, rather than a strategy for IT alone.

transformations in the ways organizations are managed and carry out work.

A Radical Change in Management Processes

The MIT Management in the 1990s programme highlighted 'management processes', such as planning and budgeting, as a central force in shaping the outcomes of interactions between the main factors shaping organizational performance: business strategy; corporate culture and structure; the roles of individuals; and technology. BPR stemmed largely from this finding.

The MIT research also identified 'stages' which an organization needs to go through in 'engineering' IT-enabled organizational change, a notion which was first popularized by three of the participants in the MIT project, Hammer (1990) and Davenport and Short (1990).[10] The early view of BPR provided an implicit 'solution' to the Alignment Problem and the Culture Gap, based on addressing two main issues. First, it explained the tendency for IT systems to lock an organization into traditional, functional structures. Then it pointed to the essential need to restructure organizations and deploy IT systems in radically new ways that would be more customer-oriented and efficient.

For example, in 1989 a utility firm in the UK had to alter its relationships with customers and competitors dramatically when it was privatized after being fully state-controlled. A new Chief Executive was appointed partly on the strength of his 'radical' vision for aligning business and IT strategies. He initially aimed to achieve rapid cost reductions in the main business unit. The cost leadership this achieved with the main unit and its close relationships with the other businesses would then be applied to differentiate the other businesses from their competitors. The main business was to be fundamentally reorganized around four core business processes. These were to be identified, co-ordinated, and developed with the aid of four large IT development programmes. Each IT project was led by a manager from the business side, who would eventually be responsible for that core process. A strong emphasis was placed on the human resources aspects of change management. In addition to short-term cost reductions, the re-engineered processes were specifically intended to 'empower' people and to enable greater co-ordination within and across the core processes.

A large number of other companies in all industry sectors followed similar BPR-inspired initiatives. These have been characterized by a twin focus on both short-term efficiency gains and the longer-term strategic development of the organization. However, our research suggests that there has been a distinctly mixed balance sheet in the achievement of those goals (Coombs and Hull 1995a). Considerable short-term cost reductions have indeed been made in many organizations through 'delayering'—stripping out middle-management functions and relying more on existing and new IT systems. But there have also been significant problems with many BPR projects, particularly when efficiency objectives have often undermined the strategic reorientation goals of simultaneous attempts to develop new organizational arrangements for supporting longer-term growth.

This has led to what we call 'Soft BPR', a significant variation on the original BPR prescriptions and techniques. Many Soft BPR approaches to modelling and redesigning business processes stem from socio-technical techniques and 'soft' alternatives to the waterfall model of IT development discussed earlier. These emphasize 'human costs and benefits' rather than just the goal of 'engineering' the organization into a new shape.[11] Soft BPR also explores new methods and practices for managing IT development which attempt to recognize the blurred boundaries between 'harder' technical issues and the 'softer' human and organizational aspects.

BPR and the Frameworks of Computing

BPR has therefore been faced with cross-currents and conflicts between the different ways that IT is understood and used through the 'frameworks of computing'. Although the rhetoric of BPR presumed that IT would enable a 'transformation' of working practices, the original tools, techniques, and actions of many organizations were oriented towards automating existing practices, seeing IT as simply a replacement for labour. The rhetoric often used with BPR also suggested that IT could be used to increase 'empowerment'—to liberate people from routine work and improve communication and knowledge-sharing. Yet many BPR tools and techniques grew from an engineering perspective on human processes and activities based on a linear-logical understanding of the ways that humans communicate information and knowledge.

For example, many early BPR projects largely ignored the emergence of significant objections and alternatives to the waterfall mode. The Technical framework of computing had 'burst through' in response to the perceived pressures for rapid change. Soft BPR attempts to resolve these conflicts by offering techniques and tools that are consistent with the rhetoric of empowerment and in tune with the Partnership and Benevolent frameworks. However, Soft BPR generally adopts an instrumental approach which sees the problems of IT and organizations as soluble through 'rational' principles assumed to be shared by all participants. In some organizations reality approximates to this, but usually the irreducibilities of politics and uncertainties in organizational life militate against this happening. Soft BPR has therefore become a rhetorical fudge for a fragile collection of concepts and techniques that is liable to disruption from organizational politics and/or continued external economic pressures (Coombs and Hull 1995*a*).

New Paradigms of Organizational Change

BPR is one manifestation of wider structural changes within and around organizations. These have necessarily been accompanied by changes in the understandings of the structure and environment of organizations, such as the important emergence of the new 'Business Process' paradigm (Coombs & Hull 1995*b*). This focuses on analysing, designing, and managing the horizontal flows within and between organizations and the organizational changes needed to achieve this, which is one of the key elements in BPR initiatives that also address wider strategic issues.

The changes which this paradigm brings into focus are exemplified by the increasing use of operational information systems in the development of organizational strategies—such as the 'informated organization' (Zuboff 1988), in which ICT-based systems generate information about the organization and its customers, and 'networked organizations' based on the use of ICT networks to link individuals across departments and organizational boundaries (Rockart and Short 1991). One of the underlying assumptions behind these kinds of strategies is the belief that the world economy is moving towards a greater reliance on knowledge resources, knowledge workers, and information, rather than capital or labour. These ideas have been linked to developments in ICTs since the late 1980s, most notably in the view that IT could either have a negative human impact through automation, or a positive impact if deployed in the correct organizational arrangements.

There have been many objections to this perspective, such as a concern that organizations will use ICTs to increase surveillance and control, which could stimulate resistance (Knights *et al.* 1993). Nevertheless, it is notable that the focus has shifted from a one-way deterministic understanding of the impact of ICTs towards an appreciation of the relationships between ICTs and firm-specific organizational arrangements. This new awareness becomes increasingly valuable as the artefacts and techniques of ICT become extremely diverse and widely diffused through-out all aspects of organizational and everyday life. This makes it ever more urgent to develop better understandings of the specific ways in which particular capabilities emerge, are used, and change within each organizational arrangement.

In this context, the Business Process paradigm can be seen as a new kind of 'received wisdom' through which enterprises make sense of their options and actions. This opens out discussions of ICTs by legitimizing a search for the right processes, rather than uncritically accepting existing organizational structures. Such 'reconceptualization through processes' can be triggered by perceived ICT potential or can itself generate demand for specific types of ICT support, thereby promoting the beginnings of a more integrated understanding of the linkages between organizational change and ICT. Nevertheless, it can overrationalize or disregard the political dimensions of this relationship.

Conclusion: The Importance of Organizational Politics

The shift to a Business Process paradigm has been bound up with a variety of pressures to restructure organizations within the highly competitive global marketplace. ICT has played a significant role in this restructuring. However, this does not mean it is feasible to propose the kinds of prescriptions for ICT-oriented organizational change which are based on a misguided faith in the ability of plans and strategies to produce predictable outcomes. Even when the 'situated' nature of plans and actions is acknowledged (Suchman 1987), there remains a fundamental depend-ence on perceptions of ICT, organizations, and the relations between them—perceptions which do not spring unproblematically from straight-forward 'observations'.

The role of ICTs in organizational change can be observed in terms of three main levels—artefacts, practices, and understandings. ICT has become embedded in organizations through the development of specific artefacts, such as personal computers, software packages, telecommunica-tions networks, and information systems. These have necessarily been accompanied by changes in a variety of practices, some directly related to ICT—such as the financial treatment of investments in ICT systems and the development of new roles and responsibilities for ICT personnel and end-users. Others are related to broader factors, such as the political manœuvring within organizations and the shift from hierarchical bu-reaucracies to 'flatter' networked organizations and business processes.

Finally, there have been changes in the understandings of, and the relations between, three key domains: ICTs; the goals, values, and identity of organizations and their employees; and broader structural change in organizations and the economy as a whole.

Our research, summarized in this chapter, argues that senior business managers as well as IT professionals need to take serious account of the fine details and unpredictable nature of organizational politics at all of these levels. Particular attention should be given to new understandings of how IT developments—including those embedded within BPR efforts—will affect the politics of organizations and, therefore, be contested. Wide structural changes in the economy need to be understood and key business pressures within organizations have to be identified and translated into effective business processes and organizational practices. This is not just a technical problem of redesigning ICTs to support new business processes. It is also a political problem of understanding how to introduce and implement change in what the organization does as well as how those activities are carried out.

Notes

1. This chapter is a major update and revision of the 1992 PICT Charles Read Lecture given by Coombs, as reported in Coombs (1992). It also draws on other work at CROMTEC, the PICT Centre in Manchester. For a detailed overview of this work, see Bloomfield *et al.* (forthcoming).

2. 'ICT' is more commonly referred to as 'IT' in business management and related literature. As explained in the Introduction, this book treats the abbreviations as synonyms and makes explicit any distinctions between 'information' and 'communication' technologies where appropriate.

3. For example, Strategic Information Systems Planning (SISP) allows goals to be set for business directions and organizational design, based primarily on identifying a portfolio of information systems and supporting technology to achieve the desired objectives (see for example Galliers 1992).

4. For more background on CSCW see for example Suchman (1987); Diaper and Sanger (1993); Easterbrook (1993); and Hull (1994).

5. A detailed background discussion on these developments is provided in Friedman and Cornford (1989).

6. The new methods suggested all sought to emphasize a more iterative, less linear approach. This has included a variety of approaches suited to different types of development, like the 'spiral' life cycle (Boehm 1988) and 'incremental', 'evolutionary', and 'prototyping' techniques (Mazza *et al.* 1994).

7. The discussion of ICT disasters in Chapter 10 suggests that failure occurs when the model for organizational change embedded in a new information system does not match the beliefs and values of key members of the organization.

8. Other social scientists often call these 'power relations' (Knights and Morgan 1991).
9. Information provided in personal communication by Kit Grindley, giving preliminary results for 1995 of Price Waterhouse (annual).
10. Hammer had previously worked on office automation in MIT's Computer Science Laboratory; Davenport worked for a consultancy firm that was one of the project's sponsors; and Short was one of the researchers at MIT.
11. A description of a Soft BPR approach is provided in Mumford and Beekman (1994).

10 Computer Power and Human Limits

Malcolm Peltu, Donald MacKenzie, Stuart Shapiro, and William H. Dutton

Disasters are exceptions, not the rule. However, extreme cases often provide new perspectives on the more routine. This chapter examines disasters involving ICT systems which vividly illustrate the many connections and interdependencies between the design of technologies and the management of organizations.[1]

The authors suggest that these exceptional disasters indicate that society is becoming increasingly reliant on ICT-based systems which are so complex and tightly integrated that it is problematic whether they can be managed safely and effectively. They use case studies of a number of specific ICT-related disasters to help highlight key points in the systems design, development, and implementation process where risks can be minimized and the likelihood of success maximized. The chapter also explores the crucial issue of why managers, system developers, and users fail to learn lessons from past failures, which have been widely formulated in a variety of 'best practice' guidelines. Guidelines are provided to the policies and practices which ensure adequate attention is given to critical human and organizational limitations and opportunities in the design and use of ICTs.

Information Disasters

Disasters involving ICTs loom large in the public mind, with the computer often featuring as a major culprit. Some public anxieties may be exaggerated because of fictional dramas like *2001: A Space Odyssey* and *Jurassic Park*. However, their fears have been reflected in the analyses of experts since the 1960s, for example in warning about a 'software crisis' causing many operational problems, ranging from annoying 'bugs' to catastrophic failures.

As computing has become more central to social and economic institutions, the onus is on managers, professionals, and public policy makers to ensure that these fears are not realized and that the lessons from past disasters are implemented effectively in practice. Yet a striking feature of most major ICT failures is that they probably could have been avoided if existing knowledge about successful systems design, development, and implementation had been applied. A key reason is that most serious problems are not primarily technical failures. In fact, they are 'information disasters'—that is, failures to learn—in the broadest sense, which stem from the interplay of a variety of organizational, management, and psychological as well as technical factors (Dutton *et al.* 1995).

For instance, a study into computer-related deaths found about 92 per cent were caused by human–computer interaction and organizational factors (MacKenzie 1994). Similarly, a strong human component, particularly management failures in procedures and policies, has been significant in major telecommunications failures, such as those affecting AT&T's long-distance US network in 1991 (Dutton *et al.* 1995: 13).

ICTs give us the power to overwhelm ourselves with information and to build systems that we cannot fully comprehend or control, creating new potentials for disasters across an economy increasingly dependent on their successful operation. We therefore need to deepen our understanding of why ICT failures occur in order to minimize and manage the disastrous consequences that could flow from them.

Studies of disasters, including the cases examined in this chapter, have revealed a number of common failures that are social and organizational problems, not technical ones (see Box 10.1).[2]

The Human Limits of Information Management

The development of ever faster and more complex information systems is stretching the limits of humans to cope with and manage information.

> **Box 10.1.** Guidelines on Actions to Avoid Common Social and Organizational Problems which Cause ICT Failures
>
> ....
>
> • Respect the organizational and human limits to comprehending and, therefore, managing large-scale complex ICT systems.
>
> • Nurture an open safety culture that can overcome the 'politics of blame' in organizations.
>
> • Balance concerns over safety and reliability with other demands, such as innovative risk-taking imperatives.
>
> • Recognize how the psychology of organizational decision making influences what happens at key points in the life cycle of an ICT system.
>
> • Build a holistic view of ICT systems that respects the distinctive contributions of specialists in different, but often narrow, areas of expertise.
>
> • Allow for the multitude of unplanned ways in which a new idea is reinvented, altered, and sometimes moved far from initial conceptions during the process from adoption through implementation to routinization.
>
> ....

This can create what some have called a 'glass-cockpit syndrome': a term originally identified by psychologists studying the stressful situation faced by pilots of highly automated aircraft (Rochlin 1991). Such an environment encourages the tying together of different units and levels of command with small allowances for error ('tight coupling'), together with a growing reliance on abstract displays from systems whose inner workings are opaque to their managers and operators.[3] The syndrome also applies to other high-risk settings where ICTs have been threaded within and between organizations in an attempt to establish better and more direct centralized real-time control over great technical and organizational complexity. This has occurred, for example, with systems to support the management and control of ambulance and other emergency services or the global trading of stocks and other financial transactions.

One characteristic of a 'glass-cockpit' environment is that users of a complex technological system will 'lose the bubble', as officers on US warships say when multiple information inputs no longer fall into place as part of a larger coherent picture (Rochlin 1991).[4] Misunderstandings and faulty performance are less easy to localize and repair in this context than in more loosely coupled systems which allow much more scope to acquire skills in dealing with problems locally. This makes operational mistakes with disastrous consequences more likely to occur in tightly coupled systems, even when the technical system performs as its designers expect.

The glass-cockpit syndrome seems to confirm the warning by computer scientist Joseph Weizenbaum (1976) that people should not place undue trust in computers and models which their users could not fully understand and manage. As another computer scientist put it nearly twenty years later:

> As soon as a manager, in the smallest particular, takes the intangibility of software as an excuse for not knowing and understanding, there is a lift off from reality—and what starts out as a loss of touch by an inch quickly becomes a mile. The 'bubble' is then lost and disaster looms (C. A. R. Hoare, quoted in Dutton *et al.* 1995: 2–3).

In order to avoid the potentially nightmarish consequences of the glass-cockpit syndrome, therefore, it is necessary to ensure managers and system developers retain a premium on both the limits and value of human judgement and skills.

The Importance of Disasters as a Focus for Enquiry

Despite great concern about failures, the actual record of ICT disasters has compared favourably with the history of general engineering developments. For instance, one study concluded that there had been about 1,100 deaths from computer-related accidents worldwide to the end of 1992, of which only about 3 per cent of the deaths identified could actually be attributed to software (MacKenzie 1994). The Network Reliability Council (NRC), established by the US Federal Communications Commission (FCC), has also found that software errors were not the most significant cause of system failures in telecommunications services (NRC 1993). For instance, the Council attributed 12 per cent of outages in switching systems to software, about the same as for hardware and the inadequate implementation of standard procedures.

The total of 1,100 software-related deaths identified by MacKenzie (1994) is fewer than the annual deaths from road accidents in a country the size of the UK, which suggests the actual safety record of computers has been better than that implied by talk of a 'software crisis'. This better-than-feared performance was probably assisted by the way alarms raised about software reliability stimulated programmers to use their ingenuity to apply defence-in-depth tactics in which, for example, a great deal of code is designed to recover from errors. Nevertheless, as more complex systems become more widely used, the ability to cope with errors in this way becomes less feasible and the risks for more disastrous failures increase—so the relative safety of computer-based systems in the past should in no way encourage complacency.

Studying the extreme circumstances involved in incidents generally perceived as 'disasters' can provide new insights and lessons that are applicable to the more routine failures and near-misses that occur in organizations (Sauer 1993). For instance, social scientists often use extreme cases as a means for better understanding the ordinary. This is true despite the difficulty of defining a 'disaster'—a label attributed to some events and not others by established social and political institutions, such as the press and public opinion. These events generate different levels and types of response than failures which receive less attention in the public arena.

It is also valid to study 'disastrous' outcomes even though they can be construed as resulting from the 'correct' expected functioning of a system. For example, in warfare one side's 'disaster' is the other side's 'success', or in health care money spent on an administrative hospital information system may be judged to have been more beneficially invested in direct patient care. The fact that 'disaster' is a socially attributed characteristic does not negate the value of studying such events as extreme cases in the use of ICTs. The judgement that a case is 'routine' is also a social attribution about which individuals might disagree.

Case Studies of Information Disasters

The following examples illustrate important aspects of how information disasters can arise at different stages in the life cycle of information systems. The vital live use of fully operational systems is illustrated by an incident involving the USS *Vincennes* warship, which also dramatically illustrates the 'glass-cockpit' environment. Problems that can go wrong during implementation are highlighted by the experience at the London Ambulance Service (LAS) with a system that combines features of a 'safety-critical application'—for which lives may depend on its successful operation—and a more general information system. Taurus at the London Stock Exchange provides an example of a system that was stopped in the design process before full implementation was completed.

Box 10.2. Timetable of Events for the USS *Vincennes* Incident in the Persian Gulf on 3 July 1987

10:13–16. The *Vincennes* opens fire on menacing Iranian boats.

10:17–20. The *Vincennes* detects an aircraft and sends warnings on military and civilian frequencies. The ship's fore gun is damaged and resultant manœuvring at high speed causes violent lurching in the ship's control room, containing key controls for the Aegis system that had identified and was tracking the aircraft.

10:21–4. The aircraft is identified as an Iranian F-14 fighter descending towards the ship. No relevant entry is found in a listing of commercial flights when checking a warning that it might be a civilian plane.

10:24. After repeated warnings, the *Vincennes* shoots down the aircraft—Iran Air Flight 655 climbing on its assigned route to Abu Dhabi after taking off a few minutes after its scheduled departure. All 290 people on the plane are killed. A few seconds earlier, the nearby frigate USS *Sides* decides correctly that it is a civilian flight.

The USS *Vincennes* and Iran Air Flight 655

In 1987, thirty-seven US naval personnel on the USS *Stark* in the Persian Gulf were killed when its computerized air defence system failed to intercept two Iraqi Exocet missiles, although it had detected the fighter which attacked them.[5] Early the next year, US warships patrolling the Gulf included the USS *Vincennes*, which had been optimized for air defence with an advanced fire-control computer system that can project an image of an air battle covering many hundreds of square miles.

On the morning of 3 July, the *Vincennes* went to investigate an incident involving armed Iranian boats. The timetable of events which ensued is summarized in Box 10.2.

A US government investigation headed by Rear Admiral William M. Fogarty found magnetic tape recordings showing that the electronic signals received by the *Vincennes* were consistent with the actual events. The Fogarty report (US Department of Defense 1988) concluded that Aegis had not failed technically as it did not have the capability to decide on the type or size of aircraft. The report notes: 'stress, task-fixation and the unconscious distortion of data may have played a major role', leading to 'scenario fulfilment' in which data flow is distorted in an unconscious attempt to make available evidence fit a preconceived scenario.

The report attributed the main blame to two relatively junior officers. In particular, the sharp warnings from one of them when he became convinced the ship was being attacked by a military jet were said to have played a critical role in the *Vincennes'* captain's decision to fire. The captain subsequently received a medal for his performance in the Gulf.

Rochlin (1991) argues that this incident is indicative of the effects of a glass-cockpit information system environment which put managers and users in a control mode, playing a well-rehearsed and set role within a large centralized system. This led them to fall back on pre-programmed scenarios instead of making a personal judgement based on the unique and detailed circumstances of the local context. On the *Vincennes*, for instance, Rochlin says Aegis was designed as air defence for a battle group in total war situations, rather than for a highly selective engagement in an arena with much civil air and sea traffic. It was therefore not surprising that a crew extensively trained and practised on simulators to play the 'games' for which it was designed should fall back into one of many pre-programmed behavioural patterns when they were under stress and severe time pressure.

The *Vincennes* saw itself as part of a large integrated command, communication, and control system covering the entire Gulf. On the other hand, the *Sides* made a correct identification—possibly because it remained an individual ship trying to fit its actions into a larger pattern. It had a more restricted span of control and was exercising more localized discretion than that involved in the centralized control environment on the *Vincennes*.

ICTs can extend the scope and complexity of any direct or indirect effects of an individual's actions. They can also raise the consequences of a failure, along with the psychological stress that accompanies this realization. In trying to build more fail-safe systems by automating individual judgement, ICTs therefore create a new set of problems with the management of complexity, generating even greater demands for a new technological fix. The *Vincennes* case highlights why 'losing the bubble' will become increasingly likely as ICTs increase the span of control and activities over which an individual can have authority.

The London Ambulance Service (LAS)

The LAS is a quasi-independent body reporting to a Regional Health Authority within the British National Health Service (NHS). LAS senior managers have a considerable degree of autonomy. In the late 1980s they decided to pursue an agenda of radical and fast-moving change as part of a major upheaval in the NHS directed at implementing a more business-oriented management approach.[6] This strategy included the introduction of a new Computer-Aided Despatch system to control automatically the allocation and sending of vehicles to incidents. Work on it began in the autumn of 1990, at a time when the service was still recovering from a damaging national pay dispute with ambulance staff.

Management consultants Arthur Andersen estimated it would cost £1.5 million and take nineteen months, but warned these figures should be increased significantly if a suitable software package was not found. The invitation to tender sent in February 1991 specified a non-negotiable implementation date of 8 January 1992, leaving less than a year to develop and implement the system. The successful bid was for slightly less than £1 million, about £700,000 cheaper than the second-lowest one. A small software house was responsible for managing the project on behalf of the winning consortium, which included a much larger computer hardware manufacturer.

Despite the existence of eighty-one known quality problems—over half of which were identified as having serious potential consequences—the system went live in full automation mode on 26 October 1992. Ambulance response times then became unacceptably long and the system stopped completely at about 2 a.m. on 4 November, when staff reverted to a fully manual system. Box 10.3 summarizes the findings of a Public Inquiry into the incident.

The Inquiry said some seemingly inexplicable actions that led to the failure, like going live with so many known errors, were caused by the existence of a 'fear of failure' culture in which 'Many managers and staff saw deadlines set by the top level of management as being rigid, inflexible and, more importantly, not to be challenged at the risk of losing one's job or being moved sideways.'

Taurus at the London Stock Exchange

In 1981, the London Stock Exchange proposed to automate trading between market makers, Share Registrars, banks, investors, and all other players in the share-settlement process.[7] However, resistance came from some stakeholders—like Share Registrars, who maintained manual records of shareholders and feared computerization would put them out of a job. Resistance led to the proposal going into abeyance. The idea was revived in 1987, when developments like the huge processing backlog at stockbrokers from the recent privatization of major UK utilities made it seem

Box 10.3. Key Contributory Factors to the Failure in 1982 of the Computer-Aided Despatch System at the London Ambulance Service (LAS)

- The computer system 'did not fail in a technical sense'. The cumulative effect of flaws in the accuracy of the data it was managing caused the main operational problems. Increased levels of automation made it difficult for staff to correct them.

- There was no evidence that certain key questions were asked about the winning bid, such as why it was so much lower than others and whether the software supplier had the resources and experience to manage such a critical project.

- When it was decided not to use a package, the warning from Arthur Andersen about increasing budgets and timescales was not heeded.

- Senior LAS managers directly involved in the project did not have sufficient IT expertise and the team's morale was undermined when a senior project manager was told he would lose his job when a properly qualified replacement was found.

- An internal management review which raised serious doubts in March 1992 was never submitted to the governing board of the LAS, although it was used as input to a report which stated: 'There is no evidence to suggest that the full system software, when commissioned, will not prove reliable.' The Inquiry stressed that such negative assurance is not enough in safety-critical software.

- Formal Quality Assurance processes were never implemented effectively.

- The UK Government's standard for managing IT projects, Prince, was not implemented thoroughly, despite an early warning from the project team.

- Poor staff relations provided an unsound basis on which to build a new system. For instance, there was no evidence of ambulance staff being given a sense of joint ownership of the system. Ambulance crews resented many changes introduced, such as a failure to take account of previous practices which aimed to ensure crews ended their shifts as close as possible to their home base.

- Training was inconsistent, not sufficiently comprehensive, and sometimes carried out so early there was 'skills decay' by the time the system was used.

- Use of the then-unproved combination of early versions of Microsoft's Windows operating system and Visual Basic application development software probably caused some early system failures and slow response times.

Source: Adapted from South West Thames Regional Health Authority (1993).

that the climate was ripe for progressing the system, which had been named Taurus (Transfer and Automated Registration of Uncertified Stock). Yet it was not until 1990 that sufficient agreement was reached between stakeholders to enable work on Taurus to be officially launched.

Subsequently, the deadline gradually slipped and predicted costs rose. On 12 March 1993, the Stock Exchange announced work on Taurus was to be abandoned following a review which decided the underlying problems were so serious the project would take another three years to finish and the cost could escalate further. By then, about £400 million had been invested in Taurus by all stakeholders.

A prime cause of the collapse was the failure to get a meaningful resolution of the diverse and often clashing interests among Taurus stakeholders. A consensus was particularly difficult to achieve because responsibilities for overseeing Taurus were shared among many groups within and outside the Stock Exchange.

The unresolved conflicting interests also caused problems at a technical level. Frequent changes in requirements from the multiple project stakeholders meant a full design was not completed by the time the system was abandoned. For example, the Structured Software Systems and Design Method (SSADM)—which is approved by the UK Government—was planned to be used but was never properly implemented. In addition, a decision to move from a centralized system to one where information is spread across hundreds of sites on many different computer systems raised the risk by requiring the use of untried distributed database technology. Difficulties also arose in trying to adapt a software package from Vista Concepts of New York using staff based in London and America, while the government's insistence through the Department of Trade and Industry on strict data encryption to protect information added costs and complexity which many experts felt were unnecessary.

Factors Affecting Risk

These and other experiences of ICT failures indicate that the main factors likely to raise the risk associated with a system involving ICTs include:

1. key decisions made at arm's length from those with responsibility for actually managing and using the system—which is particularly prevalent in the public sector (Margetts and Willcocks 1993);

2. highly interdependent systems with inherently fuzzy boundaries between diverse groups within and between organizations—which can exacerbate difficulties in reconciling conflicts between stakeholders;

3. tight coupling combined with high complexity;

4. radical changes involving a large gap between where the organization is now and where it plans to go;

5. heterogeneous changes—in which an incremental ICT development is a radical move in organizational terms, and vice versa;

6. mandatory changes—which are generally less acceptable than voluntary ones;

7. risk characteristics unique to ICTs, at least in the degree to which they are applicable:

   (a) people are at the heart of systems and therefore place limits on the reliability that can be achieved;

   (b) a vision of organization and information processes is built into software controls which may be at odds with the real processes;

   (c) software's intangibility makes it easy for managers and users to perceive incorrectly that software is infinitely malleable at virtually no cost;

   (d) there is a lack of predictability and rigour in software 'engineering';

   (e) non-linearity in the interactions and impacts of ICT systems can result in a rapid escalation in consequences from relatively tiny causes and great difficulty in tracing the sources of problems.

Critical Points in the ICT System Life Cycle

Real progress in ICT system development is generally messier and more iterative than that implied by structured software engineering methodologies based on a forward 'waterfall' movement between phases. Nevertheless, there are a number of key decision points where the seeds of ICT disasters are sown and where failures are most likely to be prevented or their effects minimized.

Initiation and Feasibility Studies

Drummond (1994; forthcoming) argues that the metaphor of an 'escalator' provides an apt analogy to organizational decision making processes, because it emphasizes the significance of the momentum that can form behind early decisions. Once they are on the escalator, individuals and organizations can find it difficult to step off it. Drummond has illustrated this from the Taurus experience:

> The sheer energy involved in the tortuous decision process—the committees and subcommittees, the arguments, the back and forth debates—was highly instrumental in making top management want to carry on once they thought they had a solution (quoted in Dutton *et al.* 1995: 24–5).

The crucial juncture where a solution is first formulated has traditionally come during the feasibility study. Yet it is rare for a feasibility study to conclude that a project would not be feasible. One reason for this is that the lack of physical engineering limits on software has allowed developers to get away relatively easily with the 'macho' desire prevalent among technical professionals to prove any problem can be solved with enough ingenuity.

Requirements Management

Delayed, uncertain, or changing requirements are common root causes of major difficulties in software development. However, organizational politics, conflicts of interest, and fuzzy organizational boundaries can mean even an agreed statement of requirements may not express real needs. Moreover, the design process may not be accessible to many stakeholders.

Although the complexities of ICT systems and their diverse implications make it inevitable that requirements will evolve continually, trying to change software during later development phases can be as difficult and costly as with physical constructions (such software rigidity is emphasized by Quintas (forthcoming) in his conception of 'electronic concrete'). This has important implications for the procurement of major long-term projects because components of the system might change more rapidly than revised procurement orders can be written (Mills 1990).

Systems Design and Development

The political and social context in which system design and development takes place cannot be separated from the technical aspects which are too often given primacy, for example through the technical bias of Computer-Aided Software Engineering (CASE) methods. As discussed in Chapter 9, this has usually given insufficient priority to human and organizational factors, for example in treating the development as a logical linear process that fails to properly acknowledge the significance of a continual evolution in users' real-world requirements. Knowledge and techniques from the social sciences, psychology, organizational behaviour, and other relevant disciplines have therefore not generally been adequately incorporated into development processes and the training of ICT professionals.

Going Live

The 'going live' point is part of a continuum of activities before and after implementation, as dramatically illustrated in the LAS case. There needs to be a migration strategy for the introduction of the new system into routine operations and properly resourced plans to complete the technical process with effective marketing and other ongoing support.

Reviews That Can Stop the Escalator

A common fault with problematic projects is a failure to stop them before difficulties overwhelm the team, who have often seen disaster clearly looming. Management is more likely to think again if there is a mechanism that forces meaningful reviews, such as the need on Taurus to renew budgetary approval annually. Project management and software development methodologies, like Prince and SSADM, generally require reviews before moving to the next phase. However, this is not always effective in practice because necessary corrective action identified by the review may not be implemented and documented properly. As the escalator model suggests, it is not the absence of decision points which can keep a bad system moving ahead—it is the psychological momentum behind previous decisions that maintains the project. A 'fear of failure' climate also encourages organizations to stay on the escalator to disaster.

Shaping Safer ICT Outcomes

A failure to follow 'good practice' guidelines, and even some basic common-sense platitudes, has characterized many ICT disasters like Taurus and the LAS. Many successful ICT applications evolve by 'organic innovation' in which benefits are related directly to locally perceived need and delivered to locally dictated timescales. Common sense and good judgement often prevail in the long run. However, the importance of local contexts means it is difficult to identify or apply any generic 'cookbook' solutions since they are usually inappropriate unless they can be tailored to suit local contexts (see for example Fleck 1988). Nevertheless, the study of disasters suggests several kinds of policies and practices which are most likely to maximize the innovative opportunities of ICT systems and minimize their risks, recognizing that there is no single prescriptive solution to all situations.

Informed Management Decision Making

Corporate and business strategies should recognize that ICTs are not simply a technical matter to be left to the computer experts. All phases of the life cycle of ICT systems involve complex interactions between political, organizational, social, and technical factors. Priority should be given to gaining and keeping the commitment and understanding of all stakeholders at all stages, including agreement from key players before a project is authorized that 'the pain of change' is worth paying. Assessments of a system's benefits, risks, and costs should go beyond quantified financial criteria to include qualitative goals, such as addressing potentially negative psychological factors that could lead to resistance during implementation—like the perception that ICT innovations are dehumanizing because they accelerate organizational 'downsizing' by cutting staff numbers.

The strategic significance of ICT applications requires top-level decision making to be informed by people with real and reasonably current ICT experience and judgement. This can be achieved effectively through 'hybrid' senior executives who combine ICT expertise with other management skills; the formation of multi-skilled teams; or the employment of external advisors who do not have internal responsibilities for enacting ICT policies. However, poorly managed or unnecessary 'outsourcing' of critical ICT responsibilities to external companies could undermine the maintenance of a necessary level of core in-house expertise.

As organizations move away from hierarchical structures to something flatter, appropriate new ways need to be found to retain the expertise and information necessary to making strategic decisions about the development of ICT-based systems.

An Open Safety Culture: Overcoming Barriers to Learning

Political scientists have emphasized the political dimension of safety cultures. For instance, Sagan (1993; 1994) has argued that most organizations will have a management climate of fear in which the 'politics of blame' is difficult to avoid. This means that even serious accidents and warnings of impending disasters are likely to be hidden, ignored, or covered up. Managers who are judged by short-term performance criteria could be tempted to estimate the probability of accidents as being very low in the immediate future so that they have to do little to prevent them—which leaves longer-term problems to accumulate. Managers may also have a natural inclination to accept optimistic estimates more readily than those which more realistically highlight the extra costs, resources, and time needed for risk management measures (Sagan 1994).

Managers should recognize and anticipate the prevalence of this pattern and try to overcome it. An effective safety culture should make it clear that management regards a successful intervention to stop a disaster as a matter for praise not punishment. Such an open organizational climate is likely to result in more reliable systems because self-reporting of near-misses and all other relevant learning experiences will provide more timely warnings about potential problems and more evidence on how to prevent and contain failures. A willingness to assume personal responsibility for systems should also be encouraged. Positive personal incentives that promote high reliability and peer reviews within teams are additional ways of helping to encourage individuals to learn how to improve the quality of their own practices. For example, people could be rewarded for reporting 'near-misses', even when they share some blame.

At the same time, management must ensure a 'safety-first' attitude complements—rather than stifles—the entrepreneurial risk-taking ethos that has driven the ICT innovations which have delivered so many benefits.

Effective Project and Quality Management

The Director of Technology for the London Metropolitan Police (Nicholas Boothman, quoted in Dutton *et al.* 1995: 32–4) has argued that the project manager plays the key role in overall system development and implementation processes:

> An effective project manager is the person who leads the adventure, stays awake at night to try to solve problems—and generally ensures that good, solid techniques are applied with creativity, skill and courage.

Successful project management must take account of important real needs, like securing sufficient resources by influencing decision makers, as well as being skilled in planning, monitoring, and other more formal tasks. This includes managing requirements by persuading those who will receive the system that a string of compromises during development is usually inevitable and that something 'good enough' is the most realistic outcome. This occurs widely in physical engineering projects. A phased implementation approach can assist migration plans and project managers must use appropriate testing and other techniques to ensure managers and users have confidence in a system's reliability before it goes live, while acknowledging that the real-world performance of complex information systems cannot be modelled precisely.

A corporate 'quality culture' which pays due regard to political, organizational, and psychological aspects of local environments provides essential support to all ICT projects. Quality inspections should be backed by the authority to stop projects if necessary although, even here, there is no guarantee because inspection teams often get captured by the systems they are monitoring (Carson 1970).

Quality and project management methods should encourage system design and development creativity within a set of well-founded processes, techniques, and tools flexible enough to fit many local settings. An important technical role in ICT-based safety-critical systems can be played by the reuse of proven software components to build in an ever-rising degree of systems reliability. Another valuable approach is the application of formal mathematical methods where computer simulations, real-world testing, or other techniques cannot cope—such as in testing distributed systems whose outcomes cannot be properly determined.

Government Roles and Self-Regulation

The appropriate role of government regulation in ICT systems development is extremely controversial. On the one hand, inappropriate or excessive regulation can add costs, slow down progress, and stifle innovation.

On the other, governments can assist in raising and monitoring ICT safety and reliability by the formulation and implementation of realistic and enforceable regulations. This is especially important for life-critical systems, where it is necessary to have some form of registration, monitoring, control, and acknowledgement of personal responsibility.[8] Governments can also encourage high professional ICT standards, say through procurement policies.

Effective cross-organizational learning can be achieved using regulatory controls. Over 150 years ago, for instance, the British Regulation of Railways Act of 1844 set up an independent inspectorate to review every incident causing injury or death, backed by statutory government authority to require companies to implement any recommendations derived from the lessons learnt. The insistence by aviation authorities that all near-misses be logged and a 'black box' recorder be carried on each flight has a similar aim.

The reluctance of companies to discuss ICT failings in public can be overcome by allowing failure reports to be made available across an industry without identifying individual companies. This was recommended for the US telecommunications industry in the report by the NRC (1993), which also encouraged competing companies to offer mutual aid and restoration capabilities when significant outages occur.

Corporate self-regulation and voluntary industry-wide initiatives have an important role to play in promoting high reliability standards. Learning could also be assisted if more litigation about ICT failures resulted in published judgements, which would require development and operational practices to deliver evidence which can stand up to forensic analyses in court (Castell 1993).

Harnessing Professional and 'Amateur' ICT Expertise

If regulations for life-critical systems are to be effective, persons who are responsible for them need to be identified. This would require the establishment of professional standards among ICT practitioners. However, 'amateur' entrepreneurs and users whose prime job is not software development are such a large source of ICT innovation that it is probably too late to establish a situation where effective sanctions can be imposed by ICT professional bodies on practitioners who fail to live up to the standards expected. In these circumstances, government and private sector policies must try as best they can to raise the quality and professionalism of ICT developers.

Staff motivation is an especially important component in these policies, as there could be an increase in destructive acts by ICT professionals who fear their expectations of ever-expanding career achievement and reward are threatened by moves to cut permanent staff levels and the status of technical experts. Apprenticeship schemes are a valuable complement to formal training for ICT professionals because they offer a unique means of imparting essential tacit (experiential) knowledge by allowing controlled mistakes to be made under the guidance of an experienced practitioner (Humphrey 1991; Shapiro 1992).

Taking Risk Management Seriously

Growing awareness of the multi-faceted nature of ICT systems is mirrored by the increasing acceptance in risk management disciplines that technical risk factors cannot be extricated from 'softer' psychological, social, and organizational influences which are less amenable to definitive solutions (Royal Society 1983; 1992; National Research Council 1991). ICT specialists can also draw on an extensive body of risk management knowledge about the lengthy and difficult process of creating a safety culture (Turner 1994). Risk specialists can similarly be assisted by ICT knowledge, say in preventing good safety cultures being undermined by a tendency to accept uncritically the action recommended by decision-support software.

Managers of all major ICT projects should carry out a systematic risk assessment and prepare detailed disaster management plans. Government regulations and corporate policies should also take account of risk management needs, such as the availability of qualified risk assessors.

The Ecology of ICT Games

Specialists from different disciplines approach the multiple facets of an ICT system with their own special lenses, each adjusted to focus on the perspective dominating their own subject area. This explains why many decisions in the lead-up to ICT disasters may be rational in terms of one specialist domain, although different domains interact to produce the failure. In such an 'ecology of games', each 'game' within a domain has its own rules and assumptions in trying to achieve a particular goal (Dutton 1992a). For a large system consisting of many games, as in any major ICT application, the broad ecology must be understood, not just the best-known domain game.

Many domain viewpoints—some contradictory, some complementary—can co-exist successfully in an ecology. This holistic perspective makes it unnecessary to search for universal panaceas or to take a dogmatic stance when faced with apparent dilemmas, such as safety-first versus innovation-driven cultures and out-sourcing efficiency versus maintaining credible in-house skills.

Respecting the distinctive perceptions, knowledge, techniques, and tools contributed by the many relevant domains and exploring ways of combining them into effective holistic policies is a major challenge facing everyone concerned with trying to exploit the full potential of ICTs. The problems posed by ICT system complexity and the limits of human understanding can be addressed successfully only by recognizing that the diversity in the ecology shaping ICT systems allows for many approaches to co-exist, with different balances suited to different local contexts.

Notes

1. The authors of this chapter are indebted to the expertise and knowledge of the business, IT, telecommunications, and risk management professionals and researchers who attended a PICT Forum on ICT Disasters in 1994. They have drawn extensively on Forum discussions in developing the chapter and apologize for not being able to identify all individual contributions. A more detailed report of the Forum is provided by Dutton *et al.* (1995).

2. Pressman and Wildavsky (1973) and Bardach (1977) are two seminal works on the politics and management of implementation of ICT systems. Similar factors have been found to be significant characteristics of disasters involving many types of advanced technologies, as illustrated in the analysis by Vaughan (1996) of the organizational culture in which decisions were made that eventually culminated in the *Challenger* space shuttle explosion in 1986.

3. Perrow (1984) is an early and seminal work on the effects of 'tight coupling' in organizations.

4. Rochlin's (1991) case study provides the basis for this description, along with his elaborations of this case, presented at the PICT Forum (Dutton *et al.* 1995).

5. This section draws extensively from Rochlin's (1991) account and analysis of this case.

6. The description of the case given in this chapter summarizes and quotes verbatim from this official report by the South West Thames Regional Health Authority (1993). The case is also examined in Flowers (1996).

7. For more on Taurus, see Waters and Cane (1993), Flowers (1996), and Drummond (forthcoming).

8. See for example Advisory Council for Applied Research and Development (ACARD 1986), whose major recommendations had not been implemented ten years later.

11 Why Geography Will Still Matter: What Jobs Go Where?

John Goddard and Ranald Richardson

Historically, technological change has had what Christopher Freeman in Chapter 1 calls a 'double-edged' effect on employment—jobs directly displaced by new technologies in established industries have been paralleled by the creation of new jobs dependent on those innovations. A question central to the long-term employment implications of ICTs is whether the role of ICTs in facilitating instantaneous communication over great distances will be used to shift the location of old and new jobs.

In this chapter, John Goddard and Ranald Richardson argue that the geographical implications for the location of work are likely to be of great importance.[1] They examine key aspects of this issue, including the main characteristics of ICTs which enable jobs to be relocated and the ways in which the technologies are implicated in organizational change. This is done mainly through case studies which examine the links between ICTs and organizational change at local, national, and international levels. The policy implications of this potential for change in the geography of information economies is examined in Chapter 19.

John Goddard and Ranald Richardson

A New Dimension to Technological Change

There are three interrelated features of ICTs which are likely to contribute to structural unemployment. Two of these are of a quantitative nature: their pervasiveness and rate of diffusion. The third and most revolutionary characteristic relates to ICT's network capabilities, which we believe represents a qualitatively new dimension to technological change.

The Pervasiveness and Diffusion of ICTs

As explained elsewhere in this book (such as in Chapters 1 and 2), ICTs have become pervasive in all areas of social and business life. This includes support for the design, development, and supply of new products and new services; the forging of new linkages with suppliers; provision of improved support services for customers; more effective central co-ordination of corporate operations; and the re-engineering of business processes (see Chapters 9 and 15). ICTs are also affecting virtually every occupation at all skill levels.

The pace of ICT diffusion has been accelerated by falling costs and improved user interfaces. Most significantly, networked interconnections have multiplied at an exponential rate the number of potential users of ICTs. This has left little time for the making of adjustments in the labour market to allow new industries to be built up or for workers to acquire new skills or migrate to areas where jobs are available. Nevertheless, the pace of diffusion has often been slower than that predicted in the more technologically optimistic visions and has proceeded at uneven paces in different sectors, applications, and geographical regions.

The Implications of Networking

As more and more work involves the processing and exchange of information, the fusing of telecommunications and computing into the networked 'telematics' characteristic of ICTs means that this work can become more portable or mobile. With the global spread of telematics, the factors that confine the supply and demand of labour to one locality or nation-state no longer apply. While the adoption of ICTs within the workplace can reduce the demand for labour in one location, telematics can simultaneously increase its supply from elsewhere.

Such job portability is an important element in social and economic policies. For example, pronounced variations in unemployment across Europe existed in the mid-1990s—against an average in the EU of 100, Andalusia in Spain registered an index of 290 compared to just 20 in Luxembourg (European Commission 1994*b*). This reflects historical imbalances, which indicates that labour has remained relatively static in terms of permanent changes in the place of employment. At the same time, capital within the EU became much more mobile after the creation of a single EU market in 1992. Such disparities are even greater in areas outside the EU, where barriers against immigration are stronger while capital flows are increasingly fluid on a global scale. This analysis raises two key questions:

1. How far might telematics ameliorate these differences by taking work to the workers wherever they are located, perhaps even by providing competitive advantages to distressed areas within nations?

2. How far is telematics responsible for creating an uneven geography of work?

In response to the first question, the widespread adoption of telematics in industry, commerce, and public services is often depicted as being essential to the realization of new employment opportunities, as in many 'information superhighway' initiatives (see Chapter 22). For example, the high-level Bangemann Group (1994) saw the promotion of teleworking as the first priority for public action if Europe is to 'seize the opportunities' of the emerging information society. Under a heading 'More jobs, new jobs, for the mobile society', the report of the Group (1994: 25) states: 'the aim is for 2 per cent of white-collar workers to be teleworkers by 1996, and 10 million teleworking jobs to be created by the year 2000.'

Similarly, a White Paper from the European Commission (1994*a*) pointed to the indirect contribution that telematics can make to competitiveness and concomitant employment growth, for instance by removing market problems resulting from the distance of 'peripheral' or rural areas from central or urban-based employment opportunities. It also acknowledged the job-destroying potential of ICTs, thereby implicitly recognizing telematics is both a threat and opportunity in terms of where jobs are located, as well as their number.

John Goddard and Ranald Richardson

The Nature of Locational Change

The successful implementation of telematics widens the 'locational repertoires' available to organizations. This does not mean that geography in the sense of differences between places no longer matters. In our highly cost-sensitive world, telematics enables organizations fully to exploit very small differences between locations—such as the cost and quality of human resources; physical infrastructure, including transport facilities; institutional infrastructure like the nature of local government; and a wide range of quality-of-life factors. Flexibility may be achieved either without major relocation within a given stock of accommodation in a number of sites or through using new locations as a means of escaping the problems of inefficient working in existing situations.

Such locational flexibility clearly does not take place on a level playing-field. One of the central paradoxes of telematics is that the less important it makes spatial barriers as such, the greater becomes the sensitivity of organizations to variations of 'place' within space and the incentive for places to differentiate themselves in ways that attract investors. This is an example of how the ability of both capital and labour to move at low cost from place to place has come to depend on the creation of fixed, secure, and largely immobile social and physical infrastructures (Harvey 1989). Developments in telematics are one of the key current means of resolving this tension between fixity and mobility, between the rising power to overcome space and the immobile structures required for such purposes. Such considerations inevitably shape and constrain the revolutionary potential of telematics, producing more conservative outcomes in geographical terms than many futurists claim. Nevertheless, these processes of adjustment are increasingly operating on a global scale, within which local differences matter more and more.

Research at the Newcastle PICT Centre demonstrates the validity of these generalizations (see for example Hepworth 1989; Goddard 1992; and Richardson 1994).[2] In the following sections we draw on that research to provide examples of how telematics is implicated in each of the conventional classifications of innovation—new products and services; new processes of production; and new ways of managing the organization and its external relations. The case studies demonstrate the part played by telematics in processes of organizational change across a spectrum of activities, which also illustrates the all-pervasive nature of the changes in progress.

Supporting Changes in Manufacturing Industries

Networked-Based Reorganization in the Building Industry

John Carr plc is a manufacturer of doors, windows, and other components for the building industry. Based in the north of England, the firm concentrated its early development in the 1960s and 1970s on being the least-cost producer in geographically defined markets, chiefly public housing constructed directly by local authorities in the north and west of England. The company's initial expansion involved duplication of production across the whole product range in different regions. The use of computer-based networks at this stage was restricted to supporting the centralization of finance and cost-control functions to reinforce the strategic objective of being 'least-cost producer' in a number of specific regions.

Between 1979 and 1982, the company's locally differentiated markets collapsed as the national government cut back on public housing, leaving the firm with an organization suited to market conditions that no longer prevailed. The new market it faced was characterized by a shift to the private sector and to 'do-it-yourself' domestic building markets in the then-booming south-east of England, which includes London. This demanded products to be manufactured in three days from order to delivery, compared to its previous ten-week cycle.

The response of the firm was interwoven with the development of its computer network. Its management decided that the much shorter order-to-delivery target, greater economies of scale in production, and other new objectives would be best met by a spatial reorganization of its production, sales, and marketing functions as illustrated in Figure 11.1. This involved reorganizing its manufacturing plants to give each one a prime responsibility for just one product range, instead of the previous policy of product diversification at individual plants. Each plant in the new set-up despatches output to central warehouses, which are responsible for deliveries to the market. The sales function was also centralized and its geographical focus reoriented towards the south-east England market.

This reorganization was based around the establishment of a new telematics infrastructure to support the efficient assembly, analysis, and integration of information from both external and internal sources. The spatially distributed functions of manufacturing, distribution, and sales are managed through this network, including the establishment of new

201

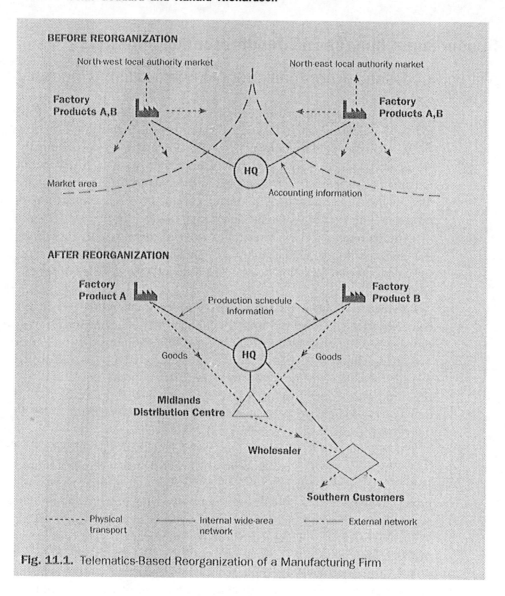

BEFORE REORGANIZATION

North-west local authority market

North-east local authority market

Factory Products A,B

Factory Products A,B

HQ

Market area

Accounting information

AFTER REORGANIZATION

Factory Product A

Production schedule information

Factory Product B

Goods

HQ

Goods

Midlands Distribution Centre

Wholesaler

Southern Customers

- - - - - - Physical transport

———— Internal wide-area network

—·—·— External network

Fig. 11.1. Telematics-Based Reorganization of a Manufacturing Firm

relationships with suppliers and customers in order to respond successfully to actual market demand. This involved aligning its sales activities with several large retail chains through the development of intercorporate networking. Overall, John Carr used ICTs to exert significant influence in securing a strong position in its newly defined geographical markets.

The telematics capabilities were therefore central to the company's ability to restructure its operations spatially and move into new geographical markets successfully. This was done from its traditional locations as the availability of the ICT network meant customers in the south-east of England could be serviced without requiring new investment in that region—where land, property, wages, and other costs are significantly higher than in its traditional northern base.

Establishing a Car Plant from Scratch

The second manufacturing example refers to the building by Nissan in 1984 of a car-making plant in Sunderland in the north-east of England, a region previously lacking a significant tradition in the vehicle production industry. An important factor in choosing the location was the abundant local supply of manual labour accustomed to heavy work, arising in part from the closure of the local shipbuilding industry. In addition, there was a suitable site at a former airfield and government regional investment subsidies. However, the main UK base of vehicle component suppliers and skilled designers were some 200 miles to the south, in the English Midlands. ICT networking was vital in the management of activities between these locations, including the creation of a 'virtual' design facility linking a test track in Sunderland with Nissan's European Technology Centre in the Midlands.

A complex logistic system was created to manage relations between Nissan in Sunderland and about a hundred component suppliers scattered around the Midlands, including many small companies. Suppliers were expected to deliver in small volumes, with opportunities for economies of scale coming from the long-term nature of their contracts with Nissan. Goods are typically collected from suppliers four times a day, then held for no more than eight hours at storage points—from where they are collected by large lorries operating on a regular shuttle service to Sunderland.

A telematics network is essential in managing the information needed to ensure the movement of goods between the geographically remote manufacturing assembly plant in Sunderland and component suppliers in the Midlands. For instance, Electronic Data Interchange (EDI) enables the supply chain to act as an extension of Nissan's production process and to help co-ordinate production processes across the chain, which aim for a minimum of buffer stocks for Just-In-Time (JIT) production processes. The use of ICTs therefore meant investment in the new plant reinforced, rather than undermined, established industrial agglomerations in the Midlands, while limiting the job-multiplier effects near Sunderland.

John Goddard and Ranald Richardson

Innovations in Services to Producers

A Skilled Workforce for Telemediated Support

Quarterdeck International is a US-based company which designs and manufactures a range of software products for personal computers (PCs), such as a successful package that helps to manage the PC's memory efficiently. It has production sites around the world and sells its products in Europe through a network of agents. The company seeks high-volume sales, mainly through multiple sales to large companies.

In the late 1980s, Quarterdeck opened a European headquarters in Ireland at Dún Laoghaire, a small town to the south of Dublin. Its principal function was to produce software and customize the product for European markets, for example by changing keyboard configuration to take account of different character sets used in different languages. Quarterdeck subsequently set up a telemediated technical-support operation at the site.

If a problem arises with a Quarterdeck product in Europe, customers call their nearest agent. A German, Scandinavian, or Eastern European customer, for example, will contact Dusseldorf by telephone, fax, or electronic mail. The incoming calls are not answered directly at the local centres, but are automatically routed to Ireland via leased telecommunications lines. Each member of staff in the Dún Laoghaire centre speaks four or five languages, which helps them to deal directly with all calls. They also have access to the firm's databases in the USA and Ireland as well as external online information sources. The Irish site services offices on both seaboards of the US to supplement support centres in Los Angeles and New York outside their local office hours.

This illustrates how the availability of a multi-lingual and technically skilled workforce together with advanced telecommunications at competitive rates can be important factors in decisions about locating telemediated support work. In other parts of the software industry, where English is the common language, India has exploited the British influence in becoming a major centre for software export. For instance, Hamilton (1992) reports how Texas Instruments in the USA uses satellite communications with its Bangalore software facility to import software used to design its semiconductors. Capabilities like these are becoming increasingly important in many industries.

Outsourcing Business Processes

The use of telematics to 'outsource' work by transferring particular internal functions to an external supplier can lead to a shift of jobs from metropolitan to distant rural areas. For example, the Paris-based Telergos company has established centres in a number of villages, mainly in France but also in Barnard Castle, County Durham in the UK.

The company was established in 1989 to provide support for companies who do not wish to take on more secretarial and processing staff just to be able to deal with peaks of activity. The village-based offices provide the necessary supplementary secretarial services for clients. Telergos started by concentrating on word-processing capabilities for dealing with mail shots and reports, particularly for Paris-based insurance companies. It has subsequently diversified into more value-added services like graphical design and translations. The Barnard Castle office deals with clients in the UK as well as France, including the preparation of English-language documents for French clients far more cost-effectively by using a similar operation in France.

Telergos established a telematics system which enables clients to send spoken or written files and to receive the final documents downloaded to their computers. Documents can also be sent by fax, dictated via the telephone, or sent by postal and courier delivery. Letters are turned round within 30 minutes of the reception of a dictation or less than 48 hours for other routine work. The rural location of the company's telecentres has a clear economic rationale. For instance, clients of the company have said that labour productivity is higher than on work previously carried out in-house within the Paris region. This is accounted for by the fact that, in comparison to in-house staff, Telergos personnel receive lower wages, spend less time commuting, remain longer with the company, and have closer relationships with their managers in smaller offices. The quality of the work is also reported to be higher.

Another example of an outsourcing centre in a remote area is the establishment by the Hoskyns Group, one of the UK's largest IT services companies, of a Business Process Outsourcing Centre at Forres, near Inverness in the far-north Highlands of Scotland. Its principal initial work when it opened in 1993 was to collect money on behalf of clients, who are typically large organizations with heavy administrative loads. For instance, Hoskyns collects property-based taxes and processes some welfare benefits for local authorities in the north of Scotland. It also collects parking fines for a number of local authorities in London, in partnership with another firm which manages the traffic wardens who can issue fines for other traffic violations. Offenders can phone a number at local London rates, which is automatically routed to Forres, or they can write to a Post Office Box number for delivery to the Hoskyns centre.

The Forres operation does not require a sophisticated, technologically skilled workforce as in the Quarterdeck case. Intensive training is carried out over a relatively short period, covering the basics of using the PC and telephone systems and instruction in effective customer relations.

A Transcontinental Operation

ICD Ltd. started life in the early 1980s as a provider of marketing information to corporate customers, initially as a specialist publisher of financial magazines. These were edited at the company's London base in the heart of the City, the financial district which included the organizations representing the main market for the magazines. Information for these was gathered primarily through personal contacts and paper records.

When the company's sales plummeted after a major stock market collapse in 1986, it refinanced itself and built a new strategy around electronic database services. The core data of around 25 million records for this is derived from paper-based electoral registers compiled by all local authorities in Britain. These give the names and addresses of people registered to vote in elections. The physical registers are brought to ICD's London headquarters, from where they are air-freighted to India for keying into electronic form by relatively low-cost labour. The data are then shipped on disk from India to a computer bureau in the USA, from where they can be accessed from London via a satellite link.

ICD supplements this basic data with a variety of other information, including data on individual consumer behaviour, house prices from around the UK, and shareholding and inheritance information lodged with official institutions in London. Many sources are used for gathering this information, from formal market research activities to relatively informal personal and business contacts. Overall, therefore, telematics has enabled ICD to totally re-engineer its business around processes involving information gathered in different localities within Britain, while there is a major labour input in another continent and a major capital item in the production process—the bureau's computer system—in a third.

Telemediated Consumer Services

An increasing number of companies are transferring previous face-to-face interactions with customers at 'front offices', like sales outlets and bank branches in city centres, to telemediated services provided from a few 'back-office' locations, typically located in out-of-town business parks.

Regionalizing Telesales Centres

Telematics has enabled British Airways (BA) to create an integrated international telesales network and a more regionalized operation in the UK. Traditionally, the use of telecommunications for BA customer enquiries and flight bookings was carried out mainly through travel agencies located in popular shopping areas, increasingly by online access to BA databases. In the early 1990s, BA started to shift its focus to direct sales to individuals. Each direct sale is worth almost twice as much as an indirect purchase through a travel agent, mainly because of the elimination of commission payments to agencies for ticket sales and 'add-on' services like hotel rooms, car-hire, and insurance.

The vast majority of BA's customers have always been in the southeast of England. Until the late 1980s, the only feasible way of catering for this market was to have almost all BA's telesales staff located in the London area—otherwise customers would have objected to making telephone calls at non-local rates. Then three ICT-based developments opened new opportunities for BA to reorganize its operations:

1. automatic call-distribution systems that can interconnect sites in different locations;

2. the introduction by BT of a value-added service which permits callers to pay only the local call rate, regardless of where they are telephoning from;

3. the availability and continuing falling costs and improving capabilities of private leased lines.

Using capabilities like these, BA set up a network of regional telesales centres which operate as a single 'virtual office' as far as the customer is concerned. The overall network is monitored and controlled from a Call Management Centre at BA's main centre at Heathrow on the outskirts of London. This centre can equalize activity across regions—for example by preparing a 'national roster' of the number of staff required at any site at any time to allow the total operation to reach performance targets as efficiently as possible. If the nearest centre is busy when a customer telephones at a local rate, the call is automatically transferred without extra cost for the customer to another centre, using a programmed routing algorithm. The system can also be 'reconfigured' to have different routing sequences if one or more centres are out of action, say because of a fire or an industrial dispute.

Confidence gained with this telematics network has encouraged BA to use geography on a global scale to optimize staff resources. It has done this by integrating its UK telesales operation with those in other countries to create an internationally based 'virtual sales office'. For example, by the mid-1990s around 15 per cent of calls generated in the USA using BA's toll-free numbers were answered in the UK through automatic rerouting procedures. This has added little to BA's costs as it uses voice data compression techniques that allow for efficient use of leased lines which were already used to carry computer data. The UK also handles calls made by customers using international freephone numbers from some European countries. This internationalization of BA's telesales operation is being continuously extended, for instance by enabling calls generated in Belgium to be answered either in Amsterdam (if originating from Flemish-speaking areas) or in Lyon (if from French-speaking areas).

The telemediated innovations within the UK enabled BA to relocate most of its telesales staff away from Heathrow. Around 900 telesales personnel were located at Heathrow in the late 1980s. By 1995 the number was down to about 200, with a likely eventual fall to no more than 100. Meanwhile, the numbers of telesales and flight information personnel at regional centres in provincial cities have grown to over 900. This shift has provided BA with a number of gains:

1. a more stable workforce with lower staff turnover than at Heathrow, where the job availability in the south-east of England contributed to a high turnover rate (about 35 per cent in the 1980s), which meant staff did not stay long enough to give a reasonable return on training and recruitment investment;

2. financial savings because regionally negotiated wages and associated costs in provincial cities are significantly lower than in the south-east— BA estimates that regionalization has saved an average of from £3,000 to £4,000 a year per employee.

3. generally better-motivated and more highly skilled staff in labour markets less competitive than in the south-east of England.

A Telebanking Pioneer

First Direct was established as a new company in October 1989 by one of the major UK banks, Midland. It provided what was then a radical concept in British banking—a service operated mainly by telephone but offering most personal account services customers would expect to find from a traditional bank with a network of branches in well-frequented locations. First Direct is 'open for business' 24 hours a day, 365 days a year. Money withdrawals and cheque encashments can take place at Midland Bank's branches and automatic cash machine network. Within about four years, First Direct employed around 1,500 staff (equivalent to around 1,100 full-time staff as many worked part-time) and had over 400,000 customers, mainly in the more affluent socio-economic groups in the 25–44 age band. This customer profile was significantly up-market compared to the traditional British bank.

First Direct has relied heavily on ICTs to concentrate its telemediated production at a single site to cover the whole of the UK, which bypasses the high costs of running a branch network. As well as creating this new type of banking service, First Direct also sought to establish a new organizational culture that moved away from the hierarchical, bureaucratic structure of the traditional UK bank. Instead, it offered flatter, more sales-oriented structures and a greater emphasis on rewarding individuals according to performance and commitment as part of its aim of developing a more flexible workforce.

This 'flexibilization' included employment policies which sought to avoid recruiting staff with traditional banking experience for its call-centre and sales operations, where it was felt new skills and attitudes were required. Some skilled banking staff are employed where their specialist skills are felt to be essential. However, the aim is to minimize their number and to develop systems that can be operated by staff who can be recruited on the basis of their behavioural skills and personality characteristics, such as telephone manner and an ability to work as part of a team.

First Direct used BT's service for accessing remote location at local-call rates to build a critical mass of customers in the south-east of England from a centre based in the north—where there is a large pool of good-quality, reasonably priced labour and much suitable office accommodation. Telematics enabled the same site to be used to support the service as it was expanded across the whole of the country.

Overall Employment and Locational Effects

The above case studies are indicative of the potential created by ICTs for broader employment and locational trends. They also provide considerable insight into the processes by which ICTs are supporting new kinds of work location. However, individual examples like these do not indicate the likely scale of the overall implications of the use of telematics networks on the number and type of jobs and their disposition.

Productivity Gains and Employment Losses

Telebanking clearly illustrates broad trends in telemediated work. For example, since the mid-1980s the number of bank branches in the UK fell from around 14,300 in 1985 to just over 11,000 in 1994, with branch employment declining from a peak of 356,000 in 1989 to about 288,000 in 1994 (BBA 1995). Such falls are likely to continue for some time. The move towards telebanking has played a growing role in this trend, with all major retail banks in the UK following the lead of First Direct in setting up telebanking services. However, many other factors have also contributed to these changes, like the increased competition arising from the deregulation of the financial-services sector in the 1980s.

Telebanking has offered substantial productivity gains over branch networks. For example, First Direct handled over half a million customers with around 1,000 full-time equivalent workers in 1994, whereas its parent Midland Bank employed 36,000 staff to service four million customers through its retail outlets. Another bank at an early stage in its telebank pilot has claimed that just sixteen staff are able to service 40,000 regular customers in an operation that would be equivalent, at a conservative estimate, of the work of four major branches employing a total of about 200 people. Similar examples of labour savings through the centralization of call functions can also be found in other sectors. For instance, one airline has been able to cut its call reservation workforce by a third through centralizing its call-centre function.

The use of telemediated call centres could also limit job growth in some countries if they were to be established 'offshore' in other countries, as in the way some US companies have sited telesales and data processing centres in the Caribbean and as in ICD Ltd.'s use of data preparation staff in India. In addition, the numbers required at call centres could start to fall as technological advances enable customers to interact directly with companies' databases, for example by home telebanking via interactive-

TV multimedia systems or by the sophisticated exploitation of touch-tone telephones and automated voice-response systems.

Potential for Employment Growth

There are a number of activities where genuine net growth in employment could be achieved through telemediated services:

1. More workers will be required to meet the demands created by the provision of genuinely better services that respond to more sophisticated consumer requirements.

2. Jobs will be created as consumers come to expect longer 'opening hours', although much of this growth will be mainly in part-time work.

3. More labour-intensive resources will be needed to exploit highly targeted and personalized marketing strategies, say by complementing or replacing mass-marketing drives with direct-response television campaigns targeted at specific audiences.

4. Employment can be created by firms which export teleservices successfully.

5. There will be continuing employment growth within those call centres which continue to recognize that the value added by a skilled person making a human contact—say in selling products and services that 'add on' to the customer's initial interest—demonstrably outweighs the efficiency gains of automated direct electronic interactions with customers.

Implications for Public Services

Public services have lagged behind the private sector in the adoption of ICTs for the kinds of organizationally innovative uses illustrated by the case studies in this chapter. However, as discussed in Chapter 15, pressures to make economies in public expenditure and to bring market criteria and a more customer-oriented ethos into the public sector have begun to close the gap through the electronic delivery of an ever-widening range of public service. Government computing services are also being contracted out to private agencies in many countries, as in the following cases:

- The US information service company Saztec uses its office in the Philippines to enter data for clients such as US hospitals and European Patent offices. It also has a contract to catalogue the Helsinki library, which involves partial data entry in Manila of information from microfilm; computer formatting in Sydney; database searching for full entries in Toronto; conversion to the Finnish catalogue systems in Dayton, Ohio; and final checking in London (Hamilton 1992).

- The UK government's Inland Revenue computers are run by IT services firm EDS and the social welfare system by IT consultancy Arthur Andersen.

- In Malmö, Sweden, the fire department reaches its database of street routes via a General Electric computer in Cleveland, Ohio.

Work in local government services has traditionally provided a buffer against cyclical variations in employment in the private sector. Once local government information jobs are provided electronically, they also become potentially mobile and part of the traded sector. This has happened, for instance, to the services of London local authorities being run by Hoskyns in Scotland. Such approaches could be extended to a wide range of local information-based services. Similar arguments apply at the national level, where electronically provided services become potentially mobile on an international scale.

Such considerations imply that the traditional 'Keynsian' view of the role of the state as a counter-cyclical provider of employment may no longer be a viable option for the local or nation-state. However, savings in the provision of services should benefit the public by either reducing taxes or permitting money to be spent on other services.

Why Geography Remains Important

Profound implications for the location of work arise from the combination of innovations discussed above. The outcomes of this are very open. Telematics could support existing urban agglomerations or provide work opportunities in new locations; a combination of the two is equally possible. Particular outcomes are therefore highly contingent on the circumstances of each organization and the characteristics of different potential locations. This geographical contingency is also matched by an historical specificity. The environmental pressures on organizations and the technological opportunities open to them are subject to continual change. Telematics-supported locational restructuring in one place might only be appropriate to the particular circumstances prevailing at the time.

It is clear from some of the case studies in the chapter that the job gains supported by telematics in one location can be associated with far greater losses in one or more other locations. However, it is also evident that the firms adopting telemediated innovations are securing the jobs that remain through their greater competitiveness. It is therefore difficult to quantify the overall effects of this example of 'two-edged' technical change. What is not in doubt is that the most significant employment effects are arising in the area of direct services to the consumer. Here the traditional close geographical relationship between the customer and supplier of the service is breaking down.

For example, customers no longer have to go physically to their local bank but can be serviced electronically from a central and distant location. As well as being 'de-localized', services are also being 'industrialized' as the skills of front-office staff are incorporated into back-office software and systems. The 'product' cycle in services has therefore gone from investments aimed at gaining efficiency, to improvements in the quality of service, and finally to a widening of the range of services. This is a reverse of the cycle in traditional factory systems, where new products are introduced and then followed by successive attempts to lower the cost of manufacture (Barras 1986). It is important to emphasize that telemediated locational flexibility of work is just one factor in the process of corporate and government reorganization. Telematics has facilitated—but not caused—changes such as the 'delayering' of corporate hierarchies to flatter organizational structures, the reduction of headquarters staff, and the out-sourcing of selected business processes.

In some instances, there may be a degree of choice as to which particular locational configuration of work to adopt. Situations could arise in which the differential private costs and benefits between one configuration and another might be quite small, but with a quite large public benefit. In such circumstances, the outcome might be amenable to influence in the public interest, say to sustain employment in one distressed area by retaining jobs or reducing unemployment in another region by attracting jobs (Porter 1995).

The deeply important nature of the geographical implications of ICTs mean that new forms of incentives and negotiations between central government and companies, and even within government, are needed. These must seek to ameliorate locational unemployment—the distinctive new form of structural unemployment which partly characterizes the ICT techno-economic paradigm.

Notes

1. This chapter originated as a paper presented to PICT's 1995 International Conference on the Social and Economic Implications of Information and Communication Technologies, held in Westminster, London on 10–12 May 1995.
2. Further case studies from the USA and elsewhere can be found in Hamilton (1992); Kanter (1995); and OTA (1995).

Part III

Living in an Information Society: ICTs in the Home, Education, and Democratic Processes

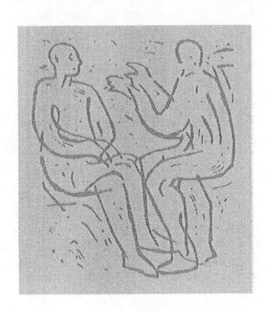

12 Future Imperfect: Information and Communication Technologies in Everyday Life

Roger Silverstone

One of the main themes of this book is that it is wrong to regard ICTs as the sole drivers of major changes in the way all people live and work. Non-technical factors can impose limits on—and extend the horizons of—the social implications of any technological revolution. In this chapter, Roger Silverstone explores the complex web of factors that could influence the social role of ICTs in one of the most critical domains of society—the household.[1] He questions the coherence of technology-driven revolutionary visions and suggests there are likely to be many possible outcomes. This is done using stories of very different 'futures' based on a practical appraisal of technological change in the context of the realities of everyday life. He explains why he believes full advantage will be taken of ICTs only if policies ensure the benefits are more equally and evenly shared throughout society.

Multiple Futures for the Multimedia Revolution

During the 1990s it became commonplace to observe that things are changing in the media world. New technologies, new delivery systems, and new industrial alliances were being announced almost daily. The apocalyptic and breathless rhetoric of revolution and crisis has been employed in describing such developments—a rhetoric of competing utopian or dystopian visions, fought out in and on the very media who are its subject. It is a rhetoric deeply engrained in the militaristic and sexual metaphors of strategic advance and big bangs.

Great changes have undoubtedly taken place in media and information technologies and their use. More and more households around the world are making use of a mix of terrestrial cable, and satellite television, video, multimedia personal computers, the Internet, and other innovations. New markets have also boomed. By 1994, for example, the computer games industry worldwide had grown to be bigger than that of recorded music. This new media world is one of converging technologies and intense competition. It is also a world which is no longer shared or so easily shareable as new and alternative delivery systems, products, and services allow consumers to express their own individual tastes much more intensely and consistently. At the same time, it is a world in which the internationalization of culture begun by Hollywood is being equally intensified as huge new multinationals fight to integrate hardware and software production and to extend the distribution of programme content—content which they themselves increasingly own—across media and across continents.

This is what became known as the 'multimedia revolution'. In this chapter, I will explain why there is nothing inevitable about that revolution and its consequences. Social change is created by how we use the technology rather than the technology itself—and that use is no simple matter. It depends on access and competence as well as desire and is influenced by gender and age, class, and culture. The difficult and contradictory nature of the processes involved means that, in looking ahead, we should consider multiple possible futures—social futures of individuals, families, and households, as well as of technologies and industries. I therefore offer an account of the supposed revolution which takes seriously the actual nature of the ways in which media and information technologies are shaped by the mundane but still complex realities of everyday life.[2]

The Key Issues: Control, Access, and Choice

Three interrelated concerns are released and intensified both by the relentless march of technologies and the particular ways they are developed and regulated:

1. **Control**. Surveillance and freedom are affected by the increasing dominance and power of major media and information industry players, as well as the possible countervailing force provided by consumers and users with greater opportunities for action. On the one hand, greater control is threatened by the increasing possibilities for surveillance in the data gathered through the introduction of interactive home-based multimedia. On the other hand, the almost entirely unpoliced (and possibly unpoliceable) Internet illustrates what the new technology might mean for freedom, or even subversion, where a vast number of interest groups have open access to communicate with each other around the world.

2. **Access**. The denial or restriction of access to groups and individuals who do not have the resources to participate in an increasingly market-dominated system has vital implications for the quality of our social, cultural, and political lives.

3. **Choice**. Issues of choice are embodied in what has been called 'Me-TV'—the increasing capacity of television to change from being the end of the line of a broadcast signal to a domestic communication and information hub through which individuals and families can command information and media products at the touch of a button (but at a price). Me-TV refers to *my* ability to determine what *I* want from *my* screen.

An important way in which these concerns are articulated is through the consumption and use of the technologies, as new and old machines and services jostle for position in the endless to-ing and fro-ing of our everyday lives. Indeed, it is within our domestic rituals and resistances that the battles for our media and information futures will be won or lost. In trying to make sense of what futures might emerge from these forces, it is also necessary to consider influential technological and industrial factors.

The Technological Story

It is difficult to penetrate the smog of claims and counter-claims that shroud the technological story. But at least two things are clear. The hype itself both signals and attempts to mask a high level of anxiety in the industry, as major players invest massive resources in a technological competition in which there are going to be some very big winners and some cataclysmic losers. Secondly, it is clear that the technology continues to change very quickly.

One thing above all makes these changes possible—the digitization of all forms of information. This enables more accurate and precise reproduction of sound and image as well as the accurate and rapid transmission of data. The use of advanced compression techniques, which allow digitized information to be squashed into ever smaller spaces, will fully release the techno-genie from the lamp. For example, compression allows telecommunications transmission media other than broadband optical fibres—even the old 'twisted copper wire' used for telephony—to be employed for multimedia applications in which people use television sets and computers to interact with a variety of services, like video-on-demand and telebanking. It also makes it possible to transmit many more discrete channels of high-quality video using cable, radio, or other transmission media—and for one CD to hold a rapidly increasing volume of full-motion video, stereo sound, and pages of text.

Compression is one of the many technological innovations that have enabled the growing convergence of previously discrete media and information technologies. Once upon a time, the telephone was a telephone and the television a television and no one had heard of computers in the home. Then hybrids like computer games entered households without the newly convergent aspects even being noted. Multimedia can now allow the user/consumer to interact with a complex of materials: gaining access, making entertainment choices, responding to, or initiating, requests for information.

Those who see in this scenario a vivid new technological future also see a number of quantum leaps in what we can expect from what were once plain old TV sets. Home shopping is one of the most obvious examples. Then there is the conversion of existing broadcasting culture into a publishing culture in which consumers will be able to select what to watch when they want to watch it. This will have consequences both for the scheduling of media content and universal provision as audiences become consumers, fragmented both in time and space.

Visions of such apparently tangible technological advances mask profound uncertainties. There are major uncertainties, for example, about the nature of key elements of interactive multimedia which are the subject of intense international competition, such as the 'set-top' box that attaches to a television to interpret digital signals and the 'delivery system' used in the transmission. But, one way or another, the technology is likely to deliver the capabilities expected.

Other real uncertainties are not strictly technological and are more profound because an eventual solution is less probable. These relate to questions like: how is the new media and information environment to be controlled and regulated, and by whom?; can a radical increase of service options (say many hundreds of cable channels) be supported effectively?; and who, if anyone, really wants or needs any of it?

The Industrial Story

The idea of convergence is a crucial dimension of the reconstruction of the media and information industry worldwide. This has involved the coming together of major companies which have previously focused on one sector, such as: telecommunications, film production, broadcasting, hardware manufacture, software development, or publishing. The driving force behind this convergence is the perceived need to control the integrative potential of the emerging lattice of technologies. The key prizes of ownership will come in two main areas:

1. **Content**. The talent to produce new materials for new media will always be at a premium. So too will be the rights to existing software— be it in the form of films, television shows, or computer games.

2. **Distribution networks**. In a world where principles of common carriage are disappearing like water in the sand, ownership provides the ability to charge others for access to the consumer and to charge consumers for access to content.

Those who can control both content production and rights as well as distribution could find themselves on a gravy train of unprecedented proportions. However, some commentators (such as Bowen 1994) argue that such consolidation and vertical integration will be counter-productive if it stifles the organizational flexibility that is essential in a constantly changing technological and commercial environment. The first moves in industrial convergence were seen in the late 1980s, for instance when Hollywood film makers were bought by Japanese hardware producers (like Sony's purchase of Columbia) and newspaper publishing groups (such as Rupert Murdoch's News Corporation buying of 20th Century Fox). Many huge takeover battles have followed, involving a wide range of enterprises from around the world which were traditionally involved in distinct and separate industries. Whatever the detailed outcomes of these battles, the industrial map is likely to change continually.

Important consequences and problems could flow from the technological and industrial convergences outlined above:

1. **There will be products and services available via TV screens**. These will create a more focused and fragmented media environment, with distinct programmes, software, or services being directed to distinct groups of consumers.

2. **Public service broadcasting, in Europe at least, therefore cannot hope to continue its traditional role of providing a universal service within a national culture**. However, the question of a universally available service cannot be left to the depredations of the marketplace. The media marketplace itself is unlikely to produce even a marginally disinterested publisher unless some principles of common carriage are implemented, say to allow access to the cable networks by content producers, programme makers, service providers, and the rest (Murdock 1990).

3. **The screen is also increasingly likely to become the site of a hybrid multimedia culture in which telecommunications, computing, and video intertwine**. An important aspect of this will be the new ways advertisers find to attract consumers who have so much choice. For example, 'advertainment' sponsored programmes may not appear to be the advertisements that they actually are. Some advertising will become more customized, even personalized, say when interactive home shopping provides retailers with important data about customers' financial and other dimensions.

The Domestic Story

There is, however, another reality to be considered—the complex, diverse, perverse reality of the everyday worlds of those who live with media and information technologies. This social context at the interface of new technologies and old social forms might contain or constrain the multimedia technological and industrial revolutions unless it is properly understood. As leading cultural critic Raymond Williams (1980) noted: 'A main characteristic of our society is a willed coexistence of very new technologies and very old social forms.'

Impacts on the Quality of Everyday Lives

Our domesticity is a product of a number of interrelated social and cultural processes in which media and information technologies have been increasingly involved. Historically, the overall shape of that domesticity has been associated with the rise of industrialization: with the urbanization and suburbanization of populations, the rise of mass education, and changing patterns and structures of work.

Throughout the twentieth century, ICTs (including physical communication technologies like the train and motor car) have enabled the dispersal of populations away from the face-to-face intensities of inner cities and rural villages. This dispersal has involved increasing mobility and reach, allowing us both to move around more and to communicate with and learn from others without moving around. If present and future generations of media and information technologies prove to be major accelerators of these tendencies, there would be significant implications for the quality of our everyday lives; our capacity to participate in the wider society; and our senses of belonging and security.

As ever, there are competing visions and competing critiques. There are those who argue that these technologies have contributed to an undermining of a sense of home, creating a new kind of rootlessness because they have the capacity to unlock and disconnect individuals from their dependence on place—a rootlessness which results in increasing social isolation and cultural fragmentation. Others have suggested the reverse: that technologies like the telephone, television, computer, and now multimedia will continue to liberate our domesticity from its dependence on physical location and enhance our social and cultural freedoms by enabling us, as active consumers and users, to create our own distinct and meaningful cultural identities.[3]

These debates are important. They go to the heart of the essential tensions that lie at the centre of our domestic lives—tensions between security and insecurity, participation and isolation, freedom and control. They are the defining tensions which any analysis of the role of media and information technologies in our everyday lives must confront.[4] Yet they are not resolvable merely by an examination of the technology. For media and information technologies, even the basic telephone, have double lives: they connect and disconnect, liberate and constrain (de Sola Pool 1977). They can do both simultaneously and contradictorily. The particular balance struck is a product, I would suggest, of the ways in which they are regulated and the ways in which they are consumed or 'domesticated'.

Domestication Processes

The domestication of new media and information technologies involves a taming of the wild and a cultivation of the tame. In this process, domestic users decide to buy (or not to buy) new technologies and services which are marketed as being 'user-friendly', although they are still unfamiliar—exciting but also threatening. They are bought or subscribed to, understood or misunderstood, used or rejected. In their ownership and their appropriation into the culture of family or household and the routines of everyday life, they are at the same time cultivated. They become familiar and are moulded and shaped to fit the expectations and values of the household. At the same time, and in that very moulding and shaping, the cultivator is also changed, as is her or his culture.

This process of domestication takes place in complex social and cultural environments: in the pre-existing and necessarily conservative cultures of families and households. New technologies have to be found a place, literally, in the home. They have to be fitted into a pattern of domestic time. They have, in short, to be valued. Such domestication is complicated by the social dynamics and politics of families and households. There are conflicts over use and location; ownership and control; rights to access. These conflicts are played out across the differences between generation and gender—as adults seek to control the media activities of their children, and boys and girls vie for control over the latest machine.

There are anxieties to be dealt with: anxieties about the disruption a new technology might create for the security of familiar routines and rituals; the challenges it might present to an individual's competence or skill; or the threat it might pose to the moral values of the family. The pressures to accept, reject, and modify the meaning of a new technology or service are not generated only by the politics of domestic life. They also come from conflicts between domestic and public values: from, for example, the competing claims of parents or peer groups, or the incompatible demands of family and work responsibilities (see also Silverstone 1994c).

It is in this sense that the 'multimedia revolution' in all its contradictions must also be seen as a 'domestic revolution', albeit on a different scale and within a different timeframe. It is in this sense too that what goes on in the everyday lives of all of us is a necessary part of the story. Answers to the crucial question of who mediates the media lie as much in the soil of everyday life as they do in the laboratories of the engineers, the offices of the regulators, or the studios of the advertisers and programme makers. The next two subsections dig a little more deeply into that soil through two brief case studies taken from research into the role and meaning of ICTs which covered a diverse social range—professional and clerical; employed, self-employed and underemployed; male and female.[5]

The High-Achieving, High-Tech Teleworkers

Jonathan and Emma Townsend live in a large house in two acres of rural Oxfordshire in the UK. Both have science or engineering degrees. They have two children: Geoffrey, aged eighteen, and Susan, fifteen. Jonathan works from home as a managing director with operations both in the UK and USA. Emma works from home designing computer software. Their combined income is over £100,000 and they vote Conservative. They have three separate telephone lines, one domestic, one business, and one fax. They have both fixed and cordless receivers, but no mobile; an answerphone, but no photocopier. They have three computers, two printers (one colour), and a modem for work use—but no electronic mail because of the amount of junk mail Jonathan worries about receiving.

Geoffrey has an old PC in his bedroom, despite the fact that it was bought originally as a Christmas present for all the family. This was typical of the presents they buy themselves in so far as it was expected to extend, and extend to, them all. Geoffrey has been a computer buff since the age of seven and his parents have promised him a £5,000 Unix workstation if he gets a place to read computing at Oxford. Susan plays the odd game on the old PC.

The Townsends have two televisions and a video recorder, used mainly for bought videos, with television connectors in most rooms. But the main television, which has teletext, is small enough to tuck away—and the old one in the bedroom is too fuzzy to use. These are supplemented by a hand-sized portable which Susan was given as a gift. There is talk of distributed video around the house and getting stereo sound, but they watch television relatively infrequently so do not express much enthusiasm for satellite or cable. However, Jonathan and Emma thought these new media could offer foreign programmes, which would help Susan with her languages. The prospect of home shopping and video on demand also appealed to the parents. Television was only really embraced when it involved activity and the opportunity to extend their control.

This is a household dominated by a work ethic and a self-confessed technophilia. Jonathan admits he is a workaholic. His arrival in the home four years earlier as a teleworker, together with the equally committed involvement of his wife, has transfixed the culture of the family. Their children are paid for the jobs they do around the house. Jonathan sets his wife deadlines for the tasks he asks her to fulfil. His life is dominated by the need to control his environment and his more or less unsuccessful attempts to maintain the boundaries between home and work, especially the temporal boundaries. His domestic life is fractured and disturbed by international telephone calls made and received at unsocial hours.

Emma's life is suffused by the deadlines set by both her husband and her own schedules for completing programming tasks. Family television watching involves, often, a shared critique of the rhetoric and argumentation presented on the programmes, informed by the family's reading of *Straight and Crooked Thinking* by Robert Thouless (1954). Jonathan sees his media and information technologies as a kind of therapeutic drug. 'I use technology to try and stay sane,' he says. The telephone and fax offer a modicum of managerial comfort in an otherwise intolerably frustrating working day. The television brings a degree of relaxation at the end of it.

But while their technology connects Jonathan and Emma both to a distant world and, to some extent, to each other, it provides a route neither to their community nor to their children. Both are fighting what they recognize is the increasing isolation from neighbours and friends which their teleworking promotes. And Jonathan in particular bewails his technologically intensified absence in the lives of his children. Meanwhile, equivalent technological skills and commitment to work have not affected the domestic division of labour. Susan is still responsible for almost all the household tasks.

This case is presented as neither exemplary nor representative. Nor is it meant to be a moral tale. But it is illustrative, I think, in a number of different ways. First, it reveals the power of a family culture to define the character of media and information use. It shows dramatically, but not exceptionally, how important the capacity to control the flow of information and images into and out of a household has become and how important it is for a family such as this one to be in control. It also demonstrates how teleworking can undermine familial closeness without to any significant degree altering the basic gender- and age-based structures of the household. Above all, it offers a dramatic example of the double life of technology, multiply expressed in the paradox of 'connective disconnection'.

This is not a case of new media technologies determining family culture, or in any direct sense transforming it. However, it is an example of the way in which a particular accommodation is reached between specific expressions of social and technological change.

The Low-Income, Low-Tech Lone Parent

Jackie Berry is a 37-year-old lone parent living with her ten-year-old son, Mark, in a two-room basement flat in the British seaside town of Brighton.

Her income from a part-time job as a school assistant is less than £5,000, though she receives family credit and housing benefit. She does not buy any newspapers and supports the Liberal Democrats. Her poverty is extremely constraining in a number of ways that have a direct bearing on both her use of media and information technologies and the consequences of that use.

Jackie is profoundly conscious of her financial situation. She has the sole responsibility for Mark, who is beginning to make increasing demands on her resources. Her involvement with advanced technology is nil. Mark has an old, no-longer-used Sinclair Spectrum computer and a more recently purchased Sega games console which Jackie bought as a Christmas present from savings made during her first year back at work. Their basic telephone is rented. There are two second-hand televisions, one colour and one black and white. The stereo is also second-hand. Both have walkmans, but Jackie rarely uses hers. They do not have a video.

The Berrys' relationship to these various media is largely determined by their limited housing space. The main television has found a place close to the dining table as the kitchen was too cramped. It is therefore on during meal times—regrettably as far as Jackie is concerned. Mark has his old black-and-white set in his room so that Jackie will not be disturbed too early on a weekend morning. In the evenings they watch the main set together. Television is a comfort and a companion, particularly for Jackie.

The impossibility of funding a baby-sitter and the cost of going out make Jackie something of a prisoner in the evenings. In this enforced isolation, occasional telephone calls and the continuous flow of the television provide company. But even this is a source of anxiety, since Jackie is constantly aware—as she hears the 'tick tick tick' of the electricity meter—of how much their involvement with the screen is costing. She tries to watch as much BBC as she can as she feels she must get her money's worth from her licence fee.[6]

Television is seen as a problem and a resource, although it is a resource of which Jackie is still not always able to take full advantage. She acknowledges how television viewing facilitates social interaction both inside and outside the home. Yet when the cooling of her night storage heaters once again raises her concern about costs, she is forced to go to bed early during the winter with a book, instead of the TV. As a result of these circumstances, she feels excluded from conversations at Gingerbread, her local support group for lone parents.

The main problems surface in her ambivalence about, and difficulty in, managing Mark's television watching. She discourages him from exchanging computer games at school because of the risk of loss or damage to someone else's game. In any case, as she points out, Mark seems more interested in computer games magazines than the games themselves—an indication perhaps of his being pushed by economic pressure to take comfort in a secondary discourse as a way of maintaining contact with his peers.

The telephone is seen as an essential lifeline and source of security, especially when Jackie is ill. She makes few calls, though admits her use increases when she feels bored and lonely. So far, Mark is not a significant user but she expects that will change. She has no desire for anything more sophisticated. The suggestion of an answerphone is appalling: 'Everybody will know if I'm out if there's an answerphone. Somebody might burgle me,' she comments. Jackie does not have a computer, but muses about buying an old one from the school. She sees it being used by both Mark and herself (she talks of writing letters and stories). But Mark is not that keen. He would much rather have something newer.

Jackie's case may not, once again, be representative in any strict methodological sense, but her circumstances are far from unique and they are not confined to lone parenthood. Her life with new media technologies is a life, as it were, without them. What she does have offers her a minimal way of keeping contact with the world beyond her front door. But lack of resources as well as lack of confidence powerfully limit her participation in a wider social and cultural life. For the Berrys, the telephone and television are technologies of survival.

Challenging the Visions of Revolution

Together, the case studies mark some of the limits of the social and cultural territory across which the multimedia juggernaut must pass. The impacts of ICTs on our everyday lives are not ones simply of bland, inevitable, or uniform acceptance. Their benefits are unevenly spread and often contradictory, their effects constantly mediated by the social and cultural circumstances of their use. They illustrate my analysis, which argues for multiple futures instead of one, thereby helping to challenge the integrity of a 'multimedia revolution' vision. Instabilities and uncertainties even within those alternative futures challenge the vision even more.

The enormous degree of uncertainty is most obvious when it comes to technological futures. It is often said that the technology of the future is available now, but its arrival is often a disappointment and premature

—as occurred with innovations like video discs, videophones, and teleshopping. Technological realities do not always match the dreams and the introduction of a new technology does not guarantee that it will be used in ways which its maker intended.

The more complex a system, the more vulnerable it tends to become. Multimedia interactivity, for example, offers a promise of genuine appropriation by users—consider the possibilities for otherwise passive consumers to send any videos they want to down the phone lines. Many consumers will have to be persuaded that they need what the new media will offer. Even a high-tech family like the Townsends rejected electronic mail and the mobile phone. So perhaps a certain amount of scepticism is justified. Careful consideration must be given to how specific applications of new technologies will be made to fit into our everyday lives, for example by providing local deliveries to supplement home teleshopping services. Old social habits die hard and there is no doubt that new technologies and services will be transformed in their consumption.

These uncertainties also intrude into the industrial story. To consumers, which of the big multinationals win or lose the competitive battles probably matters less than two other factors: the amount of media and cultural space made available for local, alternative, or individual access and use; and the effect of the dominance of the mass media market in our overall media environment. These have consequences for broadcasting's traditional role as a provider of the social cement in a nation's culture and for the continued survival of some form of public service provision.

Another form of convergence is needed to address all the issues raised in this chapter: a political convergence in the shape of an integrated national media and information policy. The possibility of establishing a coherent media policy has been fundamentally undermined by the uncertainty of technological trajectories, fragmentation of consumer markets, and, especially, the political reframing of media and information access as something to be bought rather than provided. An integrated media policy would not only have to confront the interdependence of many issues, such as the regulation of cross-media ownership, monopolies in the computer games industry, and equal access to telecommunications infrastructures for service suppliers. It would also have to take profound account of the social dimensions of media and information change, recognizing that access to media is a matter not so much of tastes or cultural difference, but of the nature of the political economy which defines the working of an industrial and commercial system (see for example Golding 1990).[7]

It is also a matter of the structured inequalities of life within

---

Box 12.1. Schoolchildren in the USA with Access to a Computer

....

At school

- 62% of whites
- 52% of blacks
- 52% of Hispanics
- 68% in households with annual incomes more than $75,000
- 53% in households with annual incomes less than $20,000

At home

- 43% of whites
- 16% of blacks
- 15% of Hispanics
- 75% in households with annual incomes more than $75,000
- 15% in households with annual incomes less than $20,000

....

Source: US Census (1993).

---

contemporary society. For instance, Box 12.1 shows the large discrepancies on racial and economic lines in the proportions of school-age children with access to a computer in the USA.

Such inequalities have also existed elsewhere, such as in the UK in the mid-1990s, where 52 per cent of professional households had a home computer and 98 per cent had a telephone—compared to 21 per cent of unskilled households with a computer and 73 per cent with a telephone. Similarly, a much higher proportion of professionals than the most unskilled owned more advanced ICTs, such as a CD-ROM player, Internet link, mobile phone, or satellite or cable link (OST 1995*d*). In the USA, there has also been a practice called 'redlining', in which some cable companies have cherry-picked prime residential areas for the roll-out of new or improved delivery systems and services.

Threats to the Quality of Life

These kinds of inequalities reinforce economic and cultural disadvantage by progressively denying those who are disadvantaged full political and cultural participation in a world which will otherwise become increasingly distant, irrelevant, and threatening. They reinforce my argument that media and information technologies are nothing if they are not social—social in production and social in consumption. If ICTs are to become increasingly the veins and arteries of a future society, then we have to find public policies and ways of imaginatively intervening in the market to make sure traditional levels of disadvantage are not increased and magnified.

At their core, these social dimensions of policy making must focus on the issues of universal service and public interest. Although media change in an increasingly market-led world will almost certainly offer greater choice, it will be choice at a price and only for those who can afford it. The quality of life for many is threatened by these inequalities because they could lead to a systematic alienation from the infrastructure of our society of those who are, for one or reason or another, systematically denied access to the ICTs and services which increasingly provide that infrastructure.

Media and information technologies by themselves cannot eradicate social ills—though they are often used as a way of escaping from their most immediate effects—any more than interactive computer voting on its own can remove endemic weaknesses in the democratic system. But their absence can substantially reinforce those ills and weaknesses while their presence can, at least, offer a resource which can be used to change things for the better.

Notes

1. This chapter updates and revises Silverstone (1994a).
2. The PICT-funded research on which the chapter is based was carried out at Brunel and Sussex Universities. It involved a series of qualitative studies into the use, and the consequences of use, of media and information technologies within a variety of British households. I am grateful to Dr Leslie Haddon, who carried out fieldwork for this research at Sussex and commented on earlier drafts of this chapter, and to Dr Eric Hirsch, who conducted the fieldwork at Brunel. For detailed reports on the research see Silverstone and Hirsch (1992); Haddon and Silverstone (1993); and Silverstone (1994b).
3. Some of the most succinct and relevant contributions to this substantial and inevitably inconclusive ongoing debate can be found in Harvey (1989) and Giddens (1990).
4. See Silverstone (1994b) for a discussion of how some of these issues precisely interrelate with the media.
5. See note 2 for the background to this research. The names in case studies have been changed to preserve anonymity.
6. Each British household with a TV set must buy an annual licence. The licence revenue is used to fund the public service BBC, which does not show commercial advertising. In 1996, the licence fee for a colour television was about £90 (US$140).
7. Chapters 6 and 13 expand on these issues.

13 The Cultural Dimension of Communication Technology and Policy: The Experience of Satellite Television in Europe

Richard Collins

Satellite television was one of the earliest manifestations of the way new ICT-based services can transcend the previously well-defined boundaries within which nation-states could develop and control their own information and communication policies. Satellite technology is also indicative of how economic and cultural issues become entwined in ICT innovations. For example, it has stimulated great expectations that large new global markets will grow which are capable of sustaining minority programming. At the same time, substantial fears have been raised that global media companies may dominate the market and undermine distinctive national cultures by appealing to the lowest common international denominator.

In this chapter, Richard Collins examines how these visions and fears have worked out in practice. He focuses on lessons that can be learnt from experiences in Europe, where many satellite television initiatives have been tried out in a variety of cultural contexts.[1] This underscores the degree to which national cultures have proved resilient to transnational programming and highlights cultural factors which should be considered in formulating and implementing communication policies.

Richard Collins

The Significance of Satellite Television

Satellite broadcasting is an important element in international information and communication infrastructures, which also encompass many other new media services and ICT networks like the Internet. Satellite technology is particularly significant because it lowers the costs of distributing television signals over a wide geographical area, which facilitates the transnationalization of television. It also makes available radio frequencies that were previously unusable for broadcasting over more conventional terrestrial systems.

These capabilities have greatly weakened the effective power of national governments and regulators to control the number and character of broadcasting services within their jurisdiction.[2] More specifically, satellite television has posed special challenges to three pillars on which broadcasting in Britain and many other European nations had rested until the 1980s:

1. **communication sovereignty** over services within distinct national markets;

2. **national regulatory control** over television content;

3. **national public service monopolies** committed to the production and transmission of culturally valuable and morally inoffensive programmes.

The effects of satellite television, however, have been different to those anticipated when they were first introduced in the early 1980s. The widespread fears raised then were rooted in economic and cultural concerns. Economically, the main anxieties were about the impacts on local audiovisual production industries when exposed to unregulated international competition. Cultural fears focused on the implications for social cohesion and cultural standards if there was a major change in the balance between programmes developed locally and externally. The cultural concerns were particularly important outside the USA, as American programming has been a strong force in satellite broadcasting.

In these debates, dystopian forecasts of pessimists tended to dominate— not least because established media interests gave much space to visions of destruction wreaked by the demonic 'space invaders'. The optimists, in contrast, fully welcomed satellite technology's power to dissolve national broadcasting monopolies and to accelerate the commercialization of broadcasting in countries where public broadcasting generally dominated the relatively small number of services then available. The optimists also saw opportunities, not threats, in satellite television's potential to target minority audiences in different countries. By agglomerating small numbers of such 'narrowcasting' viewers in many countries, it was hoped that a large enough audience could be found for specialized programmes and channels—such as educational programming—which would have been economically unviable within single national markets.

Europe provided a particularly fertile arena both for debating these issues and encouraging the introduction of satellite-based services into a variety of very different cultural contexts. This has given an opportunity to examine how a variety of complex and unexpected interactions between social factors and new technology shape the outcomes of new communication media. Before analysing that experience, it is therefore valuable to establish what is meant by 'culture'.

Cultural Attributes Relevant to Communication Technologies

British cultural critic Raymond Williams (1976) claimed that 'culture' is one of the two or three most complicated words in the English language. He distinguished three principal meanings of the word: a 'culture' that is drawn from husbandry and horticulture signifying rearing or fostered growth; an anthropological notion signifying the ensemble of practices and assumptions which distinguish one society from others; and a 'culture' which is evaluative and ranks different symbolic practices and works for their moral and aesthetic content. The last two are of particular relevance to satellite technology.

The 'anthropological' perspective of culture lies at the heart of many of the fears about satellite television eroding the distinctiveness of European culture and weakening social cohesion. This perceives culture as a bundle of attributes which integrate one social group and differentiate it from others. The attributes that unify and differentiate one culture from another were well characterized by T. S. Eliot (1948: 31) in relation to English culture:

> all the characteristic activities and interests of a people: Derby Day, Henley Regatta, the dog races, the pin table, the dart board, Wensleydale cheese, boiled cabbage cut into sections, beetroot in vinegar, nineteenth century Gothic churches, and the music of Elgar.

235

National cultures do not necessarily correspond closely to political structures and national boundaries, although there are undoubtedly politically sovereign states with strongly delineated national cultures. Yet even apparently clear-cut national cultures are qualified by a host of exceptions, such as the long-established international 'high culture' for which universal qualities have been identified. Indeed, this idea of a high culture has permeated much public service broadcasting in Europe—an idea based on an evaluative rather than anthropologically descriptive use of the term 'culture'. Instead of treating cultural characteristics as separate but equal social markings (some prefer cabbage boiled, others pickled; some their beer dark, others light), a judgement is made on their relative aesthetic and moral merits. All anthropological cultures are not equal if 'culture' is regarded as the 'best that has been thought and known in the world' (Arnold 1963 edn.: 70).

Most new communication technologies, from the book to the Internet, have at first been identified as a threat to culture in its anthropological and evaluative senses. Satellite television, for instance, has been seen as both a potentially powerful solvent of established collective identities—notably national identities—and a diluter of cultural quality. This has created worries among many that satellite television would be an agency of destructive cultural competition in which 'kitsch drives out kultur', by replacing 'high culture' public service broadcasting with what is sometimes described as 'mindless' populist programming of 'wall-to-wall' soap operas, quiz programmes, chat shows, and popular movies. This indicates that the very notion of 'culture' can become a block to clear thinking about the 'interpenetration of aesthetic practices and social processes and structures' (Corner 1994).

Why Europe was a Leader in Satellite Television Services

North American broadcasters were responsible for the main pioneering landmarks in the history of satellite television: 1962—Telstar, the first television satellite; 1965—Early Bird, the first satellite in geostationary orbit; 1972—Hermes, the first direct broadcast satellite. Yet satellite television take-up in Europe outpaced the medium in North America. For instance, true direct broadcast services—capable of being received through a 60cm diameter antenna—were established in Europe in 1989, several years earlier than in North America. This was because Europe had more to gain from an increased number of national services and from new transnational channels.

Radio frequencies for television transmission were in shorter supply in Europe, due to the large number of politically separate countries in close geographical proximity. Satellite television thus offered to extend European viewers' viewing choices. In North America, on the other hand, choice was being extended via cable television systems, which developed earlier, and satellite-linked cable television systems, for which high-powered satellites were not necessary. In Europe, transborder television also offered a means of realizing powerful political imperatives which were developing around efforts to consolidate the European Community (as the EU was originally known). These moves were strongly supported by the first directly elected European Parliament, which took office in 1979.

This was a time when the Community was continuing to expand, with Greece joining in 1981 and Portugal and Spain in 1986. Both the European Parliament and the Commission of the European Communities (the 'civil service' of the EU) saw transnational satellite television as a means of fostering European unity within this expanding political entity. Public service broadcasters and many European politicians also welcomed satellite television for its potential to disseminate European 'high culture' and to help forge a shared European cultural identity that would strengthen pan-European social cohesion. These factors helped to quicken the pace at which pan-European satellite television services were introduced.

Television and the Pan-European Political Vision

The relationship between culture, television, and the achievement of pan-European political goals was expressed succinctly by the European Commission (1984a: 10): 'By linking together European culture and the new technologies, which hold the key to future prosperity and employment, a European television policy is now a major imperative.' To support this, the Commission referred to a comment attributed to Jean Monnet, one of the EU's founding fathers: 'If we were beginning the European Community all over again, we should begin with culture.'[3] The momentum for satellite television in Europe started to build in 1982 (see Box 13.1).

The genesis of the EU's broadcasting and audiovisual policy was the 'Hahn Report' to the European Parliament (1982a), which eventually formed the basis of the Hahn Resolution (European Parliament 1982b). It presumed television to be a powerful form of social glue with the

Box 13.1. Key Events in 1982 which Helped to Build Momentum for Satellite Television in Europe

....

- The first directly elected European Parliament supports the development of pan-European satellite television by passing the 'Hahn Resolution'.

- The first commercial satellite television service in Europe is launched— the UK-based Sky Channel.

- The first trans-European public service satellite channel is launched— Eurikon.

- The Steering Committee on the Mass Media (CDMM), an intergovernmental co-ordinating body of nations extending beyond the EU, is established by the Council of Europe to ensure that the provisions of the European Convention on Human Rights, particularly in areas like freedom of expression and information, underpin the satellite television regime in Europe.

....

potential to bind the Community more closely together. The report argued that information is 'a decisive, perhaps the most decisive factor in European integration' and that the media, of which 'television is the most important', are significant instruments which 'serve to shape public opinion'. The compilers of the report hoped that, by bringing information about the political institutions and practices of the EU to its citizens and circulating the culture of Europe, television would engender a truly European consciousness and a collective European identity transcending established and limited national identities. That would foster support for the goal of 'ever closer union', as prescribed in the Treaty of Rome, which established the European Community. The Hahn Report felt this was unlikely to be achieved while 'the mass media is controlled at national level' (European Parliament 1982a: 8).

This report articulated for the first time the technological and cultural determinisms which have run through much of the EU's subsequent broadcasting and audiovisual policy. The technological determinism in the report is found in the way that particular social consequences are expected to follow from the commissioning of a new communication technology. The cultural determinism is indicated by its underlying assumption that the consumption of particular cultural artefacts will re-engineer viewers' perceptions of themselves and, thus, their collective identities.

The Hahn Report gave particular attention to the role of satellite technology capabilities as a catalyst in enabling the boundaries of the national television networks in Europe to be broken down and wider-ranging transmission areas to be created. That view was supported in the response to the Hahn Resolution by the European Commission (1983: 22):

> Viewers in one country will be able to share television programmes with viewers in other countries and will thus acquire a new feeling of belonging and involvement. This sharing of pictures and information will be the most effective means of increasing mutual understanding among the peoples of Europe and will give them a greater sense of belonging to a common cultural and social entity. The development of a truly European spirit will therefore become possible in national audiences, who will still, of course, retain their full cultural identity.

This vision was reinforced by the EU 'Television without Frontiers' directive which was adopted in 1989, came into force in October 1991, and has subsequently been strengthened (European Commission 1984b; 1986; 1994c). The directive made it illegal to impede television transmission between EU member states provided certain provisions are met, such as the duration of advertising, the protection of minors, and effective copyright controls.[4] The directive also attempted to help reinforce European cultures and industries against a perceived threat from the outside by calling on member states to try to ensure that at least 50 per cent of air time is devoted to programmes originating within the EU and that at least 10 per cent of their programming budgets is devoted to European works from independent producers.

Pan-European Satellite Television

A number of public service and commercial pan-European satellite television services were launched during the 1980s. They initially targeted 'shallow but wide' niche segments within the overall audience—small numbers of viewers in many places which would aggregate into an audience large enough to sustain the service. Public service channels aimed primarily to make a cultural impact, while commercial entrepreneurs—like Rupert Murdoch with Sky Television—hoped to achieve profitability for services which could not succeed in single national markets.

Public Service Channels

The first attempts to use satellite television to realize the political vision encapsulated in the Hahn Report were orchestrated by the European Broadcasting Union (EBU), an umbrella body of European broadcasters. Promotional material prepared for Eurikon reinforced the technological and cultural determinism embodied in that vision, for example in the statement: 'National identity fades away as common bonds are struck irrespective of frontiers.'

In April 1982 Sky Channel became the first operational satellite television channel in Europe. A month later, the Eurikon experimental service began transmissions in scrambled form to a select audience, mainly composed of members of the EBU. Sky and Eurikon started transmission from the European Space Agency's Orbital Test satellite, which used 'second-generation' technology based on relatively low-powered satellite signals that were generally relayed to viewers via cable networks.

Broadcasters from Austria, Germany, Italy, the Netherlands, and the UK each took responsibility for one week's programming on Eurikon between May and November 1982. Eurikon's programme schedule on its first evening gives a flavour of what pan-European public service broadcasters sought to offer their viewers (see Box 13.2).

Eurikon eventually developed into a full operational service called Europa, based in the Netherlands. It was transmitted to the general public and ran for a year between 1985 and 1986. Europa evolved into the EBU-sponsored channels Eurosport, which began in 1989, and Euronews, which started transmissions on New Year's Day 1993. The Franco-German culture channel ARTE is also rooted in EBU initiatives of the 1980s.

Commercial Innovations

Privately funded satellite broadcasting proved to be a high-risk investment and its viability was in great doubt at one stage.[5] This was reflected in the UK market with the establishment of BSkyB in November 1990 through the merger of Sky Television and British Satellite Broadcasting (BSB). In 1989 Sky had begun using Luxembourg's Astra 'third-generation' satellite technology to provide relatively high-powered signals which enabled transmissions to be sent directly to homes without going through a cable relay. BSB had begun such direct broadcasting in 1990. Shortly before their merger, Sky and BSB had accumulated total losses of over £1 billion.[6]

Box 13.2. Schedule for First Evening's Viewing of Experimental Eurikon Pan-European Public Service Satellite Television in 1982

1. Opening speeches by male European dignitaries.

2. About an hour and a half of 'high culture': a documentary on the composer Haydn (in German); an interview (in French) with the Romanian director of the Vienna State Opera production of Haydn's *Orlando Paladino*; and the first act of that opera.

3. Episode of the longest-running UK soap opera *Coronation Street* (in English), which was about celebrations of the Jubilee of Queen Elizabeth II and was preceded by a four-minute item on the Queen's visit to the programme's studios.

4. Thirty-seven-minute discussion (in French with English subtitles) on 'the lack of appreciation for the feminine' between a Dutch feminist, a princess of the Dutch royal house, and a French philosopher.

5. Fifty minutes of pop music, sung mainly in English, closing with 'Little Bit of Peace' (sung in Dutch, English, and German), which had won the most recent Eurovision song contest, a European Broadcasting Union event for countries across Europe.

6. A *World in Action* current affairs documentary from the UK.

7. A transvestite cabaret, *Mary und Gordy*.

Note: Dutch, English, French, German, and Spanish languages were used during the evening's programming, together with simultaneous studio interpretation into English overlaid on the original sound.

Within a few years, the fortunes of BSkyB were transformed, assisted by the acquisition of rights to major sporting events like the English soccer Premiership and Cricket World Cup, first-broadcast movies, and popular bought-in American series like *The Simpsons*. This helped BSkyB turn its operating losses of £47 million in the 1991–2 financial year into profits of £170.1 million in 1993–4 on BSkyB's nine-channel service, with the 1993–4 income of £550.5 million up 44.9 per cent on the previous year (British Sky Broadcasting 1994).

Variations within the European Television Market

Satellite television has become a significant force in Europe—by 1992 an average of 29 per cent of television households in 16 European countries had satellite television (about 32 million out of 111 million households).[7] However, impacts have varied considerably from country to country and have diverged from those anticipated by early proponents of the new medium. For instance, the percentage of television homes receiving satellite services was as high as 92 per cent in the Netherlands, but only 25 per cent in the UK.

Broadly speaking, Western European television markets in 1994 could be divided into three categories (*Screen Digest* Aug. 1994: 177–9):

1. **high** (more than 80 per cent of homes having either satellite or cable) —including Belgium, Denmark, the Netherlands, Sweden, and Switzerland, all of which have particularly high cable penetration;

2. **intermediate** (between 20 per cent and 80 per cent of households with satellite or cable)—including Finland, Germany, Ireland, Norway, and the UK, with varying mixes of cable and satellite penetration ranging from less than 1 per cent satellite and 40 per cent cable in Finland to 15 per cent satellite and 30 per cent cable in Germany;

3. **low** (less than 5 per cent new media penetration)—includes France, Greece, Italy, Portugal, and Spain.

Differences between National Audiences

In terms of audience ratings, the performance of satellite television has been more modest in some countries than the penetration figures suggest. In the UK in 1995, for instance, peak satellite programme ratings were just above one million, generally for major sports events and popular movies, which compares with typical peak audiences of fifteen to twenty million for the main commercial (ITV) and public service (BBC) channels and four to five million for BBC 2 and Channel 4.[8]

Several factors, singly or in combination, explain the variation in penetration of new media and in the balance between cable and satellite in different countries. These include relative levels of prosperity; climate (promoting or discouraging time spent indoors); the propagation of satellite signals (poor on the European fringe); levels of competition from terrestrial service; the size of the relevant language market; and, of course, different government policies towards the new media. Whatever the causes, broadcasting policy cannot be the same as it was in the days of traditional terrestrial broadcasting.

Satellite broadcasting was not the catalyst for establishing the pan-European television services that was once anticipated. However, satellite broadcasting has intensified competition within national (or, strictly speaking, single-language) markets and its transfrontier character has significantly weakened the power of national governments and regulators to conduct distinctive, independent, national broadcasting policies. Unfortunately for European unionists and proponents of pan-European satellite television services, the technological and cultural determinisms which have informed European policy deliberations have not been vindicated by events. European television viewers have proved to have dissimilar tastes, which makes it impossible to programme pan-European services in such a way as to attract a sufficiently wide spectrum of viewers for the services to be viable.

For instance, a Pan European Television Audience Research (Petar) study in 1987 of the UK-based commercial Super Channel, which programmed a 'Best of British' mix of repeats from UK terrestrial television, found a peak rating of 2 per cent out of a potential audience of 16 million. This was for *The Benny Hill Show*, which was very popular in Britain and based largely on a broad visual humour that might travel well across cultures. The audience share for this programme was as high as 6 per cent in Scandinavia, but it did not reach 1 per cent in countries like Belgium and West Germany. The top-rating programmes in each country also showed considerable differences.

Challenges Posed by Audience Differences

This illustrated a wider truth: that audience tastes are often so dissimilar that tailoring a schedule to attract viewers in one location can lose them elsewhere. In addition, pan-European satellite services have to face competition within each distinct national market from terrestrial channels which offer services in viewers' native languages and often have higher programme budgets than most satellite channels can afford (Collins 1992). The variations in audience shares between countries, even for individual programmes, suggest there are 'cultural screens' which differentiate audiences. These can militate against a unified European taste for television programming.

Such problems were a major reason behind the failure to achieve sufficiently large audiences for transnational services. This provoked a change in strategy from commercial satellite broadcasters when third-generation technology was introduced in 1989. The new approach was most pronounced at Sky, which withdrew from Europe and oriented its direct-to-home services to UK and Irish viewers—although it had previously invested substantial sums to achieve the highest access of any channel to transnational audiences. Super Channel effectively went bankrupt.

Pan-European public service channels, like the second-generation Eurikon and Europa and third-generation Euronews, were no more successful in building a viable pan-European audience. Indeed, the high-culture aspirations of these channels alienated many potential viewers. For instance, Eurikon services were felt to be worse than on each British TV network and Italian viewers' responses included terms like 'boring', 'worthless', and 'incomprehensible' (Gunter 1982: 3; RAI 1983).

The Influence of Culture on Television Viewing

The UK provides an interesting case study of cultural influences because satellite television, initially at least, had less impact on UK viewing habits and terrestrial television than in many other European countries. Britain shared general fears that satellite television would lead to a decline in television programming quality. These were intensified by the prospect of an influx of pornography and violence, given the relatively strict censorship laws in the UK compared to the USA and many of its EU partners. However, some culturally important historical factors were also highly influential.

The UK was exposed from 1955 to television competition that aimed to maximize audience sizes within an elaborate regulatory regime—about thirty years before similar developments in other European countries.[9] UK television planners and regulators sought to stimulate competition between the BBC and the commercial Independent Television (ITV) network of regional franchises, as well as between ITV companies. A dramatic fall in its share of the television audience shortly after ITV was launched stimulated the BBC to incorporate many popularizing initiatives from commercial television within its overall public service obligations. For example, its game-show formats were often borrowed directly from the USA and its drama became more oriented to the daily experience of viewers from a wider spectrum of society than the traditional BBC middle-class and high-culture emphasis.

The aspirations of UK television-policy makers were only partly fulfilled as the BBC and ITV acted largely as a duopoly until the 1990s. Nevertheless, British viewers were supplied with a set of choices closer to consumer demand much earlier than in other European jurisdictions. This gave the UK a lead in strengthening the popularity, diversity, and quality of local television production. This commitment was very different to that in most other members of the EBU, whose governments were almost uniformly opposed to broadcast advertising—and some even refused to accept any ITV contributions to EBU's jointly run Eurovision unless they were 'clean feeds' protected from advertising (Sendall 1982).

It was from these cultural roots that a distinctive—sometimes troubled—British marriage between popular and elite broadcasting cultures developed. This inheritance was an important reason why UK terrestrial television in the 1980s and 1990s was relatively resilient in facing competition from the satellite 'space invaders'. Its success highlights why outcomes from satellite television and other applications of ICTs cannot be explained solely in economic terms. The example is presented here to illustrate this point, not to assert a single-cause explanation of these complex outcomes or to defend unreservedly the traditional UK regime for terrestrial broadcasting.

Implications for Communication Policies

Economics is, of course, an important factor in shaping patterns of ICT investment and use. For example, the greater spending power of German and Scandinavian viewers has assisted the higher penetration of cable and satellite services in Northern Europe and the relatively low programme budgets of Swedish and Norwegian broadcasters have made terrestrial services in those countries particularly vulnerable to competition from satellite television. However, economic factors are only part of the full explanation of the variations in European satellite markets.

The UK experience exemplifies how cultural differences have accounted for key features of the history of satellite television throughout Europe. The general lack of success of pan-European satellite television initiatives and the preferences shown by many viewers for programmes made in their own country in their own language are other outcomes shaped by cultural dimensions. So is the growing appeal to viewers of American films, music, and other cultural artefacts, which has also led to a pronounced growth in non-European programming on European screens. For example, while national programmes often occupy top positions in the audience ratings, American has become 'the lingua franca of the European market of television fiction' and American programmes are far more popular with European audiences than those produced by European countries other than their own (Silj 1988: 199).

Richard Collins

Are Quotas a Viable Solution?

The extent and impact of the screening of non-European content became one of the most pressing and controversial international policy issues in the 1990s, for instance when provisions for the audiovisual sector were among the last to be resolved between the EU and USA in the GATT world trade negotiations in 1993. Jack Lang (1988), the former French Minister of Culture and Communication, forcefully stated European concerns in the EU's semi-official publication *European Affairs*:

> At a time when Europe, the cradle of Western civilization, loses control over one of the main areas in which contemporary culture is being made, the audiovisual, one can no longer react aesthetically to such liberal or ultra-liberal ideologies. Reality demands that concrete steps be taken.

The most contentious of the 'concrete steps' alluded to by Lang and taken up by others are revisions to the European-content import quotas for television, notably for satellite television. This includes proposed revisions by the European Commission (1994c) to the EU 'Television without Frontiers' Directive. However, there is much evidence that neither quota sanctions against imports nor subsidies for European productions will be enough to stop the Americanization process. For instance, the island of Jersey has offered facilities for European satellite programmers who wish to circumvent EU regulations (*Screen Digest* Sept. 1994: 193). Practical problems and inconsistencies have also arisen in the different ways that EU member states report information, such as in how data relating to specific channels are identified and in definitions of what constitutes an 'audiovisual work'.[10]

Guillaume Chenevière (1990), the Director General of the Swiss public service broadcaster, used his own experience to explain why a backlash from viewers could be a major barrier to the successful implementation of quotas:

> I had the idea of running a schedule *à la carte* where viewers would be able to choose a series each week from among a selection of some fifty repeats of French, British, and American productions. Not only were the American series the triumphant winners chosen by viewers, but they had considerably higher viewer ratings during the summer than those we had obtained with similar productions over the rest of the year. I was forced

to recognize the fact that American productions were preferred by our viewers, and that the problem was not one of imposing the European product but of making it competitive.

His conclusion points to the need for policies to address changes in the content, character, and perhaps mode of production in European television—rather than protection of, and support for, existing programmes and practices. The way a strong UK terrestrial base was nurtured through early experiences of competition and adaptation to viewer preferences lends support to this contention. However, European policy in the 1990s has generally not emphasized change in the character of European programming and practices. Instead it has focused on protecting existing structures and practices, such as through subsidies, while continuing to seek ways of using new communication technologies to foster a collective European cultural identity.

Combining Popular and Elite Cultural Goals

This chapter has explained why satellite television has changed the communication policy agenda irrevocably, although not always in directions originally predicted. However, new technologies do not in themselves guarantee success. Consumers are concerned much more with the character of the services they receive than the technologies used in their delivery. As discussed earlier, the demand patterns for satellite television in Europe indicate that national languages and cultures are strong determinants of what people want to see. It is also clear on the supply side that public service broadcasters have undersupplied more popular entertainment and overemphasized high culture, which appeals to fewer people.

Nevertheless, the intellectual matrix in which EU policy is made has remained, at least to the mid-1990s, that of the dual technological and cultural determinisms originally expressed in the Hahn Report and by the European Commission (1986; 1994c). Even though previous pan-European television initiatives have failed and future demand is, at best, uncertain, public service sponsorship of pan-European satellite television channels—like Euronews—has still been favoured. That commitment is based on the belief that there is a strong relationship between television viewing and the audience's developing perception of a tangible and desirable collective European cultural identity which could help to build more coherent European political and social structures.

Such national and transnational policies are likely to be effective only if they are based on a realistic assessment of what viewers actually want to see. This requires rethinking the traditional approaches to policy making in relation to satellite television in Europe. If satellites and other new media are to play a practical role in achieving pan-European political goals, more account needs to be taken both of the ways in which local cultures have been more resilient than many had feared and of the growing demand for certain kinds of internationally popular American-based cultural identities. The imposition of import quotas is unlikely to achieve this. An alternative approach would be to encourage local communication industries to find their own ways of providing distinctive programming that mixes popular appeal with more specialized cultural needs.

Notes

1. More background on Collins's research on the development and take-up of satellite broadcasting is provided, for example, in Collins (1990; 1991; 1992). The transnational and new communication media issues raised in the chapter are also explored in Chapters 6 and 22.
2. For a development of this argument, see for example de Sola Pool (1990).
3. For more on Monnet's views about European culture, see Monnet (1978).
4. Leonard (1994: 192–6) summarizes EU policy on culture and the media.
5. For example, my analyses of future prospects (Collins 1990; 1991; 1992) proved to be unduly pessimistic.
6. For more information on this background, see for example *Cable and Satellite Europe* (Oct. 1990: 8); *Screen Digest* (Dec. 1990: 270); and *Financial Times* (4 Mar. 1991: 8). All these are published from London.
7. GEAR (Group of European Audience Researchers) data kindly supplied to the author by Judith Stelmach of Oesterreichischer Rundfunk.
8. See the London-based *Broadcast* for weekly reports on viewing figures.
9. An official history of the early days of ITV is provided in Sendall (1982).
10. *Screen Digest* (June 1994: 133) offers a useful assembly of data on programme content on European screens.

14 Learning and Education in an Information Society

Michael Gell and Peter Cochrane

In Chapter 1, Christopher Freeman identifies the crucial role that education is likely to play as a source of future employment in many countries and as a key element in the evolving, sometimes turbulent, global economy—a central theme of national strategies for realizing the potential of new information superhighways. The following chapter by Michael Gell and Peter Cochrane presents a vision of how education, economic change, advanced telecommunication services, and the growth of 'knowledge' businesses are inextricably linked. They see this interlinking causing a transformation of education into a new type of industry servicing new international markets, having dramatic impacts on the established educational sector.[1]

Education in the Global Maelstrom

Education was one of the few sectors which remained relatively stable during the early decades of the all-pervasive ICT-based revolution which has been charted throughout this book. In the 1990s, however, education began to face the full brunt of a global maelstrom driven by ICT. This was because education held a near-monopoly on the important middle ground separating work and play in most advanced economies.

The way in which communications can change old ways by closing the gap between work and play was first demonstrated by the growth of teleworking in the 1990s. This kind of change makes the very concept of a distinct education sector become increasingly tenuous as community and customer requirements undermine traditional frameworks and institutions. Organizations designed to cope with stable environments and limited information flows find it increasingly difficult to cope as they move towards a new environment. In this, information, education, training, expertise, and ultimately, experience are expected to be delivered on demand at the time and place they are wanted—Just-In-Time (JIT), to use the phrase coined in the manufacturing industry (see Chapter 7). The assumptions on which such organizations were based in the past therefore no longer 'fit reality' (Drucker 1994).

Turbulence in the global economy, in which ICT plays a key role, is thus likely to trigger the absorption of much of the education sector into a new 'experience industry'. This will encompass sectors like entertainment and tourism and rely extensively on a variety of telecommunications-based 'tele-services' and the application of virtual reality capabilities. Such developments present immense opportunities for co-operative forms of global wealth creation.

They also mean many enterprises are having to adopt new organizational forms which must be resilient and able to adjust to new environments continually as all institutions have to become increasingly fluid, agile, and obsessively customer-facing in order to maintain direction and survive in intensely competitive markets. The growing uncertainties and shortening timescales in this global economy are challenging centralized organizations and structures in all their varied forms—political, economic, social, managerial, and technological (Handy 1990; Drucker 1992). Centralized control and management can no longer handle the vast and increasingly rapid information flows involved while at the same time allowing reflexive local decision making processes (Scott Morton 1991).

Turbulence in the global marketplace will continue apace as newer developing economies become comparable with North America, Western Europe, and other developed regions. The resulting escalation in the mobility of economic and technological activity across international borders will see bleak prospects for traditional industries and their old working practices. New flexible forms of industry are needed to succeed in the emerging 'super-advanced economies' operating at even higher speed than in the latter part of the twentieth century.

Telecommunications and Competition

The super-advanced economy will rely, initially at least, on a synthesis of manufacturing and servicing capabilities for 'tele-exporting' within global markets, as well as a variety of other new economic activities. The intensification of competition and rapid wealth redistribution will then become a day-by-day norm. In the transition, unstable enterprises will 'melt down' when their traditional organizational manifestations disappear. However, the people, money, and resources will metamorphose into many smaller organizations. The telecommunications industry was one of the first to do this when public telephone utilities with established national monopolies were transformed into large numbers of small, highly competitive, customer-oriented units.

The waves of meltdown will grow as digital technologies converge and competitors rush into overlapping new markets. The future of the global economy depends fundamentally on the ability to use advanced ICT capabilities to transfer and process vast amounts of information across geographical borders, markets, and organizations (Reich 1991). It is no longer possible to operate in isolation when communications across organizational and geographical boundaries become so easy and efficient. As a result, many 'virtualizing' services become feasible. For example, on-demand interaction at a distance can be mediated through 'telepresence' capabilities which allow users to experience multimedia information, communication, and processing as if they were 'real' entities. Telepresence further stimulates creativity, allows choice to multiply, and underpins advanced co-operative global wealth creation—while the inherent ability of telecommunications to act as a conduit increases with the growing capacity to combine different media.

The ICT revolution started in the factory and office, then entered the home in the form of integrated entertainment and information systems. As advances in chip, satellite, radio, and optical-fibre technologies further reach out to the car and individual, distinctions between work, education, and play dissolve (Gell and Cochrane 1994). The way business is conducted, economies are driven, and education is delivered will change dramatically as more people are able to choose where, and with whom, they carry out these activities. 'Virtual teams' can be located around the globe while working together through networked interactions. Programmes, projects, developments, creativity, and collaboration can then be non-stop and transnational, with rapid responses and very high productivity.

Transforming Education

Education is typical of those sectors likely to be caught in the second wave of meltdowns prompted by the increasing availability of communication and information capabilities. ICTs remove the constraints of distance, time, and location, which will undermine traditional educational monopolies and force a restructuring and revitalization as a new 'training, learning, and creativity' sector. In common with other industries, a hybrid of innovations both within and outside the sector will be needed to sustain growth through the global transition (Turner and Hodges 1992).

'Micro-hybridization' of detailed educational activities is evidenced by the widespread introduction of modular courses which allow the integration of previously separate subjects to meet specific industry, business, and lifestyle needs. In many technology areas, university degrees can become outdated within a few years. Lifetime learning has become a necessity and will replace the old pattern in which education occurred in school and university before a person started a career (Spoonley 1994). Meltdown in education is also likely to encompass all ages and bring remote capabilities into the home.

These developments are pushing education into extensive 'macro-hybridization', such as in the moving closer together of previously distinct education and entertainment activities to spawn an 'edutainment' sector fuelled by new consumer electronic products. Even traditionally stable domains such as mathematics and the classics are being radically changed through visualization, modelling, and animation techniques created to excite the individual learner.

Online self-learning packages fundamentally question the traditional role of the educator by giving students greater individual control. Effective learning can be realized by providing a student with a computer, loading the educational software, and walking away. As this becomes a natural teaching environment for younger people, it may be necessary to use only traditional methods with 'older' students.

Integrating the Learning Structure

New forms of economic activity must offer competitive advantages over those already established. If they do not, the hyperconnected global market will react quickly and bypass them. The requirement for new forms of activity indicates that advanced economies must invest new learning skills in their people. A super-advanced economy will work only if it is super-creative, with the ability to market and sell its creations rapidly. Economic activity relying on the deployment of unskilled labour is extremely unlikely to form the basis of healthy and sustainable social structures.

Unskilled, low-cost, low-value-added labour markets will be decimated, perhaps leading to the formation of economic and knowledge ghettos locked out from global participation and society. There is, therefore, a real prospect of the formation of a permanent underclass. The overriding requirement is for rapid and high-density learning, education, and training in support of the new rapid-creativity industries, many of which may be in, or very close to, the home (Gray *et al.* 1993). Hence education and training must be transformed into all-pervasive, boundary-crossing learning and creativity activities.

Many of the newly emerging economies have exceptionally young and massive populations, reinforcing the vital need for super-advanced economies to develop and tap the skills of every citizen. Future economies cannot afford the learning and creativity sector to be separate from the rest of society. It must permeate every aspect of society and embrace all of the people. Everyone must be given the opportunity to contribute.

Education Monopolies

In most industrialized countries education has evolved to become a monopoly employing relatively slow processes. These monopolies have been challenged by a global economic and technological turbulence. In addition, there is a substantial growth in the creation of advanced knowledge and innovation outside education in the 'knowledge businesses' (Hague 1991). The education sector is thus losing its monopoly on knowledge creation. In the UK, for example, all the university research programmes in the mid-1980s were totally overshadowed and largely outclassed by the industrial sector, with some companies investing more in R&D than government-sponsored Research Councils. The ratio of industrial to university expenditure and achievement is even greater in Japan, the USA, and some other European countries. Nevertheless, universities remain a vital and vibrant part of the system, although they provide only a small percentage of the total research activity.

Education is unable to contribute meaningfully in areas whose levels of investment necessary in the more sophisticated technological areas are too great. R&D can thus become rapidly denuded as companies seek relevant expertise and innovations beyond their national boundaries. In this situation, the involvement of all levels of industry in academic programmes is important, offering benefits to both sides. Academia brings a freshness that can be quite powerful, while industry exposes academics to the complex world of commercial R&D and operations. For example, it should be possible for students to link into industry through projects which present meaningful challenges at all levels. Work programmes should be farmed out as undergraduate and postgraduate projects, with sponsored R&D supporting researchers in industry and universities.

Knowledge businesses, with their life-long learners, have an important advantage over traditional educational institutions because their operating environment compels them to develop forward-looking and responsive capabilities. Knowledge businesses should see themselves and their customers in partnerships, with both partners playing the role of educator and learner. The synergistic relationship of education, training, knowledge, and business has become essential for their mutual survival and prosperity. The transformation of education and training will bring numerous opportunities to those active in building the new flexible learning and creativity structures. It will also provide new choices for the millions of new global customers waiting to be offered new telelearning experiences.

Virtualizing Education

Developments in multimedia, increased communication, and other ICT innovations are obviously key components of the information society. In this new era, managers must be prepared to abandon everything they know—and the same may hold for teachers, educationalists, researchers, students, and policy makers. Maintaining the *status quo* is not an option (Drucker 1992).

Numerous corporations and businesses have already become defunct or moribund through their adherence to the old markets and practices that made them. In contrast, other corporations are rapidly changing in structure and function as extended enterprises and virtual organizations emerge (Lyons and Gell 1994). These virtual organizations are not defined by physical space, but collaborative international networks linking people through integrated ICTs. For instance, the Integrated Digital Services Network (ISDN) available in many countries enables new modes of learning, working, and operation across a broad range of activities (Heldman 1988). These capabilities could make the 'virtual organization' the dominant organizational form, which is more about self-organization and emergent behaviour than planning and prediction. The advantages of moving to such a virtual approach based on tele-education and numerous novel partnerships to support training are key influences in transforming the education sector.

Technology developments needed to support such innovations can only be financed by diverting some of the enormous funds traditionally

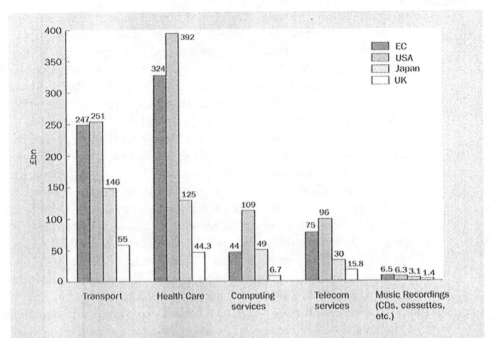

Fig. 14.1. Expenditure on Activities with a Potential for Diversion to Tele-Education

Note: All figures are for 1991, except for Music Recordings, which is for 1992.

Sources: CSO (1992); ITU (1992); Eurostat (1994).

spent on activities such as physical travel, health, ICTs, and entertainment (see Figure 14.1). Of these, physical travel is perhaps the least necessary, given its high cost in terms of raw material, energy, pollution, and time. Much of this could be avoided and largely replaced by ICT. Diverting into telecommunications-based activities even a modest percentage of this travel expenditure would enable considerable waste to be avoided through tele-activities.[2]

Revolutionizing Education

To appreciate the challenges and opportunities facing education, it is instructive to examine the specific case of education in engineering. This is one of the fastest-moving industrial sectors and has been a leader in promoting technological, managerial, and operational change. The accelerating pace of technological innovation requires engineering education to be more responsive to industry and society, while also becoming more cost-effective. However, a key problem in many countries has been the lack of critical mass, which has resulted in university departments having insufficient staff to specialize and treat topics in sufficient depth, keep up to date, supervise research students, and develop new courses and teaching material. Moreover, it is clear that the pressures will not recede. It is, therefore, inevitable and essential that more productive forms of educational resourcing are realized.

The best teachers are able to put themselves in the student's place and impart their own insight in a graphic and enthusiastic way. With the acceleration of technological development and subsequent broadening of all curricula, the professionals who are successful in this process are becoming all too rare across the breadth of education. This has been overcome to some extent in the 'hard' sciences and technologies by, for example, using mathematical and physical models combined with 'hands-on' experience which rapidly facilitates understanding. The process is far more difficult in other subjects, especially the 'soft' human and social sciences, where students face a bewildering and expanding complexity. At the same time, financial budgets are constrained, as are course durations and schedules. All this promotes the need for the quick fix and rapid turnaround, combined with pressures to become more efficient, as in other sectors of the economy. Perhaps the key issue is whether education is becoming more effective as a result.

Due to various factors, it is unlikely that departments with the necessary critical mass will be realized simply through the co-location or coalescing of existing smaller units. The danger is that the global economy is fast unleashing forces which will destroy departments, colleges, and universities in their present form. With staff numbers and funding pared to the bone, there is no visible fat. This makes the education system increasingly vulnerable. Nevertheless, there is an alternative approach to achieving order-of-magnitude improvements in the efficiency of resource utilization and the stimulation of new forms of creativity. ICT can bring students and teachers together for lectures, tutorials, and one-to-one interactions across geographic locations. Many experiments can be conducted on the screen, while visualization techniques can greatly aid understanding through simulation and modelling. Such an approach could revolutionize teaching, training, learning, and research.

Multimedia Enhances Education

There are many thousands of libraries and information sources accessible online. CDs also provide vast stores of information, such as single discs containing thousands of works of classical literatures including the complete works of William Shakespeare or comprehensive encyclopaedias. Interactive CDs can also allow students to 'visit' virtual museums, zoos, and landscapes so that they can make their own video-diaries of what they see. Such electronic capabilities continue to expand inexorably.

Compare this with the traditional world of paper. The US Library of Congress, for example, had about 24 million books in the mid-1990s and added new volumes which take about a further 3.5 km of shelving space each year. Libraries based on trying to keep pace with such volume and growth cannot be sustained. In most libraries, information is out of date, outmoded, disorganized, and irretrievable. The costs of physical searches are in themselves a major constraint, even if the existence of the required books or documents can be established. Online electronic libraries and CDs, on the other hand, can do all that much more quickly, at lower cost.

The most useful feature of a paper-based library, museum, or gallery is serendipity—the chance happening upon something you were not looking for and the fortuitous cross-correlation of thoughts and ideas. Electronic libraries are capable of achieving similar benefits. As computer and other display screens grow larger, for example, it also becomes possible to view multiple documents and pages simultaneously. The libraries of old are thus to be eclipsed as the traditional paradigm of the printed page is expanded into a virtual 'hyperspace' in which documents have multiple layers of detail, extensive and flexible cross-linking, and great adaptability. Multimedia significantly added video, sound, animation, modelling, and interactivity—while the technologies of telepresence and virtual reality introduce the richness needed to move from a world of information to an 'experience world'.

Since the Industrial Revolution, education has moved through all three lines of an old Chinese proverb:

> I hear and I forget
> I see and I remember
> I do and I understand.

We started with words, then included pictures, and finally experiments—as in university lecture theatres which traditionally have a demonstration bench right up front. Not so long ago, lectures and classes were commonly supported by physical demonstrations and 'hands-on' sessions. Sadly, that has become increasingly rare, thereby diminishing the effectiveness of much teaching. The reasons for this backward step can be found in the exponentially growing curriculum, the tightening economy, the fixed education timeframe, and static mindsets. Salvation lies with the technology itself—ICT allows a wide range of experiments to be on the screen. From the 1990s, many degree courses around the world have used the personal computer (PC) as a primary tool. To attend without access to a PC would be the equivalent of not having a pen or paper in earlier times.

Broadening Horizons

As the concept of using telecommunications to assist in education and training is increasingly accepted, environments incorporating dictums like 'you must have a PC to do a degree' and 'you must have PC skills to do the job' become intrinsic to more people's lives. Traditional educational assumptions must therefore be questioned by new educational options, as indicated in Box 14.1.

These transitions represent significant improvements over traditional methods in the utilization of educational resources, as well as indirectly assisting industrial competitiveness. In many cases, optimum benefits for individuals, groups, and communities will come from finding the most effective balance between these newer approaches and more traditional methods.

Virtual Universities for Real

Distance learning through ICT has been increasingly practical since the early 1990s, when successful experimental systems were established in many countries. This included the Open University in the UK, which in the 1960s pioneered the use of television for enabling mature students to get degrees. It conducted its first summer school over the Internet in 1994. In early 1993, the Robert Gordon University in Scotland conducted night-school classes over the telephone by broadcasting to over 250 students. In 1995, Stanford University in California launched its first online postgraduate degree course.

The distributed university clearly increases overall efficiency by teleporting students, teachers, and 'experience explorers' to virtual lecture theatres and environments. The notion that many students need to meet at the same physical place at the same time to watch one overworked teacher copy material from a book onto a blackboard, then allow it to

Box 14.1. New Educational Opportunities Opened by Advanced ICTs

- Lecturing and teaching do not necessarily have to take place in real-time. Interactive multimedia databases and lectures could be accessed around the clock from the virtual electronic classroom.

- Lecturers in numerous colleges and universities need no longer deliver substantially the same material. Instead, students and staff can be 'teleported' through telecommunications networks to common work spaces where they can interact. This releases valuable time which educators can use for activities such as research, consultancy, and generating new knowledge, understanding, and revenues.

- Students will not have to be constrained to one university. They will have access to hundreds of different specialists, units, and centres across national borders and will be able to select the best and most inspirational teachers.

- Student 'customers' can choose to build individualized courses engineered to suit their own lives, companies, and development. This could undermine national curricula.

- Education and training can become a major export business by teleporting educational experiences to other countries.

- Educational establishments can reduce investments in new buildings and halls of residence when their customer bases are extended globally, enabling state-of-the-art laboratories and libraries to be programmed, accessed, and shared in a virtual environment.

- School, college, training course, and university 'opening hours' can be extended to 24 hours, seven days a week through virtual enterprises offering simulation technologies, teaching aids, and computer-based self-assessment.

- Unhelpful distinctions between arts and sciences can be dissolved through the use of synthetic ICT-based environments which integrate teaching and research in disciplines such as choreography, acoustics, dynamics, and theatre design.

- Students in 'virtual universities' can also work as company associates who contribute to designing and constructing real systems and products, as part of a synthesized process of training, learning, and experience acquisition.

be recopied into many separate notebooks, is archaic in comparison. Students are also likely to fare better if they are treated to individual expert lectures by specialists in each topic, combined with backup from local or remote tutors, mentors, counsellors, and guides.

As part of the growing demand for perpetual learning, there is also an increasing requirement in industry for online first and higher degrees, refresher courses, and higher levels of 'instant' understanding, Company staff are often too busy to spare time to travel to a college or university. Distance learning allows them to mix and match lectures and tutorials to create a learning portfolio of their choice, at times that fit with their other commitments.

For example, BT started to implement this concept in 1991 in the form of a 'distributed university' which offered Master's Degrees via interactive lectures using Integrated Digital Services Network (ISDN) services, with students gathered together physically in common locations to access each class. In 1995 BT opened the first virtual university, which enables teams of students in different locations to use the ISDN for interactive classes and tutorials. Students generally find this helps them to learn quickly, explore new areas without limiting subject demarcations, and, perhaps most important, develop their teamworking capabilities. Classes, lectures, tutorials, and experiments for this virtual university are presented and prepared by many universities and industrial organizations around the world, selected because they are regarded as the best of the best—not just because they are close by and convenient.

As the global market becomes more competitive, the ability of organizations to bring teams together to tackle new problems for their customers will become crucial to survival. Business problems will come to resemble research problems as enterprises and their customers accelerate into the unknown. The ability to tap into virtual educational, learning, and training resources is thus a key strategic element. The virtual university, college, and school will be the hub by which learning organizations will begin to buzz with 'can-doism'.

Adding Substance to Virtualization

Simulation software and multimedia products offer animation, 'interactive theatre', and other capabilities which can help students understand and analyse complex issues. Experimentation and interaction with simulations on the screen also reduce the need for expensive physical laboratories. In addition, Artificial Intelligence (AI) techniques can be used to build systems that provide built-in expertise and knowledge to assist the student to learn or to create 'software agents' that anticipate their needs and are pro-active on their behalf. Such intelligent agents can, for example, search databases and libraries to assemble and format information which meets an individual's requirements, thereby freeing us to spend more time on productive processes. In medical systems, for example, a combination of all these types of automation is essential to enable the latest information to be sifted and symptoms correlated in order to identify causes, improve diagnostic accuracy, and provide effective treatment.

Telepresence systems enable students and experts to 'be there together' and learn, instruct, and guide in a wide variety of at-a-distance situations. These products are exciting, providing encouragement to all ages to enjoy learning. For instance, the CAMNET telepresence product developed at BT Laboratories enables people to learn, create wealth, and help others in ways unimaginable without modern communications (Cochrane *et al.* 1992).

CAMNET has a headset incorporating a microphone, miniature video camera, and display screen. The person at the far end of the communications link sees precisely what the user of the headset is seeing and can communicate verbally and visually through images and data sent to the user's display screen in the headset. All of these experiences can be augmented by traditional and other learning methods, such as those based on multimedia PC packages.

Examples of actual CAMNET applications include:

1. a student and expert communicating about chemical engineering—the student learns while gaining telepresence experience through 'tours' and plant 'visits' around the world;

2. a student of Egyptian archaeology and architecture taking a virtual visit to all the tombs in the Valley of the Kings and an architectural student exploring virtual worlds including new building designs;

3. a student and veterinary expert examining a horse, with the remote vet helping the student diagnose potential problems.

Educational organizations will atrophy and entire national or regional educational sectors will fail if they do not rise to the challenge provided by the powerful array of ICTs available. Other enterprises around the world will seize any opportunity to increase their own customer base. National boundaries will be increasingly bypassed as universities and companies provide education and training direct to customers through global networks. To be successful, economies must create and harness a distributed learning and creativity infrastructure using the technology and know-how available. This is the only way to tap fully the energies and abilities of all the people, each of whom needs to discover ways of learning, creating, and selling new skills which will help them survive in this advanced global economy.

Towards the Creativity Enterprise

People and organizations will need to be ruthless in their decisions about what remnants of the old systems and organizations should be perpetuated into new approaches designed to meet the needs of the emerging experience society. An obsession with keeping and doing old things could become a major cause of 'overload', leading to system breakdown. Universities are particularly vulnerable as they have little financial stock to cushion the mistakes of holding onto a great deal of unnecessary institutional baggage.

Most of these traditional methods were paper-based. This meant many people spent the majority of their time collecting and gathering information before being able to perform any analysis, gain understanding, form a view, take decisions, and act. Most of this work can be eliminated by recording, publishing, and disseminating information electronically and using software agents to do our tedious searching—rather than buying, consuming, storing, shifting, collating, filing, searching, stacking, burning, posting paper, and devastating increasing amounts of rain-forest. Instead, books, journals, lecture notes, business briefings, ideas, research results, business games, on-screen experiments, market analyses, animations, video, and other multimedia information can be handled in purely electronic forms.

Young people brought up with digital ICTs often exhibit a great excitement, willingness to learn, and ability to move into the new worlds of electronic information and experience. Older people frequently find all of this bewildering. Making the technology acceptable and friendly to those who are resistant to change, or find it difficult to adapt, is a vital ICT engineering objective (Cooper 1994). Technology must integrate seamlessly into our lives and surroundings to allow us to feel comfortable in letting go the habits of a lifetime.

An important characteristic of the ICT-based experience society will be the emergence of 'creativity enterprises', such as international virtualized education and training operations. The timescale for which a typical customer may be engaged with such an educational enterprise is likely to be shorter than that traditionally spent in a university, college, or school. The concept of a university having a monopoly over a customer for a period of three or four years will seem increasingly absurd. It will become the norm for people to use the services of a learning company for perhaps one or two hours—then move on to another for further sessions at times convenient to them.

In the experience society, we could accumulate thousands of different learning sessions from thousands of different creativity enterprises and individuals. The basic educational notions of 'term-time', standardized 'qualifications', and 'curricula' such as a degree may break down under such dynamic conditions. The development of round-the-clock creativity enterprises, including entertainment as well as education, spearheads the drive to acquire work- or play-related experience. This is being delivered by the services of an experience industry which is implicitly dependent on ICT for its opening up of international markets and wide-ranging possibilities for co-operative wealth creation.

Education is likely to be a focal point for the wave of economic transformations triggered by turbulence in the global economy. This is because the education sector straddles the traditional middle ground between work and play—and because virtualization increasingly mixes sectors, enterprises, and services to reinforce and increase the level of systemic integration in the global economy.

Notes

1. This chapter originated in the PICT lecture 'IT in Education and Learning: The Virtual University' given by Cochrane at the Policy Studies Institute, London on 14 Dec. 1994. He and Gell have substantially developed and updated the ideas contained in that talk.
2. See Chapters 11 and 19 for details of the research findings at Newcastle University on the geographical implications of ICTs.

15 Innovation in Public Service Delivery

John Taylor, Christine Bellamy, Charles Raab, William H. Dutton, and Malcolm Peltu

Cultural, economic, and organizational constraints on the diffusion of ICTs are starkly illustrated by comparing the way the technology has been used for innovations in service delivery in the public and private sectors. Although electronic information and communication media offer rapidly growing potential to enhance services in both sectors, from the 1970s onwards public agencies generally fell behind private enterprises in the way ICTs were applied.

This chapter explores key factors which help to explain why this has happened, identifying the main barriers to innovation and the most significant drivers.[1] It discusses, in particular, the different ways in which ideas about business process re-engineering described in Chapter 9 are being played out in public and private organizations in order to understand how technological innovation can be harnessed to assist in the management and delivery of public services.

Opportunities for Public Service Innovation

The public sector led many private enterprises during the 1960s in the use of computers for supporting basic administrative functions, including management information systems, payroll processing, and accounting applications. Subsequently, governments have tended to fall behind private industry, particularly in Electronic Service Delivery (ESD) systems that give direct access to information and services—a situation captured in a comment from the US Vice President Al Gore (1993a): 'When it comes to information technology, horror stories abound in both the public and private sectors. In some cases, the federal government is woefully behind the times, unable to use even the most basic technology to conduct its business.'

This situation is changing. Many innovative local and national government agencies around the world have begun to apply ICTs to a growing range of public services.[2] The specific objectives of such public sector ESD projects vary greatly but generally revolve around two main aims. One is to implement major improvements in the speed of response, efficiency, and accuracy of public services, often by emulating techniques that have been well proved in the private sector. The other is to bring government closer to citizens and to encourage broader and more active participation in decision making by developing an infrastructure for 'electronic democracy' capabilities (Chapter 16).

However, modernizing government requires more than simply employing computers and telecommunications in innovative ways. Managers must anticipate and respond to issues like privacy and public access—some of which are unique to the public sector—which threaten the effective use of ICTs (Bellamy and Taylor 1994).

New Electronic Approaches to Delivering Public Services

Modern relatively low-cost ICT networks, of which the Internet is one example, can lay a foundation for the development of a broad spectrum of decentralized communication and information processing opportunities on which a 'public information utility' could be founded.[3] Table 15.1 summarizes the main types of public sector ESD applications which started to be widely implemented in the 1990s.

Although changes in technology are an obvious springboard for these kinds of innovation, new ESD services are often based on technologies with a long tradition in public services, such as computerized administrative systems and databases. They also incorporate capabilities—like automated teller machines and electronic funds transfer—which have been proved over a long period in banking, retail, and other private industries.

For example, in one of the first experiments of its kind in the early

Table 15.1. Types of Public Electronic Service Delivery Applications

ICT Task	Sample Applications	Systems that Could be Used
Narrowcasting	Public meetings; education	Cable and satellite networks
	Up-to-date information (including multi-lingual)	The Internet; multimedia kiosks; CD-ROMs; bulletin boards; videotex
Transactions	Welfare benefits advice; electronic benefits transfer; payments for services, licences, transport, etc.	Multimedia kiosks; expert systems; smartcards; automatic tellers; electronic funds transfer
	Voting; referenda; public opinion polling	Interactive TV; voice mail; screen phones; the Internet
	Criminal parole checking	Fingerprint-check kiosks
	Electronic tax returns	Phone + voice check; PCs
	Road charging systems	Automatic vehicle monitors
Information retrieval	Access to government information	The Internet; online databases
	Answering routine public queries	Voice response; electronic mail
	Supporting public officials and professionals to deliver services	Executive information services; expert systems; electronic mail
Remote communication	Forums on public issues; help for voluntary and professional groups	The Internet; computer conferencing; bulletin boards
	Citizens' complaints, requests; emergency support	Low-cost access to ICT networks; the Internet; kiosks; voice mail
	Intercommunity meetings; consultation with voters	Video and audio conferencing; videophones; local cable networks
	Parent-teacher interaction	Voice mail

Source: Adapted from Dutton (1994).

1990s, the state of Wyoming in the USA introduced an electronic 'smartcard' as a means of distributing welfare benefits electronically instead of by paper. This 'Wyocard' is used for payments at a store's checkout counter as if it were a credit or cash card (OTA 1993*a*: 91). A microchip on the plastic card is encoded with data that enables welfare recipients to buy certain goods and the system can also automatically bar the card's use for buying items, like alcohol, which are not available on the programme. Similar approaches based on various forms of smartcard have subsequently been adopted around the world. The use of security checks, such as password codes or fingerprint checks, is being incorporated in a growing range of secure ESD applications which require personal identification of the user. The important questions about surveillance and privacy raised by such checks are examined in Chapter 16.

Multimedia Kiosks

Integrated ICT-based systems provide further opportunities for public service innovations. These capabilities are illustrated by the development and use for many different public service requirements of electronic kiosks which can include a personal computer and a variety of media for interacting with users, such as a keyboard, touch-sensitive screen, pre-recorded video, and audio and videophone. Moreover, some kiosks are linked to external computer networks to provide wider access to information sources and other services. Kiosks are generally sited in well-used public locations, such as shopping malls, libraries, and health clinics.

The diverse range of applications offered by such kiosks includes:[4]

- Direct access to a wide variety of information from local and/or national government agencies, covering topics like jobs, health, and the environment. These are provided, for instance, by INFOCID in Portugal and the multi-lingual Hawaii Access in the USA.

- Online transaction services as well as information. This is exemplified by Info/California, one of the first large-scale public systems to include transactions, like requests for copies of birth certificates or renewals of driving licences, using electronic security checks to identify individuals.

- Help with applying for services. Such capabilities could be based, for instance, on an 'expert system' containing knowledge about procedures to provide an automatic response or give information about where to go for further help, as in the Tulare Touch welfare-advisory system in Tulare County, California. A direct videophone link to a human adviser could supplement automatic responses. A number of legal-advice services have been developed, such as multimedia kiosks in Long Beach and Ventura County in California which provide automatic guidance on legal procedures, and the QuickCourt kiosk in Arizona, which can complete automatic do-it-yourself divorces.

- Access to both public and commercial services. Project Vereda in Spain is an example of this mix of applications. Its kiosks encompass facilities for public service information and transaction capabilities—like renewing a vehicle licence—as well as private sector facilities, such as arranging a private insurance policy or booking a theatre ticket with a credit card.

- Systems for individual agencies. Singapore Post's 'automatic post office' kiosk, for example, allows the public to weigh letters and purchase stamps automatically.

Box 15.1. Key Benefits of Electronic Delivery of Public Services

....

- Faster and more appropriate responses to requests and queries, including the provision of services outside normal office hours.

- Lower administrative costs, releasing the savings to enhance 'front-line' support.

- Access to all departments and levels of government from any location.

- More efficient and effective prevention of fraud or misuse of public services and benefits, resulting in increased public confidence in welfare and taxation services as well as saving substantial sums of money.

- Assistance to local and national economies by facilitating the government-to-business interface.

- Improved services to remote rural areas.

- Enhanced emergency-support services.

....

Source: Dutton *et al.* (1994).

Benefits of Electronic Service Delivery in the Public Sector

Apart from the electronic-democracy applications discussed in Chapter 16, ESD offers many benefits to the public as 'customers' or 'clients' of services produced by public agencies (Dutton *et al.* 1993; Dutton, Blumler, *et al.* 1994). These are summarized in Box 15.1.

Barriers to Innovation in Public Organizations

The US Office of Technology Assessment (OTA) warned that the potential public service benefits from ESD are often wasted because of failures in government policies. The main problems identified by the OTA (1993*a*; 1993*b*) include inadequate attention being paid to the human element in systems development; insufficient priority being given to the need for affordable, accessible, user-friendly applications; allowing the gap to widen between the advantages that educated, technically proficient citizens have over those less so; and failure to forge effective partnerships between government agencies and the private sector.

Box 15.2 summarizes a number of other barriers to innovation in the

Box 15.2. Barriers to Innovation in the Provision of Public Services

....

- Defence of functional organizational boundaries by agency 'barons'.

- Fragmentation caused when departments or agencies develop systems exclusively for their own clients, although integrative multi-functional and cross-departmental 'one-stop-shop' applications have greater long-term potential.

- Constraints and demotivation faced by champions of innovation in the risk-averse bureaucratic cultures which typify many public agencies.

- Overcentralization of government, leading to a weakening of local government and fewer opportunities for local innovation.

- Limited financial resources for introducing technological innovation.

- Anxieties among staff caused by fears of employment cuts, job reorganization, and geographic redistribution.

- Perception among many staff and citizens that cost-cutting is the overriding objective of ESD initiatives and that claims about improving services fulfil a primarily rhetorical role.

- A narrowly focused 'business case' for ESD investments that fails to identify as key priorities the kinds of benefits which will build a broad constituency to support the continuing introduction and use of new ESD applications.

- Negative reactions from citizens who do not want to be treated purely as 'customers' or 'clients' and who might see ESD as a wedge for the introduction of inappropriate business methods into public services.

- Experiences of past ICT failures, making users reluctant to be involved in new ventures.

- Difficulties in scaling up to larger operational systems from small pilot projects.

- Practical incompatibilities when communicating between systems in different departments, local authorities, levels of government, and private enterprises.

- Prevention of flexible, multi-functional uses of data by the introduction of privacy regulations in response to public fears about those uses of personal information held within ESD systems.

....

Source: Dutton *et al.* (1994).

public sector which have been identified by researchers, public officials, and others involved in attempting to implement novel ESD initiatives.

Organizational Constraints

Many of the main barriers to the development of public service ESD are organizational in character. Overcoming these barriers requires an awareness among all concerned that new methods of service delivery cannot be successfully implemented unless the organizations which support those services also take on new forms, just as many companies have sought to transform their organizations through Business Process Re-engineering (BPR) exercises (see Chapter 9).

Changes for which BPR techniques are being brought forward in public services seem, at face value, to mirror innovations in private enterprises. For example, the questioning of boundaries of conventional administrative structures and the forging of new business processes which integrate public service organizations and their customers are similar to the changes being undertaken in private companies where cross-functional organizational forms are being introduced to enhance the quality of services and products. Public service managers are therefore faced with distinctive and enormous challenges involving profound changes in the design and management of the traditional processes and structures of public administration. Increasingly, as in BPR approaches, the use of ICTs is advocated to facilitate organizational solutions to these problems.

In most discussions on ESD, the underpinning technologies have been given primacy as the source of quality improvements, economic gains, and opportunities for innovations. A simple and appealing linear narrative often follows from this viewpoint which suggests that the diffusion of ICTs will lead to a set of specific consequences of these kinds (Scarbrough and Corbett 1992). This narrowly construes organizations which have a responsibility for public service provision as 'production and transmission systems'. From this perspective, such organizations are seen as developing electronic services in response to requirements laid upon them by the political system or by professional interpretation of the needs and wants of customers—then acting merely as the transmission system to ultimate consumption.

A more complex perspective understands the nature of these organizations of governance as complex social entities, with a bundle of mediating forces acting as a set of powerful influences on the adoption, deployment, and application of new technology systems. Once this view is accepted, it follows that optimizing technology-intensive innovations like ESD requires organizational changes which will support, sustain, and successfully carry out those service innovations. This is a more holistic concept of change, founded on the intrinsic interrelatedness of organizational outputs—the services provided—and the organization itself. As service innovations are designed and prepared for implementation, so organizational changes must occur to support them.

Re-engineering Public Service Processes

This holistic view of organizational change has been widely recognized both through developments known generically as 'New Public Management' (NPM) and through the adoption of the language and methods of BPR.[5] The British Government, for instance, has explicitly referred to the importance of BPR in both sustaining, and moving on from, its first wave of NPM change programmes in the early 1990s (OPSS 1994). NPM has led to an increasing separation of policy making from administration, which takes the form, for example, of the introduction of 'market testing' of services by a process of competitive bidding to run specific public services—such as hospital cleaning, the transport of prisoners, or the operation of IT systems for public agencies. In addition, a greater customer orientation and commitment to targeted quality improvement goals were encouraged through 'Citizen's Charter' initiatives, a UK Government innovation which defines the levels of service citizens and clients can expect from public service providers (Cabinet Office 1991).

Similar NPM-style changes have taken place elsewhere in the 'developed' world and are creating appropriate conditions for a second wave of innovations involving a search for deeper changes in the organizations of governance. This began with broad exhortations and commitments from US Vice President Al Gore (1993b) to 'reinvent' government so as to serve its citizens more effectively and developed into the 're-engineering' approach that ascribes a clear and powerful role to ICTs in the enabling of organizational changes (Gore 1993a; Hutton 1995).

Much of the potential of ESD derives from systems which offer multi-service and information-intensive capabilities that require new coalitions between public and private organizations together with newly integrated forms of working within public agencies. This move towards more integrated structures and processes, at least in the form of 'back-office' administrative integration, reflects a key priority in BPR techniques as well as a fundamental underpinning for ESD. However, the twin logics of ESD and BPR raise two key interrelated issues.

First, there is the degree to which the hierarchical and functional structures of public administration are amenable to redirection. Existing organizational forms in public administration have emerged over long periods and reflect a particular vision of the necessary processes, norms, and values which should be embedded in governance, particularly in response to the demands of public accountability. Powerful resistance to change and fierce organizational battles will be more likely if this vision is abruptly assaulted through the application of 'hard' forms of BPR, crystallized in the exhortation of Michael Hammer (1990)—'Don't automate, obliterate!'

A second issue arises if public administration is taken as a supreme example of a knowledge-based 'industry', with public organizations as 'intelligent enterprises' (Quinn 1992). If this perspective is accepted, then that knowledge-base must be respected. At the very least, such a view suggests uncertainty about the desirability of Hammer-like obliteration strategies (Taylor 1995). Public administration has often been likened more to an art than to a science (Vickers 1965) because it is based on learning from the organization's history and memory as well as from direct experience of policy and administration. To 'obliterate' the existing organization through BPR is to run the risk that irreparable damage will be done to the knowledge-base of public administration and its unique repository of knowledge—its experienced workforce. The obliteration of existing organizations could then scatter or remove the intelligence resident in public administration.

Policies to Promote Successful ESD Innovations

Given this formidable array of forces and arguments set against innovation, it is critical to the success of ESD projects that government at all levels, including its senior managers, develop a clear understanding of the reasons for such resistance and bring forward appropriate policy responses. The following sections highlight the key elements that should be considered in formulating ESD policies which address the many deeply rooted barriers to change.

A Political Climate that Supports Risk-Taking

Successful innovation requires a willingness to take risks. However, traditional public-service cultures are 'risk-averse', in part because scarce public funds are at stake. A senior British civil servant has remarked: 'The only

273

risks I take are the ones I am confident are not risky.' An American administrator put it this way: 'People don't join the civil service to be entrepreneurs'.[6] Although the variety of ESD experiments in the 1990s demonstrates that there are many entrepreneurs and innovators in public agencies, change is likely to evolve only incrementally unless a political climate is created which promotes and rewards risk-taking.

Top-level encouragement is important in creating this environment and in giving legitimacy to innovatory ideas. The best-known contemporary example is provided by the Clinton Administration's development of policies to 'reinvent' government and promote the 'information superhighway', with both being seen as providing a top-down impetus for innovative ESD experiments (Gore 1993b). Other governments have developed similar initiatives (see Chapter 22). In the more traditional and common 'bottom-up' approach to technological initiatives, innovations in computing and communications were generally delegated to IT managers and departmental heads because they were rarely seen as innovations in the organization and processes of government. During the 1990s, awareness has grown that ICT innovations have such crucial implications for managing the organization and delivering services that they need to be overseen directly by the top-management team (see also Chapter 9).

Encouraging Local Initiatives

Risk-taking also has to be supported at local levels. Local agencies can more easily nourish innovations relevant to their communities because they are closer to the public, community groups, and businesses. In addition, the large number and diversity of local governments in many countries can greatly facilitate the emergence of innovative ideas, provided a political climate and organizational arrangements are established which will nurture them. Moreover, reorganizations of local government structures can offer a 'window of opportunity' for authorities to rethink and change the way they do things, including how they deploy ICTs (FITLOG 1994).

A major constraint on local innovation is that available budgets and resources may be too small to support investment in significant long-term innovation programmes. One way around this problem is to develop collaborative ventures and multiple funding sources, which could involve a mix of public agencies at the local, national, and international (such as EU) levels, together with private investments. It might also be feasible to establish a set of common funds, such as a 'Universal ESD Fund', to promote innovation in the development of applications.

Gaining Commitment to Re-engineer and Reinvent Government

There is little evidence by the mid-1990s that BPR has taken root in public organizations, indicating that the management challenge posed by many ESD applications has rarely been met. Unless a better understanding grows of the broader transformations of government which ESD makes possible, any exercises in 're-engineering' public services run the risk that at worst they will cause the severe dislocation to which we refer above—and at best they will merely rewrite old procedure manuals and result in narrow-gauge changes. This low level of BPR take-up in government, as well as the inability of BPR to deliver radical transformation in many large-scale business firms (Grint and Willcocks 1995), confirm the view that public sector organizations should be cautious about 'hard' approaches to BPR.

Strongly integrated forms of ESD can pose profound challenges in public services because they suggest that existing forms of governance may prove to be high barriers to the achievement of optimal benefits from using ICTs. BPR's apparent potential for lowering these barriers and enabling change and improvement will be realized only if the 'radical transformation' approach is adopted cautiously and if the existing strengths of public administration—its repositories of knowledge, skill, and memory—are nurtured.

Public sector change programmes are more likely to succeed if transformations are seen as long-term processes. ICTs should be used to create a readiness for organizational innovation, through the development of information and knowledge resources, in ways that are sensitive to the needs of its knowledge workers. In turn, public service staff should be trained to understand and communicate the nature of the new services they are providing and of the logic of organizational changes made to support them. Enhancing knowledge and encouraging organizational learning in this way will strengthen the foundations for the organizational changes necessary for effective ESD.

Making a Public Service Business Case

The traditional Cost–Benefit Analysis (CBA) techniques which have been the basis for making many 'business cases' for ICT investments have tended to focus on narrow financially oriented criteria, like the search for cost savings and improved efficiency. Such approaches do not encourage risk-taking, nor do they allow for vital investments where the financial payback is assessed over a long-term period of perhaps six to eight years. Whilst the setting of financial goals is essential in public services to demonstrate that care is being taken with taxpayers' money, the focus of appraisals of public sector ESD applications should be broadened so that genuine priority is given to identifying and meeting the needs of users and stakeholders.

This widening of vision should be assisted by the trend in the public sector to shift the focus of ICT projects from 'backroom' administrative support to direct improvements in the quality of front-line services offered to 'customers' and 'clients'. Citizens increasingly expect the providers of public services to offer the flexibilities derived from ESD techniques that are routinely applied in private enterprises, such as those in electronic banking. A new approach to justifying public sector investment should combine traditional, financially oriented, appraisal criteria with the need to take account of enhancing service quality, including the provision of tangible solutions to citizens' problems. For instance, should electronic support for one-stop services in welfare benefits administration be appraised only for its capacity to produce savings on the internal management costs associated with maintaining clients' files, or should such appraisal include qualitative intangibles related to improvements in customer service?

The complexities of this issue are highlighted by differing approaches to pricing ESD services. For example, in some instances government agencies pay private vendors for the running of some multimedia kiosks through per-transaction charges. This aims to give the vendors an incentive to ensure that their ESD systems are useful in practice. However, some types of application might actually *reduce* the number of transactions overall, for example by offering better initial advice. Other applications could increase (or be perceived to increase) public expenditure as they become more successful, say by encouraging citizens to take up more of the welfare benefits to which they are entitled. Where charging for individual services becomes more explicit and profit-oriented, it could be more difficult politically to support socially desirable but non-profitable ventures, such as schools' access to libraries and the provision of health information to low-income families.

The ESD projects which are easiest to get off the ground generally have a single focus, such as helping job seekers. Yet these projects could achieve less than is feasible unless they are introduced as part of a longer-term strategy of moving towards multi-functional applications that span departments and agencies.

Appreciating the Value of Champions and Sponsors

Behind most successful ICT projects there is usually a 'champion' with the vision, management skills, and staying power to steer the development. Champions in the public sector will need to be aware of the power structures of government and must be sensitive to the motivations of elected politicians and officials. They must be able to forge partnerships across the traditional 'baronies' represented by long-established functional and jurisdictional boundaries.

Champions can usually be successful in starting pilot projects, but they need the backing of senior 'sponsors' with political will if they are to have their systems introduced as mainstream applications. For instance, the INFOCID project in Portugal was brought forward by middle-level management in the Secretariat for Administrative Modernization, which is directly accountable to the Prime Minister. Having an appropriate sponsor can be particularly important for IT professionals. It is difficult to use specialist expertise and become agents of change if champions are isolated within a specialized IT department; particularly since, as explained earlier, ESD innovations require the redesign of service delivery, not just the purchase of new equipment or software.

In view of these substantial potential barriers to public service innovation, it is essential that ESD champions build a broad base of political support, including backing from citizens, community groups, public sector staff, and politicians. Sponsors and champions must align the disparate and conflicting self-interests of a variety of stakeholders, perhaps canvassing and debating the issues publicly to help mobilize opinion towards commonly agreed aims. These are formidable tasks which are unlikely to be realized easily or quickly. Their accomplishment may be assisted by educational and communication campaigns to strengthen the public's awareness of the potential of ICT in public services, for example by pointing to successful applications of similar techniques in the private sector or in other countries, and by directly addressing fears that are generated by the prospect of change.

Harnessing Private Sector Support

The private sector is a crucial influence on the electronic delivery of public services, as it acts to create familiarity with similar capabilities in daily life. These everyday experiences of electronic services establish benchmarks against which citizens may judge public sector ESD.

Furthermore, the introduction to public services of competitive tendering, privatization, and 'outsourcing' has meant that business ICT know-how is being applied directly to public services.

The take-up of technology is also stimulated by vigorous marketing efforts by ICT suppliers, for whom the public sector market is a major source of business, dwarfing most private markets even in a recession.[7] Suppliers can also provide direct support to public projects. For example, BT assisted the Scottish development organization Highlands and Islands Enterprise in building an advanced digital telecommunications network in the north of Scotland involving a total cost of about £20 million (Taylor and Williams 1990).

Policies to Encourage Success Factors in Public Sector ESD Projects

ESD can be applied to such a diverse range of services to the public that no single approach is relevant to all projects. For instance, some systems are large, long-term developments covering many functions, agencies, geographical areas, and types of users; others are small, self-contained, relatively low in risk, and have a limited lifespan. Safety-critical applications whose failure could threaten the functioning of whole parts of government have vastly different rationales from those which are peripheral to everyday operations, such as services offering access only to non-controversial information. Services provided for business users, such as the provision of online access to land records, have very different requirements from those offered to the general public. However, systems which collect and maintain personal information, for example to verify a user's identity, raise different concerns over access and privacy that are absent in systems which employ privacy technologies (Chaum 1992), or otherwise preserve anonymity.

Although this diversity makes it difficult to generalize about the success factors for ESD, analyses of the lessons learnt from actual developments provide widely applicable general guidelines, such as those highlighted in the remainder of this chapter in relation to key ESD-related activities and roles.[8]

Strategic Public Policies

In order to ensure that diverse ESD capabilities are harnessed effectively to meet overall goals, a coherent public policy framework towards ESD needs to be established. Such a framework would set out a clear vision which would provide a focal point for debate and action aimed at ensuring innovative ESD applications meet social as well as economic goals. To turn the vision into systems that meet practical goals, many countries and regions have developed a strategic framework covering all government levels which encourages and supports the use of ESD for delivering a wide variety of services to clients, and in some instances facilitates democratic political processes.

This strategic framework would co-ordinate telecommunications policies with those of closely related areas, such as regionalism, industrial development, employment, privacy, data protection, and regulation of the mass media. For example, policies which offer all citizens equitable access to vital facilities are crucial to gaining widespread commitment to such ESD innovations. The framework would also seek to develop charging policies for ESD applications which are anchored in principles that are defensible in the light of public service obligations, including provision for subsidized services. This could include guidelines on how, and under what circumstances, government information and services should be paid for by users. In addition, appropriate legislation and regulations could be developed in areas like editorial control over networked information, public access to information, privacy and data protection, and intellectual property rights. A clear distinction could also be made between the provider of ICT infrastructures and the suppliers of information and services on them.

Maintaining an appropriate balance between central and local responsibilities and services would be a vital aspect of such a strategy. This would include designing the technical architecture so that it is capable of delivering the mix between central co-ordination and local autonomy which suits each particular political and cultural context. As these requirements change over time, and as the ICTs supporting them are subject to continual innovation, architectures must allow for efficient and reliable system evolution. They must also be flexible and powerful enough to support the implementation of a broad spectrum of multimedia applications involving many agencies and organizations.

The Role of Senior Management

Top management in public agencies must provide strong leadership and guidance in implementing ESD strategies and priority should be given to cultural, political, human, and organizational issues. ESD applications should be promoted as a means of complementing and enhancing, rather than substituting for, traditional approaches to the delivery of public services. In addition, as we have seen, in building a business case for ESD account should be taken of public service factors as well as of the financial criteria common in business enterprises.

Overall, the aim must be to create a positive attitude towards ICTs in general and ESD in particular, while remaining receptive to criticism and open to debate about their uses and implications. Progress in developing ESD services can be facilitated if areas of common ground between political parties, such as improved service delivery and administrative efficiency, are clarified and distinguished from those which might cause divisions. This can be done, for example, in determining the balance between public and private service provision, or that between efficiency and equity.

Managing Project Development and Evolution

ESD innovation is best viewed as a continuing and iterative process. This process should include regular evaluations using relevant qualitative and quantitative criteria and the creation of a mechanism to help disseminate lessons learnt from ESD experiences among public agencies, communities, and business groups. Project plans should describe lucidly and specifically how technology can deliver the services required, including an outline of the main issues and options to be considered. Effective communication must be maintained between the project team and all the stakeholders who will use, and be affected by, the system. New ESD systems and their benefits should be explained clearly for potential users in practical and understandable terms, perhaps using multimedia awareness and training material.

The Importance of Grassroots Partnerships

Finally, a key element in effective public ESD projects has been the establishment of effective working partnerships among citizens, community groups, business enterprises, ICT vendors, and public agencies at all levels and across all functions. This has been particularly evident in the USA, where local agencies have taken a strong role in leading innovation. Such experiences have helped to establish an understanding of how to build a political climate which addresses this participatory issue effectively (see Box 15.3).

The forging of partnerships along these lines can, however, be

> **Box 15.3.** Guidelines on Supporting Citizen-Centred ICT Initiatives
>
> - Involve the grassroots: local citizens; community groups and other not-for-profit organizations; national and local government agencies; business enterprises; and all others who are significantly affected by ICT-based innovation.
>
> - Develop community infrastructures that can help facilitate the use of new electronic facilities, including the provision of adequate training, education, and implementation support, for example through schools, libraries, community centres, and town halls.
>
> - Set up a planning task force and explore ideas and alternative futures using techniques like community workshops and technology demonstrations.
>
> - In the pre-operational phase, ensure there is a co-operative development of operating rules and attempt to resolve key issues, like how costs and risks are to be shared. Pilot projects and demonstrations can also be particularly valuable at this point in testing participants' understanding of the system and the ease with which it can be used.
>
> - In the operational stage, scale up resources and clarify the roles and responsibilities of the selected lead agencies and participants.
>
> - Establish directories and other information about relevant public agency and electronic democracy services.
>
> - Ensure budgets are allocated specifically to support the above activities.
>
> *Source:* Derived from OTA (1993a: 105–32).

extremely difficult to achieve in practice. Some ideas generated at the grassroots may not coincide with the aims of senior policy makers, and vice versa. Champions of projects can become opponents if they feel they are losing control and that their original intentions are being marginalized. To avoid these kinds of problems, senior management must keep in regular contact with all constituencies in order to ensure key individuals and groups remain committed to achieving successful outcomes for public sector ESD developments.

Notes

1. The authors have used their own extensive research in the field in developing this chapter, which also draws on discussions at the PICT Forum on electronic service delivery in the public sector (see Appendix 2) as reported in Dutton, Taylor, *et al.* (1994).

2. Evidence of this trend is provided by a variety of studies by government agencies, public interest groups, and academics (Abramson *et al.* 1988; OTA 1993*a*; Doulton *et al.* 1994; FITLOG 1994).

3. The concept of a public information utility was first envisaged in the late 1960s (Sackman and Boehm 1972).

4. More information on the examples mentioned and other applications using similar capabilities is provided in OTA (1993*a*); and Dutton (1994); and FITLOG (1994).

5. See for example Davenport (1993) and Hammer and Champy (1993).

6. Quotations drawn from the PICT ESD Forum (Dutton, Taylor, *et al.* 1994: 7).

7. For example, according to Donald Marchand, Dean of the School of Information Studies at Syracuse University, $20 billion had been invested in ICT developments in 1989 by state governments in the USA and nearly as much—about $15 billion—by county governments in 1991 (Dutton, Taylor, *et al.* 1994: 9).

8. These guidelines are based on those identified at the PICT ESD Forum on which this chapter is based (see Dutton, Taylor, *et al.* 1994). The issues mentioned are also examined elsewhere in this book, particularly in Chapters 6, 16, 21, and 22.

16 The Information Polity: Electronic Democracy, Privacy, and Surveillance

Charles Raab, Christine Bellamy, John Taylor, William H. Dutton, and Malcolm Peltu

ICTs could have profound implications for politics and governance. The technologies offer opportunities for realizing visions of a new 'electronic democracy' in which government and citizens are brought into closer dialogue, as well as for enhancing opportunities for political organization and debate. For example, they can facilitate the forging of new 'virtual' groupings which transcend traditional social and political boundaries, like the city and nation. They can also give individuals access to information on a scale that adds substance to 'freedom of information' legislation. However, the same technologies could reinforce control and surveillance powers of centralized authorities which pose threats to individual privacy and democratic rights.

This chapter analyses the sharp divisions which exist about these issues and explores the emergence of an 'information polity' in which the development of tools for use in an electronic democracy is intertwined with those involved in the electronic delivery of public services. While Chapter 15 examines aspects related specifically to such service delivery, this chapter focuses on the wider issues of citizenship.[1]

Electronic Democracy in the Information Polity

The effectiveness of democratic institutions and processes could be greatly enhanced through developments in what has been called 'teledemocracy' —the use of ICTs to improve communication and the delivery of services to individuals and groups from governmental and political organizations.[2] A variety of trials and experiments have sought to realize this vision since the 1960s (Sackman and Nie 1970; Sackman and Boehm 1972). However, it has only been since ICT-based Electronic Service Delivery (ESD) applications began to grow significantly in the 1990s that this vision has come closer to widespread realization (see Chapter 15).

The prime motivation for many ESD initiatives has been to improve the efficiency and effectiveness of public services in furthering governments' obligations to citizens. However, these initiatives may also introduce significant second-order changes in the provision of 'electronic democracy' capabilities to enhance the quality of citizenship more broadly. ESD and the potential for electronic democracy are therefore intrinsically related factors in making ICTs central to all aspects of politics and governance. This may be leading to the emergence of the 'information polity', in which the use of a variety of electronic capabilities becomes a central feature of the relationships between government and citizens and among citizens themselves (Taylor and Williams 1991; Bellamy and Taylor 1994; Taylor forthcoming).

Within this broad interpretation, the term 'electronic democracy' can be seen as encompassing all the various ways in which technological innovations can be used to alter relationships between governments and citizens as well as in providing new communication opportunities among citizens. Two kinds of development are of particular relevance to these aspects of electronic democracy (Taylor *et al.* 1995):

1. The provision of improved support for elected representatives through enhanced access to expertise or information via ICT networks, like the planned installation of a data and video network in the UK to link Parliamentary offices in Westminster with government departments and the homes and constituency locations of Members of Parliament.

2. The support of efforts to enhance democracy by stimulating more direct participation in decision making through the use of electronic networks, as illustrated by the community information and 'digital cities' initiatives discussed in the next section. The establishment by the US Clinton Administration of electronic-mail links between the White House and

the public over the Internet, which has subsequently been followed by similar services elsewhere at local and national levels, are further examples of this.

Nevertheless, in addition to supporting greater democratic control, the technology could also undermine democratic values. One crucial concern is that access to the information should be equitable to help reduce, rather than widen, the substantial gap between information 'haves' and 'have-nots'. It was this concern which contributed to the advocacy by the US government's Office of Technology Assessment (OTA) of an information superhighway that would support advanced community-access networks, including better access for the citizen to the agents and agencies of government (OTA 1993a). But another danger, which is less often discussed, is the opening of new and enhanced avenues for the invasion of personal privacy and increased surveillance and control. These potential abuses can be avoided by timely and appropriate public policies and by the public's continuing awareness and understanding of the importance of democratic processes which rely on thoughtful deliberation and the protection of minority views against the tyranny of majorities. How this could be achieved is explored in the rest of the chapter.

New Tools of Electronic Democracy

ICTs provide the potential for a variety of capabilities that can underpin an electronic democracy in which there is wider and more direct participation in elections and other decision making processes than has been possible with traditional modes of political activity (Arterton 1987). The following examples give a flavour of the wide and ever-expanding range of new 'tools of electronic democracy'.[3]

In Amsterdam in the early 1990s, projects sponsored by public agencies included:

- 'City-talks', using a local cable television network for interactive discussions between politicians and citizens and for polling opinions;

- the 'Digital City' system for discussing political issues via Internet, with access available from terminals in public places (Schalken and Tops 1995); and

- the use of interactive links via TV sets to a voice-response computer to consult Amsterdam citizens on topics such as the city budget.

A great deal of innovation in electronic democracy also originated in the USA in the early 1990s. For instance, the Freenet system in Cleveland, Ohio was established with a networked information service offering customized services, including medical advice, information on bills going through Congress, and a real-time 'chat' function. At a Federal level, the White House's electronic mail (e-mail) capability enables citizens to send messages directly to the offices of the President and Vice President, while the 'Ask Congress' project for the House of Representatives has provided touch-screen kiosks for answering commonly asked questions and to get some public opinion feedback.

The Media and Democracy Project run by the Centre for Governmental Studies in Los Angeles included the Interactive Multimedia Political Communication initiative which, for instance, created a package of voters' information on a broadband test bed for the national elections held in 1994. This enabled voters to 'click' through full-motion video on candidates' statements, press conferences, endorsements, opponents' replies, and databases on topics like voting records and campaign contributions. Another project at the Centre has examined how ESD can offer information to low-income families on subjects like health, child care, employment opportunities, and job training.

In the UK, little had been done by the mid-1990s to provide citizens with interactive ways of participating in public decision making processes beyond some e-mail capabilities with a few members of Parliament and some government departments. However, more has been done in terms of electronic information provision. For instance, many government departments and agencies have established 'Web sites' on the Internet to disseminate press releases, ministerial statements, and other policy-related information. In addition, by 1994 about 120 local authorities provided electronic community information systems using videotex technology to disseminate information about local government, community groups, and other local facilities (Horrocks and Webb 1994). The most advanced of these, like Oxfordshire Council's OXCIS, have stimulated a major rethinking of the way local government agencies use and manage information—a process which, in turn, has caused attitudes to 'open government' to be reconsidered.

The stimulus for innovative local uses of ICTs in the UK has also come from groups concerned with community, educational, and economic development. Some of these highlight the ways ICTs can provide the technological basis for changes designed to bring economically, socially, or politically marginalized groups within the compass of the information polity (Bellamy et al. 1995). Manchester City Council, for example, has sponsored 'Electronic Village Halls' that offer people from disadvantaged groups access to ICT-based services such as e-mail, desk-top publishing, and online information about job vacancies and electronic trading. The South Bristol Learning Network has been funded by the government's Department of Trade and Industry with private sector support to exploit new kinds of electronic networks, especially cable, to develop opportunities for training and 'lifetime learning' within a relatively deprived neighbourhood.

Case Study: An Electronic City Hall

The practical issues regarding an electronic democracy can be illustrated by looking in more detail at the Public Electronic Network (PEN) in Santa Monica, California. PEN started in February 1989 with the aim of creating an 'electronic city hall' that would enhance democratic communication by facilitating local residents' access to public information, government agencies, and public officials (Dutton and Guthrie 1991). It is owned and developed by the City of Santa Monica, which has fostered a culture of participation in local politics (Guthrie and Dutton 1992).

Once residents have registered to join the network, they can access PEN without charge from a home computer or from terminals sited in many public locations around the city, where free training is provided. About 20 per cent of accesses are made from public terminals. Non-residents were also eventually allowed free access to the system. PEN users (known as 'PENners') are offered four main types of services (see Box 16.1).

Use of the network to communicate with others has generally been more popular than retrieving specific information. For instance, nearly half of the accesses to PEN in the first few years were to about a dozen computer conferences on public affairs topics. Surveys of city staff and PEN users also suggested that the system was of value in several ways. It stimulated discussion, allowed many facets of issues to be expressed, and provided communication with key opinion leaders. Moreover, it offered opportunities for new sets of people to become involved in local government, particularly those whose schedules or commitments would not otherwise permit them to participate (Guthrie *et al.* 1990; Dutton *et al.* 1993). PEN also seems to have overcome barriers to participation that are found in face-to-face and other, more conventional, forms of interpersonal communication. This further facilitated the inclusion of some who might otherwise be left out (Sproull and Kiesler 1991).

Compared to other residents of Santa Monica, PENners were more likely to be active and interested in local politics. The provision of public

---

Box 16.1. Services Provided by the Public Electronic Network (PEN) in Santa Monica, California

....

• Read-only links to over 250 categories of information, ranging from the council's agenda to details of how to obtain services.

• The ability to complete some transactions with the city, such as applying for a dog licence.

• Provision of facilities to allow citizens to send messages to city departments, public officials, elected representatives, and other PEN users.

• Access to a conference feature enabling users to participate in a wide variety of electronic meetings in which they can read entries already in the system and add their own comments on a wide variety of topics, ranging from local and national public affairs issues such as homelessness to specialist interests like Star Trek.

....

---

terminals helped the city to create a community of participants that was more diverse than the population of home-computer users. For example, PENners have included the unemployed as well as managers and professionals, the homeless as well as home owners and renters, and a larger proportion of women than would have been expected on the basis of computer ownership, although the majority of users have been male (Guthrie *et al.* 1990). Although fewer than 5 per cent of Santa Monica's population of about 87,000 have registered to use the system at any one time, this represents about 10 per cent of households and a far greater number than proponents originally expected. In addition, PEN was able to sustain from four to six hundred active users in any given month, at least during its early years. That is a large group compared to the numbers participating directly in local public affairs as measured, for example, by attendances at council meetings.

Notwithstanding these benefits, a number of citizens and public officials became disenchanted with interpersonal communication over PEN, particularly the conferences and forums. Their main concern was the lack of civility, such as occasional personal attacks and the use of obscenities (Dutton 1996). Over time, the city de-emphasized the role of PEN in supporting communication among citizens through e-mail and forums. Instead, it focused more attention on the use of PEN to support the dissemination of information and the provision of services, for instance by making the service available through multimedia kiosks and the Internet's World Wide Web. These innovations build on technological trends in ESD and move PEN away from earlier visions of an electronic city hall.

The experience with PEN helps to illustrate a crucial question relating to ICT-based electronic democracy developments: Who can contribute to decisions about priorities in the provision of electronic services? Citizens' initiatives and broad public acceptance were central to the launch of PEN. The close involvement of targeted users in the design and management of applications has also been an essential characteristic of other initiatives, like the Lambda project sponsored by the European Union's Race telematics research programme to develop multimedia terminals for rural communities in Scotland, Greece, Germany, and Ireland (Taylor *et al.* 1995).

Innovations to Facilitate Direct Democracy

New electronic tools could be used to make fundamental and positive changes in democratic processes by offering a significant means of overcoming a growing disillusion with traditional representative democracy.[4] For instance, public opinion polls have shown that those who believe government in the USA 'does the right thing' slipped from 62 per cent in 1967 to 26 per cent in 1992. A California poll in 1992 also showed that 50 per cent believed government generally ignores citizens; over three-quarters felt that too much influence was held by large interest groups and by contributors to political parties and election campaign funds.

Disenchantment with representative government has fuelled the growth of 'ballot initiatives' in the USA, where citizens vote directly on specific propositions. The number of ballots remained unchanged between 1900 and 1980, but since then the volume has grown by 400 per cent. In California such balloting has supported the reduction of property taxes, introduction of capital punishment, regulation of toxic materials, and limitations on politicians' terms of office. All these decisions went against the declared wishes of elected representatives.

This long-term trend in the USA has also become evident elsewhere in the world. Electronic democracy could accelerate this because it has the potential to overcome some major failings of representative democracy, such as: imprecise choices offered to voters; weak control over politicians caused by the infrequency of elections; and the sometimes excessive influence of pressure groups. The deliberate use of ICTs to encourage direct democracy could lead to a fundamental reinvention of government, involving a shift from representative government to a more participatory democracy.

In an extreme version of this scenario, ad-hoc coalitions linked by multimedia networks would largely replace existing legislative bodies and the traditional functions of political parties. Multimedia interaction would be used to form broadly based panels to deliberate on public policy, instead of elite 'blue ribbon' commissions. Major impacts might result from such changes in the political process. The influence of financial backers of specific parties or candidates might be counter-balanced. The topics receiving attention on the political agenda would become more diverse because the capacity for handling issues might expand. Day-to-day government might be improved by providing citizens with more information in more accessible forms. It would be easier to highlight single issues and to increase the frequency and scope of polling citizens' views. Finally, the role of legislative bodies and public administrators would be reduced or altered.

The Challenges Facing Electronic Democracy

Potential Negative Implications for Democratic Processes

Whatever the likelihood of the scenario outlined in the previous section becoming a reality, the desirability of the changes envisaged by proponents of electronic democracy can be questioned. Sceptics hold that, despite the flaws in representative processes, democracy could be seriously weakened by problems arising from ICT-based electronic democracy innovations. For instance, electronic democracy could alter valuable and well-established processes of decision making in which consensus emerges from hearing what others have to say in debates, not just from registering opinions electronically (Laudon 1977). By putting citizens in direct touch with the centre, ICTs might cut out important consensus-building intermediaries, such as local political parties, community and pressure groups, and trade unions.

This process would remove the basis for deliberation which helps to create a sense of political community. It would also lead to a fragmentation of publics that would damage the development of a democratic consensus. The notion of people voting and being polled directly through electronic networks raises the undesirable spectre of 'couch-potato politics' and 'push-button democracy', in place of the possibilities for discourse and learning that are afforded by traditional democratic processes.

However, it is arguable that electronic media such as the PEN system can be used for the same purposes as are valued by supporters of these traditional processes. PEN was implemented in ways that supported dialogue and discussion, but discouraged voting and polling. This indicates that the fear of 'disintermediation'—the elimination of intermediaries—might be based in part on a simplistic view of technical options and a romantic view of the present, if not the past, because it has become increasingly difficult in practice to gather people together for public meetings and debates. The alternative to telemediated interaction in these circumstances may be no interaction at all.

Nevertheless, both sides of this debate agree that the interaction between citizens and groups is an important part of the political process and so should be encouraged when moving to ICT-oriented environments. Networked conferencing, e-mail, and other capabilities popularized by the Internet have been widely used on electronic democracy projects like PEN and Amsterdam's Digital City. Such facilities are seen by many as providing a positive practical contribution, mobilizing a 'virtual polity' that can give more power to individuals and groups. Yet the degree to which these new virtual constituencies of interest represent 'public opinion' is a key issue that will be difficult to resolve.

Developing Fair and Equitable Democratic Processes Using ICTs

It is possible for elected politicians to dismiss the results of electronic opinion polls on the grounds that they are unrepresentative. This has happened with some polls in Digital City, in the same way as traditional public opinion polls are routinely dismissed by interest groups and politicians on a variety of grounds. The fact that electronic networks are independent of location could also introduce new requirements to define who can vote on particular topics and how voters can (or should) be identified. For example, PEN was originally limited to residents of the city but its co-ordinators were continually challenged to expand membership to other groups, such as those working but not living in the city.

Some of the initial high hopes about the ability to send e-mail directly to politicians and civil servants began to decline when better-quality interaction did not necessarily result from the technical ability to increase the flow of messages. Instead, the practical limitations imposed by time, resources, and the commitments of political elites prevented more meaningful interactions. Although most letters sent to elected officials have always been handled by office staff in more or less automatic ways, word processing permits routine correspondence to be dealt with using more sophisticated automation capabilities, tailoring each response to the profile of the person who made the initial contact. E-mail makes it easier for some citizens to write to elected officials and enables requests and replies to be transmitted more rapidly. However, it does not create more time for officials to consider letters on an individual basis. Hence, many replies to e-mail messages have been standardized and automated, which has disappointed many who hoped it would make officials and politicians more responsive.

One of the most important features of electronic democracy is the use of ICTs to target the needs of specific client groups, both in terms of delivering services and in obtaining feedback. However, the benefits of tailoring of public services more efficiently are seen by some to be offset by the possibility that such differentiation is discriminatory and stigmatizing. ESD systems which rely on cross-relating detailed personal data to help target services could also be open to potentially serious abuses of privacy and data protection rights.

Arguments like these pose major challenges to the movement towards more direct electronic democracy. Technology itself will not determine the outcome. Policies must be formulated to steer a course between the dangers of popular impulsiveness and the elitism of unresponsive representative government. These must ensure that any newly emerging, more direct methods are implemented in ways that are fair and equitable for all citizens and that include protecting the rights of minorities.

Privacy and Surveillance in an Information Society

The growing use of ICTs in all walks of life means that increasing amounts of personal information are being gathered, processed, stored, and disseminated via electronic media. Ethical conduct with respect to these data is at stake as ICT networks spread (Forester and Morrison 1993). Many concerns are voiced about the degree to which their use contributes to invasions of privacy and to an unwarranted surveillance of individuals that is incompatible with liberal democracy (Lyon 1994).

Civil libertarians have taken the lead in bringing these concerns onto the political agenda and into the thinking of those who provide services or who pursue democratic goals through the use of ICTs. Nevertheless, it is arguable that many 'information superhighway' proponents and ICT suppliers and professionals have acknowledged privacy as an important issue more on pragmatic grounds (Raab 1995). This is because public support and trust in ICT developments is seen as being dependent on governments being able to protect essential privacy rights as part of developing the necessary conditions for 'capturing' personal data for public service, electronic democracy, and commercial applications.

Privacy Risks in a Changing Technological Environment

The early use of computers did not fundamentally change the record-keeping practices of organizations, as computerized systems often contained far less information than was held in equivalent manual files (Westin and Baker 1972). However, continuing advances in ICTs, coupled with economic, administrative, or political goals, have led organizations to make more fundamental changes in their information-management practices. These facilitate the collection and use of vast quantities of personal data, posing greater threats to the privacy of individuals (Laudon 1987; Flaherty 1989; Gandy 1993).

On the one hand, individuals willingly undertake an increasing number of electronic transactions for which they gain tangible personal benefits, such as payment by credit card. The collection and matching of information collected through different transactions and stored in different databases is an efficient and perhaps inevitable practice in commerce and public administration. Some have argued that attempts to prevent or control it could inhibit the growth of ESD, raise the cost of services, and thus be to the disadvantage of customers, citizens, and national economies. On the other hand, these information processes can also throw a net of surveillance over these same individuals by tracking their movements, purchases, work habits, and lifestyle preferences, often without the person's awareness and frequently in breach of rules or codes of fair information practice.

Resolving Conflicting Interests

A reconciliation between such conflicting interests is made more difficult because the public often displays ambivalent attitudes towards privacy (Dutton and Meadow 1987). For example, the use of personal data is frequently regarded as risky and needing regulation when it involves government, but is treated with less apprehension in commercial applications, where computerized data are collected through everyday transactions which are perceived as convenient and beneficial. Techniques that could be used for privacy-invasive surveillance and control purposes, such as personal identification numbers or fingerprint checks, might also be welcomed by some people if they prevented fraudulent use of their credit cards or reduced the chance of delivering services to the wrong individuals. The proposed introduction of personal identity cards into the UK (Home Office 1995) brought these matters to the fore, as it has done elsewhere.

The conflict of values involved in ICT applications is sharply illustrated by the use of a multimedia kiosk in Minnesota to ensure that criminals comply with their probation conditions. The probationer registers at the kiosk through a fingerprint identification device. His or her breath can also be tested automatically to check the alcohol level, although the person may not be aware of this. This type of system opens the door to many potential breaches of civil liberties, but it is typical of innovations that are being widely welcomed as many citizens give greater priority to efforts aimed at controlling crime. The growing use of video surveillance in private and public spaces is also indicative of an approach to the prevention of crime and public disorder which poses risks to personal privacy, but which is proceeding apace in many locations without widespread public debate about the trade-offs involved and without the development of adequate safeguards against abuse.

Another arena in which there are privacy-related trade-offs is the 'one-stop-shop' concept, which offers single-point access to a variety of services (Bellamy forthcoming), for example using a multi-functional, multimedia kiosk (see Chapter 15). The advantages of this approach are offset by the threat to personal privacy, as the rationale for many such systems is based on expected economic and service improvements derived from the efficiencies of communicating and sharing data across otherwise fragmented bureaucratic domains. Organizations in the public and private sectors involved in such integrated systems might follow information practices and adhere to rules in ways that vary, or fall short of the requirements of good data protection.

However, fears about invasions of privacy through increased computerization have lessened in many countries as the uses of ICTs become more commonplace in everyday life and are perceived to deliver real personal benefits, resulting in a popular willingness to accept trade-offs. An intriguing possibility is the 'privatization of privacy', based on the premiss that 'If someone is making money from data about me, why shouldn't I charge for allowing the information to be disseminated to others?' Yet the opposite is also occurring: the possibility of paying extra for privacy, for instance unlisting your telephone number from directories available to the public or installing 'call-line blocking' systems to stop the transmission of your phone number to be used for identification purposes (Dutton 1992c).

Formulating Effective Policies to Safeguard Privacy

There are many personal, commercial, and public service imperatives which are likely to continue to drive the growth and diversification of ICT-based services. However, this expansion, involving increasing interconnections between systems, will make it increasingly difficult to implement comprehensive regulations concerning the collection and use of information. At the same time, citizens' expectations that some safeguards will be provided to control what can be done with their personal data create an impetus towards strengthening privacy protection as ICTs expand into ever more applications. For this, there are a number of strategies on the policy agenda.

Data protection and privacy laws, principles, and guidelines aim to provide 'rules of the road' for the 'information superhighway', helping to establish good information practices without necessarily prohibiting information-processing activities. Such regulations have been enacted in a large number of countries since 1970 as well as in a Directive applicable to all members of the EU. These include controls over the following aspects of the operations of data users:

- the fairness and lawfulness of obtaining and processing personal data;
- the purposes for which data are gathered, processed, and disclosed to others;
- the adequacy, relevance, accuracy, longevity, and amount of data;
- the 'transparency' of the data operations, the accessibility of the data to the individuals concerned, and the remedies available for inaccuracy or for the breach of rules.

Although the physical security of personal information and the authorization of access to it are also important elements of data protection, the aspects itemized above go beyond them. They require decisions to be made about what kinds of privacy protection and control are not negotiable in order to prevent economic, administrative, or political imperatives from overriding all other considerations—and from transforming the 'information society' into the 'surveillance society'. Balancing these imperatives with individuals' rights involves many difficult judgements and decisions. Whether such 'balancing' is conceptually and practically possible, and who is to do it, are among the thorny issues to be faced (Raab 1993a).

In most European countries, this 'balancing' role is performed by an enforcement agency, such as the Office of the Data Protection Registrar in the UK, often accompanied by guidance and advice (Raab 1993*b*). These agencies, and the laws they interpret and enforce, are based upon internationally agreed guidelines and principles—such as those of the OECD (1981) and Treaty No. 108 of the Council of Europe (1981)—which seek to ensure data users apply the good information practices mentioned above. These arrangements might place constraints on ESD and electronic democracy applications. But the existence of requirements like the right to know what information is held on you and to correct inaccuracies could also help to gain the trust that is essential to make a success of these practices.

Such rules should ideally involve a consideration of their requirements at early stages of systems design, for example by allowing an option for anonymity of some information. If the ICTs used in specific applications—such as in highway control systems, interactive purchasing transactions, electronic polling, or call identification—are designed without taking privacy requirements sufficiently into account, individuals are likely to have their privacy invaded. Redesigning these systems to 'bolt on' data protection will generally be costly and disruptive. Self-regulation by the users of personal data is also finding favour and many codes of practice have been adopted by private and public organizations. Whether or not these codes are actually implemented is less certain, especially as specific actions are needed to achieve this, such as the training of relevant staff in the maintenance of rigorous privacy safeguards.

Finally, another strategy that is compatible with others mentioned is the use of encryption to address problems of data confidentiality, security, and access. Such 'privacy technologies' in the hands of individuals could facilitate privacy-friendly applications of ICT (Chaum 1992). However, the process of formulating effective regulatory policies at any level requires detailed analyses of who is at risk from privacy invasions, who pays, and whether those risks are fairly distributed between different groups. These analyses have scarcely begun.

Political and Cultural Dimensions of Electronic Democracy

Fears of Cultural Imperialism

The political implications of ICTs also include the cultural forces that can shape, and be shaped by, the use of electronic media (see also Schiller

1989 and Chapters 6 and 13). Many Europeans and others argue that American industrial policy has given US suppliers a strong home base from which to go 'cherry-picking' in high-income areas elsewhere, raising fears of 'cultural imperialism'. An example cited to support this claim is the building up in the 1990s of a strong presence by American companies in the provision of local cable networks in the UK (Dutton, Blumler, *et al.* 1994).

Critics of this view contend that American companies have been filling a vacuum created by British banking and other investment companies who have failed to invest in cable and other new media. Moreover, they argue that this inward investment has benefited the public interest, and that the location of the national headquarters of a company does not determine the look or feel of the technology. They claim that it does not matter who builds the 'black boxes' through which services are delivered because users will shape the applications. The growing availability of open systems, which lessen the dependence on any particular supplier, reinforces the argument that hardware, at least, is not a major problem in this area. However, some companies acknowledge the importance of cultural contexts by seeking to transfer their technological know-how to partners around the world who understand local needs (Dutton, Taylor, *et al.* 1994: 17–19).

The main fear which remains is that, by dominating the supply of communications infrastructures, foreign companies could determine the cultural content of electronic media. Similar anxieties exist concerning the computer programs which control ESD applications. The prime concern here is that ICT suppliers will use their marketing muscle to promote those television programmes, films, software packages, and systems which are most profitable to them rather than those most needed by local citizens and communities. Moreover, all software—not just television programming and films—can have cultural biases, such as in the use of the English language in computer programs that are not designed for multiple audiences.

Open Government and the Information Polity

Debates and discussions about electronic democracy illustrate the complex relationships between ICTs and political processes. While the introduction of integrated electronic communication networks offers the opportunity to make fundamental changes in long-standing organizational arrangements in government and to improve public service delivery, those same arrangements can act as powerful forces in shaping the nature of the 'information polity'. The social settings in which public ESD applications are developed and used will strongly influence the nature and results of the innovations. This is why there are many open questions about the implications of the use of ICTs, even when the technological potential seems clear-cut. One example is whether direct democracy or greater social control is best served by interactive communication networks (Van de Donk and Tops 1992).

It is insufficient simply to possess the technological mechanisms to access and deliver information. 'Open government' also depends on the degree to which public agencies wish, or are obliged, to make information available to citizens. 'Freedom of information' legislation, which would require government agencies to provide reasonable access to their records and to foster a culture of openness in public life and government, is therefore thought by many to be an important complement to public ESD strategies.

The political, social, and organizational forces which determine the outcomes of ICT developments and applications mean that new electronic relationships often fail to make the radical change to the fundamental order suggested by much of the rhetoric surrounding ICTs (Taylor *et al.* 1995). Conceptions and hopes about the information polity or electronic democracy should therefore reflect both the qualities associated with the revolutionary promise of ICT and the evolutionary nature of political systems (Taylor forthcoming). Even in periods of apparent revolutionary change, the strong forces for the *status quo* that derive from the institutions of governance and established administrative and democratic practices could powerfully determine the form of the information polity.

This point does not challenge the validity of envisaging what a radical new electronic democracy could mean, although it does suggest that realistic predictions cannot be derived primarily from extrapolations based on anticipated advances in technological capabilities. What actually happens will be the outcome of a struggle between proponents of change and of stability, each more or less aware of the opportunities and threats posed by technical change.

Notes

1. The chapter draws on discussions at the PICT Forum on electronic service delivery in the public sector (see Appendix 2). The report on that Forum (Dutton, Taylor, *et al.* 1994) has been substantially developed and updated to reflect the authors' own research.

2. This section draws on the extended discussion of teledemocracy in Dutton (1992b) and Taylor *et al.* (1995).

3. For more examples see Dutton, Taylor, *et al.* (1994).

4. Professor Tracy Westen of the University of Southern California's Annenberg School for Communication and President of the Centre for Governmental Studies argued this case strongly at the PICT Forum which is one of the main sources for this chapter. The views and statistics in the section on direct democracy are based primarily on Westen's comments and the information provided by him at the Forum (Dutton, Taylor, *et al.* 1994). For a broad discussion of the trend towards declining levels of trust in government, see Ranney (1983).

Part IV

Public Policy and Regulation: Actors, Goals, and Strategies

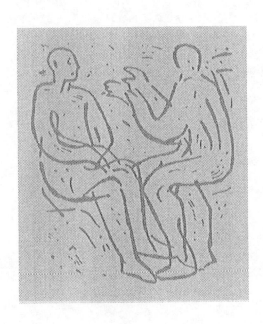

17 The Strategic Value of Policy Research in the Information Economy

William H. Melody

The evolving global information economy is based increasingly on the management and communication of information and knowledge using ICTs. Yet the implications of the fundamental changes in these processes opened by ICTs have often received far less attention than the technological opportunities as such.

In this chapter, William Melody explores the pivotal role that policy research can play in understanding how such changes affect the global economy.[1] He emphasizes that the implications of ICTs for society are great because of the close link between information and communication processes and the structure of economic and social institutions—a theme supported by a variety of contributions in this book, such as Chapter 11. It is therefore essential that public policy development *be* as 'informed' as possible, which will require the backing of appropriate research programmes.

The Importance of Public Policy Research

Major public policy decisions influence the course of development of the economy and of society, promoting some avenues while constraining others. They provide direction and guidance for day-to-day decisions by organizations and individuals operating within their ambit, which in aggregate have pervasive effects that ripple throughout society.

Although policy formation is often thought to be the prerogative of governments, in reality it is much more broadly based. Policy is made by those organizations which are in a position to make major decisions affecting the course of development of society. In modern capitalist societies, this means policy in some vital areas—say in relation to investment and employment—is determined as much by the larger corporations in key industries as by the central government. In most countries, a degree of influence over certain areas of domestic policy is exercised by transnational corporations, national governments of other countries, and international agencies.

Most new scientific and technical knowledge is obtained because of a sustained policy commitment to long-term programmes of research, often involving great effort and expense. But the knowledge from which major economic and social policies are developed is frequently not informed at all by new research, or even by research which already has been completed. There is a widespread belief that policy making on these issues is largely the implementation of personal preferences and ideologies, not requiring a serious assessment of alternatives or implications—a belief that received a major stimulus during the Reagan–Thatcher era in the 1980s. This lack of awareness by policy makers of the severe limitations of their knowledge about the economic and social implications of policy choices can make them oblivious to the need to undertake research in order to become more informed. Even worse, it allows policy makers to be wrong with confidence. As the American humourist Will Rogers observed: 'the trouble isn't what they don't know; it's what they do know that isn't so.'

Information, Communication, and Institutions

The structure and character of all institutions are significantly influenced by the state of information. Institutions are created from the development of a need or desire to share information, thereby cultivating patterns of interaction—of communication or information exchange. Institutions become structured in particular ways to achieve the desired internal and external information flows. The institutional structure changes when, for whatever reason, the communication processes and information flows are changed. And institutions die when the incentive or the ability to maintain the information flows and communication links ceases.

Informational Characteristics of Organizations

Institutions can therefore be described according to their informational characteristics. One way to study institutional dynamics is to focus directly on an institution's changing information and communication structure. Equally significant for economic analysis is the fact that institutions also generate information for the external environment that is then employed by other organizations and individuals for decision making. For any particular institutional structure in society, there will be an associated information and communication structure which will influence how that society functions. Some institutional structures will provide stronger incentives for the creation and diffusion of information than others. Moreover, the type and quality of information are likely to change as a result of changes in institutional structure. If institutional change is desired, it may therefore be necessary to change the information structure as a prerequisite to, or as an essential aspect of, effective institutional change.

The importance of information flows and communication patterns to the establishment and maintenance of particular institutions has been well understood, at least by some policy makers, since earliest times. Trade routes and communication links were deliberately designed to maintain centres of power and to overcome international comparative disadvantages. For example, Britain still benefits substantially from its historically established communication links with its former colonies, long after the empire's formal demise. Universal telephone service has been adopted as a policy objective in many countries to encourage economic and social interaction within the country in order to help promote national unity. The EU is attempting to foster a new European identity by promoting increased communication and information exchange as a basis for stimulating greater trade between its member countries and for the creation of both a European market and a European culture (see Chapter 13). Thus, those factors that influence information and communication structures are central to the study of all institutions—and are sometimes controlling with respect to economic institutions.

The Information and Communication Sector

The information and communication sector of the economy consists essentially of the new electronic ICTs as well as the more traditional forms of information and communication, such as libraries, publishing, and the postal service. Stimulated by rapid and continuing technological change, this sector has experienced a high rate of economic growth over a long period. Moreover, the direct economic effects are compounded by the fact that major parts of this sector provide important infrastructure services or enabling functions which affect the operation and efficiency of manufacturing, agriculture, government agencies, and almost all other industries and institutions. Many analysts believe that information gathering, processing, storage, and transmission over efficient telecommunication networks will provide the foundation on which technologically advanced nations will close the twentieth century as so-called 'information economies' or 'information societies'—societies that have become dependent on complex ICT networks and which allocate a major portion of their resources to information and communication activities.

The expansion of the information and communication sector helps to integrate domestic economies more easily into the international economy by means of efficient international ICT networks. As international economic integration expands, the impact of domestic public policies in all nations becomes more complex and their objectives more difficult to achieve. Control over the domestic economy by national governments is weakened. These developments are forcing governments to recognize the need for a full range of international trade policies addressed not only to direct trade in information and communication equipment and services, but also to the implications of world-wide information and communication networks for other industries.

In addition, growth opportunities are opening in a wide variety of information and communication content and service markets, trading in both public and private information. Although these markets are adding value to information, they are very imperfect markets which are often characterized by international monopoly. They raise important policy issues concerning government regulation of monopoly power in national and international information markets and government activities with respect to access by the public to traditional types of public information. Determination of the appropriate limits to place on the commoditization of information requires in-depth research, public debate, and the crafting of wise public policy if the citizenry is to be more informed—rather than less—in the information economy.

ICTs and the Limits of Markets

The convergence of rapidly improving computer and telecommunication technologies has had a profound impact upon economic institutions. The growing significance of electronic information and communication networks is fundamentally altering the nature of markets and the structure of industries, as well as the competitiveness of firms and the prosperity of regions. They are affecting the internal structure of organizations and the information environment through which consumer behaviour is formed. We can follow the latest strategic developments in the newspapers daily. But what is the significance of these developments?

When information and communication networks undergo fundamental change, traditional explanations of economic and social processes may be rendered obsolete. The new ICT systems are often more complex than the old. Ironically, in an age where information and communication systems are more sophisticated and comprehensive than ever before, the planning horizons for decision makers of all kinds are continuously being reduced because of a growing inability to forecast even short-term future developments. Seldom has a subject attracted such attention, yet yielded so little critical insight into its long-term implications for society.

Major technological advances in telecommunication are pushing back the extensive geographical limits of markets to global dimensions in an increasing number of industries. Major technological advances in microelectronics and the computer industry have pushed back the intensive limit of information markets by reducing the cost of generating more and more kinds of data. What are the implications of markets without geographical limits and of an enormous expansion of information in the so-called information economy?

Conventional economic theory would suggest that more information and better (and cheaper) communication can only improve the functional efficiency of markets. It should lead to expanded competition and an increased role for the market in allocating resources in society. More considered research and experience since the 1970s, particularly in currency and stock markets, suggest that this analysis is oversimplified. In particular, it suggests that improved information and communication networks may be fundamentally altering the structure of markets so that, at least in many instances, they become more unstable, function less efficiently, and play a less significant role in allocating resources. If this is true, stable economic growth and development will require an increased role for informed public policy direction of markets, resource allocation, and economic activity more generally.

The Extension of Market Boundaries: Theory and Practice

According to conventional market theory, an expansion of available information, together with enhanced and improved telecommunication, should permit more efficient decision making and the extension of markets across geographical and industry boundaries. This should increase competition. It should allow resources to be allocated more rapidly and efficiently. The conditions of real markets should approximate more closely to the assumptions of theory, where markets are frictionless and operate under conditions of perfect information. Indeed, much of the literature on the information economy considers these developments to provide unmitigated benefits to society (Melody 1985).

However, closer examination indicates that the benefits of these technologies are not likely to be distributed uniformly across markets; that certain segments of society will be made poorer both in absolute as well as relative terms; and that the structure of markets in many industries will be made less competitive. Although these new technologies permit many markets to be extended to the international and global level, it is the largest national and transnational corporations and government agencies which have the greatest need for, and the ability to take full advantage of, these new opportunities. For them, the geographic boundaries of markets are extended globally—and their ability to administer and control markets efficiently and effectively from a central point is enhanced. These changes have been a significant factor in stimulating a wave of mergers and takeovers involving the largest transnational corporations throughout the 1990s. The application of ICTs can reduce substantially the economic disadvantages of increasing administrative costs and reduced effectiveness of information processing and communication in very large organizations.

Oligopoly Tendencies

The manner in which these technological developments are being implemented opens possibilities for creating significant barriers to entry for all but the largest firms, thereby accelerating tendencies toward concentration. In fact, smaller firms in many industries are likely to find themselves disadvantaged because of the new technological developments. For example, telecommunication systems in many countries are being redesigned to meet the technically sophisticated digital data requirements of high-volume, multipurpose, global users. When it comes to traditional, simpler communication requirements—such as basic telephone services and narrowband digital services like those available on the Internet in the mid-1990s—the newer upgraded systems will serve quite well, but at substantially increased cost to smaller users.

Unless there is public policy intervention, the telecommunication options available to small, localized, and even regionalized businesses are not likely to reflect their unique needs. Rather, their range of choice among services and prices on the common telecommunication network is likely to be dictated by the global needs of the largest firms and government agencies (see Chapter 21). In a similar fashion, the terms and conditions for access to many new databanks provide substantial benefits to transnational corporations with high-volume information needs—but the costs are prohibitive to small domestic companies, non-profit organizations, and individuals, particularly in developing countries.

The new competition that has developed in most major industries from the globalization of markets is intensifying oligopolistic rivalry among transnational corporations. The firms which can leap across market boundaries are already dominant in their respective product/service and geographical markets. Their entry has a considerable impact on the structure of the supply side of the market just entered, which stimulates a major strategic response from the established dominant firm(s). This is not dynamic competition responding to the invisible hand of market forces reflecting consumer sovereignty, as assumed in economic theory. Instead, it is a type of medieval market jousting, an oligopolistic rivalry for the control of market territory. The rivalry is directed to obtaining a long-run position of market entrenchment and dominance in particular domestic or foreign national markets. Well-publicized illustrations of this are the strategic positioning of the world's largest telecommunication operators with respect to constructing fibre-optic cable links to households in many developed countries and of the largest media conglomerates to acquire the world's stock of entertainment video content.

Transnational corporations are often assisted in attempting to achieve these long-term dominant market positions by their respective governments, who sometimes even participate in international marketing. Thus, the oligopolistic rivalry among such corporations involves a strong element of nationalism and direct government involvement on both the demand and supply sides of the market exchange. This is increasingly evident in the continuing negotiations between Europe, the USA, and Japan about the conditions of market access in industry after industry.

In addition, adoption of the new ICTs has tended to increase the significance of fixed overhead costs in many industries, not only for information and telecommunication activities, but also with respect to greater centralization of functions and capital/labour substitution. For example, increased R&D and software costs in many areas are requiring significantly higher sales volumes to reach profitability. Therefore, the inherent instability in oligopolistic markets, long recognized in economic analyses of older industries like oil, is magnified by the instability created by an increased proportion of overhead costs.

Increasing Risk and Uncertainty

Taken collectively, the changes discussed above introduce new elements of risk and uncertainty into the economic system. However, the greater the geographical coverage of a transnational corporation, the more its risk and uncertainty can be diversified, although not for the particular production locations dependent on it. Indeed, major structural imbalances in regional economic development have been well documented by the UN (1994; annual), the IMF (1994), and the World Bank (1994).

These developments have dramatically exposed the contradiction inherent in the market theory that 'perfect' information may not, in fact, promote markets which function efficiently. Rather, with 'perfect' information markets may not function at all. Market exchanges recognize different perceptions—presumably based on different information—of the value of the items being exchanged. After all, there must be both buyers and sellers. As the range and diversity of their perceptions is narrowed by improving information and communication, greater instability may be built into the market system. For instance, if virtually all major financial analysts receive the same new information at the same time and plug it into what are essentially similar generic economic models, they are likely to reach the same general conclusion. A 'lemming' effect can then take hold, as was recognized first in the 1987 stock market crash and is being observed in increasing currency and stock market fluctuations.

The current revolution in telecommunication technology can be compared in certain respects with the effect which the introduction of the telegraph had on the structure of markets in the nineteenth century. For instance, a detailed study of these developments in the USA concluded (DuBoff 1983):

> The telegraph improved the functioning of markets and enhanced competition, but it simultaneously strengthened forces making for monopolisation. Larger scale business operations, secrecy and control, and spatial concentration were all increased as a result of telegraphic communications . . . increasing market size helped 'empire builders' widen initial advantages which at first may have been modest.

This assessment provides a useful benchmark for examining global developments in the 1990s. If the direction of change indicated here is correct, there will be a paramount need for sound public policy at both the national and international levels. The future global information economy is likely to require policy guidance and economic management of a higher order if reasonably stable economic and social development is to occur in the future information economy. Indeed, the 1990s have seen a major restructuring of the role of government policy in the direction of more specialized and sophisticated policy making at both national and international level. The role of government regulation remains strong, despite the rhetoric of deregulation and privatization that has been popular in many countries—and the many applications of these approaches in telecommunication, broadcasting, and other industries. In fact, the deregulation movement created many regulatory agencies, but abolished few. For example, the deregulation of BT in the UK required that the Office of Telecommunications (Oftel) be created to provide a more detailed, knowledgeable, and sensitive kind of regulation and general economic management of a more complex industry environment. By the mid-1990s, there were about a dozen new regulatory agencies created in the UK, several of which have jurisdiction over some aspect of the information and communication sector. The UK experience is representative of the trend in many countries.

At the European level, several steps have been taken toward the establishment of EU-wide regulation of both telecommunication and broadcasting. For example, the European Telecommunication Standards Institute (ETSI) seeks to facilitate the establishment of common technical standards in a fully integrated European telecommunication system. The EU is also increasingly active on matters of economic regulation. The USA has retained both federal and state regulation of telecommunications. Current debates about the future roles of international agencies like the GATT, GATS, and the new World Trade Organisation are really not about the necessity for regulation, but rather how best to adapt and restructure international regulation for the services and information-based economy of the future.

Research as a Strategic Resource

There has been a growing recognition that research capability may be a strategic resource which can provide significant benefit to the economy. Scientific and technical research has been seen as a stepping stone to the creation of new technologies which will provide firms and nations with a competitive advantage in the global market economy. The information and communication sector is viewed by many government policy makers as the key to national industrial and economic policies. Economic growth, employment, and the 'wealth of nations' are seen as following directly from investment in R&D applied to technological advance in this area. Massive research initiatives in Europe, Japan, and the US have been premissed upon an unwavering faith in a chain of causal links that connect R&D investment with economic prosperity.

Investment in R&D has actually become a competitive arena for the development of commercial strategies directed to achieve economic success in global markets. However, the chain of reasoning that links investment in R&D to scientific advance, technological development, innovative applications, increased efficiency, market advantages, and the generation of jobs and economic growth involves substantial uncertainty at every step. There is much more to economic prosperity than investment in R&D.

A second category of strategic research encompasses the human, social, and institutional aspects of the information technologies, including the effects of investing in technological R&D and of applying new technologies, and the range of economic and social implications. These technologies must be used by humans working in organizations for the efficient provision of public services or the efficient production of goods and services that will command acceptance in the marketplace. Research which examines the economic and social policy dimensions of changes in ICTs is as important to economic success as investment in technical R&D. There is no way that R&D can compensate for an inadequately trained labour force, inefficient management, unresponsive bureaucratic institutions, or inadequate understanding of market demands and social needs.

Historically, it has been extremely difficult for policy research to be undertaken unless the researcher is employed by, or is a consultant to, an organization that has a direct vested interest in particular policy issues, i.e. the government policy making agency or an organization directly affected by its decisions. It has been particularly difficult for most academic researchers, although they are in a unique position to provide a substantial contribution to the policy process in at least two important respects (Melody 1990).

First, the absence of a close connection with institutions having a direct vested interest in the immediate results provides a detachment that permits them to address the long-term societal implications of issues more thoroughly, independently, and continuously than even the policy making agencies. Second, by training and vocational practice, the perspective of academics should be more compatible with the conduct of research on long-run implications for society than that provided by any other institutional environment. For many types of policy questions, independent academic enquiry can provide an assessment of particular aspects of reality that elude special-interest research.

Due in part to the slow development of a significant body of such research by the mid-1990s, a great deal still has to be done in the development of a conceptual and descriptive map by which we can measure the size, structure, and implications of the information economy. Without this background information, neither policy decisions by government nor market decisions by corporations are as informed as they should be—or could be. This is certainly one contributing factor to the limited planning horizons that constrain both corporate and government decision making.

The major difficulty to date has been developing a thorough understanding of the important dimensions of information and communication policy issues, particularly when it comes to assessing the long-term implications. There has been a tendency for governments to recognize only those immediate issues which have been thrust before them, generally in fragmented fashion, outside either a long-term or a systemic context. There are, and will continue to be, many important issues of short-term policy that can be separated from the long-term total system context. Nevertheless, the unique aspect of developments in the information and communication sector is that there are so many fundamental issues that cannot be separated in this way. The long-term economic and social implications of information and communication developments provides the challenge for policy research.[2]

Growth and Development in the Information Economy

The concept of the information society owes much to the well-publicized speculations of Daniel Bell (1973) about the future 'post-industrial' or 'information society'. People working in such long-established and well-settled sectors of society as education, libraries, printing, consultancy, administration, and the entire bureaucracies of every organization in the world were suddenly reclassified as part of the information sector and transformed into pioneers in the progressive and futuristic information society.

Difficulties in Analysing the Information Economy

Did the information sector really grow without anyone recognizing it? Or has there always been a very large information sector? Its creation essentially was a relabelling exercise. But it did help to focus attention on the important and unique role of information in society. At about the same time, major studies of the US economy were under way at the US Department of Commerce (Porat 1971). This built on the pioneering work of Machlup (1962; 1980), which attempted to document the size and proportion of the labour force involved in the information sector. Similar studies were done in other countries, by the OECD, and by other organizations. These have demonstrated that a majority of the labour force in many industrialized countries is employed in the information sector (OECD 1986).

There is a serious difficulty in interpreting these statistics because they have not been developed within a theoretical or conceptual framework that permits substantive economic analysis. ICTs create new jobs, but they also substitute for old jobs (Freeman and Soete 1994). The substitution effect may be the greater—but surely the most developed information economy is not the one with the most bureaucrats and administrators. In addition, most information workers are also workers in other industries, including manufacturing and agriculture.

A widespread belief has existed that information technology has been providing a basis for major increases in productivity for the past two decades. Yet Robert Solow (1988), Nobel prize winner in economics for his work on growth theory and productivity, has observed that the information technology revolution shows up everywhere but the productivity statistics. There are essentially two conclusions that can be drawn from this. One is that ICTs have not provided a significant basis for productivity improvement, which mounting evidence appears to discount (see Chapters 1, 18, and 20). A second, which deserves more serious attention, is that the underlying economic theory is not capable of capturing the productivity effects of ICTs.

One crucial weakness of current economic theory in dealing with information and communication is the tendency to assume that it is both perfect and costless. Moreover, as a commodity it is almost impossible to quantify information output in any meaningful way. We can count printed pages, hours of television production, minutes of conversation, numbers of business lunches, and lectures. But these are measures of the information packaging unit, not the information content. It has been observed that what economic analysis needs is a unit of information comparable to the 'bit' from information theory, a unit of knowledge that was once called a 'wit' (Boulding 1966). Unfortunately, such a unit has not yet been defined. Clearly we have a long way to go in our attempts to develop an understanding of the evolving information economy and its implications.

The Economy of Knowledge and Learning

We might seek counsel from one of the founding fathers of economics as a basis for directing appropriate policy in relation to the evolving information economy. The first chapter of Adam Smith's *Wealth of Nations* (written in 1776), often cited as the philosophical bedrock of economic policy being applied in many industrial countries today, emphasizes that knowledge is the most important single factor in economic development. In simple terms, economic development is reflected in a growth in per capita output, which in turn derives primarily from an increase in the productivity of labour. Whether this comes from new technologies or from the greater skill, dexterity, and industriousness of the workforce, it represents an improvement in knowledge. Development therefore cannot be achieved by the simple accumulation of physical capital. It requires a change in the structure of both material and human capital which derives from an increase in knowledge.

Unfortunately, a recognition that economic development is primarily a process of acquiring and diffusing knowledge has not penetrated mainstream economic analysis. The economics of knowledge and of learning in the development process remain at the fringe of economics. It is not incorporated into the economic models that have traditionally dominated policy thinking and prescriptions.

Certain rudimentary principles would appear to be self-evident in any dynamic economic system. First, the total stock of knowledge is constantly being dissipated by changing social conditions, age, death, and, sometimes, emigration. Unless a programme of knowledge maintenance is in place (i.e. education and training), the stock of knowledge will decline, retarding economic development. Second, increased productivity and economic development require both the acquisition of knowledge and its diffusion throughout society. The acquisition of new knowledge is essential, but the major stimulus to economic development comes from its widespread dissemination.

In modern times, the rapid development of the USA and Japan, for example, has been associated with the allocation of a relatively large proportion of economic resources to the knowledge sector, with a major emphasis on diffusing knowledge throughout the population via a variety of formal and informal education and training programmes. Studies of productivity improvement in the USA since the 1940s attribute about 40 per cent to the maintenance and improvement of educational qualifications of the average worker and about 33 per cent to the growth of new knowledge, i.e. new technologies (Denison 1985). Despite evidence like this, the expansion and diffusion of knowledge across the population has not been the cornerstone of national economic development programmes in most countries in the 1990s.

Research to Assist Policy Decisions

As subjects of study and research, the core ideas of 'knowledge', 'information', 'communication', and even 'technology' have always been very difficult to grasp. They have been far too pervasive and elusive to fit comfortably within the conceptual framework of any established discipline—and multi-disciplinary efforts have had to proceed without a common theoretical foundation. Initiatives have therefore tended to be very limited and heavily constrained by the parameters of a particular academic discipline (such as biology, psychology, or information processing) or by a specific industry interest (like journalism, broadcast media, or telecommunication).

As information and communication have become more central to economic and social activity more recently, there has been a gradual recognition that these core ideas must be moved from the periphery of social science research to the centre. Moreover, new initiatives cannot be developed solely within the framework of traditional academic disciplines because the newly developing knowledge is also urgently needed by policy makers in industry and government. A number of major programmes, policy research centres, and other initiatives were established in the 1980s and 1990s to help shape the evolving core disciplines which will be central to education, training, management, policy development, and citizenship in the information economy of the twenty-first century.[3]

PICT's comprehensive foundation of research literature, which forms the basis of this book, played a significant role in policy debates on many issues in the UK and Europe, as well as acting as a catalyst for related activities elsewhere. For example, PICT researchers helped form a formal European network of research centres focused on ICT.[4] Later, an informal global network of researchers and research centres began working through the Internet. Despite such continuing activity, we still understand far too little about the essential characteristics of the information economy. However, there are some key things we do know:

1. knowledge as an economic resource will be more central to the information economy than to the industrial economy of the twentieth century;

2. sound public policy will be essential to provide guidance and direction in a more complex and potentially more unstable economic and social environment; and

3. economic and social research will be an essential ingredient to the development of informed public policy.

Those nations and sectors of the economy which establish a commitment to long-term policy research will have a clear advantage over those that do not. The serious pursuit of 'knowledge about knowledge' must therefore be central to all successful information economies of the twenty-first century.

Notes

1. This chapter is an up-date and extension of PICT's Inaugural Charles Read Lecture given by William Melody in 1988 (see also Melody 1988).
2. This challenge was taken up by PICT and an increasing number of research centres around the world.
3. When PICT was established in the mid-1980s, there were few social science research and training programmes focused on ICTs (Melody and Mansell 1986).
4. This group of affiliated research centres in the field, the European Network for Communication and Information Policy Perspectives (ENCIP), is headquartered in Montpellier, France.

18 IT and Economic Development: International Competitiveness

Kenneth L. Kraemer and Jason Dedrick

Christopher Freeman in Chapter 7 explains that the perceived 'productivity paradox' in the 1980s was based on evidence which—contrary to expectations that IT would boost productivity—pointed to a fall in productivity in some activities in organizations and nations which had invested heavily in the technology.

In this chapter, Kenneth L. Kraemer and Jason Dedrick argue that there was no longer such a paradox at the national level by the early 1990s, even if it appeared valid at an earlier point in time. They summarize their research, based on extensive cross-national comparative analyses and qualitative case studies, which shows a strong positive association between investment in IT and national economic growth. They also explain the implications of their conclusions for government policies towards the production and utilization of ICTs.

The Promise of IT-Led Development

There has been a growing recognition among economic development specialists that investments in technology can play a critical role in stimulating economic growth and productivity. The rapid economic expansion of Newly Industrializing Economies (NIEs) in East Asia is at least partially attributable to their investment in technologies to upgrade the productivity and competitiveness of export-oriented industries (Amsden 1989; Ranis 1990). The economic stagnation of other developing countries has been blamed in part on government policies which restricted the importation of advanced technologies from abroad (Lall 1985; Dahlman and Frischtak 1990).

IT represents a set of generic technologies with the potential for stimulating substantial economic growth and productivity because they are all-pervasive in their implications for industrial and economic development.[2] Some researchers have therefore made a specific case for the value of investment in IT as a stimulus for economic development and a means of enhancing national competitiveness, including studies that suggest IT development may have led or anticipated economic growth in the East Asian NIEs (see for example Rahim and Pennings 1987; OECD 1988; APO 1990; Mody and Dahlman 1992). Such arguments for IT-led development are based on the notion that investments in IT can accelerate economic growth by enhancing worker productivity and increasing the returns on investment in other capital goods.

Our study described in this chapter examined the factors influencing investment in IT and the payoffs they have achieved between 1984 and 1990 in twelve Asia-Pacific countries. These can be classified as:

- **newly industrializing economies**: Hong Kong, Singapore, South Korea, and Taiwan;

- **'developing' countries**: India, Indonesia, Malaysia, Philippines, and Thailand;

- **'developed' countries**: Australia, New Zealand, and Japan.

The study explored the effects of IT investment on the countries' economies to see whether the notion of IT-led development had validity for them. It also examined evidence that would help to shed light on the so-called 'productivity paradox'—the notion that investment in IT has not paid off in productivity improvements. We focused our quantitative analysis for this chapter on investment in IT use as measured by investment in computer products and services. A companion study takes a quantitative approach to the factors determining levels of IT production (Dedrick and Kraemer 1995). The IT sector was defined for the study as covering computer hardware, software, and services. Telecommunications, semiconductors, and other electronics industries are treated as part of the IT infrastructure—supporting and complementing the production and use of computer products and services.

Investigating the Productivity Paradox

Belief in the ability of an IT-led development policy to spur economic growth runs contrary to empirical research that identified the apparent productivity paradox (see for example Baily 1986 and Loveman 1988). That research showed productivity gains in the aggregate economy from the use of IT have been limited, despite the rapid improvement in the price–performance ratio of computers and heavy investment in IT. The identification of the paradox was based largely on the fact that the USA invested heavily in IT during the 1970s and 1980s, yet productivity growth slowed during that period compared to the earlier post-war years.

For example, Roach (1988) showed that IT investment in the USA in the service sector from the early 1960s to 1987 grew tremendously relative to IT investment in manufacturing, with 84 per cent of the nation's multi-billion-dollar IT investment going into services. However, productivity in manufacturing increased during this period, while productivity in the service sector remained stagnant at a level no higher than it was in the mid-1960s.

Other researchers have responded to such 'productivity paradox' findings with disbelief and offered three main explanations for why the expected payoffs might not show up. First, some have argued that errors have arisen because productivity measures based on the level of output for a given level of input fail to account for gains like the availability of new services or improved product quality and variety. Rapid declines in the price of computing power also make it difficult to measure the value of IT stock. In addition, part of the value of IT is that it allows business to be more flexible and do new things, rather than just reducing costs or increasing output (Applegate *et al.* 1988).

A second possibility could be that insufficient account has been taken of the way in which new technologies require a learning process and organizational changes before significant benefits are realized. As a result, there is likely to be a lag between the time of investment and the time that benefits show up in productivity gains while organizations learn to exploit IT and make necessary adjustments in management practices and incentives (Brynjolfsson *et al.* 1988).

These two explanations suggest that we only need better data or a longer timeframe to identify productivity gains from IT investment. The third proposes that IT investments will not increase output: they will only redistribute the pie, benefiting individual firms but not the economy as a whole. This would indicate a global zero-sum game—but with the potential for redistribution among nations as some of them benefit from using IT to make their firms more competitive against foreign enterprises.

Each of these explanations is plausible, but not very reassuring to business managers or public officials concerned about the return on their large investments in IT. Newer studies attempt to deal with measurement errors and time lags by using larger samples over longer timeframes. Such research has been discovering evidence of significant payoffs from IT investment at the firm level. For example, Brynjolfsson and Hitt (1993) of MIT's Sloan School studied data from 380 of the 500 largest US companies from 1987 to 1991, representing over $2 trillion in output (which is about one-third of US GDP). They found a return on investment of 54.2 per cent for computer investments, compared to 4.1 per cent for all other investments.

At the national level, previous studies of the economic impacts of IT have been limited primarily to data from some developed Western economies which compared one time period to another. The claims of productivity stagnation were actually based on comparisons with earlier years when productivity gains were greater. Our study pursued the question of returns from IT investment for Asia-Pacific countries at different levels of economic development, measuring relationships between IT investment and output by comparing data across countries over time, rather than relying on comparisons of data on only one country at different time periods.

Environmental Factors Affecting IT Investment

In carrying out the study, we were interested primarily in the answers to two main questions about investment in IT use: 'What environmental factors affect the level of IT investment in a country?' and 'Does investment in IT lead to increased productivity and economic growth?' We examined these using quantitative analytical techniques to measure the relationship between environmental factors and investment in IT and the effects of IT investment on national productivity and economic growth.

We hypothesized that the level and growth of investment in IT at the national level are influenced by four key factors:

1. **National wealth**. This covers the resources to make initial and subsequent technology investments, measured by: GDP level, GDP growth, and savings as a percentage of GDP. Wealthier countries with growing economies and high savings rates should have more capital and more

efficient markets to provide investment capital at a lower cost. A lower cost of capital means a higher return on investment.

2. **Wage levels and growth rate**. Wage rates are expected to be correlated with return on IT investment, as organizations paying higher wages stand to gain a higher return from replacing labour or improving labour productivity.

3. **IT infrastructure**. This involves necessary support for the productive application of IT including human resources, capital availability, telecommunications networks, and a dependable power supply. The presence of an adequate infrastructure is expected to be related to the return on investment in IT because the technology is complex and requires supporting networks of electricity, telecommunications, and skilled people.

4. **Price/performance of IT products**. Improvements in the value-for-money gained from IT products make returns on IT investments more attractive because more computing power can be purchased for a given amount of investment. It has been estimated that for every 1 per cent drop in price in IT products there is a 1.5 per cent increase in demand. The costs and benefits of investment in IT should include relevant taxes, tariffs, and all other factors which affect the price/performance of IT in a given country.

Investment in IT use can improve productivity in two ways. First, IT increases labour productivity directly by substituting for labour or enhancing the productivity of workers. The gains in labour productivity can be seen most easily when computers are installed to perform routine data processing functions and replace workers carrying out those functions. Less visible are the gains in productivity achieved by providing workers with timely information and tools for planning and carrying out their work.

Secondly, IT improves capital productivity by complementing other investments. Plants and equipment can be made more productive through the use of computerized control systems that allow automation of processes and greater flexibility in production. The entire production system can be made more productive through the use of computers for planning and co-ordination of activities within the firm and externally with suppliers and customers. In the service sector, assets can be employed more productively, such as through computerized reservation systems that maximize the usage of airplane capacity. Improved capital productivity should also increase labour productivity, as workers with more productive tools should be more productive themselves.

Kenneth L. Kraemer and Jason Dedrick

Payoffs from IT Investments

The analyses in this chapter measure the relationships between environmental factors and IT investment, as well as between IT investment and growth in GDP and productivity.[3] Table 18.1, for example, presents data for each country on key environmental factors affecting IT investment:

1. national wealth is measured by GDP per capita, growth in GDP, and savings rates;

2. IT infrastructure is gauged in terms of human resources (adult literacy, secondary school enrolment, scientists, and engineers), telecommunications, scientific capacity measured as R&D spending, and capital availability (investment as a percentage of GDP);

3. productivity is measured by the level and growth rate of GDP per employee and wage rates by average hourly wages in manufacturing and services.

To compare these data across countries, we use IT investment as a percentage of GDP and of total capital investment in 1990, as well as growth rates for these figures from 1984 to 1990. These provide common measures across countries and over time.

We first looked at the effects of environmental factors on diffusion. To assess the effects of environment, we conducted correlation analyses using measures of the four factors affecting IT investment discussed earlier—national wealth, wages, IT infrastructure, and IT price/performance. These were correlated with IT investment as a percentage of GDP and of total capital investment across the countries to find relationships at a given time. Where a statistically significant correlation was found, we concluded that a relationship exists between the two.

Then we carried out correlation analyses of growth rates in IT investment against growth in GDP and labour productivity (GDP per worker) in order to quantify the dynamic relationships among those variables. An especially important aspect was measuring the correlation of growth in IT investment as a percentage of total capital investment against increases in productivity and GDP. These measure the extent to which a shift in capital spending towards IT and away from other investments is related to increases in productivity and GDP, as the proponents of IT-led development suggest it should.

Table 18.1. Key Environmental Variables Related to IT Investment

	Japan	Aust/NZ	Singapore	Hong Kong	South Korea	Taiwan	Malaysia	India	Thailand	Philippines	Indonesia
NATIONAL WEALTH											
GDP per capita, 1990 ($US)	22,879	155,283	10,521	10,897	4,968	7,509	2,050	300	1,194	740	520
Average GDP growth, 1984–90	4.62	0.56	6.66	6.68	9.65	8.47	5.81	5.72	8.61	1.18	5.85
Savings as % of GDP, 1988	33	24	41	33	38	23	36	21	26	18	25
INFRASTRUCTURE											
Human Resources											
Adult literacy (%)	99	99	86	88	95	91	74	43	91	86	74
Secondary school enrolment	96	95	71	69	95	75	53	35	29	66	41
Scientists/Engineers per 10,000 pop.	33.8	22.4	23	na	14.9	18	3	12.8	na	1.1	4
Telecommunications											
Telephones per 1,000 pop., 1988	403	435	340	360	209	262	68	4.9	16.8	7	4.3
R&D Capacity											
R&D as % of GDP, 1988	2.8	1.27	0.9	0.6	1.6	0.9	0.3	0.9	0.3	0.12	0.2
WAGE RATES (US$)											
Average hourly wage in manufacturing, 1990	11.95	12.43	3.36	2.95	3.95	3.50	0.76	0.50	0.78	0.80	0.40
PRODUCTIVITY (US$)											
Productivity, GDP per employee, 1988	47,301	32,550	19,277	19,895	10,155	14,388	5,694	1,093	2,298	2,067	1,175
Average productivity growth, 1984–90	3.34	0.76	4.70	4.82	6.30	6.02	3.30	4.29	3.84	-0.96	2.23

na = not available

Sources: Department of Labor (1989); IMD International (1990); DGBAS (1991); IMF (1991); UNDP (1991).

Table 18.2. IT Investment in Asia-Pacific Countries

	IT investment as % of GDP, 1990	IT investment as % of total investment, 1990	Average growth in IT investment, 1984–90
Japan	2.18	6.52	13.90
Australia/New Zealand	2.03	8.24	15.43
Singapore	1.84	3.89	18.06
Hong Kong	1.19	5.18	15.22
South Korea	0.91	2.19	24.49
Taiwan	0.83	3.60	21.64
Malaysia	0.67	2.30	10.77
India	0.37	1.36	22.21
Thailand	0.36	0.83	25.00
Philippines	0.25	2.43	12.21
Indonesia	0.23	0.56	18.09

Source: Database at CRITO, University of California, Irvine.

Main Findings from the Quantitative Analyses

Investment in IT Use

Table 18.2 shows for twelve Asia-Pacific countries as of 1990 the total IT spending (hardware, software, services) as a percentage of GDP and of total capital investment. It also specifies their average annual growth rates in spending from 1984 to 1990. In this analysis, we used spending as a percentage of GDP as a comparative measure because it is related to the size of a country's economy. This is a better measure than IT spending per capita, since it is based on buying power rather than population. (Data for Australia and New Zealand are combined in the original source, so they are treated as one unit using a weighted average of the two countries based on the relative size of their economies.)

Two points are clearly illustrated by Table 18.2:

1. Spending is related to national wealth. The developed countries are the heaviest users of IT, followed by the NIEs and then the developing countries.

2. Growth in spending is fastest in the rapidly growing NIEs and Thailand and Indonesia, all of which are playing catch-up with the developed countries.

Environment and Investment

From the data in Table 18.1, we found six variables which have a statistically significant correlation with IT spending:[4]

- *national wealth* measured as GDP per capita;
- *average wages* in manufacturing and services;
- *telecommunications* measured as telephones per 1,000 population;
- *structure of economy* relating to services as a percentage of GDP;
- *human resources* in terms of secondary school enrolment and scientists/engineers per 1,000 population;
- *R&D capacity* as a percentage of GDP.

The first three of these directly overlap with the four main environmental factors determining IT investment hypothesized earlier. In each case, they are strongly correlated with IT investment as a percentage of GDP. Each of the other variables is also strongly correlated with GDP per capita, suggesting that level of wealth may be the key determinant of IT investment. While the other variables might be correlated only with IT spending because of their relationship to wealth, we also found all but two variables (service wages and investment as a percentage of GDP) are correlated with IT investment as a percentage of total investment. This shows that in countries with a favourable environment for IT use, a larger share of total investment goes to IT.

This important fact is not as easily accounted for by the simple argument that richer countries can afford the investment. That does not explain precisely why they choose to invest more heavily in IT as opposed to other investments. A plausible explanation is that these countries can earn a higher return on investment in IT, due to favourable environmental factors. It is also possible that the relationship is the other way around. That is, the reason for the correlation might be that the wealthier countries invested more heavily in IT in the past, so that their current wealth is at least in part a reflection of that investment, rather than the key determinant.

Given the many historical influences which determine relative levels of economic development, it is unlikely that the causality runs in this direction on a static level. Australia, for example, is not likely to be richer than the Philippines because of its higher investment in IT. However, it is possible that there is a dynamic relationship between IT investment and growth in productivity and GDP. This relationship, which is at the heart of the productivity paradox debate, is the focus of the following section.

Table 18.3. Pearson Correlation of Growth in IT Use with Growth in GDP and Productivity

Variable	Average annual growth in IT investment, 1984–90
Average annual GDP growth, 1984–90	0.76**
Average annual productivity growth, 1984–90	0.61*

* Significance level = 0.05
** Significance level = 0.01

Environmental Change and Growth in IT Investment

We now come to the critical question of whether IT investment has measurable effects on productivity and economic growth. We found compelling evidence that both GDP growth and productivity increases are highly correlated with growth in IT investment (see Table 18.3). More importantly, we discovered that productivity and GDP growth are also correlated with rises in IT as a percentage of total investment. This demonstrates that countries which increase their investment in IT relative to other investments experience higher growth rates in productivity and GDP.

That conclusion challenges the productivity paradox claim that there is no evidence of a relationship between IT investment and productivity growth. It further provides evidence that investment in IT may actually be more productive on average than other non-IT investments. While correlation is not evidence of causality, the findings presented here are consistent with the hypothesis that investment in IT pays off in gains to productivity and economic growth.

Figure 18.1 illustrates the relationship between growth in IT investment as a percentage of total investment and growth in productivity by country. It shows that Thailand, South Korea, India, Taiwan, Indonesia, Singapore, and Hong Kong have experienced the most pronounced shift in investment toward IT, with an average annual growth of over 15 per cent. These countries also have had the highest rates of productivity growth. Australia/New Zealand and the Philippines are the countries in Figure 18.1 for which productivity growth is low (less than 2 per cent) and appears to lag relative to growth in IT investment. Case studies suggest that the problem in Australia and New Zealand is that both countries depend heavily on exports of agricultural and mineral products, which experienced major price drops in the late 1980s. This factor

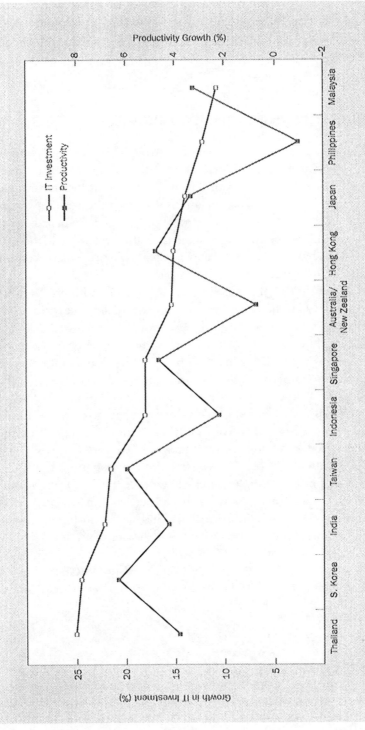

Fig. 18.1. Growth in IT investment, Asia-Pacific Countries, 1984–1990

is likely to have overshadowed productivity gains in the manufacturing and service sectors, driving down overall GDP growth. In the Philippines, political upheaval and natural disasters shook the economy for several years.

Challenging the Productivity Paradox

Our study's finding that there is a strong correlation between growth in IT investment and productivity in national economies is consistent with the notion of IT-led development. However, it does not provide conclusive evidence of a causal relationship, given the relatively small proportion of IT in the overall investment picture and the broad array of factors which affect economic growth. It is also true that if there is a causal relationship, the causation may run both ways between economic growth and IT investment.

Nevertheless, this evidence challenges the notion of the productivity paradox. Our quantitative analysis and qualitative case studies of the countries examined lend much support to the view that IT investment, especially in conjunction with investments in the supporting infrastructure, has a positive impact on productivity and economic growth. This is supported by findings of Brynjolfsson and Hitt (1993) on the relationship of IT investment to increased productivity in large US companies, which also challenged the 'productivity paradox' by its strong evidence of productivity gains from IT investment. Their information base had the virtue of having a large number of data points, with quite detailed information on both IT investment and company output.

Our findings complement and reinforce those of Brynjolfsson and Hitt. We identified a relationship using data at the national level across a diverse sample of countries. They find a relationship between IT investment and corporate productivity at the company level across a diverse sample of companies within a single country. However, given that the firms in their sample represent one-third of US GDP, they can also be considered representative of the relationship between IT investment and national productivity.

Policy Implications

Our research clearly shows a significant positive correlation over the eight-year period studied between investment in IT and growth in both

GDP and productivity. Countries that invested more in IT as a percentage of GDP and of total investment achieved consistently higher growth rates of GDP and productivity. These conclusions have important implications because national governments in many countries have developed, or are developing, policies to promote investment in the production and use of IT, including investment by the government itself.

The development of national industries to produce IT hardware and software has been an important goal of government policies in countries like Singapore, Japan, Korea, Taiwan, and India. Other countries, such as Hong Kong and New Zealand, have taken a hands-off approach, preferring to let the market determine the levels of production and use. The questions facing policy makers are whether there is more value in developing an IT industry or in applying IT to other sectors of the economy—and whether promotion of one will be detrimental to the other.

The benefits of IT use, as well as the high costs of policies which would depress demand for IT, are also clearly demonstrated by the evidence summarized in the chapter. Others have also argued that the use of IT offers greater economic benefits than IT production and that the presence of sophisticated users is vital to developing the production of IT, both to provide a market and because of the importance of close interaction between producers and users (see for example Flamm 1987 and Schware 1992). These points of view argue for policies favouring use. If production is to be promoted, it should be done without trade barriers or other policy instruments which protect domestic producers but discourage investment in use by increasing the cost of IT products.

There are still questions as to what the trade-offs are from policies which limit use to encourage production. Japan clearly followed such a policy, especially in the 1960s and early 1970s, by limiting access to its domestic market and requiring foreign companies to license their technology to Japanese companies in return for access to the Japanese market. Japan now has a large, technologically advanced computer industry —but lags behind the US in IT use. One may reasonably ask what the costs have been to the Japanese economy in terms of lost opportunities to apply IT in other sectors. More importantly, policy makers must consider what the likelihood is of repeating Japan's success in developing a competitive computer industry, given the enormous capital and technology requirements of the industry.

Trends in the 1990s in countries such as Brazil, India, and Mexico have been to remove restrictions on imports, technology transfer, and foreign investment in order to gain access to low-cost IT products and advanced technologies. This trend seems to be an acknowledgement that previous policies to promote production were too costly to user industries in those countries. Countries which have been successful in IT production, such as Singapore, Taiwan, and Korea, have done so largely through attracting multinational computer companies to invest in production facilities or subcontract with local firms. Of these countries, only Korea has used protectionism as a tool for promoting IT production—and it did so only for a limited period when it banned imports of microcomputers from 1982 to 1987.

Government officials can be encouraged by the finding that IT investment on a national level is correlated to productivity gains and economic growth. Given the importance of a strong information infrastructure, governments can promote IT investment by investing in human resources and telecommunications networks. This should include broad-based investments such as support for general education and widespread provision of basic telephone services, both of which provide high economic and social returns in their own right.

The development of a good information infrastructure, however, also requires investments in specialized human resources—such as electronics engineers, computer scientists, systems analysts, and programmers—as well as specialized telecommunications services, like digital switching, high-speed data transmission, and value-added networks. Such investments may be made in co-operation with the private sector, although experience shows that a government role is usually needed in building infrastructure, especially in NIEs and developing countries.

Our firm overall conclusion is therefore that every country would be well advised to promote investment and training in the use of ICTs— and discourage any trade barriers to the importation of ICT hardware and software, which would undermine efforts to promote greater utilization.

Notes

1. This chapter has been developed from a PICT lecture given by Professor Kraemer at the Policy Studies Institute, London on 16 Dec. 1993, which also formed the basis of Kraemer (1994) and Kraemer and Dedrick (1994). The research into the effects of IT investment in Asia-Pacific countries that forms the foundation of the chapter was sponsored by the US National Science Foundation, the University of California Pacific Rim Research Program, and the National University of Singapore. It was carried out by Kraemer and Dedrick at CRITO at the University of California, Irvine.
2. The research on which we have based this chapter defined the elements of 'IT' in specific ways, which we explain where relevant. Otherwise, 'IT' and 'ICT' can be taken as synonyms in the chapter.
3. The data for these analyses were collected from our own case studies of each

country—the CRITO database—and secondary sources (including IMD International 1990; ILO 1991; IMF 1991 and other years; UNDP 1991; PECC 1992). The CRITO database includes information on IT flows between 1984 and 1993, detailing IT investment for each country by technology (hardware, software, services) and by industry (government, finance, distribution, manufacturing). The case studies were conducted through field interviews and a literature review (see for example Dedrick and Kraemer 1993; Kraemer and Dedrick 1995).

4. Spearman rank correlations were calculated between each of the environmental variables and the level of IT spending as a percentage of GDP and of total capital investment in 1990.

19 Telecommunication Infrastructures and Regional Development

Andrew Gillespie and James Cornford

Chapter 18 highlighted the many connections between investment in IT and economic development. This relationship also extends to the telecommunication networks and services, which are critical components of national information infrastructures.

In this chapter, Andrew Gillespie and James Cornford provide a synthesis of many case studies and surveys which demonstrate that the development of telecommunication infrastructures is linked to national and regional economic development. In doing so, their analysis highlights the uneven nature of economic development tied to telecommunication infrastructures and the locational strategies of firms, which is discussed by John Goddard and Ranald Richardson in Chapter 11. This leads into a review of public strategies and policies which merit consideration in efforts to stimulate the development of new telecommunication infrastructures, particularly in relatively distressed or underdeveloped nations and regions.

Telecommunications and Regional Development

Many firms have used ICTs to expand the range of organizational and geographical repertoires available to them, which creates opportunities for some regions and locales to benefit from the relocation of jobs and firms (see Chapter 11). A lack of adequate telecommunication infrastructures is therefore likely to disadvantage some regions in this process, as firms choose whether to expand or relocate. Nevertheless, the existence of such infrastructures does not necessarily guarantee that the new opportunities will be grasped.

Telecommunications and Decisions about Work and Business Location

As ICTs are becoming increasingly central to the competitiveness of firms, variations in the quality of telecommunications infrastructures are likely to exert a growing influence on corporate decision making about the location of work and facilities (Bar *et al.* 1989; Keen 1991).[1] Evidence which indicates the existence of such causal links has been provided by a variety of researchers and consultants.

For example, a survey of European business decision makers found that 43 per cent of companies regarded the 'quality of telecommunications' to be an 'absolutely essential' factor in considering where to locate their business (Healey and Baker 1992). The 'quality of telecommunications' was placed above the 'cost and availability of staff' and the 'availability of office space' in the ranking of important location factors in this survey. However, 'ease of access to markets, customers and clients' and 'transport links with other cities and internationally' were judged more important. In terms of the quality of telecommunications, the survey's responses ranked London, Paris, and Frankfurt as the best three and Moscow, Athens, and Rome rated as the worst. This is consistent with the findings of another study (Ireland 1994) that 'the high quality and comparatively low cost of telecommunications in London have encouraged financial firms to make London a major hub for communications links into Europe'.

Variations in the significance of telecommunications as key factors influencing locational decisions were identified in a survey for the European Commission (1993) by the Netherlands Economics Institute and Ernst & Young. As shown in Table 19.1, telecommunications was of notably greater relevance in the choice of country in relation to distribution activities compared to manufacturing plants. In terms of decisions about regions within countries, the quality of telecommunications was of substantially more relevance in office and services activities than in manufacturing and distribution. With the exception of manufacturing plants, telecommunications was seen as critical or important to location decisions for at least 15 per cent of the firms surveyed and was identified as an

Table 19.1. The Importance of Telecommunications as a Location Factor

Proportion of companies considering decisions about the location of facilities and work who identified the quality of telecommunications as a critical or important factor

	Country		Region within country	
	Critical %	Important %	Critical %	Important %
Manufacturing plants	5	12	2	11
Head offices and other offices	15	15	39	15
Distribution activities	20	15	10	10
Service activities	27	7	27	7

Source: European Commission (1993).

increasingly important location factor for services, European Head Offices, European distribution activities, R&D, and high-tech manufacturing.

Telecommunications and Regional Economic Performance

In addition to telecommunications provision becoming an increasingly significant location factor, there is evidence to suggest that investing in telecommunications infrastructures has a positive effect on economic growth and levels of development. For example, a strong positive association between per capita telephone penetration and GDP per capita has been found within Europe (Biehl 1982; Gillespie *et al.* 1984). In the USA, an analysis of rural counties in the states of Oregon and Washington, for example, found that the deployment of more advanced telecommunication infrastructures, such as those using modern computer-based digital switches, tends to be greater in counties with higher levels of economic performance (Parker and Hudson 1992).

As noted in Chapters 1 and 18, these associations do not establish the ordering of any causal relationship between telecommunications investment and economic growth. Telecommunications investment could bring about economic growth, or economic growth could bring about increased investment in telecommunications. Most studies have supported a reciprocal relationship over a period of time between economic development and telecommunication investment and use (see for example Hardy 1980;

Cronin *et al.* 1991). Although returns on telecommunication investments seem to diminish as economies become more developed (Hardy
1980), a bi-directional causality has been supported even in the world's
most developed nations. For example, studies of the USA (Cronin *et al.*
1991; Cronin, Parker, *et al.* 1993) strongly suggest that—at both national
and subnational levels—increases in GNP or output lead to increases in
telecommunications investment and, conversely, increases in telecommunications investment stimulate overall economic growth (see also
Chapter 20).

The Uneven Geography of Telecommunication Infrastructures

Given the economic significance of variations in the quality of telecommunication infrastructures between different locations, there has been
increased concern over an apparent widening of regional disparities in
terms of the level of telecommunication services provided. In the era of
traditional basic telephony, it was possible, given sufficient resources and
political will, to establish policies for 'universal' service which could reduce
or even eliminate any gap between the provision of telecommunications
infrastructure in urban cores and rural peripheries.

In the USA, for example, a strong political commitment to universal
service was enshrined in the 1934 Communications Act and implemented
through a combination of regulatory policy and the availability of interest-
free loans to rural telephone companies. These efforts reduced the gap
in the quality of telephone infrastructures between urban and rural areas,
although geographical differences remained. In 1987, for example, only
80 per cent of Mississippi's households had a telephone, compared with
more than 96 per cent in Connecticut, Massachusetts, and Pennsylvania
(Hills 1989). One estimate suggested only 3.2 per cent of US households
do not have access to a telephone due to remoteness (Parker *et al.* 1989).
Most households without telephones are in metropolitan areas and 36
per cent are in rural areas served by telephony. In both cases, poverty is
the major explanation for the lack of service (ibid.).

This evidence suggests that a 'universal service' policy can prevent
core–periphery infrastructure differentials from becoming marked within
a nation. However, differentials can be considerable between countries.
Within the EU, for instance, a number of studies have identified lower
levels and quality of telecommunications provision in its economically
weaker regions, which are heavily concentrated in Greece, Portugal,

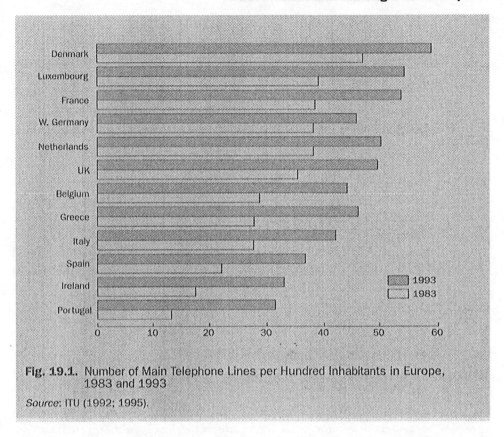

Fig. 19.1. Number of Main Telephone Lines per Hundred Inhabitants in Europe, 1983 and 1993

Source: ITU (1992; 1995).

Spain, Ireland, and Italy. Even in terms of the provision of basic telephone services, a substantial gap exists between the prosperous core and the poorer periphery, despite efforts by the periphery to catch up (European Commission 1994*b*). For example, although the number of main telephone lines per 100 inhabitants in Portugal increased from 13 in 1983 to 31 in 1993, it still had the lowest density of any EU member state (see Figure 19.1). Ireland, Spain, and Greece also have telephone penetration below the EU average.

As Figure 19.1 shows, a significant gap is likely to remain for some time, although the differences between the most- and least-developed countries have narrowed. The same core–periphery pattern is also evident with respect to the quality of service. In the more developed member states, for instance, there are fewer than 0.2 faults per line per year. In the four weakest member states, however, equivalent rates vary from 0.3 in Spain to 0.5 in Greece and Portugal, despite intensive modernization which halved fault rates in these countries between 1987 and 1992 (European Commission 1994*b*). A report to the European Commission

(NERA 1993) estimated that 67 billion ECU (about $50 billion) would be required to close the gap in telecommunication infrastructure levels between the most and least prosperous regions. This figure was about twice as much as the actual planned investment.

The reasons for regional disparities lie partly in the differentiated ability of telecommunications operators to invest in upgrading their networks, which is related both to the level of national wealth and to the relative priority attached to telecommunications while it has been run by national governments as a state monopoly. The disparities also reflect the differentiated nature of demand, with concentrations of more sophisticated users, particularly multinational corporations, imposing much higher requirements on the supply side than small manufacturing enterprises or domestic subscribers. This reinforces the dominance of information-rich regions by producing a kind of 'virtuous circle', in which strong demand for advanced telecommunications produces innovation and higher levels of service, which in turn enhances demand (Hall 1990).

Key Factors Affecting Disparities in Telecommunication Provision

A combination of technological and regulatory changes are serving to increase this interdependence between the level and nature of demand and the level, diversity, and quality of infrastructure provision.

The Role of Technological Change

New switching and transmission technologies are increasing the functionality and capabilities of telecommunications networks, while simultaneously reducing the maintenance costs associated with the network. In order to gain these advantages, telecommunications operators are required to make major investments in upgrading their networks with features like digital switches, advanced software systems, and fibre-optic cable. This investment does not take place all at once, but new services and capabilities are 'rolled out' on the network over a period. As a result, technological innovation often leads to an uneven geography of telecommunications supply.

Analyses of disparities are complicated by the plurality of networks and infrastructures being developed. New wireless transmission technologies, such as satellite communication and cellular radio, now provide viable and, in some cases, highly desirable alternatives to fixed 'wired' networks. Such wireless transmission can assist in spreading technological innovations more quickly over a wide area without requiring new cables or optical fibre to be laid. Much of the impetus behind the emergence of such multiple networks also comes from the demand of major users whose applications of ICTs have become integral to their core business strategies (Chapter 9). This has led to demands from large organizations for specialized and optimized networks supporting high data-transmission rates that allow Local Area Networks (LANs) within their enterprises to be interconnected to networks covering wider areas. Specialized networks such as these cannot be provided on a universal basis, so have been introduced only where a sufficient concentration of users require such services, which are typically in major urban areas and industrialized regions. It requires special public policy initiatives to target the development of advanced infrastructures in other areas, as discussed later in the chapter.

The Impact of Regulatory Liberalization

The widespread liberalization of telecommunications provision interacts with technological innovation to shape the regional disparities we have identified. In regimes based on a state-owned or closely regulated private monopoly, investment decisions could be made primarily on the basis of political or engineering imperatives. Commercial considerations obviously become more important in a competitive liberalized market, which creates pressures on the operator to relate the charges for a service with the costs of providing it.

The drive to minimize the costs of provision and to maximize revenues from new investments becomes stronger as competitive conditions increase. New private operators therefore tend to make their investment in the most profitable market segments, such as leasing telecommunication lines and enhancing long-distance communications. These services are of particular interest to large businesses, which are typically concentrated in the central business districts of major cities and in business parks on the periphery of urban areas. By targeting such agglomerations of large customer groupings, telecommunications operators can lower the costs of providing their services—while maximizing their potential revenues—because fewer locations need to be serviced. These locations therefore tend to receive new investments well in advance of smaller towns, residential urban areas, and rural districts.

For example, the landscape of telecommunications provision has become highly differentiated in the UK, which has one of the most competitive telecommunications regimes. Firms in the central business districts of major cities, business parks, and other concentrations of business activities can choose from a range of competing suppliers offering access to advanced telecommunications services (Ireland 1994). Firms have a more restricted choice of supplier in the remaining urban areas, in some cases only from BT, the former state-owned public telecommunication operator (PTO), and the local cable operator, if the appropriate infrastructure has been built. In many small towns and rural areas, customers are confronted with BT as a *de facto* monopoly supplier, while customers in some, mainly rural, areas did not even have access by the mid-1990s to digital exchanges capable of providing the high-speed and functionally rich Integrated Services Digital Network (ISDN). The general pattern is one of 'hot spots' of intense competition and investment, surrounded by 'warm halos' of duopolistic competition giving way to 'cold shadows' of *de facto* monopoly (Gillespie and Cornford 1995).

Policies for Infrastructure Provision

The installation of new advanced telecommunication services which are not used would be the electronic equivalent of building cathedrals in the desert. Conversely, the availability of new infrastructures and services can be an important element in stimulating new ICT applications and users, as well as in helping to attract inward investment. In the longer run, if firms in the core regions widely adopt new services like ISDN, then companies in areas where such services remain unavailable or are prohibitively expensive will be at an increasing disadvantage in their ability to interact with partners, suppliers, and customers in the core regions. The following subsections examine the main policy actions and initiatives which have been undertaken with the aim of enabling information and communication infrastructures to contribute to urban and regional development.

National Information Infrastructure Strategies

National telecommunications policies have often been framed with economic development objectives in mind. Motives for pursuing liberalization agendas, for example, can include seeking benefits from attracting foreign companies and the conferring of some competitive advantages upon indigenous enterprises. The UK government, for instance, has identified clear economic benefits associated with being the most liberalized telecommunications regime within the EU (Harrison 1994), while the USA's National Information Infrastructure initiative was at least in part justified as a means of supporting American business in a global economy (Schiller 1995; Chapter 22).

Several other countries have promoted investment in telecommunication infrastructures as a key component of their economic development strategies. Singapore is one of the most prominent success stories (Corey 1995; Chapters 1 and 18). Another is Ireland, which since the 1950s has pursued an economic development strategy based on attracting export-oriented overseas companies. Until the late 1980s, its focus was on manufacturing firms. Since then, export-oriented service activities have been targeted. This shift in emphasis has been greatly assisted by the considerable investment made by the state-owned PTO Telecom Eireann in modernizing and upgrading its network. By 1992, 60 per cent of its subscribers were connected to digital exchanges—one of the highest proportions in Europe (European Commission 1994*b*). In addition, the cost of telecommunication services is relatively low; there is a good supply of well-educated, low-cost labour, including many multi-lingual workers; and low rates of corporation tax apply. This combination has enabled Ireland to attract many teleservice companies, primarily in call-centre projects involving US-owned companies (see the Quarterdeck example in Chapter 11). As a result, thousands of jobs have been created in teleservice projects (Richardson 1995).

Spreading the Benefits of Competition

Newly competitive environments require new regulatory mechanisms to sustain universal-service goals of minimizing or eliminating the gaps in telecommunication infrastructure provision between geographical areas. The least controversial of these policies relate to establishing and maintaining the technical interconnectability between different operators' networks. A more difficult challenge concerns the complex systems of hidden cross-subsidies which sustained the expansion of networks in the era of monopoly PTOs.

In a competitive environment in which new operators can selectively enter particular markets, there are strong pressures for 'tariff rebalancing', in which the tariffs charged for a service directly reflect underlying costs. This is especially important in the most profitable long-distance, international, and business-oriented markets, where strong competitive pressures created by new operators drive down prices towards the real costs of providing the services. This results in a counter-pressure to raise the prices charged for local access, which had traditionally been cross-subsidized from the surplus made in the most profitable services. In order to prevent such increases from deterring new customers or causing some subscribers to drop off the network, regulatory regimes have tended to establish price controls that seek to manage the process of tariff rebalancing in a gradual manner.

From the point of view of regional development, a potentially important implication of telecommunications competition is the threat that, given the geographically uneven pattern of competition, the former monopoly PTO will raise tariffs in areas where it still enjoys a monopoly. This would be used to subsidize tariffs in those areas where it faces competition. In order to counter such a strategy, national regulatory agencies have tended to impose a requirement for tariffs to be averaged across the national territory, so that efficiency benefits are shared across all customers.

However, in a situation where tariffs have been rebalanced but remain geographically averaged, any customers or areas which fail to generate enough revenue to cover the costs of serving them will become 'uneconomic' from the point of view of the telecommunications operator. The clear commercial imperative on such an operator would then be to cease to serve such customers or areas. This danger has been dealt with by national regulations which impose a Universal Service Obligation (USO) that requires operators to make available a specified level and quality of service to all at prevailing tariffs, regardless of whether or not customers are deemed to be 'uneconomic'. The costs of this USO are then shared out among all relevant telecommunications operators.

Defining Universal Service Obligations

At first, the scope of USOs were restricted to simple voice telephony, with criteria set for the minimum quality of service to be delivered. Increasingly, questions have been raised about the adequacy of focusing only on voice telephony (Mueller 1993). For example, the European Commission (1995) has proposed USO standards that are adequate for voice and a low-speed facsimile service, but are well below that demanded by many business and residential computer users who wish to access state-of-the-art services, such as over the Internet.[2]

Although there is little agreement about what the precise scope of a USO should be, it is widely accepted that definitions of universal service should be periodically reassessed to take into account technological and market developments. For example, the European Commission (1995) has identified in a discussion paper three concepts of universal service:[3]

1. universally available services at an affordable averaged price;

2. universally available services at prices which reflect underlying costs; and

3. providing access to all by making services available at specified institutions, such as at schools, hospitals, and libraries, which would help to widen public availability without imposing the major costs associated with universal service provision in the telecommunications industry.

Other regulatory strategies have sought to move beyond definitions of minimal service, for example by specifying that particular advanced services, such as electronic mail, are widely spread or, simply, that virtually all potential users are offered a choice of suppliers offering network access (Anderson *et al.* 1995).

One well-established mechanism which has been adopted to achieve universal service objectives is to incorporate coverage targets into the licences for new operators to prevent them from concentrating only on the most profitable business 'hot spots'. This was done, for instance, in the UK when Mercury Communications was granted a licence to be a PTO in 1982. This stipulated that Mercury should provide service in a given number of cities by a certain date. Similar licence conditions have been imposed on operators of mobile communications networks in many countries, including the UK, Portugal, and Spain. Some cable network operators in the UK have been penalized for breaching their licences by not meeting 'build milestones'—targets for the proportion of households within the franchised areas which have been offered service by a given date. The UK has also been a pioneer in the granting of special 'local delivery operator' licences to help ensure a range of advanced technologies and services reach a particularly sparsely populated or otherwise disadvantaged area (DTI 1995).

A variety of funding mechanisms have been developed to support different elements of universal service strategy. Payments to cover USOs can be bundled with interconnection charges, or explicit universal service contributions can be made into a separate fund which is then used to support operators who are obligated. One approach designed to minimize the burden placed on industry by USOs involves an auction in which operators bid for subsidy to provide a clearly specified level and quality of service within a given area, with the contract awarded to the operator making the lowest bid. A similar mechanism is the so-called 'pay or play' strategy, in which an operator can either serve a specified area or group of consumers itself—or pay a penalty that is used to subsidize the provision of that service by another operator.

Some key regulatory issues relate to institutional forms rather than the substantive content of regulations. For instance, threats are posed by the possibility that the regulator could be 'captured' by the dominant telecommunications operator(s), or that large, well-resourced companies from metropolitan areas will be more successful in lobbying the regulator than smaller firms and consumer representatives, especially those based in peripheral areas (see Chapter 21). A number of countries have therefore attempted to incorporate some mechanism for giving the regions a voice within the regulatory machinery, such as the Spanish Telecommunications Advisory Council and regional UK Advisory Committees on Telecommunications. In the USA, state-level governments go beyond such an advisory or monitoring role to participate actively in regulatory decision making.

Direct Infrastructure Provision

There have been a variety of territorially focused infrastructure support measures at regional, national, and local levels. Within the EU, for instance, investments in telecommunications infrastructure 'ahead of demand' have been justified on the grounds of stimulating the economic development of peripheral or remote areas and less-favoured regions.

An important expression of this approach was the Special Telecommunications Action for Regional (STAR) development programme between 1987 and 1991. Sponsored by the European Regional Development Fund, it aimed to accelerate the rate of advanced telecommunications infrastructure investment in some regions, where demand for such services was too low to justify supply on purely commercial criteria (European Commission 1991). About 80 per cent of the budget was spent on improving infrastructure services, such as network digitalization, public data networks, and cellular mobile radio. The programme was judged to be successful in bringing forward the investment plans of the PTOs, for example by accelerating network digitalization in Greece by two years and bringing forward the launch of a cellular radio network in Portugal, again by two years (Ewbank Preece 1993). While these advances hold the potential for improving economic development, it was difficult to be precise about the more indirect and long-term outcomes.

One implication of geographical differentiation in levels of telecommunications infrastructure provision which follows from liberalization is that a role is created for pro-active regional and local telecommunications strategies, as occurred in the USA. The importance of telecommunications to local economic and social development has been recognized in a number of states, for instance by the establishment in New York, California, and Ohio of task forces or 'blue ribbon panels' to develop telecommunication strategies which go beyond the regulatory role which state governments can play through Public Utility Commissions.

Strategic infrastructure initiatives at a city level in the US have also met with some success. For instance, city leaders in Heathrow, north of Orlando in Florida, went into partnership with Southern Bell, which installed a fibre-optic electronic highway, and Northern Telecom, which provided specialized digital switches to create a 'state-of-the-art' telecommunications infrastructure to attract business (Keen 1991). Omaha, Nebraska provides a good example of a co-ordinated state and city strategy. Omaha is at the intersection of several major fibre-optic north–south and east–west trunk networks and has some of the lowest toll-free '800' phone rates in the US. In partnership with Northwestern Bell, Omaha has become the '800 capital' of the USA, with more than 100 million calls being handled for many companies which are heavily dependent on telecommunications, such as credit card and hotel reservation services (ibid.). However, it is not entirely clear in such instances what role governments have played with respect to infrastructure provision *per se*, as opposed to support measures—like labour-force training or marketing the infrastructure to potential inward investors. It could be argued that, despite increasing awareness of the economic importance of telecommunications infrastructure to their economic futures, the capacity of city governments to influence outcomes from infrastructure investment in the market-driven telecommunications era is little different to the earlier period of federally regulated monopoly provision (Schmandt *et al.* 1990).

This tension between the increasing interest in the quality of telecommunications provision in local areas and the lack of mechanisms available to local government to influence outcomes has also been seen in the UK in the wake of telecommunications liberalization. The licensing of alternative telecommunications providers through cable TV franchises might have helped 'recreate the scope for local control of the communications infrastructure' (Mulgan 1989: 21). In practice, however, few local authorities have successfully exercised such control. As the only statutory regulatory role with respect to cable networks rests with a national cable authority, the main lever which local authorities can use to influence infrastructure provision is through their own power as a potential major customer. For example, Nottinghamshire County Council ensured widespread coverage of the emerging cable network by contracting with Diamond Cable to connect up their many sites across the county, including schools.

The role for regional and city governments in the provision of telecommunications infrastructures is, therefore, limited and contingent on the particular contexts. Nevertheless, local governments can and should play an active role in encouraging private investment in this infrastructure through activities like making rights of way available for fibre-optic systems, providing incentives to make the infrastructure serve all parts of a community, and identifying opportunities for public–private co-operation (Moss 1992).

Public–Private Co-operation: The Example of Teleports

An important opportunity for public–private co-operation is the 'teleport', which seeks to exploit a site-specific advanced telecommunications infrastructure and its services and applications to enhance the development prospects of a city or part of a city as part of a wider urban context (Graham 1994). The Osaka Teleport in Japan, for example, forms the centrepiece of a broader project designed to reclaim land from the harbour and modernize the city's trade, transportation, and telecommunications infrastructure' which serves users in the greater Osaka area by an integrated digital fibre-optic network and links with Pacific and Indian Ocean satellites for wider communication (Moss 1992).

The teleport concept has been espoused most vigorously in Japan and Europe as a policy tool, although it first emerged in the deregulated telecommunications environment of the USA in the 1980s, with New York Teleport on Staten Island being the first to open in 1985. Within seven years, over 100 teleports were said to be in operation or development around the world (WTA 1992). Teleports take many forms, but a report for the European Commission (IBEX 1992) defines three basic models:

1. **sector-specific teleports**, which respond to distinct commercial demands, such as Teleport Bremen in Germany, which is heavily dependent on the shipping industry;

2. **infrastructural teleports**, such as in Osaka, Lisbon, and Amsterdam, in which a high-technology business area has its own advanced telecommunications infrastructure which can connect to the existing national network;

3. **applications-oriented teleports**, which aim to act as a catalyst for telematics R&D and service provision by promoting telematics projects in an area, for example as provided by the Twente teleport in the Netherlands.

The need for teleports is a matter of debate. Particular doubts exist about the second type, as few of the teleports initially established in Western Europe provided infrastructural facilities that could not be obtained on other sites (Richardson *et al.* 1994). Amsterdam Teleport, for example, has a dual-routed fibre circuit around the business park, but access to national and international telecommunications networks is via the 'normal' PTO network. BT abandoned a proposed teleport in Edinburgh in the early 1990s because it felt there was no longer a need for the development, as its recent investments in the city had already provided one of the most advanced telecommunications infrastructures in the world (ibid.).

Within Europe, teleports are mainly a transitional policy form lying between tightly regulated monopoly and liberalized telecommunications provision. This can be seen particularly clearly in France, where teleports are planned or under development in a number of cities and regions, including the Île de France, Roubaix, Poitiers, and Bordeaux (Graham 1995). A key element of the French approach have been the Zones Télécommunications Avancées (ZTA), which are small areas in cities designated by central government in which local government subsidizes the telecommunications provider, France Télécom, to provide advanced telecommunications services ahead of demand. However, their value has been much debated, particularly while the degree of 'advancement' remains strictly limited and competitive operators are not allowed (ibid.).

The Components of an Effective Regional Development Policy

From the evidence reviewed above, there can be little doubt that telecommunications infrastructures are becoming increasingly important to processes of urban and regional economic development. With respect to the location of mobile investment and to the overall performance of regional and local economies, the quality of telecommunications infrastructures seems to differentiate successful regions from less successful ones. The precise nature of the relationship between infrastructure quality and economic development, however, displays considerable complexity. This creates difficulties for policy makers wishing to influence economic development prospects through infrastructure measures. For instance, at the same time that the use of telecommunications infrastructures is conferring a degree of location-independence upon corporate users, it is making the quality of telecommunications infrastructure provision an increasingly important factor in locational decisions of firms (see Chapter 11).

There is relatively limited scope for public policy intervention in an environment when decisions about investments in infrastructures are driven mainly by the needs of private firms and national regulatory instruments only rarely allow for local or regional interests to be represented in the regulatory process. Moreover, high-quality infrastructures are insufficient in themselves to guarantee economic development. Many other factors have to be favourable before the infrastructure can exert a more than marginal positive influence. By far the most significant of these is the quality of the local labour force in relation to its cost. Areas possessing a favourable labour quality–cost ratio can benefit appreciably from inward investment, assuming that telecommunications infrastructures allow these assets to be mobilized effectively.

Telecommunications infrastructure therefore plays a reasonably direct and significant facilitating role in relation to inward investments. For indigenous economic performance, however, the role of infrastructure, and by implication the justification for infrastructure policies, is rather more hazy. There is a substantial body of evidence (see for example Ó Siochrú et al. 1995) which suggests that the translation of investments in high-grade telecommunications infrastructures into enhanced economic performance is intermittent and, on occasions, non-existent. Even providing services and tailoring them to the assumed needs of indigenous enterprises often proves insufficient as the real needs of users are too often taken for granted or misspecified in the initial design process.

Ó Siochrú et al. (1995) have also demonstrated that the same application can have widely differing outcomes in differing organizational and socio-economic contexts. This illustrates why the success of policies to stimulate telecommunications infrastructure supply and demand are dependent on 'complementary requisites', such as skills, education, organizational and institutional capacities, and investment resources. It follows that telecommunications-related policies will meet economic development goals only if they are integrated with policies that mobilize and upgrade these other local organizational and socio-economic factors (see Chapters 1 and 14). For firms and territories without these complementary requisites, or who are not committed to their constant upgrading, inadequate telecommunications infrastructures will be but one more signifier of economic failure.

Notes

1. This chapter draws on a range of in-depth research into the geographical implications of ICTs conducted by ourselves and colleagues at the University of Newcastle's Centre for Urban and Regional Development Studies (CURDS).
2. A draft EU Directive specifies a minimum of 2,400 bits per second.
3. Similar 'multi-level' conceptions have emerged in national discussions of telecommunications policy (IITF 1993; Hudson 1995; Nexus Europe 1995; Oftel 1995).

20 Telecommunication Infrastructure Competition: The Costs of Delay

Walter S. Baer

Competition has been introduced into many telecommunications activities that were once the preserve of monopolistic suppliers. In some countries, this liberalization has extended beyond the provision of services to also include competition to the basic telecommunications infrastructure and facilities. Since the first moves towards liberalization in the 1980s have had time to settle down, evidence has grown to demonstrate how gains that can flow from increased competition are at least as important as those that can flow from improvements to the technology itself. Such technological innovations are themselves spurred on by competition.

In this chapter, Walter Baer reviews the experiences of countries which first liberalized their telecommunications markets.[1] He provides a conceptual framework for assessing the economic costs and possible benefits associated with delaying moves towards greater competition. An important question he focuses on is whether the costs of delay are simply the negative of the benefits of liberalization. Baer also discusses the degree to which past experience in this field can be extrapolated to other countries.

Walter S. Baer

Assessing the Costs of Delaying Telecommunication Competition

During the 1980s, after long and heated debates, the USA, the UK, Japan, and New Zealand opened their long-distance trunk telephone markets to various forms of competition which reduced the monopoly power of their public telephone operators (PTOs). By the mid-1990s, virtually all OECD countries had introduced competitive markets for customer premises equipment (CPE), such as telephones and automatic exchanges. A growing number had also permitted competition for network equipment, mobile communications, and packet-switched data services. However, most OECD countries still retained their PTO monopolies on the infrastructure facilities for providing basic services over the public switched telephone network (PSTN).

Figure 20.1 summarizes the status of telecommunications market competition in OECD countries in 1994. The fact that market competition is permitted by law does not necessarily mean effective competition actually exists. The incumbent PTO still holds a dominant market share in virtually all PSTN markets.

Levels of Market Competition

Telecommunications networks and facilities are used for a variety of switched and private-line voice, data, and video services. In developing an analysis of the outcomes from competition, it is important to distinguish between markets for service-based and facilities-based competition.

In service-based competition, the PTO retains monopoly control over facilities but other firms may lease lines from the PTO to offer their own services. Depending on what the regulatory regime permits, competitive services can include the resale of basic voice and data circuits or of value-added services such as packet-switched data, electronic mail, electronic data interchange (EDI) among businesses, information retrieval, and transaction processing. From 1993, competition was mandated within the EU for value-added services and resale of all but basic voice telephony. Voice services will subsequently be opened to service-based competition towards the end of the 1990s.

In contrast, facilities-based competition means that firms offer services on their own networks to compete with the PTO. This can also take several forms: tightly controlled entry, open entry with the PTO retaining considerable market power, and open entry with no dominant firm.

Country	PSTN Local	PSTN Trunk	PSTN Int'l	X.25 Data	Leased Lines	Mobile Analogue	Mobile Digital
Australia	D	D	D	D	D	M	C
Austria	M	M	M	M	M	M	M
Belgium	M	M	M	C	M	M	M
Canada	M	C	M	C	C	RD	D
Denmark	M	M	M	C	M	D	C
Finland	C	C	C	C	C	D	D
France	M	M	M	C	M	D	D
Germany	M	M	M	C	M	M	C
Greece	M	M	M	M	M	M	C
Iceland	M	M	M	M	M	M	M
Ireland	M	M	M	C	M	M	M
Italy	M	M	M	C	M	M	D
Japan	C	C	C	C	C	RD	C
Luxembourg	M	M	M	C	M	M	M
Netherlands	M	M	M	C	M	M	D
New Zealand	C	C	C	C	C	C	C
Norway	M	M	M	C	M	M	D
Portugal	RM	M	D	C	C	C	C
Spain	M	M	M	C	M	M	M
Sweden	C	C	C	C	C	C	C
Switzerland	M	M	M	M	M	M	M
Turkey	M	M	M	M	M	M	M
United Kingdom	C	C	D	C	C	D	C
United States	PC	C	C	C	C	RD	C

C = Competition Permitted   D = Duopoly   M = Monopoly
PC = Partial Competition   R = Regional

Fig. 20.1. Status of Telecommunication Services Competition in OECD Countries, July 1994

Source: OECD.

An OECD Working Party on Telecommunication and Information Services Policies found that substantial advantages had been reaped from introducing 'facilities-based' competition and commented that countries who followed the example of pioneers in this area would make similar gains (OECD 1994).

These classifications enable five main levels of market competition to be identified:

1. PTO monopoly on facilities and services;

2. service-based competition with PTO monopoly on facilities;

3. duopoly or tightly controlled facilities-based competition;

4. open entry involving facilities-based competition with a dominant firm;

5. open entry involving facilities-based competition with no dominant firm.

By the mid-1990s facilities-based competition typically occurred mainly at Level 3, especially for mobile communications, or Level 4—where PTOs still retain strong market power. Transitions to facilities-based competition among the pioneering countries were generally complex and time-consuming, with many procedural problems and delays.

In the USA, for example, the first application to construct private-line long-distance facilities competitive with AT&T was filed by MCI in 1963. The Federal Communications Commission (FCC) approved MCI's route linking Chicago and St Louis in 1969 and authorized additional private-line competition in 1971; but the FCC subsequently refused to order interconnection and resale that would permit MCI to compete for switched long-distance services. It was not until 1978 that the US courts overturned the FCC and permitted MCI to resell services over lines leased from AT&T. A more general FCC order authorizing long-distance resale was issued in 1980. Equal access interconnection to the PSTN for long-distance competitors was ordered along with the divestiture of AT&T in 1984, but it was not substantially completed until 1989. Thus a period of twenty-six years elapsed between MCI's initial filing to compete with AT&T and the successful implementation of equal access interconnection for US long-distance competitors.

The UK and Japan were among the countries which implemented facilities-based competition more quickly than the USA—but the working-out of interconnection agreements and regulatory arrangements also took a considerable time in these areas. Other countries can learn from these experiences and need not repeat the convoluted processes undertaken in the past, although they will certainly encounter delays in implementing infrastructure competition even after the necessary political consensus to do so has been forged.

A Conceptual Economic Framework

One of the main costs of delaying competition in telecommunications is the loss of benefits that can be gained from liberalization. Such lost benefits may include:

1. lower prices to telecommunications users;

2. more variety of, and faster innovation in, service offerings;

3. greater usage of telecommunications services;

4. more investment in the telecommunications sector, which may bring above-average economic returns;

5. productivity gains by telecommunications users, leading to increases in growth and output in other sectors;

6. increased overall GDP growth arising from positive externalities associated with telecommunications networks.

The added costs of regulation and co-ordination that are required in a competitive environment and the possible loss of economies of scale as the PTO monopolist loses market share must be subtracted from these benefits. Many would argue, however, that competitors using new technologies or employing more efficient practices will enjoy lower costs than the incumbent PTO, and in fact will force the PTO to reduce its facilities and operating costs.

Estimating the economic costs of delay involves comparing streams of benefits and costs over time for different competitive and monopoly scenarios. Conceptually, we must estimate the benefits and costs in future years for each scenario, appropriately discount them to the present, and then compare the present values among the scenarios. Although the available data are insufficient to support precise calculations, it is nevertheless useful to have this framework in mind when considering the economic consequences of introducing or delaying competition.

The Effects of Competition: Benefits and Costs

I will now consider the putative benefits and costs outlined above, principally looking at the lessons learnt from the USA, UK, and other countries that have introduced facilities-based competition.

Price, Quality, and Variety of Service Offerings

OECD countries with competitive markets reduced overall telecommunications prices between 1990 and 1994 more than those with non-

Table 20.1. Tariff Trends in Competitive and Non-Competitive Telecommunications Markets, OECD Countries

	1990	1991	1992	1993	1994
Business tariffs					
Fixed Charges					
Competitive	100.00	104.94	109.40	109.43	107.92
Non-Competitive	100.00	111.71	114.72	118.72	125.12
Usage Charges					
Competitive	100.00	101.64	97.14	93.86	85.48
Non-Competitive	100.00	100.92	95.26	94.69	92.94
Total Charges					
Competitive	100.00	100.73	99.37	97.73	91.43
Non-Competitive	100.00	102.34	98.88	98.42	96.88
Residential Tariffs					
Fixed Charges					
Competitive	100.00	102.77	101.81	103.84	101.64
Non-Competitive	100.00	120.50	129.74	130.36	134.19
Usage Charges					
Competitive	100.00	105.73	99.30	92.39	91.06
Non-Competitive	100.00	102.36	97.43	98.77	96.18
Total Charges					
Competitive	100.00	102.17	100.30	98.82	96.93
Non-Competitive	100.00	106.69	106.68	107.67	108.65

Source: OECD.

competitive markets (see Table 20.1). This holds true for both residential and business sectors and for both fixed and usage charges.

Rate reductions for long-distance telephone services among those OECD countries with the longest histories of infrastructure competition have been particularly significant. For example, the reduction in Japan amounted to 50–55 per cent between 1985 and 1992; in the UK, the index of charges for trunk calls dropped more than 25 per cent between 1990 and 1994; and according to the FCC, US interstate toll prices fell more than 40 per cent between the divestiture of AT&T in 1984 and 1992. Service quality has improved along with these price reductions and basic subscriber connections to the network have not been adversely affected (see for example Hausman and Belinfante 1993).

It is difficult to untangle price reductions due to competition from those stemming from technological advances and other factors. For long-distance telephone service in the USA, for instance, some observers contend that the rate decreases since 1984 simply continue the downward trend resulting from technology improvements that has held steady for more than seventy years (Noll 1994). Others have argued that the post-divestiture rate reductions have been driven primarily by lower access charges paid by long-distance carriers to local exchange carriers (Taylor and Taylor 1993). There have also been studies which conclude that competition has been a significant factor in rate decreases (see for example Hall 1993 and Porter 1993). One (Sievers 1994) suggested that price competition has been responsible for 60–77 per cent of the long-distance price reductions between 1988 and 1993.

Most of these studies were commissioned by US long-distance or regional carriers and filed with their pleadings in regulatory proceedings. It is more difficult to find studies of telecommunications competition whose support does not reflect some commercial point of view.[2] However, one such independent review (Kaserman and Mayo 1994) assessed the contending arguments about competitive behaviour, price changes, and other economic results following the AT&T divestiture. It concluded that

> [the] goal of creating a 'truly competitive industry' has been realized and that fears expressed in the early 1980s were, in fact, misplaced. The industry has not evolved back toward monopoly; there has not been a mass exodus of smaller firms; there is no indication of tacit collusion, co-ordinated pricing behaviour, or predatory pricing; actual prices have fallen considerably; and neither local rates nor universal service have suffered any apparent harm.

Competition also brings pricing innovations that reduce the actual prices paid by users well below published tariffs. Competitive long-distance carriers routinely offer volume discounts, lower rates on frequently called numbers, and other special promotions. As a consequence, analyses based on published tariffs will generally understate, often substantially, the price reductions users actually experience. The situation is similar to that facing analysts of commercial air travel in the USA, where most passengers fly at considerable discounts to standard published fares.

The number and diversity of service offerings have multiplied in competitive markets. The major US long-distance carriers—AT&T, MCI, and Sprint—provide dozens of pricing and service options to their residential and business customers. There is also a wide range of competitive data service providers offering a rich variety of ways for homes and businesses to link to the Internet. Of course, monopoly PTOs can be innovative, too, as France Télécom demonstrated in the 1980s with its introduction of Minitel and related data services. But the predominant view of those who have studied innovation is that competition greatly stimulates the development and deployment of new products and services.

Competition has also brought significant improvements in performance-to-price ratios for telecommunications equipment for both customers and carriers. In the first half of the 1990s, for instance, basic fax machine prices fell about 75 per cent, cellular telephone rates by more than 60 per cent, and videoconferencing charges by more than 50 per cent. The price per line of digital switches has also fallen about 50 per cent since 1989. However, tracking equipment-price data alone can be misleading, because many technological advances translate into improved performance at a given price. In 1989, for example, a standard modem transmitting data at 2,400 bits per second (bps) cost about $200. About five years later, similarly priced modems transmit at eight times the speed (19,200 bps).

Since telecommunications equipment is now built around microprocessors, memory chips, and related microcircuitry, its price–performance trends generally follow those in computers and microelectronics. However, government telecommunications data until at least the mid-1990s consistently underestimated the real economic benefits purchasers of telecommunications equipment in competitive markets have enjoyed, as the data did not take account of both price and performance changes.[3]

Expanded Usage

Customers generally respond to lower prices by increasing their calling rates and their use of other telecommunications services. In the USA, FCC usage figures between 1984 and 1991 show the greatest increases in interstate toll and toll-free 800 calls (by average annual rates of 4.4 per cent and 6.7 per cent respectively), which were also the services where prices fell furthest (by an average of 5.3 per cent and 4.8 per cent a year). On the other hand, local residential usage dropped by an average of 1 per cent a year as costs rose by 5.2 per cent annually. Moreover, calling rates have been stimulated by innovations in, and lower costs of, equipment such as telephone answering machines, facsimile devices, cordless phones, pagers, cellular telephones, and personal computers (Mitchell and Tenzing 1994).

Internationally, OECD data show that countries with facilities-based competition averaged higher long-distance traffic growth per main line than others between 1985 and 1991. It is again difficult to separate the relative influences of competition and other factors in increasing usage. Yet the data strongly suggest that competition, leading to lower prices and faster innovation, is a significant driver of increased usage. As a consequence, delaying the introduction of competition will dampen traffic growth and deny both customers and carriers the benefits they gain from higher network utilization.

By focusing primarily on profit margins and contributions of various services, PTOs often underestimate the traffic growth that lower prices will bring. Price elasticities are relatively high for most services beyond the basic telephone service. Thus, between 1984 and 1992 AT&T saw its total revenue increase by 2 per cent and its message toll revenue grow by 14 per cent, while basic tariffs fell an average of 44 per cent and its market share decreased from 85 per cent to 60 per cent. OECD data show that as a percentage of total GDP, PTO revenues stayed remarkably steady after the introduction of facilities-based competition and remained considerably higher in countries where competition is permitted than in those where it is not.

Investment in the Telecommunications Sector

The introduction of competition increases investment in the telecommunications sector, with positive spillover effects on the general economy. In the USA, facilities-based competition has brought greater investment in fibre-optic and other long-distance networks. For example, the total number of fibre-optic route miles constructed by long-distance carriers increased 339 per cent between 1985 and 1990; AT&T alone doubled its spending on long-distance construction during those years. An analysis by the US President's Council of Economic Advisors (CEA 1994) estimated that facilities investment would increase by $9 billion annually from 1995 to 2000 if permission were granted to the Regional Bell Operating Companies (RBOCs) and other local exchange carriers to compete in the USA long-distance market. The analysis by the CEA (1994: 6) also argues that introducing more competition in the telecommunications sector results in higher-than-average returns to both capital and labour, because the regulation prevailing in the mid-1990s 'restricts entry and otherwise creates distortions limiting sector output'.

The emerging competition for local services has also spurred investment by local-exchange carriers and cable TV operators, who now enjoy near-monopoly positions in their respective markets, as well as by new mobile carriers and competitive access providers. More liberal regulatory environments lead to greater incentives to deploy modern equipment, and local-exchange carriers respond to those incentives. On the other hand, such investments paid for by current monopoly services may also be an effort to pre-empt future competitors.

Of course, there is also an argument that higher levels of investment under competition result in unnecessary and wasteful duplication of facilities. This natural monopoly argument, however, no longer seems persuasive for long-distance services, wireless communications services, or telecommunications equipment. Although these services remain capital-intensive, new facilities are significantly cheaper to install and to operate per unit of capacity than were the old. Incumbents thus may still have greater economies of scale, but operate on a cost curve substantially higher than that of their new competitors. Moreover, economies of scale with the new technologies seem to saturate at relatively low levels compared to past investments in copper-wire plant.

Density economies seem more important than scale economies in the construction of new fibre-optic or coaxial cable plant. Using a single conduit or duct for fibres or cables owned by different entities (for example, local or long-distance telephone carriers, cable television operators, and electric utilities) may also bring economies of scope. But such economies do not lend much support to arguments for a natural monopoly in telecommunications or video distribution services. Finally, if resale and workable interconnection arrangements are in place, competitors can minimize their costs of entry and build new facilities incrementally as their businesses expand.

Increased Growth and Output in Other Sectors

Probably the most powerful argument against delay is that it stifles economic growth throughout the entire economy, not just within the telecommunications sector. With lower prices, and greater availability and variety of service, telecommunications will substitute for more expensive inputs, decrease transaction costs, and spur innovation in other industries. This will result in productivity gains, higher output, and (in some cases) more employment by firms. Service sector firms will particularly benefit, since they are among the most intensive users of telecommunications, but the gains will accrue in all economic sectors (Cronin, Colleran, *et al.* 1993).

Examples abound of firms in many countries that have improved efficiencies and expanded sales through more and better use of telecommunications (see for instance Churbuck and Young 1992 and Gleckman 1993). These improvements include the following:

1. Easy access to, and lower costs of, toll-free 800 services have fuelled the steady growth in the USA of catalogue [mail-order] sales firms and

have become essential to the rapid growth of mutual-fund distributors. When AT&T alone offered the 800 service, only large firms could afford it. In a competitive market, however, prices have come down and 800 services have been introduced to appeal to medium-size and small businesses. Toll-free numbers are even marketed to residential subscribers who receive calls from children away at college or other out-of-town relatives.

2. Fashion firms now routinely send new designs to manufacturing sites worldwide by fax or videoconference.

3. Networked Point-of-Sale (PoS) terminals have become ubiquitous among retailers. Although most PoS systems use the switched telephone network, some rely on competitive transmission facilities.

4. Many manufacturing and services companies have substituted EDI for paper transactions to place orders, expedite deliveries, and pay suppliers. EDI first became routine among large firms before spreading quickly to small and medium-size ones in some industries.

5. Despite some unresolved problems like data security, many firms are beginning to use the Internet to offer a wide variety of products and services, ranging from specialized newsletters to compact discs and gourmet food.

Such examples do not necessarily result from facilities-based competition *per se*, but rather from the cheaper, faster, more innovative services that competition encourages. Compared to monopoly PTOs, competing telecommunications service providers appear much more aggressive in helping their customers to find ways to boost revenues and lower costs.

With this rich store of anecdotal evidence, can analysis quantify the overall economic benefits that result from more intensive use of telecommunications services? For many years economists have observed that GDP and other measures of national economic output are positively correlated with telecommunications infrastructure development and investment. But correlation does not necessarily imply causation. A growing economy will demand more telecommunications at the same time that telecommunications may be stimulating economic growth.

Quantitative Approaches

Different quantitative approaches to linking telecommunications to economic growth and the problems involved in clearly ascribing causality to the results are illustrated by three US studies:

1. The CEA (1994) estimated there would be a $9 billion annual increase in telecommunications investment from permitting open competition, initially ascribing a GDP multiplier of 1.6 to that investment. It then assumes that shifting investment into a 'high value-added sector' will result in a higher multiplier. Finally, it assumes that productivity for the total economy will increase by 0.03 per cent per year, starting in 1998. Using these three factors, the study projects 'a stream of annual GDP increases over the next decade [from 1994] with a present value of more than $100 billion. More than $30 billion of the increases will come from the multiplier effect of increased investment. Economy-wide productivity increases account for more than half of the remainder.'

2. In a study filed in 1993 on behalf of the RBOCs, The WEFA Group (1993) projected that permitting the RBOCs and other local carriers to compete in long distance, cable TV, and other sectors would increase US GDP by $247 billion (3.6 per cent) by 2003. This result comes from comparing competitive and baseline scenarios using WEFA's proprietary input–output model of the US economy. WEFA forecasts that the US economy will gain 3.6 million additional jobs by 2003 under the competitive scenario, in which the key assumptions driving the GDP increase are:

   • larger price reductions, especially for cable TV service, where WEFA predicts a price decrease of 5 per cent by 2003 in the competitive scenario compared to an increase of 27 per cent in the baseline scenario;

   • greater economy-wide increases in the rate of technological change, which translate into productivity gains;

   • greater 'productivity gains and quality improvements in the usage of information services [which] average 2 per cent more per year from 1994 through 2003';

   • greater 'labour force participation [which] averages nearly 0.2 per cent higher per year from 1994 through 2003 as employers and employees take advantage of new, lower priced technologies and services that enhance the viability of telecommuting'.

3. In studies also supported by the RBOCs and other local-exchange carriers (Cronin, Colleran, *et al.* 1993), DRI/McGraw-Hill investigated historical relationships between telecommunications usage and output in thirty individual industry sectors, and between telecommunications investment and total US GDP. This analysis showed that, between 1965 and 1987, the radio and TV sector was the only US industry which did not purchase more telecommunications services as a percentage of

total output. The study estimated the contribution of telecommunications to productivity in each sector and concluded that, for the US economy as a whole, advances in telecommunications accounted for about 25 per cent of productivity gains between 1967 and 1991. It found direct causal linkages between telecommunications investments and later-year GDP using a series of statistical tests.

Like many of the pricing investigations discussed earlier, these three studies were commissioned or conducted by stakeholders with clear public positions on competition issues. The studies can be criticized for making unsupported and perhaps heroic assumptions which drive their models' results. For example, the CEA and WEFA assumptions of significantly greater productivity gains, as well as the WEFA assumptions of increased technological change and labour force participation under their competitive scenarios, seem open to question. As a consequence, their quantitative estimates of productivity, GDP, and employment gains may be substantially too high. Critics have also questioned the statistical and econometric methodologies used by DRI, and thus the causal relationships reported in their studies (see NTIA 1991: appendix C, C-1 to C-26). Nevertheless, these studies point to positive, if not easily quantifiable, effects of telecommunications competition on productivity, and economic performance at industry and national levels.

The OECD telecommunication and information services working party has attempted to separate the impact of telecommunications investment on economic growth from the increased demand for telecommunications brought about by higher GDP. This involved developing an endogenous growth model that simultaneously estimates both of these effects, using data from thirty-five countries over a twenty-year period from 1970 to 1990 (Roller and Waverman 1994). Its preliminary results showed strong positive effects in both directions, leading to the conclusion that 'Investments in telecom infrastructure do then lead to spillovers and to increments to growth.'

The Costs of Competition

Competition, of course, brings with it a series of real costs and problems, such as:

- the costs of implementing interconnection terms and procedures;
- the increased costs of standard-setting and other co-ordination;
- administrative costs to regulate competitors;

- the loss of market share and employment by the former monopoly PTO;

- the need to rebalance PTO prices;

- the impacts of reducing cross-subsidies and restructuring universal service;

- lessened control of the telecommunications sector by government.

Avoiding these problems might be termed 'the benefits of delay'. Both service-based and, especially, facilities-based competition require workable interconnection arrangements between competitors and PTOs, and among the competitors themselves. Establishing fair terms and conditions for interconnecting competitors' facilities has proved to be a difficult and time-consuming task, involving both transitional and ongoing costs to PTOs, competitors, and governments.

Much has been learnt from experience with interconnection in the USA, the UK, Japan, Australia, and New Zealand, as documented in a study for the European Commission (Arnbak *et al.* 1994). This concluded that the technical feasibility of interconnection has now been demonstrated under many network configurations and that viable interconnection usually requires a combination of commercially negotiated and regulation-enforced agreements. Once established, an interconnection regime can itself reduce barriers to entry and promote effective competition in telecommunications.

Employment trends are of great concern to all countries. Organizational restructuring and downsizing are occurring in virtually every industry, including telecommunications, and firms that formerly enjoyed protected markets face particular pressures to downsize. In the USA, for example, total employment in the telecommunications services sector fell from 982,000 in 1984 to 895,000 in 1992, an average annual decline of 1.2 per cent (see Table 20.2). Employment fell significantly faster both among the RBOCs (down by 2.5 per cent), who retained near-monopoly dominance of their local markets, and AT&T (a drop of 3.8 per cent), whose manufacturing and long-distance businesses faced strong competition. However, MCI, Sprint, and other long-distance competitors to AT&T have increased employment substantially. Total employment in the competitive US long-distance market appears to have risen, despite significant productivity gains and capital-for-labour substitutions by all the participants.

Employment data in other countries generally focus on PTO job losses and do not include job gains among facilities-based competitors, resellers, providers of value-added services, private network operators, or other

Table 20.2. Employment by US Telecommunications Carriers

Company	Employment (000)		
	1984	1988	1992
Telecommunications services total	982	918	895
RBOCs	497	467	416*
AT&T total (including manufacturing)	427	365	313
AT&T Communications	na	85.5	79.9
MCI	na	17.6	30.9
Sprint	na	37.7	43.4

*1991 data   na = not available

Sources: Company annual reports; US Bureau of Labor Statistics; and US Federal Communications Commission.

beneficiaries of liberalization. By spurring faster growth, competition can create new jobs in areas such as mobile communications, data transmission, and cable television. Nevertheless, facilities-based competition undoubtedly will accelerate the pace at which a PTO must introduce more efficient management and labour practices, as well as rebalance prices and otherwise adjust to a more volatile and hostile environment. Managing such organizational change is never easy.

Lessons from Experience

In the early days of telecommunications competition, it was not evident that the introduction of facilities-based competition brought sufficient net economic benefit to justify the disruption to established organizations and relationships. The costs of competition—both monetary and non-monetary—were highly visible and focused on PTOs, their suppliers, and subsidized users. The benefits of competition were more diffused throughout the economy. Consequently, enough uncertainty existed for many observers to rationalize a wait-and-see approach.

As evidence from the experience of competition has accumulated, the gains from lower prices, more service innovation, higher usage, and increased user productivity seem significantly to outweigh the costs in the countries which have introduced facilities-based competition. Most of the 'early adopters', like the USA, the UK, and Japan, may well have had larger, relatively robust economies that could better absorb the costs and shocks of liberalization. But their experiences have reduced the uncertainties surrounding the introduction of competition.

Other countries can learn from that experience to reduce the costs and avoid many of the delays and diversions that the pioneers encountered in areas such as entry restrictions and interconnection arrangements. For developed countries, the net benefits seem clear. Even countries with less well-developed infrastructures can introduce facilities-based competition to spur investment in the telecommunications sector and speed the growth of network access.[4]

Some key questions still remain, like: is moving to facilities-based competition really necessary to achieve the economic benefits? and could a monopoly PTO not introduce innovative new services, lower its costs, and reduce and rebalance its prices to achieve the gains seen elsewhere? Of course it is theoretically possible for a PTO to do this. However, it does not appear to happen easily in the real world. The empirical evidence indicates that competition certainly accelerates the process, and may be needed to set it in motion. Similarly, experience to date suggests that competition more than privatization is responsible for the economic benefits observed.

Establishing a telecommunications environment that encourages competitive, market-driven behaviour generally requires privatization of the government-owned PTO, as well as a public infrastructure that can effectively oversee the competitors. Introducing service-based competition—resale and value-added services—can often bring early benefits and speed the adjustment to facilities-based competition.[5]

The Costs of Delay

The above analysis demonstrates that the principal economic costs of delay are now clear:

- higher prices and less innovation in products and services;
- less investment in and modernization of the telecommunications sector;
- slower productivity gains by telecommunications users;
- slower economic growth.

To these can be added other costs of delay, which are more difficult to quantify:

- monopoly PTOs and suppliers being less competitive in international markets;

- growing friction between monopoly PTOs and large users;
- business decisions to locate or expand elsewhere;
- isolation from dynamic innovation in other markets;
- greater time and cost to catch up.

By retaining high-cost, high-tariff structures monopoly PTOs will find themselves more vulnerable to competitive cream-skimming from outside, as in the growth of international call-back services in the mid-1990s. Meanwhile, PTOs in countries that have introduced facilities-based competition are adjusting to the changes, difficult as the process may be, and are becoming ready to compete both domestically and internationally. Major competitive international alliances have been formed, with more in the making. As is often said in discussions of the US information superhighway: 'If you're not part of the steamroller, you're part of the road.'

Business and other large users who represent the PTOs' most profitable customers are growing increasingly impatient with high telecommunications costs and slow responsiveness to their needs (see for example OTA 1993c: 91–108). Multinational firms have gained much direct experience with the benefits of telecommunications competition and will continue to put pressure on other countries to liberalize monopoly regimes. Telecommunications service costs and availability have also become key factors in some business location decisions, particularly in telecommunications-intensive industries such as financial services.

Perhaps the greatest cost of delay is growing isolation, for both PTO carriers and their customers, from the dynamic innovation occurring in other competitive markets. Firms that do not adopt efficient production and distribution practices, including heavy use of telecommunications and networked computing, will be left behind as international competition intensifies. The barriers protecting national markets for goods and services are falling, just as technology is lowering entry costs and otherwise undermining the foundations of former natural monopolies.

The International Dimension

Competition in telecommunications services, both across and within national borders, seems inevitable. As the pressures for change mount, so too do the costs of delay. The report by the Bangemann Group (1994) to the European Council on the global information society states this point well:

Those countries that have already opted for faster liberalization are experiencing rapidly expanding domestic markets that provide new opportunities for [telecommunication operators], service providers and industry. For the others, the price to pay for a slower pace of liberalization will be a stiffer challenge from more dynamic foreign competitors and a smaller domestic market. Time is running out. If action is not accelerated, many benefits will arrive late, or never.

These competitive pressures seem analogous to the seismic forces responsible for earthquakes along the San Andreas Fault in California. We know that the longer the stresses build, the more violent will be the quake. Stresses are now accumulating along the fault lines of PTO monopolies. Releasing them will undoubtedly cause some disruption. But the longer the stresses build without relief, the greater will be the shocks—and aftershocks—and the more difficult the transition to a new dynamic equilibrium. Any delays in introducing telecommunications competition will therefore reduce the benefits to telecommunications users and make them, as well as the monopoly suppliers, less competitive internationally.

Notes

1. This chapter has been developed from Baer (1995a; 1995b), which was derived from a PICT lecture he gave in London on 15 Nov. 1994. Primary sponsorship for the research on which the chapter is based came from RAND's European–American Centre for Policy Analysis and its Centre for Information-Revolution Analysis. The views expressed are his own and do not necessarily reflect the opinions or policies of RAND or any of its research sponsors.
2. For a broad view of the first five years following the AT&T divestiture, see Cole (1991).
3. Price and performance data can be combined in what is known as 'hedonic prices', an approach first introduced for computing equipment (see Mandel 1994).
4. Some of the complex issues involved in the timing and sequencing of liberalization in developing countries are outlined in Smith and Staple (1994).
5. See, for example, the chapter on the privatization of British Telecom in Galal et al. (1994: 51–106).

21 Innovation in Telecommunication Regulation: Realizing National Policy Goals in a Global Marketplace

Robin Mansell

The way in which rapid technological change contributes to pressures for innovation in public policy and regulation is illustrated by the move from a telecommunication era centred around 'plain old telephone services' to one focused on a diverse array of new voice, data, and video services. This has taken place at a time of great change in the global marketplace. The new environment resulting from these developments has raised vital questions about the roles of public policy and market-led initiatives. Among these, the issue of how to balance equity of access for suppliers and customers with the need for improved efficiency in the provision and use of advanced ICT capabilities lies at the heart of many other crucial policies for an information society.

This chapter by Robin Mansell examines the main public policy and regulatory options that have been adopted in pursuing equity and efficiency aims.[1] She explains why, whatever the option chosen, there will be a need for political and regulatory processes that can help to reach consensus on who should be able to access and use ICT services in an increasingly complex and global marketplace.

Robin Mansell

Understanding Technical and Institutional Change

Some people are beguiled by the myth that digital information processing technologies are impelling communication networks towards a future in which competition flourishes to the benefit of all users. However, the problems of transforming technical innovations into commercially viable services are complicated by the fact that there is generally an uneven distribution of the benefits. As markets are imperfect, there is a need for public policy intervention to complement the pressure to increase competition in infrastructure and services. This is necessary to handle the mix of voice, data, and video capabilities, which many refer to as 'telematics', that has been a dominant force since the 1980s.

Access to the advanced telematics networks and services of the future may need to be at least as pervasive as access to voice telephony has become in many parts of the world. In order to achieve this, significant innovations in regulation are likely to be required to address emerging disparities in access to common public networks. There are also many unresolved issues concerning the timing and definition of universally accessible advanced networks and services. Questions about who has the power to take decisions with regard to these aspects of the new electronic communication environment are fundamental to the ways in which technical innovations will combine with changes in the regulatory environment. They are essential to the changing balance between:

- co-operation and competition in the telecommunication industry;
- the economic prospects of suppliers; and
- the way people use and control information in their business and social lives.

Public and private institutions will need to find improved ways of coping with the rapid pace of technological innovation. The relatively slow evolution of communication technologies from signalling using drums and smoke to Alexander Graham Bell's ushering in of the era of telephony in 1876 has been followed by an acceleration in the scope and complexity of new systems that integrate telecommunication and computing technologies. This has involved a move from analogue to digital switching and transmission—and from limited computerized control to intelligent software-based functions both within and peripheral to networks. These changes, together with electronic digital media, have radically altered information production, communication, and use.

This has led to an all-pervasive paradigm shift, where widespread benefits are associated with the capacity to apply and integrate advanced telematics services in business organizations and in everyday life (see Chapter 7). Communication policy responses to the new paradigm have been based generally on the assumption that the development of telematics infrastructure and services would be stimulated by increased competition in the marketplace. One of the early initiatives towards liberalizing telecommunication markets was the creation in 1984 of the Regional Bell Operating Companies (RBOCs) in the US, which broke AT&T's monopoly as a public telecommunication operator (PTO). Walter Baer (Chapter 20) demonstrates that certain macro-economic benefits have accrued from the introduction of such competition and case studies in many industry sectors (Mansell and Morgan 1990) have shown the benefits at the firm level.

The overall quantitative and qualitative evidence may point, on balance, to gains from liberalization. However, this evidence generally documents aggregate economic gains associated with competition and the diffusion of telematics services. These can hide uneven developments in different geographical, social, and economic areas (see Chapters 11 and 19). Public policy and regulatory processes therefore need to monitor disparities more closely in order to address issues regarding disparities in network development and service diffusion patterns. These issues include, for example, the degree to which access to advanced telematics services should approach universality and who should make decisions about how to balance the equity and efficiency considerations.

Regulatory innovations to meet these challenges will emerge from continually negotiated compromises among all actors with a stake in the benefits of an information society. Different national and regional policy traditions, combined with the rapidity of technical change, mean there could be multiple 'correct' answers as to how to organize and manage technical innovation in the communication field.

The Transformation from Telephony to Telematics Services

Comprehensive telematics services—from the basic voice telephone connection to very high speed data exchange—are the 'nervous system' of an information society. They act as a major determinant of whether regions, countries, firms, and individuals can participate fully in social, cultural, political, and economic life. However, the support needed for more advanced telematics services, such as interactive multimedia applications, often requires performance characteristics that far exceed the capabilities of the public and private networks which reached into the homes of most consumers and businesses in the mid-1990s. The potential users of such innovations range from numerous smaller firms and individual consumers to large multinational business customers, who have much more sophisticated knowledge about all forms of communication services and the applications they need to support them.

Incremental versus Radical Change

Rapid technological change, the unpredictability of consumer demand, and the diversity of innovative applications have created much uncertainty about the speed of development, the diffusion, and the social and economic effects of advanced networks and services. They may evolve incrementally through the gradual interlinking of isolated islands of test-bed activity, making access to advanced networks available first to larger businesses, wealthier consumers, and the elite scientific and research communities. Alternatively, a radical upgrading of the public communication infrastructure could precede any clear evidence of strong demand in the marketplace for new applications. The actual rate and timing of the investment needed to achieve ubiquitous access to advanced networks and services will lie along this continuum between incremental and radical change.

Those who favour a predominantly market-led, incremental process of change argue that demand for advanced applications must be clearly demonstrated before steps are taken to create the necessary infrastructure. There are also those who suggest that the early introduction of high-capacity ubiquitous networks would stimulate experimentation and the more rapid take-up of commercially viable advanced services. The assumption is that 'technology push' will create opportunities for innovation and the growth of service markets.

The linking of public policy objectives to a rhetoric which assumes that advanced broadband networks are essential to all forms of social and economic activity was present in the 'information superhighway' debates in the USA and elsewhere in the world (see Chapter 22). But the vision of an information superhighway itself does little to resolve highly politically charged efficiency and equity debates about how, when, and by whom the necessary investment should be undertaken.

Regulatory Innovations

The combination of rapid technological change and shifts in policy towards creating more competitive market environments has blurred the distinctions between generally available switched networks and dedicated leased network systems, as well as between public and corporate networks. The resulting 'network of networks' is becoming a way of responding to the requirements of businesses of all sizes and to the mass consumer market.

The innovations in regulation and in the structure and organization of governance institutions are taking place at regional as well as national levels in Europe.[2] In the EU, the European Commission is attempting to shape the overall market environment by introducing directives to stimulate terminal equipment competition, create more transparent procurement rules, and open service and network provision to competition (European Commission 1992; Cullen and Blondeel 1995). National regulatory institutions are also being established, including the British Office of Telecommunications (Oftel), the Swedish National Telecommunication Council (STN), and the Direction de la Réglementation Générale in France.[3]

Nevertheless, the competitive era in communication has made it increasingly difficult to reach consensus among the many interested parties on a number of key issues such as what the goals of policy should be; the powers and processes of decision making; and the consequences of alternative policy, and regulatory and enforcement mechanisms. It is no longer possible, for example, to advocate simply that traditional public interest or universal service goals should be met.

Questions immediately arise as to what these terms mean and whether they should be abandoned or redefined. For instance, should universal service obligations be placed on network operators to provide services for which there is as yet no proven demand? Variations and changes in these definitions could have critical consequences for consumer lifestyles and the competitiveness of suppliers and business users. These changes will need to be addressed continually.

Historical analyses of the development trajectories of earlier innovations in ICTs will not be sufficient to obtain an understanding of the implications for equity and efficiency in a marketplace characterized by rapid structural and technical innovation. Public policy and associated regulations will also need to be based on analyses that use effective methods of forecasting how these innovations will shape social and economic change and the evolution of networks and services.

Robin Mansell

The Political Economy of Telecommunication

Expectations about the role of technical change in the restructuring of markets need to take account of the degree to which technologies and markets are themselves shaped by the political and industrial environment in which they develop. Change is seldom locked into a technologically determined path. It is therefore useful to examine the political economy of telecommunication and analyse the power relations embedded in processes of technical and institutional change. This perspective offers insights into likely market developments that analyses of behaviour in idealized competitive markets are unable to provide.

The Global Strategic Environment

The technical and regulatory changes described earlier have led to such major changes in the global market environment that the domestic arena can no longer be the main focus of national communication policy makers. For instance, Porter (1992) argues that the main barrier delaying the arrival of pervasive competition is the time needed for the PTOs of old to learn how to compete in a fully open market where power now resides more with the buyers of telematics services than with the suppliers. However, such claims for the supremacy of 'buyer power' across all segments of the new communication markets are questionable when the magnitude of the equivalent 'supplier power' is considered.

Many larger companies who are major users of communication service are moving towards fully integrated regional structures and are redesigning their core business practices around integrated systems that cross national borders (Tang and Mansell 1993). For example, companies like DuPont, Shell, and Reuters are creating 'logical computing utilities' and building network environments with standardized user interfaces. However, interoperability and other problems continue to make it difficult to obtain services, like billing, on a transparent basis across Europe and to achieve secure network administration and management. Such problems are caused, for example, by the use of proprietary signalling systems, differing leased-circuit prices, and the difficulties of transferring applications between incompatible systems from various computing and telecommunication vendors.

The new order of the telecommunication marketplace is characterized by global oligopolistic rivalry. This is far from a perfectly competitive marketplace in which no individual supplier or buyer can exert undue power (Mansell 1993*a*). Traditionally, PTOs provided services in foreign markets through bilateral agreements to originate and terminate services and share the resulting revenues. These arrangements have been challenged by a wide range of alliances and ventures that allow operators to enter distant markets directly, including investment in network facilities where liberalization permits. The main players in these initiatives are the small number of major operators who populate global communication markets.[4]

For instance, BT has opened sales offices in the USA to provide end-to-end global corporate telematics services and has invested in MCI, the second largest American long-distance telecommunication carrier. AT&T has maintained its historical bilateral relations with BT while opening sales outlets and facilities in the UK and establishing a variety of other facilities across Europe. In Germany, substantial investment in the early 1990s in building up the telecommunication infrastructure in the newly reintegrated eastern states is being followed by investment in Central and East European countries and a search by Deutsche Telekom for alliances with major suppliers in other countries, such as with France Télécom.

At the same time as looking increasingly to international markets for the expansion of their services to serve multinational customers, major PTOs retain considerable 'supplier power' in their domestic markets. For instance, BT dwarfs its competitors in the UK domestic market, which is one of the most liberalized in Europe. In 1995 its network provided some 96 per cent of the total exchange line connections in the UK and generated about 85 per cent of all local, national, and international call revenues.

Nevertheless, the strength of 'buyer power' in shaping the technical and investment decisions of suppliers is often assumed to be increasing as business customers become more vocal in calling for diversity and change in the communication industry. These customers have become much more visible, for example, as participants in industry standards-making activities. Yet there are a wide variety of justifications for such user participation and very little evidence of substantial buyer influence or user consensus on technical standards. Users face substantial difficulties in funding their standards-setting activities and this is not indicative of substantial 'buyer power' in the telematics marketplace (Hawkins 1995).

Co-operation and Competition in the Telecommunication Market

Regulatory institutions can bias strategic management decisions in one direction or another. The main challenge to regulatory innovation in the face of the substantial power of telecommunication suppliers is how to achieve efficiency and equity goals, both of which aim to maximize participation in the electronic communication environments of the future. Significant innovations in regulation are not likely to surface until a serious effort is made to reach consensus on the terms and conditions of network access in a way that gives consideration to both the equity and efficiency concerns of end-users and suppliers. This is not an issue that can be resolved by recourse to straightforward technical modes of regulation.

Seeking to obtain the best possible conditions for the user in terms of quality, choice, and value for money is generally one of the main tasks undertaken by regulators. The most common way of approaching this has been by promoting effective competition and by introducing directives and regulations that are intended to make it impossible for dominant telecommunication operators to prohibit the interconnection of competing networks or to charge unduly high prices for access to their networks. The public statements of incumbent PTOs are like those of any competitor in a marketplace. They all claim to want to compete fairly and to provide world-class telematics services (Mansell and Credé 1995). Nevertheless, the dominant suppliers are fully aware of the market power they can wield. For example, Mannesmann Mobilfunk took two years to agree network access charges with the dominant mobile operator, Deutsche Telekom, despite intervention by the German Government.

Network operators and public policy makers often strike uneasy alliances in the pursuit of their goals. For instance, national public policy generally supports attempts by the traditional monopolistic PTOs to develop positions of strength from which to attack global markets with a high growth potential, such as network management services. Yet public policy initiatives to stimulate competition in domestic markets could merely serve to weaken these PTOs by stimulating intense competition by new entrants who are investing in advanced infrastructure and services (see for example Trade and Industry Select Committee 1994).[5]

There are arguments that need to be resolved on both sides of the debate about the degree to which dominant PTOs should be unleashed from domestic restrictions or restrained from engaging in anti-competitive behaviour. This is just one example of the difficult questions arising in the context of the distribution of equity and efficiency gains resulting from market liberalization. The outcome is decisively influenced by regulatory measures affecting pricing, standardization, and—most crucially—network access.

The issue of network access is particularly significant because communication networks and applications like electronic banking have systemic characteristics which make reaching agreements between competing players on a range of technical and procedural agreements a precondition of their diffusion and use. This is similar to the way the integration of railway networks requires a consensus on line gauge, tunnel height, signalling voltage, and other operational factors.[6] Agreements on network interoperability and access for telematics services must, for example, cover costs, transfer payments among operators, and network maintenance. Prices for interconnection and services must not so confuse, or exclude, the customer that the efficiency gains due to competition outweigh equitable access to public networks and new services.

Most suppliers, customers, and regulators also recognize the need for co-operation on issues like national and regional dial-code numbering plans; infrastructure capacity where it is cost-effective; and the technical information required to establish standards and plan the roll-out of new networks. However, they have not reached a consensus on the role of public policy or regulation in ensuring that co-operation actually occurs. Although such co-operation is essential to competition in the new telematics environment, history suggests that firms are not always willing to do so in practice. It is therefore vital that agreement also be reached on the role of public policy or regulation to ensure that co-operation actually occurs.

Regulation may be imperfect, but it will continue to play a crucial role in monitoring, guiding, and sometimes controlling the decisions by major players in the communication market. For example, traditional investment patterns, customer–supplier agreements, and information about networks and customers are especially important to the competitive positions of telematics suppliers. The influence in the market of former monopoly PTOs is strengthened by the advantages conferred by the historical accumulation and control of a strong base of tangible and intangible assets which helps them to protect their market positions. There are very few signs, however, that regulatory innovations are keeping pace with changes in technologies and markets.

Prospects for Innovations in Regulation

In the past, equitable access conditions to the telecommunication network were implicit in the concepts of 'public service' provided under monopoly conditions. Technical innovations have made it possible for network operators to move beyond the control of traditional modes of regulation. This has contributed to an undermining of the consensus on what constitutes the 'public' network or the terms and conditions of access that should be extended to diverse communities of users. If the regulatory process is to keep pace with such changes, it will have to introduce consensus-building measures on actions needed to define and enforce 'universal access' conditions to advanced telematics networks.

Attempts to achieve this consensus have relied on two recognized traditional communication policy and regulation roles. One is to constrain the market power of dominant operators where their activities are anti-competitive or exclusionary; the other is to create incentives for new entrants when market liberalization begins. A third role is necessary to ensure co-ordination in the supply of complex communication systems to prevent equity goals from being jeopardized by the uneven development of the competitive marketplace. This role must seek to provide fair terms of network access to all users by building social and economic objectives into the technical, organizational, and operational conditions that govern market entry.

Liberalization Experiences in the USA and Europe

The USA was the first country to liberalize its telecommunication environment. Its experience has therefore been closely monitored by other countries fearful of 'falling behind'. In considering possible options the significant differences, as well as similarities, between US and European regulatory experiences and environments should be taken into account.

The first signs of competitive entry in the US market were felt in the 1950s, when a small device called the Hush-a-Phone allowed a caller to shield sound from nearby listeners. Full terminal equipment competition took two more decades to establish. In public network service supply, AT&T was challenged in the late 1950s by private telecommunication users who won access to the radio spectrum to provide microwave services. Discount pricing strategies, proprietary standards, and reluctance to interconnect competing networks were the tools used by AT&T to rebuff challenges to its market.

By the 1990s there was a growing tendency in the USA to rely on regulation of technical standards with, for example, the dominant carriers having to submit network architecture plans to the regulatory agency, the Federal Communications Commission (FCC). This followed numerous inquiries, the break-up of AT&T, and the introduction of Open Network Architecture (ONA) arrangements which require the Bell Regional

Operating Companies to unbundle their services, with competitors having access to their networks (Temin and Galambos 1987).

Such technical approaches to regulation have not succeeded in prising open public networks, at least not in the way many customers and competitors would like. Services have not been sufficiently unbundled to eliminate barriers to new entry, especially in local or regional markets. Rivalry in the marketplace has still favoured the larger telecommunication users in terms of choice and the costs of services. And US regulatory institutions are continuing to have difficulty coping with technical change.

In the EU, market liberalization came later and moved comparatively more rapidly in some member states, like the UK, and regions, such as Northern versus Southern Europe. Nevertheless, there are similarities, such as the way competition has created an increasing need for co-operation and imaginative regulatory innovation. There are glimpses of such innovation in the British Government's policy of promoting local network competition in advance of the US market.[7] But there are few signs of innovation in the way regulators are attempting to control the market power of dominant PTOs. For example, the 'level playing-field' is being sought in the UK mainly through the use of technical standards and price regulations, which is an approach similar to that adopted in the USA.

However, the USA may not provide a good model of regulatory innovation for Europe. The USA has produced detailed procedures of administrative oversight and cost-accounting methods for assessing whether service prices are fair. In turn, this system has built a vast edifice of information requirements and an immense bureaucracy of legal experts, economists, and public interest advocates. European policy makers appear to be moving down a very similar path in grappling with the increasing plurality of networks, motivated by the belief that regulation of this kind can help to avoid what Baer (Chapter 20) calls the 'costs of delay' in introducing competition. This runs the risk of recreating the features of American public utility regulation which have been found wanting.

In both the USA and Europe, public policy making institutions have found it difficult to promote debate on how, and for whom, the public telematics infrastructure should be designed. Public networks generally are being designed to meet the stringent requirements of large customers, which outstrip the average quality and capabilities of the public network and have a high implementation cost. Historical discrepancies are likely to continue between the technical standards and pricing structures needed to meet the requirements of the majority of smaller customers and those required to support advanced services for transnational corporations (Gabel 1969; Trebing 1969).

The dominant PTOs have an incentive to invest heavily to meet the needs of the multinational firms who generate a significant proportion of their revenues. This is not a conspiracy or the result of collusion among these operators. It is a pragmatic response to the internationalization of markets. The outcome of rivalry among the major operators will obviously make a difference to consumers, but the technical and public policy design principles under which the winners operate are even more important. These principles will affect whether a network is open or closed in respect of who may have access to it; who determines the network's specific uses; who may supply content; who can provide the equipment used; how interfaces and standards are formulated; and whether the technical details are made public or kept private (Kapor 1993).

The Need for Radical Regulatory Innovation

Technical modes of regulation cannot on their own resolve such issues in a way that gives adequate consideration both to equity and efficiency concerns. A serious effort to reach consensus on the public service goals to be met in a competitive market environment must be based on significant innovations in regulations that take account of the political and economic environment in which new technologies are applied.

One practical step which could help to achieve this would be to require incumbent network operators to separate structurally the provision of a public access network from their other global and domestic operations. This would unleash these companies to confront the full force of oligopolistic rivalry in international markets, perhaps causing some PTOs to withdraw from certain parts of the domestic infrastructure. All network operators licensed to provide access to end-user customers would then face the same set of incentives to negotiate interconnection arrangements to complete the systemic features of their networks, which involves being able both to originate and terminate services. Their choices concerning service portfolios, network configurations, and the ubiquity of network access would become more transparent a function of the costs of network access and of market characteristics. This contrasts with the opaque result of the impact of the market power of dominant vertically integrated PTOs.

An alternative to structural separation would be the use of accounting mechanisms which are being explored in the EU. However, as the US experience has illustrated, the accompanying bureaucracy which proliferates under this approach and the extent to which methodologies are subject to dispute suggests that this is by far a second-best option.

Either of these steps would represent an incremental innovation, but this would not be a sufficient response to the transformations in telematics service markets. There is also a necessary corollary measure. As liberalization and competition take hold, the larger operators will pursue their goals in international markets and new entrants will begin to provide alternative network access services—but the quality and characteristics of services will be uneven. This means there will continue to be a need to ensure that a common public network evolves. Failure to address this issue is likely to result in the exclusion of certain users from what many regard as essential access to the 'information highways' of the future. This could arise from the larger operators' pursuit of business goals in international markets and the uneven diffusion of alternative network access services provided by new entrants.

The problem is not one of specifying which network configurations, features, or services must be accessible to various communities of users. It is one of creating the institutional environment in which such issues can be meaningfully debated on an ongoing basis as technologies change and markets are restructured. Radical regulatory innovation is necessary to build such an environment. Too often the process of consensus formation becomes stalled in highly charged debates about interpretations of the 'relevant' costs of service supply, the impact of pricing strategies, and the details of technical standards. Conflicting views of the appropriate unfolding of a balance between equity and efficiency considerations are deeply embedded in these debates.

Achieving Consensus on Equity and Efficiency

One major goal of radical regulatory innovation is to institutionalize a means of establishing a consensus over time on the minimum set of telematics services needed to meet public service requirements. At one extreme, for example, it might be decided that simple access to a copper wire pair at a reasonable price is all that is needed. At the other, access to fibre-based networks and very high speed information applications could be required on a universal basis. In between lies the reality of network and service investment decisions guided by the pressures of a global marketplace and economic efficiency considerations.

Radical regulatory innovation would redirect activity to a minimum set of essential and manageable tasks, such as promoting the development of telematics networks designed to optimize access for the majority of users. Dominant PTOs in liberalized markets are likely to agree with such an approach as an alternative to regulation which seeks to manage or replicate the decisions of network operators through the detailed scrutiny of their commercial strategic decisions. Other regulatory priorities include:

1. monitoring where gaps are appearing geographically and demographically as a result of uneven market development;

2. investigating the degree to which public access to telematics networks and services is technically or economically feasible;

3. encouraging effective and ongoing supplier and user participation in decision making forums with a clear remit to recommend intervention to redress imbalances in network access.

Any such policies will be politically controversial as they have far-reaching economic consequences, including consideration of when, how, and to what extent public financing is needed to strengthen incentives for investment in infrastructure and services. Nevertheless, public intervention in the name of public service and equity considerations is not only possible; it is essential. To paraphrase Mumford (1934: 367), the problem of integrating the machine in society is not merely a matter of making social institutions keep in step with the machine. The problem is also one of altering the nature and rhythm of machines to fit the actual needs of the community. A machine, like a telematics network, is a good example of where it is necessary to ensure that network design and implementation reflect the broadest possible range of user requirements.

Network Interconnection: A Focus for the Future

The strong forces of global competition often appear to be moving regulation of communication markets beyond the control of individual countries. However, communication traffic originates and terminates within national boundaries. It will therefore remain feasible to establish a policy and regulatory apparatus to shape the design of national or regional markets in the interests of a wide range of social and economic goals. These include the desirability of dislodging the traditional monopoly players as well as ensuring that competition does not erode resources for innovation and for social and economic experimentation with new advanced applications. The link between such issues is being recognized at the level of general policy, for example, in discussions on the information-'poor' and the information-'rich' (see Chapters 2, 12, and 22). Nevertheless, there is a lack of consensus on how to bring about policy and regulatory innovations in practice.

There is a vital need for policy and regulatory institutions to co-operate closely in jointly addressing innovation, competition, and social objectives. Network interconnection issues are central to the ways communication markets evolve. They provide a focus for creative institution-building on a regional basis. Interconnection policies and practices can be used to promote incentives for investment; the wider geographical distribution, accessibility, and affordability of services; and the provision of specialized and other services to meet social and regional requirements.

Policy and regulatory developments along these lines will be effective only if they are given the highest political priority. Regional institution-building brings fears of the rise of a labyrinthine centralized regulatory apparatus. These fears can be countered by showing that a concentration on resolving interconnection issues can reduce the need for traditional forms of policy and regulation which are increasingly ineffective in markets populated by many suppliers. Any benefits gained by some suppliers and users from a failure to engage policy and regulatory re-sources in this way are likely to be short-lived. Focusing on interconnec-tion will be a sign of radical innovation in the regulatory process, rather than the withering away of regulation.

Ricardo (cited in Stark 1944: 24) suggested that 'where there is free competition, the interests of the individual and that of the community are *never* at variance'. However, there is evidence that 'information high-way' markets are not truly free, because of the history of public policy measures in many countries and the need to co-ordinate complex net-works. While there is increasing choice and diversity and a downward pressure on some prices in telematics services markets, the need to re-cover co-ordination costs and the monopolization strategies of certain suppliers also lead to cost increases. Public policies are needed to build a consensus on the need for, and the means to achieve, 'universal' telematics services. This would avert a tragedy in the form of the demise of an accessible and affordable public network.

Notes

1. This is a substantially updated and revised version of Mansell's PICT Charles Read Memorial Lecture in 1993 (see also Mansell 1993*b*).
2. Within the EU, the principle of 'subsidiarity' means the European Commis-sion must consider whether the objectives of any proposed action can be best

achieved by devolving powers and controls to member states. Actions at EU level should be taken only when this is required by the scale or efforts involved in achieving the goals.

3. For a history of the liberalization of telecommunication networks and services in the USA and Europe, see Mansell (1993*a*: 46–109) and Arnbak *et al.* (1994).

4. The different patterns of collaboration between telecommunication rivals are described in Mansell (1993*a*: 183–7).

5. For more background on these issues see Mansell and Credé (1995).

6. This railway analogy is based on a comment by Charles Read.

7. See the discussion in Chapter 22 on the 'BT v. cable' debate in the UK.

22 The Politics of Information and Communication Policy: The Information Superhighway

William H. Dutton, Jay G. Blumler, Nicholas Garnham, Robin Mansell, James Cornford, and Malcolm Peltu

Two of the most fundamental issues that arise over the emergence of a new technology are the extent to which the public interest would be best served by promoting or restricting innovation and the extent to which the public sector can and should take a lead in furthering an appropriate strategy. This chapter uses debate over the major information and communication policy initiative of the 1990s—what has become known as 'the information superhighway'—to identify the main enduring issues over the promotion and regulation of technological change.[1]

The authors argue that the resolution of the sometimes conflicting forces underlying these issues requires creative public policies which balance the encouragement of innovation in the production and utilization of ICTs with protection of the public interest and the effective regulation of national and international business competition. They also discuss the relevance of the Internet as a model on which the highways and byways to the information society can be based.

Dimensions of the Policy Debate

The election of US President Bill Clinton and Vice-President Al Gore in 1992 saw the metaphor of an 'information superhighway' emerge as a topic of worldwide debate and action. Within a month of taking office, the Clinton Administration announced its 'information superhighway' initiative, the National Information Infrastructure (NII). This deployed the vision of an 'information superhighway' as the centrepiece of a co-ordinated government strategy encompassing many social, economic, and technology policy areas. For example, the NII plan argued for a dramatic shift in US telecommunications policy away from a previously limited role for government as regulator. Instead, the government's involvement was seen to be a broader one of promoting the development of new ICT infrastructures, services, and products in order to help address major social and economic objectives, such as improving public services, democratic processes, and national competitiveness.

This Democrat-inspired NII vision became the focus of political dispute when its initial momentum was challenged by the election of a Republican-dominated US Congress in 1994. However, after a long debate, the US Congress approved a bundle of important revisions to related legislation in 1996. A central aim of this Telecommunications Bill was to introduce deregulation that would stimulate greater competition in cable TV and local telephone services. It also addressed significant socio-economic issues, such as offering a $20 billion subsidy to reach regions where the costs of providing advanced telecommunications services are relatively high. In addition, it required makers of TV sets to include a 'V-chip' which parents can use to block material they deem to be too violent or sexually explicit.

Overall, the Bill diluted aspects of the early NII vision as the tensions created by the political divide structured the compromises needed to get the Bill agreed. Nevertheless, the Clinton Administration was delighted with its passage and its potential for spurring both competition and employment. But as one US reporter (Andrews 1996) put it:

> **Even the politicians who wrote the communications law stumble as they try to explain just what it will actually do, reverting to clichés about the 'information superhighway' and the 21st century.**

That may indicate how yesterday's vision becomes today's cliché. Yet the NII was a vision that drove policy change. Similar visions have also influenced policy formulation in many other countries and in transnational

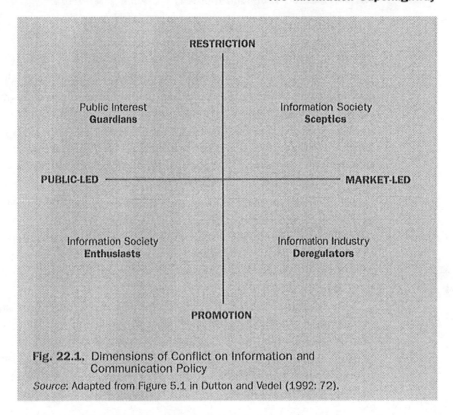

Fig. 22.1. Dimensions of Conflict on Information and Communication Policy

Source: Adapted from Figure 5.1 in Dutton and Vedel (1992: 72).

institutions (Dutton, Blumler, *et al.* 1994). At the same time, the political divide so evident in the USA also reflects deep and enduring cleavages in public policies towards major new technological ventures and industrial strategy more generally.[2]

These divisions in information and communications policy are typified by attitudes to the desirability of public- or market-led policies and to the balance between promotion and restriction of ICTs. They are illustrated in Figure 22.1, which identifies four contending viewpoints within this policy space: public interest 'guardians', information society 'sceptics', information industry 'deregulators', and information society 'enthusiasts'. This typology reflects specific instances of continuing perspectives on the information society more broadly, as defined in Chapter 2.

There are frequently expressed conflicts between the positions shown in Figure 22.1. 'Enthusiasts' typically see the public sector playing a key role in fulfilling their belief in the importance of promoting the use of ICTs (see for example Mackintosh 1986; Bangemann Group 1994; and IITF 1994). Although 'guardians' also see the need for public-led policies to harness the real momentum and potential of ICTs, they tend to see the public interest threatened by the development of an information superhighway, say in failing to share the benefits of the ICTs equitably across all sections of society (see for example Blumler 1992 and Mansell 1993*a*). The 'sceptics' generally have argued that the superhighway is little more than 'hype', driven by the supply industry and technological visionaries—rather than by real market demand from business or the public at large (see Chapter 6 and, for example, Noll 1996 and Stoll 1995). 'Deregulators' are also 'enthusiasts' in terms of promoting the technology, but argue for 'government to get out of the way' by removing constraints on business behaviour through the undertaking of comprehensive deregulation or preventing the introduction of new administrative regulation. They also wish to see the removal of the constraints of public sector ownership—such as public sector borrowing limits—which act as barriers to private investment in, or public use of, ICT infrastructures and services (see for example de Sola Pool 1983*a*; Noam 1991, 1992; and Vallance 1995).

The remainder of this chapter explores how the outcomes of debates across these perspectives may shape the evolution of the information superhighway and its related concrete policy initiatives in the USA, European nations, and transnational institutions. The future of telecommunications infrastructures will unfold as local areas, nations, and regions react to these contending viewpoints of the information superhighway.

The 'Information Superhighway' Vision

Raising Public Awareness

Telecommunications policy involves so many interconnected legal, economic, and technical details that it seldom excites much interest in the general public or mass media, as illustrated by the relatively low popular awareness of plans in the 1980s to create trans-European ICT networks that many see as a forerunner of the NII superhighway concept (see for example Mackintosh 1986 and Mansell 1993*a*). Yet a tremendous amount of mass-media coverage and public debate was stimulated by the Clinton Administration's promotion of their information superhighway vision. One reason for this was the way the NII vision of the social and economic importance of new telecommunication infrastructures was followed by strong leadership from the White House in pursuing a policy agenda to turn the vision into reality.

In addition, the 'information superhighway' is a powerful image, crystallizing issues surrounding telecommunications infrastructures into a concept which can be readily understood by non-specialists. The popularizing effect was reinforced by the subsequent growth in worldwide popularity of the Internet, which gave the mass media a tangible peg on which to hang stories about what the superhighway could mean in practice.

This widespread publicity is of great strategic importance because decision making about related policies should not be left just to the 'experts'. Public involvement is important because the issues at stake encompass so many important areas of society—such as education, health, employment, welfare services, relationships between citizens and government, industrial productivity, trade, and land planning. Without a broadly based engagement in discussions, politicians are likely to give priority mainly to economic and trade aspects of technology policies. Nonetheless, the continuing schisms and conflicts highlighted in Figure 22.1 often mean that even visions which start with a wide initial consensus may not easily be transformed into the planned realities of policy and practice.

Defining the Metaphor

In general terms, the 'information superhighway' can be defined as an ICT network which delivers all kinds of electronic services—audio, video, text, and data—to households and business. It is usually assumed the network will allow two-way communication which can deliver 'narrow-band' services like telephone calls as well as 'broadband' capabilities such as video-on-demand, teleshopping, and other 'interactive TV' multimedia applications.[3] Services on the superhighway can be one-to-one (telephones, electronic mail, fax, etc.); one-to-many (broadcasting, interactive TV, videoconferencing, etc.); or many-to-many (typified by bulletin boards and forums on the Internet).

There remain a number of competing views on the most appropriate architecture or network model on which the information superhighway should be built. For instance, the UK promoted a 'two wires into the home' model in the early 1990s—one from a public telecommunication operator (PTO) such as BT and the other from a cable TV supplier. Single-wire, more-than-two-wires, or even wireless approaches are also feasible. The superhighway could also be based on one of a number of different models derived from the traditional practices and experience of different industries, with the approaches developed in computer data communications and traditional telephone networks being the main rivals.

However, the motorway imagery of the superhighway could imply a traditional telecommunications model of a single homogeneous network in which traffic goes from A to B using fixed links between locations, with switching 'roundabouts' to choose the right roads. On the other hand, the data communications model, typified by the Internet and many other networks in use since the 1970s, allows a 'network of networks' to transmit information in 'packets'. These are routed by flexible computer-based switches to reach their destination in the form in which they were sent. Although experts disagree over the best ways of transmitting and switching information and communication services, the packet-switching model is likely to be the most widely adopted approach (Gates 1995). It has proved to be effective in a broad range of networks as a means of building ICT infrastructures which enable many types of public and private networks to function. For the Internet, packet switching combined with the use of a common standard for communicating between different systems—known as Transmission Control Protocol/Internet Protocol (TCP/IP)—offers a seamless interconnection between many old and new public and private information 'highways, main roads, and avenues'.[4]

The Internet and the Metaphor

The Internet has become associated in the popular imagination as an exemplar of the information superhighway. Although many of its capabilities would be available on the superhighway and its underlying packet-switched architecture is of value to other information infrastructures, the Internet's conception and evolution are unlikely to be a ready-made cultural and economic model on which to base a more market-driven infrastructure. The Internet could be seen as one of the most successful examples of government-inspired innovation in the latter part of the twentieth century. It was initially funded, from 1968, by substantial public investments from the US Department of Defense's Advanced Research Projects Agency (ARPA) (see Denning and Lin 1994: 123–36 and NRENAISSANCE Committee 1994: 237–53 for more on the background to the Internet). Its growth to cover tens of millions of users in the 1990s was encouraged largely through the provision of 'free' access to academic and research users, who also receive much support from public funds.

These communities are infused with a culture based on sharing information and results as freely and widely as possible. In a commercial environment, however, the realization of market potential often depends on protecting exclusivity using a definition of value involving Intellectual Property Right (IPR) agreements. It has been argued (Dutton, Blumler, *et al.* 1994: 31) that the Internet reflects 'important historical American values of sharing, generosity, and neighbourliness which are the antithesis of modern market values'. This derives not only from the public funding provided to it but also from the investment of a great deal of intellectual labour and creativity that was given for free by users from research-oriented communities.[5] While these public and personal investments are unlikely to be forthcoming in a more commercial market, the US government has placed a high priority on commercializing the Internet as an example of how public support can be translated into a viable commercial enterprise.

Politics of the Metaphor

The strength of the information superhighway as a political metaphor is that it combines apparent simplicity with considerable ambiguity. The simplicity makes it easy to understand at one level and the ambiguity allows individuals and groups room to make their own interpretations. The hype surrounding this kind of vision can—and did—lead to a mobilization of a broad spectrum of society for and against the policy and to forecasts that veered between over-optimistic images of a cyber-paradise and unduly pessimistic fears of a dystopian automated hell (which also reflects the continuism–antagonism spectrum of viewpoints towards technological change discussed in Chapter 2). A similar process occurred in the 1970s with the popularization in the USA of the 'wired nation' concept along with the many promises and fears that surrounded the development of interactive cable television.[6]

Although the articulation of a strong technological vision can be followed by many disappointed hopes, it is also often followed by steady, incremental developments which add up to substantial long-term advances. Thus, words like 'information superhighway' can really matter because they influence actual developments. Even then, strategies built around the vision may not always produce the outcomes their promoters and originators expected or hoped. For example, in its early years the Clinton Administration employed the information superhighway metaphor to encourage politicians and the public to support proposals to extend government involvement in technology policy to include strong roles as public service innovator, public interest protector, and general ICT cheerleader. The Republican-dominated US Congress elected in 1994 continued to endorse the NII's high-technology vision, but it reversed the original goals of the strategy by introducing legislation to reduce the regulatory role of government by measures such as lessening constraints on media ownership.

Taking the metaphor of a 'superhighway' too literally could have important policy and political implications. Its image of physical roads could bias plans and developments towards a hardware-driven view of the ICT infrastructure, despite the fact that many social, political, and business uses depend more on the development of a variety of software applications that meet their needs. The metaphor can also cause substantial distortions in the expectations which can be raised for the scope of government action and ownership in relation to an ICT infrastructure. This is highlighted by the political resonances in the USA between the information superhighway imagery and the popular 1950s policy of building interstate highways across America, in which Vice-President Gore's father had played a key role as a US Senator. Michael Nelson, one of the Vice-President's key advisors on telecommunications policy, explained (Dutton, Blumler, *et al.* 1994: 6–7):

> This metaphorical connection between interstate highways and information superhighways was a useful means of implying that many beneficial secondary economic impacts would result from the NII, which helped to gain support for the programme . . . However, the [information superhighway] metaphor might have also suggested that the government's role could be the same as in the 1950s when the federal government contributed 75 per cent of the funds that built the interstate roads. That is absolutely not the case with the information superhighway . . . The government simply cannot exercise dominant leadership in these circumstances.[7]

National and Transnational 'Information Superhighway' Initiatives

The US National Information Infrastructure

The broad social and economic information superhighway vision embodied in the NII set an agenda for information and communication infrastructure policies that became a benchmark against which others have been measured. The blueprint for turning the vision into reality was developed by the Information Infrastructure Task Force (IITF) reporting directly to the White House. The 'Agenda for Action' published by the IITF (1993) emphasized that there are also 'essential roles for carefully crafted government action' while acknowledging that private sector investment in developing and deploying that infrastructure should be encouraged through appropriate tax and regulatory policies. The government actions proposed included ensuring that advanced ICT resources are available to all, at affordable prices—and that any company can provide any service to any customer.

Another important NII-related activity was the National Performance Review, better known as the 'Reinventing Government' programme (Gore 1993b), which is discussed in Chapter 15. The federal government also provides NII-related R&D investment through the High Performance Computing and Communications (HPCC) programme at an initially planned rate of about $1 billion a year, although this and other NII funding was reduced by the Republican Congress.[8] Innovative projects in non-profit sectors like schools have also been sponsored on a much smaller scale than the HPCC.

A number of IITF Committees fleshed out the policy, for instance by encouraging a decision to charge for government information at the cost of dissemination rather than acquisition. This opened the way for a great increase in distributing government information through electronic media, where dissemination costs are very low. A detailed policy was also developed on how the NII could be 'put to work' (IITF 1994) in activities like industrial competitiveness, interbusiness communication, government administration, health, education, libraries, and environmental monitoring.

Transnational Initiatives

ICT networks have profound transnational and global implications because of the way they can create electronic connections that cross national and regional boundaries. Within Europe, the political vision of creating a united community within the EU has therefore given much priority to the development and use of transnational networks and services.[9]

The European Commission (1994a) White Paper on growth, competitiveness, and employment used the vision of an 'information society' to help give a fresh impetus to its evolving policies towards the application and development of ICTs. Dr Martin Bangemann, the European Commissioner responsible for industrial policy, information technologies, and telecommunications, has explained:[10]

'the information superhighway' metaphor was deliberately avoided because it indicates only the infrastructure, which is just one part of the whole system . . . and maybe not the most important one . . . The notion of a European information society comes closer than the information superhighway metaphor in reflecting the Commission's belief that the political and social consequences of using modern ICTs go far beyond just economic or technological reforms. These innovations are changing societies as a whole . . . the way in which we live, learn, and work.

This recognizes the importance of having a strong vision to help articulate strategic policies, even when different words and metaphors are used to describe similar approaches. For instance, the EU strategy makes similar connections between ICTs and social and economic issues as did the NII. The European Commission (1994a) predicted a budget of about 150 billion ECU (over $180 billion) between 1994 and 2004 would be required to fund its 'European information society' plans. These include promoting the innovative social and public-service uses of ICTs, provision of a basic trans-European ICT infrastructure, and an EU-wide Research and Technology Development (RTD) effort for the information society focused on the 'Fourth Framework' programme.[11]

Full support for the Commission's White Paper was given in December 1993 by the heads of EU member states. A group of experts led by Dr Bangemann then started the process of developing detailed plans and actions. The Bangemann Group (1994), like the IITF, recommended that the private sector should take prime responsibility for deploying and financing the information infrastructure, with public authorities setting and controlling 'new rules of the game' to encourage competition and ICT innovation while protecting citizens and businesses from potential negative impacts. The European Commission (1994d) has developed an action plan to ensure there is a consistent response across the EU to the information society strategy.

The EU and USA recognize the need for coherent, balanced, and mutually supportive transnational measures to supplement their own initiatives. This approach to a 'Global Information Infrastructure' (GII) was endorsed at a meeting in 1995 of ministers from the G7 group of leading industrialized countries. Multinational negotiations on issues relevant to the GII are being co-ordinated with the assistance of global bodies like the World Trade Organization (WTO), World Intellectual Property Organization (WIPO), and International Telecommunication Union (ITU). The GII is also regarded as a key ingredient in industrial policies in many developed countries as it opens up vast international markets.[12] However, there is a general acceptance that a GII will take a long time and be very complex to implement because there are so many players involved, including countries requiring very large investments to catch up with others.

The UK: A Lack of Consensus

Sharp divisions exist about the effectiveness of the UK's approach to 'information superhighway' and 'information society' policies.[13] One strongly held critical perception is that too much time, energy, and resources were devoted in the 1980s and early 1990s to a relatively narrow range of regulatory issues, such as the timing of BT's entry into entertainment provision in the UK, when there is so much more at stake in the development of new telecommunication infrastructures. An equally forthright positive view is that the Conservative government, which had been in power since 1979, achieved an outcome similar to that sought by the NII and EU information society programmes, albeit by a more piecemeal strategy based on regulated competition.

In terms of the social and economic dimensions of the policy, the main technological vision in the UK had been built around the image of the 'microchip', which had been emphasized in a BBC Television programme 'When the Chips are Down' in 1978 that triggered a widespread debate on the employment and other implications of IT innovation. The momentum created by the 'microchip debate' was an important factor in the Government giving a high priority to policies promoting IT production, such as sponsoring an IT awareness campaign in 1982 and funding many IT applications, technology developments, and research initiatives (which included the PICT programme).

However, the Conservatives' general political vision of switching resources and priorities away from the public sector to market-driven policies was the dominant force which motivated a series of policy decisions that reshaped the UK telecommunications environment, for example, by privatizing BT and introducing competition into many areas of telecommunications provision. The two-wired model of network connections into the home was encouraged by preventing BT and other PTOs from competing directly with cable TV suppliers in the carrying of entertainment services, which gave an investment incentive to the cable companies that helped their networks to expand in the mid-1990s and created competing infrastructures for the provision of telephone as well as video services.[14] Supporters of the government's ICT policies point to a survey by PA Consulting (Harrison 1994) which found that the UK's overall telecommunications infrastructure compared favourably with those of other leading industrialized countries.

Such optimistic perspectives are open to challenge. For instance, the degree to which regulatory controls on their own can facilitate user innovation is questioned by those who argue that determined UK leadership in encouraging telecommunications competition has not been reflected in practical innovations—particularly in public services, where Britain lags behind countries like the USA. The cross-party House of Commons Trade and Industry Select Committee (1994) claimed that the entertainment restrictions on PTOs could damage Britain's international competitiveness by preventing BT from gaining experience in the mass provision of broadband services and limiting customer choice in the long run by creating entrenched local monopolies in some areas and inadequate services in others.[15]

The way a popular vision can move technology policy up the political agenda was demonstrated when Tony Blair, leader of the opposition Labour Party, placed the 'information superhighway' at the centre of his proposals for regenerating a 'new, younger Britain'. He announced a plan at his party's 1995 conference, in the lead-up to a general election, which aimed to wire up schools, hospitals, and other public facilities. He said BT had agreed to assist in reducing the cost of linking these organizations to advanced ICT networks, provided restrictions on BT's capacity to deliver broadcast entertainment services using its existing network were removed by a future Labour Government. This turned the 'BT v. cable debate' into a major mass-media issue, with the government counter-claiming that it was already implementing 'information superhighway' policies.[16]

Superhighways to the Information Society: The Key Policy Questions

Initiatives to exploit the undoubted economic gains that can be delivered by new ICT infrastructures and services require a broad policy consensus in order to succeed. National and transnational initiatives are likely to unravel if information society 'enthusiasts' fail to enlist the support of their critics—'sceptics', 'deregulators', and 'guardians'. Achieving a consensus requires finding a satisfactory resolution of three broad questions, which are examined in the remainder of the chapter:

1. How can critical social, cultural, and economic values be protected?

2. What useful roles, if any, can be played by legislation and regulation?

3. What balance should be struck between freeing market forces and intervening through public policies?

Facing Up to the 'Information-Rich/Information-Poor' Divide

'Guardians' of the public interest point out that technology and policy often have unanticipated consequences which can put at risk important social and economic values. For example, ICTs open enormous opportunities for new electronic outlets for distributing media—but the growing involvement of large multinational media conglomerates in information superhighway activities could make control over the media more oligopolistic rather than more open (see Chapters 6, 13 and 17).

One of the main threats to the public interest is the potential for the information superhighway to exacerbate inequalities across socio-economic groups by creating widening divisions between the 'information-rich' and 'information-poor'. This could occur if information becomes viewed primarily as a commodity charged at market prices, even in areas where it was once treated as a public good to be provided for free or at low subsidized costs by libraries or other publicly funded sources. This threat could be reduced if, for instance, electronic equivalents of the public library are developed.

A closely related question is 'Who will be on and off the information superhighway?' There is a real danger that the lack of access to important new information and communication infrastructures will cause serious disadvantages to large numbers of people, resulting in immense social and economic problems. That is why the definition of a guaranteed 'universal service'—the minimum capabilities available to everyone and how these should be financed—have become central issues in ICT-related public policies (Mansell 1993a; Anderson et al. 1995). For example, universal service was a core requirement of the NII strategy, which originally aimed to achieve at least about 95 per cent national coverage compared to the 60 to 70 per cent coverage that was expected to be delivered on a purely economic basis.[17]

The financing of advanced public interest information services is a critical challenge facing governments. Suitable mechanisms for this could include: direct subsidies to users; indirect budget allocations to public agencies or service providers; a 'universal service fund' to which all network suppliers contribute as part of their social obligations; or the provision of socially desirable but non-profitable applications on networks also seeking commercial success. Disputes about the best way of balancing commercial imperatives with societal needs continue. Many believe any subsidies should be provided to the end-user, otherwise applications might be developed for which people are unwilling to pay. On the other hand, the Internet grew rapidly at a time when few of its mainly research-based users paid directly for services—or even knew who paid for them.

In the past, as some have argued, many public interest services, such as telecommunications links to sparsely populated areas, were funded by substantial—if never accurately calculated—cross-subsidies between profitable and less commercially viable sectors. This will be difficult to continue in deregulated markets where individually charged, profit-based services are the norm and the commercial temptation is to make advanced capabilities available only in more prosperous areas. As a result, historical social divisions between the information-rich and -poor could worsen.

These cleavages carry distinct geographic implications because the poor are often concentrated in specific distressed or run-down areas (Chapters 11 and 19).[18] 'Universal service' regulations should therefore be backed by appropriate monitoring methods aimed at preventing 'redlining' practices that demarcate areas of social deprivation as places where a service will not be provided. Although most telecommunications licences forbid this, it has often taken place when regulators have had insufficient local knowledge to realize it has happened.

The information superhighway also threatens traditions of socially responsible 'public service' broadcasting which have sought to provide high-quality services to all citizens. The main challenge to this comes from a multiplicity of commercially driven communication channels and new electronic media dominated by global conglomerates. The fear is that these new offerings could eventually lead to an emporium principally of 'fun and games' rather than the 'cyberworlds' of knowledge and enlightenment envisaged by many proponents of the technology.

The Role of Regulation

Many information industry 'deregulators' question the future role of governments in regulating the information superhighway because they believe regulation is a barrier to innovation. Some also argue it is an anachronism because so much telecommunication capacity and power are now available that there is no longer a need to ration and control available channels (de Sola Pool 1983*a*). However, others make a clear case for a continuing need for government regulation (see Chapters 20 and 21). For example, regulation is the most effective way of maximizing the benefits of competition by ensuring there is a 'level playing-field' in which all providers of information, product, and service applications have unimpeded and fairly charged access to networks.

Regulation and legislation also have roles in protecting public interests, like privacy and data protection (see Chapter 16), freedom of expression, and the rights of consumers of ICT products and services.[19] In order to give firms confidence in using the information superhighway, government should also give high regulatory priority to issues like IPR, network security, and the prevention of hacking, viruses, and other violations. But these issues are not easy to resolve. For instance, companies look to effective IPR rules to ensure that investments they make in advanced multimedia and network distribution capabilities are protected. To achieve this, agreed international conventions are required which acknowledge the significantly increased potential for abuses made possible by networks that could effectively abolish national frontiers (de Sola Pool 1990). On the other hand, many multimedia applications could be delayed if each element, such as a single photograph or a brief piece of music, has to be licensed. Such overprotection could give advantages to the largest content providers, who have sufficient resources to cope with the related legal and administrative costs.

Integrated electronic digital flows on communication networks will generally require substantial rethinking of regulatory systems originally developed for other technologies. The uniquely integrated and widely distributed nature of ICTs means that controls on the content of transmissions over computer and other electronic networks cannot simply mimic those used traditionally for television, radio, telephony, and manual postal services. Government must therefore find new ways to address new types of problems, such as trying to maintain the Internet's original commitment to freedom of speech while providing individuals the ability to protect themselves from personal harassment and children from electronic pornography (Denning and Lin 1994).

Appropriate regulations should also seek to encourage new creative uses, a wide choice for consumers, and sufficient financial incentives to help fund the infrastructure. Under certain circumstances, market forces are likely to create incentives for limiting access to information and communication infrastructures, so governments should support appropriate standards-setting processes to generate the necessary degree of 'open architecture' flexibility that will allow smooth interoperability between systems. This can be done only if standards are developed and implemented in a framework which is sufficiently flexible and responsive to keep pace with rapid technological innovations and changing user needs.

Regulation also has a role in assisting industry to find suitable pricing structures for new services. For example, the traditional pricing structure of the telecommunications and broadcasting industry is challenged by the delivery to the home of affordable broadband services like video-on-demand and interactive multimedia. This could mean that telephone calls are priced so that they are virtually free because so much bandwidth becomes available. At the same time, the pricing of broadcasts and services received on the TV set could move more to a 'per service' or 'per transaction' basis, which treats the set as if it were a multimedia computer accessing entertainment and information from many sources. National and international infrastructure tariffs therefore need to be sufficiently flexible to enable suppliers to find appropriate pricing levels and structures for different networked services, taking into account competition from stand-alone devices like interactive CD-ROMs.

Defining Appropriate Government Roles

There has been a widespread acknowledgement, as shown in the US and EU policies discussed earlier, that government cannot generate most of the necessary finance and innovation required to achieve the full social and economic potential of new ICTs. Private investment and competitive market forces are therefore seen as crucial engines for driving information infrastructure developments and many ICT applications, products, and service enhancements. Within this context, government can encourage effective investment in several ways, such as creating the conditions for experiments and field trials to help industry discover if there are any trigger services to fuel the motor for future infrastructure investments—the so-called 'killer' applications, typified by the Internet. However, promoters of new technologies have too often generated excitement about their potential long before any real demand for them is evident, causing general disillusion about innovation and much financial loss among technology pioneers and their users (Elton 1991; Dutton 1995).

Government can also play an important role as a catalyst in purchasing ICT products and services which encourage social and technical innovation to support new ways of living, working, and governing. Suitable co-ordinated efforts between local public agencies, educational establishments, and business enterprises can help to ensure the benefits of new telecommunications infrastructures are widely shared and help to improve local expertise of new networking cultures, which could possibly be scaled up into larger regional or national projects (see Chapters 15 and 16). Public-supported R&D programmes and education and training initiatives are also important facilitators in encouraging innovation. For example, an NII demonstrator project required librarians to be trained in how to operate systems themselves and to assist people to use those available directly to the public.

In addition, government can act as a unique force for orchestrating a vision and mobilizing broad support for policies that connect social, economic, and personal aspirations to what might otherwise become an arena only for a limited group of specialists. Policies articulated vividly to make connections between technology and human and cultural developments can generate excitement and stimulate debate which encourages inventive practical progress, even if the rhetoric used may be questionable and raise some unrealistic expectations. An example of this comes from the NII Agenda for Action (IITF 1993):

> All Americans have a stake in the construction of an advanced information infrastructure which . . . can transform the lives of the American people, ameliorating the constraints of geography, disability and economic status and giving all Americans an opportunity to go as far as their talents and ambitions will take them.

Shaping the Future

The debate over the information superhighway is essentially about how competing visions and forecasts of the enthusiasts, sceptics, deregulators, and guardians will shape the future social and economic realities which will be the outcomes of widespread applications of modern electronic digital technologies. This involves facing up to some enduring public policy issues in the context of current ICT developments. The roles that government plays in this process are critical, even though there is little consensus among policy makers, practitioners, and researchers (including contributors to this book) about how this should be done. Their viewpoints fall within different cells of this policy space shown in Figure 22.1 and as the development of technologies, markets, and policies unfold, the positions of groups and individuals within that framework will change. However, the roles of government in ICT-related strategies are likely to remain central issues in social research for policy and practice.

As explained in Chapter 2 and discussed throughout this book, the social impacts of technology are not predetermined. They are influenced by the way we design, implement, and regulate technological change in organizations and society at large. New infrastructures, for example, can be developed in ways that centralize or decentralize control over the media, protect or erode personal privacy, and exacerbate or mitigate inequalities in access to important services.

The government's role in formulating a powerful vision to promote the more socially desirable and equitable outcomes has been shown to be of crucial significance. Such a vision can mobilize a wide spectrum of society towards commonly accepted aims—rather than exacerbating divisions—only if it goes beyond a primarily technical or market focus to address important social, cultural, and economic issues. On the other hand, a government which plays the orchestration role effectively can unleash a wealth of talent, energy, and resources committed to address with imagination and skill the wide range of cultural, economic, personal, and social issues discussed in this book.

Notes

1. The chapter originated as a report (Dutton, Blumler, *et al.* 1994) on discussions at a PICT Policy Research Forum (see Appendix 2) on information superhighway initiatives in the USA and Europe. It has been substantially developed and updated to reflect the authors' own research as well as the many, sometimes conflicting, views expressed at the Forum.
2. These divisions are also illustrated by developments in cable television since the late 1960s (Dutton and Vedel 1992).
3. 'Narrowband' and 'broadband' are measures of the capacity of a telecommunication connection, usually expressed in terms of the speed with which information can move along it. This 'bandwidth' determines what kind of networks are best suited for particular applications. For example, voices involve the transmission of much less data than moving images, which is why telephones can operate on traditional narrowband links like twisted pairs of copper wires. Multimedia, particularly motion video, needs broader bandwidths, such as that offered by coaxial copper cable and optical-fibre connections. Data compression techniques permit services normally carried on broadband links to use narrower bandwidth connections, such as copper wires for some video applications.
4. OTA (1993*d*), Drake (1995), and Gates (1995: 89–111) provide informative and readable overviews of the technology for non-experts including, for example, the Asynchronous Transfer Mode (ATM) technique, an example of broadband packet-switching approaches which is particularly effective for interactive multimedia applications.

5. This view of the unsuitability of Internet as a model for a commercially based service, including the quotation, come from comments made at the PICT Forum by Martin Elton, Professor of Communication at New York University, who articulated the views of many others.

6. Dutton *et al.* (1987: 3–26) gives a detailed description of the historical background to these earlier developments.

7. According to Nelson, an investment of at least $100 billion is needed to build the NII. This is only about 20 per cent to 25 per cent higher than the annual expenditure by the US telecommunications industry in the early 1990s on upgrading their network—but far greater than the total investment (in 1994) of $4 billion in ICT systems purchases and electronic dissemination by the US government (Dutton, Blumler, *et al.* 1994: 16).

8. For more on the HPCC see for example Executive Office of the President (1994) and Vernon *et al.* (1994).

9. Chapter 13 explores in detail how this political vision has helped to shape satellite television policy and practice in Europe.

10. Dr Bangemann's comments quoted here are taken from his 1995 PICT Charles Read lecture (see Appendix 1), as reported in Bangemann (1995*a*).

11. The Fourth Framework Programme was allocated 3.4 billion ECU (about $4 billion) from 1994 to 1998.

12. The Clinton Administration's attitude to the GII is summarized in Dutton, Blumler, *et al.* (1994: 25–6).

13. UK policy developments and differing evaluations of their effectiveness are examined in more detail in Dutton, Blumler, *et al.* (1994: 18–22).

14. Key reports which supported these decisions on telecommunications policy included ITAP (1982) and DTI (1988). A 1991 Government White Paper (DTI 1991) maintained the entertainment restrictions on PTOs until 2001, with the possibility of review in 1998.

15. The 'BT versus cable' focus of UK telecommunications policy has blurred important distinctions between the promotion of the interests of nationally based ICT suppliers and users of the networks. Chapters 18 and 20 indicate that the latter may be more critical to economic growth.

16. See for example CCTA (1994) for a statement of government policy applying the information superhighway to public services.

17. Michael Nelson, quoted in Dutton, Blumler, *et al.* (1994: 43).

18. For instance, in 1993 only 26 per cent of households in one distressed housing estate in inner Newcastle in the UK had their own telephone (Goddard and Cornford 1994).

19. Priority consumer issues identified in a consultative document for the European Commission (Graham *et al.* 1996) included access and affordability; consumer consultation; contractual conditions; privacy and security; pricing; content and service quality; and choice of services and suppliers.

Appendix 1

The Programme on Information and Communication Technologies (PICT)

The UK's Economic and Social Research Council (ESRC) launched the Programme on Information and Communication Technologies (PICT) in 1985 to conduct and disseminate research on the long-term economic, social, managerial, and policy issues posed by advances in ICT. This national social science research initiative was inspired by debate within the UK and abroad about these topics and was dedicated to help shape related policy and practice.

PICT evolved into a ten-year programme involving six university research centres, as well as numerous other researchers in the UK and abroad. It was sustained until 1995 by two phases of research grants from the ESRC, a public agency established by Royal Charter in 1965 to support research and training in UK higher education and research institutes. This funding permitted the research to be independent of commercial interests and the agenda of particular government agencies.

PICT researchers also generated additional support from a wide variety of public and private organizations for activities organized by the PICT National Office—which directed programme-wide activities—and PICT research centres. The independence of PICT was reinforced by the fact that sponsorship was distributed across a large number of agencies and firms and that funding was accepted only on the understanding that decisions about the research would rest with the research team, not with the sponsoring organizations.

Work at the PICT centres covered a diverse range of research projects and workshops, conferences, forums, lectures, and publications. The dissemination actions were an essential part of achieving PICT's objective of bringing the results of its research to the attention of policy makers, IT and telecommunications practitioners, government, and the public at large.

The PICT Centres

PICT developed a decentralized, federal network of social scientists which could span the UK and build bridges to colleagues in other countries. In many respects, the six university research centres that made up the PICT network began and remained quite distinct. Each brought a different mix of multidisciplinary skills, took a unique approach to its work, and was funded at different levels to conduct research in separate but interrelated areas of enquiry. Nevertheless, ongoing communication and co-ordination across the centres was maintained through the PICT National Office, the PICT Committee, the PICT Management Group, and a variety of PICT-wide activities.

The six PICT centres were at:

- **Brunel University, Uxbridge**. The Centre for Research into Innovation, Culture and Technology (CRICT) explored the social and cultural dimensions of science and technology, with particular reference to ICTs. Its ethnographic research on technology and, in particular, software development provides insights into the ways in which the beliefs, language, and practices of producers and users—such as developers' preconceptions of users—affect the way information technology is designed and used (see Chapters 5 and 12).

- **University of Edinburgh**. This was based at the Research Centre for Social Sciences (RCSS), which investigated the social shaping of ICTs—how technical choices in the design, development, and use of advanced computing and telecommunication systems are influenced by the players involved and their particular social and economic setting. Edinburgh researchers have pursued this line of enquiry with respect to the generation of enabling technologies, such as microprocessors; the development of high-performance computer hardware and software; and the application of ICTs, particularly within industry (see Chapters 3, 4, and 8).

- **University of Manchester Institute of Science and Technology (UMIST), Manchester School of Management**. The Centre for Research on Organisations, Management and Technical Change (CROMTEC) studied the role of information technology in business and management practices, with particular emphasis on the ways in which an organization's informal social arrangements and formal structures change as they become more committed to the use of new ICTs (see Chapter 9).

- **University of Newcastle**. The Centre for Urban and Regional Development Studies (CURDS) has injected a geographical concern for space and place into debates about the emerging information economy. The work of CURDS focuses on how the use of ICT influences what tasks are carried out where—within and between organizations—and on the changing supply and demand of advanced communication services in cities, regions, and rural areas (see Chapters 11 and 19).

- **University of Sussex**. The Centre for Information and Communication Technologies (CICT) in the University's Science Policy Research Unit (SPRU) carried out research on international and regional policy and regulatory issues, innovation and technical change in the communication field, and the production and consumption of new products and services for consumers and businesses. This research considered telecommunication policy, standardization practices, software development, and consumer ICTs from social and economic perspectives, making SPRU one of the leading contributors to European information and communication policy research (see Chapters 1, 2, 7, 12, and 21).

- **University of Westminster.** The Centre for Communication and Information Studies (CCIS) focused on the regulation of broadcasting and telecommunications and the development of the information and communication industries. Initiated through PICT funding, CCIS has generated support outside of PICT that has sustained the centre's work and contributed to Westminster's high profile among those UK universities specializing in media and communication studies (see Chapters 6 and 13).

Structure of the Programme

PICT was directed and co-ordinated by the PICT Committee, appointed by the ESRC's Research Programmes Board. The Director of PICT made recommendations to the PICT Committee and took responsibility for ensuring that the mission and objectives of the programme were met by the combined efforts of a federal network of PICT centres. The research centres made recommendations to the Director and PICT Committee through the PICT Management Group, consisting of the heads of PICT centres and the Director of PICT. There were four directors of PICT: Professor William Melody (1985–8), Nigel Gardner (1988–92), Professor John Goddard (1992–3), and Professor William Dutton (1993–5).

Over sixty research projects and assignments were conducted during the course of Phase I (1986–90) and Phase II (1991–5) of PICT. All six centres received major research assignments in the first phase. During the second, the ESRC concentrated its funding on research at Edinburgh, Newcastle, Sussex, and UMIST. However, all six centres continued to function as a network through funding from other sources, the continued role of the PICT Management Group, a variety of joint activities, such as conferences and policy forums, and the development of PICT-wide strategies to synthesize and disseminate the research.

Disseminating PICT Results

The PICT programme sought to use its research to inform and stimulate policy debate through several complementary activities, which included (see PICT 1995*b* for full details):

1. **The Charles Read Lectures.** These ran annually from 1988 to 1995 and were sponsored by BT from 1991. They commemorate Charles Read, who was highly influential in the establishment of PICT when he was an Advisor to Prime Minister Margaret Thatcher's Cabinet Office in the early 1980s. He also worked at the Inter-Bank Research Organisation, where he fostered the co-operative use of IT systems, and was head of IT at the British Post Office, after its telecommunications operations had been moved into what became BT. The lectures were:

Appendix 1. PICT

- 1988: William Melody, 'The Changing Role of Public Policy in the Information Economy'.

- 1990: John Goddard, 'The Geography of the Information Economy'.

- 1991: Roger Silverstone, 'Beneath the Bottom Line: Households and Information and Communication Technologies'.

- 1992: Rod Coombs, 'Organizational Politics and the Strategic Use of Information Technology'.

- 1993: Robin Mansell, 'From Telephony to Telematics: Equity, Efficiency, and Regulatory Innovation'.

- 1994: Alan C. Kay, 'The Best Way to Predict the Future is to Invent it'.

- 1995: Martin Bangemann, 'Policies for a European Information Society'.

2. **Conferences**. These events brought together researchers from within and outside PICT centres to discuss findings relevant to the programme's goals. A Doctoral Conference was held in 1994. The final PICT conference was held 10–12 May 1995 at London's Queen Elizabeth II Conference Centre with co-sponsorship from AT&T (UK), BT, Cable & Wireless, IBM (UK), ICL, Northern Telecom, and NYNEX.

3. **The Policy Research Paper (PRP) Series**. A total of 33 PRPs were published, providing a summary of results from PICT research in a concise and readable format accessible to policy makers, practitioners, and researchers.

4. **Policy Research Forums**. These are discussed fully in Appendix 2.

5. **Occasional Lectures**. During the last two years of PICT, eleven lectures open to a broadly-based invited PICT mailing list were given by leading experts from the UK, the USA, and East Asia.

6. **Research Workshops**. Also in PICT's final two years, specialists from around the world in the fields covered by PICT were invited to workshops to assist PICT researchers in developing a synthesis of their work during the programme.

7. **Books and other publications**. Researchers in the PICT network have published a large number of books and research papers. Many are cited in this book and Dutton (forthcoming).

8. **Synthesis books**. This book and Dutton (forthcoming) provide an overall synthesis and summary of key research findings from the PICT programme. Many of the chapters in this book have been updated and developed from Charles Read Lectures, PRPs, forums, and lectures.

Appendix 2
PICT Policy Research Forums

PICT launched a series of Policy Research Forums in its last two years. Their aim was to move away from traditional lecture-discussion formats, with all the assumptions they make about the producers and users of knowledge. In contrast, the forums sought to establish a neutral meeting ground for constructive dialogues across academic, practitioner, and policy communities. This was felt to be an environment within which researchers could become better informed, as well as helping to convey the results of their research in terms that directly relate to topics of long-term relevance.

Three forums were held in 1994, with about forty participants in each. PICT Policy Research Papers (PRPs) were produced to summarize discussions at the Forums and related background reports and position statements from participants. These PRPs aimed to bring to a wider audience the insights and wide-ranging evidence provided by experts at the forums. They are written in an easily accessible reporting style, combining research findings with the practical day-to-day experience of participants from business, industry, special interest groups, public agencies, and professional bodies. All three forum reports have been updated and redeveloped as chapters in this book.

Electronic Service Delivery in the Public Sector

The first forum was held at Hamilton House, London on 4 March 1994. It focused on issues concerned with the opportunities of and barriers to the innovative use of electronic information and communication media to improve the delivery of a growing range of public services. It also explored the challenges posed by these radical changes to traditions surrounding public services and the institutions that provide them, as well as a host of key political issues, such as the implications for democratic processes, privacy, and data protection. This forum's PRP (Dutton, Taylor, et al. 1994) is the basis of two chapters in this book. Chapter 15 concentrates on aspects concerned primarily with the electronic delivery of public services. Chapter 16 explores the factors involved in the development of an 'electronic democracy'.

Participants at the Forum on Electronic Service Delivery

Inigo Baten, Netherlands Organization for Technology Assessment; Professor Christine Bellamy, Nottingham Trent University; Jenny Brogden, Highland

Regional Council, Nairn; Bob Crichton, The Home Office Partnership; Dave Denison, ICL; Niesco Dubbelboer, Gemeente Amsterdam, the Netherlands; Professor William Dutton, PICT; Mark Gladwyn, CCTA, the UK Government Centre for Information Systems; Professor Paul Frissen, Tilburg University, the Netherlands; Professor John Goddard, University of Newcastle; Stephen Graham, University of Newcastle; Jill Johnson, Kent County Council; Paul Kennedy, North Communications (USA); Robert Kerslake, London Borough of Hounslow; Walter Klein, Gemeinde Wallenhorst, Germany; Professor Dr Herbert Kubicek, Universität Bremen; Denise Lievesley, ESRC Data Archive; Mark Lucas, North Communications (Europe), France; David McLean, CCTA; Colin Muid, Home Office; Professor Donald Marchand, Syracuse University; Malcolm Peltu, PICT; Charles Raab, University of Edinburgh; Claire Shearman, University of Salford; Joan Stonham, Oxfordshire County Council; Professor John Taylor, Glasgow Caledonian University; Luis Vidigal, Lisbon, Portugal; Steve Walker, Manchester Metropolitan University; Professor Tracy Westen, Centre for Governmental Studies, USA; Dr Robin Williams, University of Edinburgh; Dr Fred Wood, US Office of Technology Assessment, Congress of the United States; Dr John Woulds, Office of the UK Data Protection Registrar.

The Information Superhighway: Britain's Response

The second forum took place at the London headquarters of Cable & Wireless (who co-sponsored the event) on 16 June 1994. It sought to assess the implications of the 'information superhighway' vision of US President Bill Clinton and Vice-President Al Gore for the development of telecommunications around the world. Particular attention was given to exploring the relevant policy implications for Britain in addressing the wide range of socio-economic, political, and cultural areas central to the development of new telecommunication infrastructures. The meeting's PRP (Dutton, Blumler, *et al.* 1994) has been revised in developing Chapter 22 of this book, which moves beyond the more immediate issue of Britain's response into a more general examination of the underlying issues dividing participants in the debate over information superhighways.

Participants at the Forum on Information Superhighways

Professor Jay G. Blumler, University of Leeds; Daniel Brenner, US National Cable Television Association; James Cornford, Newcastle University; Jon Davey, UK Independent Television Commission; John Drew, BT; Professor William Dutton, PICT; Professor Martin C. J. Elton, New York University; Professor Nicholas Garnham, Westminster University; Professor John Goddard, Newcastle University; Professor Brian Groombridge, University of London; Dr Richard Hawkins, SPRU, Sussex University; Robert Harrison, PA Consulting; Richard Henfrey, Mercury Communications Ltd.; Ruth Kerry, CCTA, the UK Government Centre for Information Systems; Professor Dr Herbert Kubicek, Universität

Bremen; Dr David Lytel, US Office of Science and Technology Policy; Professor Ian Mackintosh, European Foundation for Technical Innovation; Professor Robin Mansell, SPRU, Sussex University; Andrew Mewes, CCTA; Jeremy Mitchell, International Consumer Policy Bureau; Geoff Mulgan, Demos; John Neilson, DTI; Michael Nelson, US Office of Science and Technology Policy; Dr Michael Norton, Parliamentary Office of Science and Technology; Richard Paterson, British Film Institute; Malcolm Peltu, PICT; David Pullinger, IOP Publishing; Dr Stuart Shapiro, Brunel University; Steve Sim, BT Laboratories; Raymond Snoddy, *Financial Times*; Thomas Spacek, Bellcore; Dawson Walker, Cable & Wireless plc; Suzanne Warner, Cable & Wireless plc; Dr Robin Williams, Edinburgh University; Dr Jim Wilson, US House of Representatives.

Learning from IT and Telecommunication Disasters

The final forum took place at the Policy Studies Institute and Imperial College in London on 20 October 1994. Its aim was to illuminate the multi-faceted organizational, social, business, and technical processes which contribute to the effectiveness and safety of ICT systems. Particular attention was paid to identifying the lessons that can be learnt from past disasters. An overall theme emerged about the significance of being aware of human limitations in building and using computer-based systems, which give us the power to overwhelm ourselves with information—sometimes with disastrous consequences. The forum's PRP (Dutton *et al.* 1995) is the primary source for Chapter 10 in this book.

Participants at the Forum on IT and Telecommunications Disasters

Stuart Anderson, Edinburgh University; Stephen Bagnold, Stephen Bagnold Communications; Martin Barnes, Coopers & Lybrand; Brian Bloomfield, CROMTEC, University of Manchester Institute of Science and Technology; Professor Robin Bloomfield, Adelard; Nicholas Boothman, London Metropolitan Police Service; Professor John N. Buxton, Room Underwriting Systems Ltd.; Bernard Carré, Program Validation Ltd.; Dr Steven Castell, Castell Computer and Systems Telecommunications Ltd.; Michael Cavanagh, UK National Computer Centre; Dave Denison, ICL; John Dobson, University of Newcastle; Dr Helga Drummond, University of Liverpool; Professor William Dutton, PICT; Robert Erskine, Glasgow Caledonian University; David Firnberg, David Firnberg Associates; Ewen Fletcher, Context Systems Ltd.; Dr Stephen Flowers, University of Brighton; Paul Gibson, Hursley Laboratory, IBM UK; Professor Patrick A. V. Hall, The Open University; Professor C. A. R. Hoare, FRS, Oxford University; Barrie T. Jones, Portsmouth University; Dr Matthew R. Jones, Cambridge University; Emeritus Professor Frank Land, London School of Economics and Political Science; Professor Beverly Littlewood, City University; Mhairi Macdonald, University of Glasgow; Professor Donald MacKenzie, University of Edinburgh;

Appendix 2. PICT Policy Research Forums

Mahal Mohan, AT&T (USA); Geoff Morgan, Nationwide Building Society; Dr Gordon Mousinho, KPMG Management Consulting; Malcolm Mills, Data Sciences Ltd.; Professor A. Michael Noll, University of Southern California; Brian Oakley, Logica Cambridge Ltd.; Malcolm Peltu, PICT; Felix Redmill, Redmill Consultancy; Professor Gene I. Rochlin, University of California, Berkeley; Professor Scott Sagan, Stanford University; Dr Chris Sauer, University of New South Wales, Australia; Dr Stuart Shapiro, Brunel University; Colin South, BT Laboratories; Professor Barry A. Turner, Middlesex University; Mike Tyler, IBM UK Ltd.; Sir Kenneth Warren, former Chairman of the House of Commons Science and Technology Committee; Christopher Webb, BDO Binder Hamlyn Consulting; Dr Robin Williams, University of Edinburgh.

Glossary

Advanced Research Projects Agency US Department of Defense agency responsible for initial sponsorship of the Internet.

analogue Information represented as a continuously changing physical quantity, such as a radio signal.

artificial intelligence Techniques to enable computer-based systems to respond in similar ways to intelligent human beings.

Asynchronous Transfer Mode Network communication technique capable of handling high-bandwidth multimedia information applications, including video.

automatic teller machine Device for delivering cash and carrying out other transactions for authorized customers using, say, a bank or credit card.

bandwidth Indication of amount of information a telecommunication channel can carry (usually measured in bits per second).

bit (Bi)nary digi(t) used in a mathematical system that recognizes only two states, typically represented as '0' and '1'.

broadband Telecommunication medium, like optical fibre, which can cope with the large volumes of data required for multimedia applications.

bulletin board system A computer system allowing users of an electronic network to leave messages that can be read by many other users.

business process re-engineering Approach to restructuring organizations by optimizing the processes needed to meet specific goals, which often requires changing existing departmental boundaries.

CCITT International standards-making body representing telecommunications operators, suppliers, and other interested parties.

cellular radio A mobile-telephone service which divides the areas covered into small cells to assist in managing the network efficiently.

circuit switching Way of linking systems and devices on a network by directly connecting transmission circuits, as with traditional telephone exchanges.

coaxial cable Transmission medium used for cable networks, with a bandwidth narrower than optical fibre but broader than copper wires.

common carrier Telecommunications network supplier which carries communications from others.

computer-aided software engineering Set of methods, techniques, and tools which seek to apply engineering rigour to software development.

computer conferencing Group discussion based on the exchange of electronic messages on a computer network.

computer integrated manufacturing Use of computers and networks to support all aspects of the manufacturing process.

computer numerical control machine Software-controlled machine tools.

convergence Coming together of all information and communication forms into common underlying approaches based on digital techniques.

cross-ownership Where one company owns many different major media operations, such as television, films, and print publishing.

cross-subsidy Use of revenues from a profitable activity for less profitable ones, for instance to support telecommunications services to remote areas.

cultural imperialism Strong influence by one country over other nations through a domination of electronic media and computer software production and distribution.

cyberspace Term indicating the virtual universe created by networked information flows.

dial-up access Connecting to a network by dialling a number, rather than being connected to it permanently.

digital Represented by strings of 1's and 0's, such as the bits (0/1 or on/off) used by digital information and communication technologies.

digital compression Techniques which enable large volumes of information to be sent using fewer bits.

direct satellite broadcasting Transmission of television or radio programmes directly from a satellite to an antenna connected to viewers' TV sets.

distance learning Use of electronic networks to deliver educational services.

download To send an electronic document, software, or other computer file across a network.

electronic data interchange Ability to exchange documents and other information, such as orders and invoices, between organizations electronically.

electronic democracy Applications of electronic networks to support democratic processes.

electronic funds transfer Using electronic networks for money-based transactions.

electronic mail Network service allowing typed messages to be sent between people using personal electronic mailboxes to store messages until they are read.

electronic service delivery Using electronic networks to provide customers and clients directly with a variety of public and commercial services.

ethnography Social science method for analysing group behaviour through observation, for example to observe a work environment when new technology is introduced into it.

ethnomethodology Form of ethnography employing a range of systematic techniques for recording and studying group behaviour.

expert system Artificial intelligence technique for developing software incorporating human expertise on particular subjects.

file transfer protocol Standard for exchanging computer files across the Internet.

flexible manufacturing systems Application of information and communication technologies to tailor production relatively easily to different customer requirements.

Fordism Rigid, routinized assembly-line work processes, based on Taylorism, which Henry Ford introduced in the early twentieth century to build cars.

graphical user interface Use of icons and pointer devices to simplify users' interaction with a computer, as in Microsoft Windows and Apple Macintosh systems.

hacking Accessing a computer-based system unlawfully.

high-definition television Television pictures with a high resolution involving the presentation of more information on a screen to give sharper images than traditional lower-resolution images. This requires higher bandwidth networks.

information and communication technologies All the kinds of electronic systems used for broadcasting, telecommunications, and computer-mediated communications.

information economy An economy in which the processing and transmission of information is a prime activity.

information infrastructure Provision of underlying network capabilities to support a variety of services based on computing and telecommunications capabilities.

information service provider Organization, group, or individual who creates and packages information content carried by electronic networks.

information society Refers to the increasing centrality of ICTs to all forms of social and economic activity.

information superhighway Term coined by US Clinton Administration for an advanced information infrastructure accessible to all individuals, groups, and firms.

information technology Computer-based techniques for storing, processing, managing, and transmitting information.

Integrated Digital Services Network Service using digital techniques throughout the network.

interactive television Networked service allowing TV sets to be used for two-way communication with various services, such as for teleshopping.

Internet International 'network of networks' offering electronic mail and database services to millions of people.

Just In Time Use of information and computer technologies to co-ordinate deliveries from suppliers to ensure a minimum of locally stored inventory is needed to support production processes.

leased line Link from a telecommunications operator dedicated to a particular customer for the payment of a regular fee.

liberalization Opening up of public telecommunications supply to competition.

local area network Computer-based network which serves a particular room, building, or campus.

magnetic stripe Method of storing digital information, as on most bank and credit cards.

modem MOdulator/DEModulator which converts between analogue and digital techniques to allow computers to be connected via non-digital networks.

Mosaic Simple graphical user interface, developed for World Wide Web, which has influenced interface designs of many other tools for exploring information networks.

multimedia Integration of text, video, and audio capabilities in computer and telecommunication systems.

narrowband Telecommunication channel which can handle only relatively small volumes of data, such as copper wires used for voice-only telephony.

narrowcasting Targeting communication media at specific segments of the audience.

numerically controlled machine Machine tool controlled by a paper-tape loop.

online Activity involving direct interaction with a computer-based system via a telecommunications link.

open system The aim of enabling any computer system to interconnect and be compatible with any other.

Open Systems Interconnection Model for open-system compatibility developed by the International Standards Organization and CCITT.

operating system Software, such as Microsoft DOS and Windows, Unix, and IBM MVS, which manages the computer's basic functions so they can be exploited effectively by users.

optical fibres Broadband telecommunication links using light to transmit information.

packet switching Method for coding and transmitting digital information as small packets of information rather than a single continuous stream and then reassembling them at their destination.

Plain Old Telephone Service Basic voice-only telephony services.

political economy The overlap and interaction between economic and political power in the context of prevailing control structures.

post-Fordism New forms of work organization which move away from the automated mass-production line of Fordism.

preferred reading The interpretation which a producer of media content or software would like the audience or user to follow.

Private Automatic Branch Exchange System located on a user's premises which links phones inside the organization and connects them to the public network.

privatization Opening up of the public telecommunications supply industry to private ownership.

protocol Detailed definition of the procedures and rules required to transmit information across a telecommunications link.

PTT Monopoly public telecommunication operator, generally owned by a national government.

Public Switched Telephone Network Telecommunication network available to the public.

public telecommunication operator Supplier offering telecommunication infrastructure capabilities to individuals and companies.

Regional Bell Operating Company Local US telecommunication companies created after the break-up of AT&T in 1984.

semiotics Study of the underlying meanings of symbols and metaphors.

share of voice Measurement of cross-media ownership based on the proportion of total media consumption rather than technologically defined markets, such as newspaper circulation or television audience shares on their own.

smartcard Credit-card-sized device including a microprocessor for storing and processing information.

social shaping of technology Research discipline which acknowledges the importance of global and local social and economic forces in determining the outcomes of technological innovation.

tariff rebalancing Shifting the basis of telecommunication charges to reflect the direct costs of each service, without allowing for cross-subsidies.

Taylorism Way of organizing work which emphasizes routinization as a means of optimizing productivity, originally developed by engineer F. W. Taylor in the late nineteenth century but also often employed in modern computer-based automation.

telebanking Interactive networked service allowing transactions with banks to be undertaken from home.

telecommuting Using telecommunications to perform work at home or a work centre that would otherwise involve commuting physically to a more distant place of work.

teleconferencing Meeting involving people in different locations communicating simultaneously through electronic media.

telematics Information and communication networks and their applications.

teleport Site-specific telecommunication infrastructure, such as a land-station link to a satellite, associated with related land and building development.

teleshopping Ability to order goods and services from home directly through an interactive network.

teletext Service transmitted by television signal which allows users to call up a wide variety of information on a TV screen.

television licence Required in some countries for the use of a TV set, as in the UK, where the public service BBC is funded from annual TV licence fees.

telework Use of an electronic network to enable individuals to work from home or a decentralized work centre.

Transmission Control Protocol/Internet Protocol Interconnection standard used for the Internet.

universal service Provision of a minimum set of telecommunication services to all households.

Usenet International collection of electronic discussion groups on a multiplicity of topics, accessible through the Internet.

value-added network An enhanced service built on the basic telecommunications network, such as electronic mail and telebanking.

V-chip An electronic device that can be installed in a TV set to block out 'objectionable' material, which is detected by a rating that must be encoded in the television signal.

videoconferencing Teleconferencing involving video communication.

video-on-demand Interactive network service which allows customers to view a video whenever they wish.

videotex Computer-based network service which delivers textual and graphical information, typically as pages of information stored on remote computers.

virtual organization Operation involving many individuals, groups, and firms in different locations using electronic networks to act as if they were a single organization at one site.

virtual reality Computer-based visualization of a total environment that gives the user a perception of being within the environment rather than viewing it on a screen.

voice mail The ability to store spoken messages on a network for subsequent retrieval by the recipient.

wide area network Telecommunications network that extends beyond individual buildings or campuses.

World Wide Web System which allows information sites around the world to be accessed via the Internet through the Mosaic interface.

Bibliography

Abramson, J. B., Arterton, F. C., and Orren, G. R. (1988), *The Electronic Commonwealth* (New York: Basic Books).

ACARD (1986), Advisory Council for Applied Research and Development, *Software: A Vital Key to UK Competitiveness* (London: HMSO).

Adam, A., Emms, J., and Owen, J. (1994) (eds.), *Women, Work and Computerization: Breaking Old Boundaries, Building New Forms* (Amsterdam: North-Holland).

Agre, P. (1995), 'Conceptions of the User in Computer Systems Design', in Thomas (1995), 67–106.

Allen, T. J., and Scott Morton, M. S. (1994) (eds.), *Information Technology and the Corporation of the 1990s* (Oxford: Oxford University Press).

Altshuler, A., Anderson, M., Jones, D., Roos, D., Womack, J. (1985), *The Future of the Automobile* (Cambridge, Mass.: MIT Press).

Amsden, A. (1989), *Asia's Next Giant: South Korea and Late Industrialization* (New York: Oxford University Press).

Anderson, D. (1978), 'Some Organizational Features in the Local Production of a Plausible Text', *Philosophy of the Social Sciences*, 8: 113–35.

Anderson, R. H., Bikson, T. K., Law, S. A., and Mitchell, B. M. (1995), *Universal Access to E-Mail: Feasibility and Societal Implications* (Santa Monica, Calif.: Rand).

Andrews, E. (1996), 'Congress Votes to Reshape Communications Industry, Ending a 4-Year Struggle', *New York Times*, 2 Feb.: 1.

Aoki, M. (1986), 'Horizontal versus Vertical Information Structure of the Firm', *American Economic Review*, 76: 971–83.

APO (1990), Asian Productivity Organization, *Information Technology-Led Development* (Tokyo: APO).

Applegate, L. M., Cash Jr., J. I., and Mills, D. Q. (1988), 'Information Technology and Tomorrow's Manager', *Harvard Business Review*, 88: 128–36.

Archer, M. S. (1987), 'Resisting the Revival of Relativism', *International Sociology*, 2: 235–50.

Arnbak, J., Mitchell, B., Neu, W., Neumann, K.-H., and Vogelsang, I. (1994), *Network Interconnection in the Domain of ONP*. Study for DG XIII of the European Commission (Bad Honnef, Germany: Wissenschaftliches Institut für Kommunikationsdienste (WIK) and The European–American Center for Policy Analysis).

Arnold, E., Huggett, C., Senker, P., Swords-Isherwood, N., and Zmroczek Shannon, C. (1982), *Microelectronics and Women's Employment in Britain: Women and Technology*. Occasional Paper No. 17 (Brighton: SPRU, University of Sussex).

Arnold, M. (1963, 1st pub. 1869), *Culture and Anarchy* (Cambridge: Cambridge University Press).

Arterton, F. C. (1987), *Teledemocracy: Can Technology Protect Democracy?* (London: Sage).

Bibliography

Ayres, R. U. (1987), *Future Trends in Factory Automation*. IIASA Working Paper 87–22 (Laxenburg, Austria: IIASA [International Institute for Applied Systems Analysis]).

Baba, Y. (unpub. diss. 1986), *Japanese Colour TV Firms: Decision-Making from the 1950s to the 1980s*. Unpub. Ph.D. dissertation (Brighton: University of Sussex).

Baer, W. (1995a), *Telecommunication Infrastructure Competition: The Costs of Delay*. PICT Policy Research Paper No. 31 (Uxbridge: PICT, Brunel University).

—— (1995b), 'Telecommunication Infrastructure Competition: The Costs of Delay'. *Telecommunications Policy*, 19: 351–63.

Baily, M. N. (1986), 'What Has Happened to Productivity Growth?', *Science*, 234: 443–51.

Baldamus, W. (1961), *Efficiency and Effort: An Analysis of Industrial Administration* (London: Tavistock).

Bangemann Group (1994), High Level Group on the Information Society, *Europe and the Global Information Society: Recommendations to the European Council* (Brussels: Commission of the European Communities).

Bangemann, M. (1995), 'Policies for a European Information Society', in PICT (1995a), 5–12.

Banister, D., Capello, R., and Nijkamp, P. (1995) (eds.), *European Transport and Communications Networks* (Chichester: John Wiley).

Banker, R. D., Kauffman, R. J., and Mahmood, M. A. (1993) (eds.), *Strategic Information Technology Management* (Harrisburg, Pa.: Idea Group Publishing).

Bar, F., Borrus, M., and Coriat, B. (1989), *Information Networks and Competitive Advantage: Issues for Government Policy and Corporate Strategy Development. Berkeley Roundtable on the International Economy, Vol. 1* (Paris: OECD; Brussels: Commission of the European Communities DG XIII).

Bardach, E. (1977), *The Implementation Game* (Cambridge, Mass.: MIT Press).

Barker, J., and Downing, H. (1980), 'Word Processing and the Transformation of the Patriarchal Relations of Control in the Office', *Capital and Class*, 10: 64–99.

Barras, R. (1986), 'Towards a Theory of Innovation in Services', *Research Policy*, 15: 161–73.

—— (1990), 'Interactive Innovation in Financial and Business Services: The Vanguard of the Service Revolution', *Research Policy*, 9: 215–37.

Bauer, M. (1995) (ed.), *Resistance to New Technology* (Cambridge: Cambridge University Press).

BBA (1995), British Banking Association, *Annual Abstract of Banking Statistics* (London: BBA).

Bell, D. (1967), 'The Year 2000—The Trajectory of an Idea', *Dædalus*, 96: 639–51.

—— (1973), *The Coming of Post-Industrial Society: A Venture in Social Forecasting* (New York: Basic Books; Harmondsworth: Penguin).

—— (1980), 'The Social Framework of the Information Society,' in Forester (1980), 500–49.

Bellamy, C. (forthcoming), 'Transforming Social Security Benefits Administration for the Twenty-First Century: Towards One-Stop Services and the Client Group Principle', *Public Administration*.

—— and Taylor, J. A. (1994), 'Towards the Information Polity? Public Administration in the Information Age', in *Public Administration*, 72: 1–12.

—— Horrocks, I., and Webb, J. (1995), 'Exchanging Information with the Public: From Community Information Systems to One-Stop Shops', *Local Government Studies*, 21: 11–30.

Benet, M. K. (1972), *Secretary: An Enquiry into the Female Ghetto* (London: Sidgwick & Jackson).

Beniger, J. R. (1986), *The Control Revolution* (Cambridge, Mass.: Harvard University Press).

Berg, A.-J., and Aune, M. (1994) (eds.), *Domestic Technology and Everyday Life—Mutual Shaping Processes* (Brussels: Commission of the European Communities).

Berg, J., and Schumny, H. (1990) (eds.), *An Analysis of the IT Standardisation Process* (Amsterdam: Elsevier).

Berger, S., and Piore, M. (1980), *Dualism and Discontinuity in Industrial Society* (Cambridge: Cambridge University Press).

Berry, B. J. (1991), *Long Wave Rhythms in Economic Development and Political Behavior* (Baltimore: John Hopkins University Press).

Bessant, J., Guy, K., Miles, I., and Rush, H. (1985), *IT Futures Surveyed: A Study of Informed Opinion concerning the Long-Term Implications of Information Technology for Society* (London: National Economic Development Office).

Biehl, D. (1982) (ed.), *The Contribution of Infrastructure to Regional Development. Final Report to DG XVI* (Brussels: Commission of the European Communities).

Bijker, W. E. (1995), *Of Bicycles, Bakelites and Bulbs: Toward a Theory of Sociotechnical Change* (Cambridge, Mass.: MIT Press).

—— and Law, J. (1992) (eds.), *Shaping Technology/Building Society: Studies in Sociotechnical Change* (Cambridge, Mass.: MIT Press).

—— Hughes, T. P., and Pinch, T. (1987), *The Social Construction of Technological Systems: New Directions in the Sociology of Technology* (Cambridge, Mass.: MIT Press).

Bjerknes, G., Ehn, P., and King, M. (1987) (eds.), *Computers and Democracy: A Scandinavian Challenge* (Aldershot: Avebury).

Bloomfield, B., and Best, A. (1992), 'Management Consultants, Systems Development, Power and the Translation of Problems', *Sociological Review*, 40: 532–60.

—— and Coombs, R. (1992), 'Information Technology, Control and Power: The Centralisation and Decentralisation Debate Revisited', *Journal of Management Studies*, 29: 459–84.

—— and Vurdubakis, T. (1994), 'Boundary Disputes: Negotiating the Boundary between the Technical and the Social in the Development of IT Systems', *Information Technology and People*, 17: 9–24.

—— Coombs, R., Cooper, D., and Rea, D. (1992), 'Machines and Manœuvres: Responsibility Accounting and the Construction of Hospital Information Systems', *Accounting, Management and Information Technology*, 2: 197–219.

—— —— and Owen, J. (1994), 'The Social Construction of Information Systems—The Implications for Management Control', in Mansell (1994a), 143–57.

Bibliography

Bloomfield, B., Best, A., Knights, D., and Littler, D. (forthcoming) (eds.), *Information Technology and Organisations* (Oxford: Oxford University Press).

Bloor, D. (1973), 'Wittgenstein and Mannheim on the Sociology of Mathematics', *Studies in the History and Philosophy of Science*, 4: 173–91.

—— (1983), *Wittgenstein: A Social Theory of Knowledge* (London: Macmillan).

—— (1994), 'What can the Sociologist of Knowledge Say about 2 + 2 = 4?', in Ernest (1994), 21–32.

Blumler, J. G. (1992), *Television and the Public Interest: Vulnerable Values in West European Broadcasting* (London: Sage).

—— McLeod, J. M., and Rosengren, K. E. (1992) (eds.), *Comparatively Speaking: Communication and Culture across Space and Time* (London: Sage).

Boehm, B. (1988), 'A Spiral Model of Software Development and Enhancement', *IEEE Computer*, May: 61–72.

Boulding, K. E. (1966), 'The Economics of Knowledge and Knowledge of Economics', *American Economic Review*, 56: 1–13.

Bounine, J., and Suzaki, K. (1987), *Juste à temps: Les Sources de la productivité industrielle japonaise* (Paris: Masson).

Bowen, B. (1994), *Multimedia: Now and Down the Line* (London: Bowerdean Publishing).

Boyer, R. S., and Moore, J. S. (1984), 'Proof Checking the RSA Public Key Encryption Algorithm', *American Mathematical Monthly*, 91: 81.

Brady, T., Tierney, M., and Williams, R. (1992), 'The Commodification of Industry Applications Software', *Industrial and Corporate Change*, 1: 489–514.

Braverman, H. (1974), *Labor and Monopoly Capital: The Degradation of Work in the Twentieth Century* (London: Monthly Review Press).

British Sky Broadcasting (1994), *Annual Report* (Isleworth, Middlesex: British Sky Broadcasting).

Brock, B., and Hunt, W. A. (1990), *Report on the Formal Specification and Partial Verification of the VIPER Microprocessor* (Austin, Tex: Computational Logic, Inc.).

Brook, J., and Boal, I. A. (1995) (eds.), *Resisting the Virtual Life: The Culture and Politics of Information* (San Francisco: City Lights).

Brynjolfsson, E., and Hitt, L. (1993), 'Is Information Systems Spending Productive? New Evidence and New Results', *Proceedings of the 14th International Conference on Information Systems* (Orlando, Fl., 1993), 47–64.

—— Malone, T., and Gurbaxani, V. (1988), *The Impact of Information Technology on Markets and Hierarchies*. Sloan School of Management Working Paper No. 2113–88 (Cambridge, Mass.: MIT).

Burnham, D. (1983), *The Rise of the Computer State* (New York: Random House).

Burstein, D., and Kline, D. (1995), *Road Warriors: Dreams and Nightmares along the Information Highway* (New York: Dutton).

Cabinet Office (1991), *The Citizen's Charter: Raising the Standard*. White Paper, Cmnd. 1599 (London: HMSO).

Callon, M. (1980), 'The State and Technical Innovation: A Case Study of the Electric Vehicle in France', *Research Policy*, 9: 358–76.

Carson, W. G. (1970), 'White Collar Crime and the Enforcement of Factory Legislation', *British Journal of Criminology*, 10: 192–206.

Castell, S. (1993), 'Computers Trusted and Found Wanting', *The Computer Law and Security Report*, July–Aug.: 155–6.

Castells, M. (1989), *The Informational City* (Oxford: Basil Blackwell).

Cawson, A., Haddon, L., and Miles, I. (1995), *The Shape of Things to Consume* (Aldershot: Avebury).

CCTA (1994), The UK Government Centre for Information Systems, *Information Superhighways: Opportunities for Public Sector Applications in the UK* (London: CCTA).

CEA (1994), Council of Economic Advisors, *Economic Benefits of the Administration's Legislative Proposals for Telecommunications* (Washington, DC: Executive Office of the President).

Central Policy Review Staff (1978), *Social and Economic Implications of Microelectronics* (London: HMSO).

Chambliss, W. (1973), *Sociological Readings in the Conflict Perspective* (Reading, Mass.: Addison-Wesley).

Chaum, D. (1992), 'Achieving Electronic Privacy', *Scientific American*, 267: 96–101.

Checkland, P., and Scholes, J. (1990), *Soft Systems Methodologies in Practice* (Chichester: John Wiley).

Chenevière, G. (1990), 'The Europe Co-production Association is Five Years Old: Towards a European TV Drama Industry', *European Broadcasting Union Review: Programmes Administration Law*, 41: 17–20.

Churbuck, D. C., and Young, J. S. (1992), 'The Virtual Workplace', *Forbes*, 23 Nov.: 184–90.

Cleland, G., and MacKenzie, D. (1994), *Inhibiting Factors, Market Structure and the Industrial Uptake of Formal Methods*. Working Paper No. 57 (Edinburgh: University of Edinburgh, Research Centre for Social Sciences, Dec.).

Cochrane, P., Heatley, D. J., Fisher, K., Cameron, K., and Taylor-Hendry, R. (1992), 'CAMNET—The First Telepresence System', *Interlink 2000 Journal*, Aug.: 38–41.

Cohn, A. (1989), 'The Notion of Proof in Hardware Verification', *Journal of Automated Reasoning*, 5: 127–39.

Cole, B. G. (1991) (ed.), *After the Breakup: Assessing the New Post-AT&T Divestiture Era* (New York: Columbia University Press).

Collins, H. M. (1982), 'Special Relativism: The Natural Attitude', *Social Studies of Science*, 12: 139–43.

—— (1985), *Changing Order: Replication and Induction in Scientific Practice* (London: Sage).

—— and Yearley, S. (1992), 'Journey into Space', in Pickering (1992), 369–81.

Collins, R. (1990), *The Second Generation: The Lessons of Satellite Television in Western Europe*. PICT Policy Research Paper No. 12 (Uxbridge: PICT, Brunel University).

—— (1991), *Direct Broadcasting by Satellite in the UK—From Sky to BSkyB*. PICT Policy Research Paper No. 15 (Swindon: Economic and Social Research Council).

Bibliography

Collins, R. (1992), *Satellite Television in Western Europe* (London: John Libbey).

Committee on Women in Science, Engineering and Technology (1994), *The Rising Tide* (London: HMSO).

Comstock, G., Chapple, S., Katzman, N., McCombs, M., and Roberts, D. (1978), *Television and Human Behavior* (New York: Columbia University Press).

Cooley, M. (1981), 'The Taylorization of Intellectual Work', in Levidow and Young (1981), 46–65.

—— (1987), *Architect or Bee? The Human Price of Technology* (London: Hogarth).

Coombs, R. (1992), *Organisational Politics and the Strategic Use of Information Technology*. PICT Policy Research Paper No. 20 (Uxbridge: PICT, Brunel University).

—— and Cooper, D. (1990), *Accounting for Patients?: Information Technology and the Implementation of the NHS White Paper*. PICT Policy Research Paper No. 10 (Uxbridge: PICT, Brunel University).

—— and Hull, R. (1995*a*), 'BPR as "IT-Enabled Organisational Change": An Assessment', *New Technology, Work & Employment*, 10: 121–31.

—— —— (1995*b*), *The Wider Research Context of Business Process Analysis*. Report for the Economic and Social Research Council (Swindon: ESRC).

—— Saviotti, P., and Walsh, V. (1992) (eds.), *Technical Change and Company Strategies* (London: Academic Press).

Cooper, G., and Bowers, J. (1995), 'Representing the User: Notes on the Disciplinary Rhetoric of Human–Computer Interaction', in Thomas (1995), 48–66.

—— and Woolgar, S. (1993), *Software is Society Made Malleable: The Importance of Conceptions of Audience in Software and Research Practice*. PICT Policy Research Paper No. 25 (Uxbridge: PICT, Brunel University).

—— —— (1994*a*), 'Software Quality as Community Performance', in Mansell (1994*a*), 54–68.

—— —— (1994*b*), *A Sociological Study of Changes in Research Culture*. CRICT Discussion Paper No. 46 (Uxbridge: Brunel University).

—— —— (forthcoming) (eds.), *Technography* (Uxbridge: Brunel University).

—— Hine, C. M., Low, J., and Woolgar, S. (1995), 'Ethnography and HCI', in Thomas (1995), 11–36.

Cooper, M. (1994), 'Human Factors in Telecommunications Engineering', *British Telecommunications Engineering*, 13: 98–107.

Corey, K. E. (1995), 'Information Technology and Telecommunications Policies in Southeast Asian Development'. Paper presented at the Workshop on Informatics and Telecoms Tectonics: Information Technology, Telecommunications, Policy and the Meaning of Space (Michigan State University).

Corner, J. (1994), 'Debating Culture: Quality and Inequality', *Media Culture and Society*, 16: 141–8.

Council of Europe (1981), *Explanatory Report on the Convention for the Protection of Individuals with Regard to Automatic Processing of Personal Data* (Strasbourg: Council of Europe).

Crew, M. A. (1994) (ed.), *Incentive Regulation for Public Utilities* (Boston: Kluwer Academic Publications).

Cringley, R. X. (1992), *Accidental Empires* (London: Penguin).

Cronin, F. J., Parker, E. B., Colleran, E. K., and Gold, M. A. (1991), 'Telecommunications Infrastructure and Economic Growth: An Analysis of Causality', *Telecommunications Policy*, 15: 529–35.

—— Colleran, E. K., Herbert, P. L., and Lewitsky, S. (1993), 'Telecommunications and Growth: The Contribution of Telecommunications Infrastructure Investment to Aggregate and Sectoral Productivity', *Telecommunications Policy*, 17: 677–90.

—— Parker, E. B., Colleran, E. K., and Gold, M. A. (1993), 'Telecommunications Infrastructure Investment and Economic Development', *Telecommunications Policy*, 17: 415–30.

CSE Microelectronics Group (1980), *Microelectronics: Capitalist Technology and the Working Class* (London: CSE Books).

CSO (1992), Central Statistical Office, *Input–Output Balance for the United Kingdom 1992* (London: HMSO).

Cullen, B., and Blondeel, Y. (1995), 'Union Measures Taken in the Telecommunications Area and Results Achieved'. Paper presented at the Conference on Implementing European Telecommunications Law (Brussels: Commission of the European Communities).

Curran, S., and Mitchell, H. (1982), *Office Automation: An Essential Management Strategy* (London: Macmillan).

Curtis, B. (1993), 'Maturity from the User's Point of View', *IEEE Software*, 10: 89–90.

Dahlman, C., and Frischtak, C. (1990), *National Systems Supporting Technical Advance in Industry: The Brazilian Experience*. Industry Series Paper No. 32 (Washington, DC: The World Bank, Industry and Energy Department).

Daniels, W. (1986), *Technical Change and Industrial Relations* (London: Frances Pinter).

Danziger, J. N., Dutton, W. H., Kling, R., and Kraemer, K. L. (1982), *Computers and Politics* (New York: Columbia University Press).

Davenport, T. (1993), *Process Innovation: Re-engineering Work through Information Technology* (Boston: Harvard Business School Press).

—— and Short, J. E. (1990), 'The New Industrial Engineering: Information Technology and Business Process Redesign', *Sloan Management Review*, 31: 11–27.

David, P. (1975), *Technical Choice, Innovation and Economic Growth: Essays on American and British Experience in the Nineteenth Century* (Cambridge: Cambridge University Press).

de Sola Pool, I. (1977) (ed.), *The Social Impact of the Telephone* (Cambridge, Mass.: MIT Press).

—— (1983a), *Technologies of Freedom* (Cambridge, Mass.: Harvard University Press).

—— (1983b), *Forecasting the Telephone* (Norwood, NJ: Ablex).

—— (1990) (ed.), E. M. Noam, *Technologies without Boundaries: On Telecommunications in a Global Age* (Cambridge, Mass.: Harvard University Press).

Bibliography

Dedrick, J., and Kraemer, K. L. (1993), 'The Quest for Self-Reliance: Information Technology Policy in India', *Asian Survey*, 33: 463–92.

—— —— (1995), 'National Technology Policy and Computer Production in the Asia-Pacific Countries', *The Information Society*, 11: 29–58.

Delgado, A. (1979), *The Enormous File: A Social History of the Office* (London: John Murray).

DeMillo, R., Lipton, R., and Perlis, A. (1979), 'Social Processes and Proofs of Theorems and Programs', *Communications of the ACM*, 22: 271–80.

Denison, E. (1985), *Trends in American Economic Growth, 1882–1982* (Washington, DC: The Brookings Institution).

Denning, D. E., and Lin, H. S. (1994) (eds.), *Rights and Responsibilities of Participants in Networked Communications* (Washington, DC: National Academy Press).

Department of Labor (1989), *Handbook of Labor Statistics* (Washington, DC: Department of Labor).

Derrida, J. (1992), *Mochlos; or, the Conflict of the Faculties*, in Rand (1992), 1–34.

Derthick, M., and Quirk, P. J. (1985), *The Politics of Deregulation* (Washington, DC: The Brookings Institution).

DGBAS (1991), Director-General of Budget, Accounting, and Statistics, *Statistical Yearbook of the Republic of China* (Taipei: DGBAS).

Diaper, D., and Sanger, C. (1993) (eds.), *CSCW in Practice: An Introduction and Case Studies* (London: Springer-Verlag).

Diebold, J. (1952), *Automation: The Advent of the Automatic Factory* (New York: Van Nostrand).

Dijkstra, E. W. (1972), 'The Humble Programmer', *Communications of the ACM*, 10: 859–66.

Dosi, G. (1982), 'Technological Paradigms and Technological Trajectories: A Suggested Interpretation of the Determinants of Technological Change', *Research Policy*, 11: 147–62.

—— Freeman, C., Nelson, R., Silverberg, G., and Soete, L. (1988), *Technical Change and Economic Theory* (London: Frances Pinter).

Doulton, A., Sandford, N., and Wilson, R. (1994) (eds.), *Government and Community Information Services: EIP Report 1994* (London: Dragonflair).

Drake, W. J. (1995) (ed.), *The New Information Infrastructure: Strategies for US Policy* (New York: The Twentieth Century Fund).

Drucker, P. (1992), 'The New Society of Organizations', *Harvard Business Review*, Sept.: 95–104.

—— (1993), *Post-Capitalist Society* (London: Butterworth-Heinemann).

—— (1994), 'The Theory of the Business', *Harvard Business Review*, Sept.: 95–9.

Drummond, H. (1994), 'Escalation in Organizational Decision Making', *Journal of Behavioral Decision Making*, 7: 43–55.

—— (forthcoming), *Escalation in Decision-Making: The Tragedy of Taurus* (Oxford: Oxford University Press).

DTI (1988), Department of Trade and Industry, *The Infrastructure for Tomorrow: Communications Steering Group Report* (London: HMSO).

—— (1991), *Competition and Choice: Telecommunications Policy for the 1990s*. White Paper, Cmnd. 1461 (London: HMSO).

—— (1995), *Fixed Radio Access: Increasing the Choice* (London: HMSO).

DuBoff, R. (1983), 'The Telegraph and the Structure of Markets in the United States, 1845–1890', *Research in Economic History*, 8: 253–77.

Ducatel, K. (1994) (ed.), *Employment and Technical Change in Europe* (Aldershot: Edward Elgar).

Dutton, W. H. (1992*a*), 'The Ecology of Games Shaping Telecommunications Policy', *Communication Theory*, 2: 303–28.

—— (1992*b*), 'Political Science Research on Teledemocracy', *Social Science Computer Review*, 10: 505–23.

—— (1992*c*), 'The Social Impact of Emerging Telephone Services', *Telecommunications Policy*, 16: 377–87.

—— (1994), 'Lessons from Public and Nonprofit Services', in Williams and Pavlik (1994), 105–37.

—— (1995), 'Driving into the Future of Communications? Check the Rear View Mirror', in Emmott (1995), 79–102.

—— (1996), 'Network Rules of Order: Regulating Speech in Public Electronic Forums', *Media, Culture and Society*, 18: 269–90.

—— (forthcoming), *Society on the Line: The Information and Communication Revolution* (Oxford: Oxford University Press).

—— and Guthrie, K., (1991), 'An Ecology of Games: The Political Construction of Santa Monica's Public Electronic Network', in *Informatization and the Public Sector*, 1: 1–24.

—— and Meadow, R. (1987), 'A Tolerance for Surveillance: American Public Opinion concerning Privacy and Civil Liberties', in Levitan (1987), 147–70.

—— and Vedel, T. (1992), 'The Dynamics of Cable Television in the United States, Britain, and France', in Blumler *et al.* (1992), 70–93.

—— Blumler, J., and Kraemer, K. (1987) (eds.), *Wired Cities* (Boston: G. K. Hall).

—— Wyer, J., and O'Connell, J. (1993), 'The Governmental Impacts of Information Technology', in Banker *et al.* (1993), 265–96.

—— Blumler, J. G., Garnham, N., Mansell, R., Cornford, J., and Peltu, M. (1994), *The Information Superhighway: Britain's Response*. Policy Research Paper No. 29 (Uxbridge: PICT, Brunel University).

—— Taylor, J., Bellamy, C., Raab, C., and Peltu, M. (1994), *Electronic Service Delivery: Themes and Issues in the Public Sector*. Policy Research Paper No. 28 (Uxbridge: PICT, Brunel University).

—— MacKenzie, D., Shapiro, S., and Peltu, M. (1995), *Computer Power and Human Limits: Learning from IT and Telecommunications Disasters*. Policy Research Paper No. 33 (Uxbridge: PICT, Brunel University).

Easterbrook, S. (1993) (ed.), *CSCW: Cooperation or Conflict?* (London: Springer-Verlag).

Edge, D. (1994), 'The Social Shaping of Technology', in Heap *et al.* (1994), 14–32.

Bibliography

Edwards, R. (1979), *Contested Terrain: The Transformation of the Workplace in the Twentieth Century* (London: Heinemann).

Ehn, P. (1989), *Work Oriented Design of Computer Artefacts* (Stockholm: Arbetslivscentrum).

Eliot, T. S. (1948), *Notes towards a Definition of Culture* (London: Faber & Faber).

Elliott, B. (1988) (ed.), *Technology and Social Process* (Edinburgh: Edinburgh University Press).

Elton, M. C. J. (1991) (ed.), *Integrated Broadband Networks: The Public Policy Issues* (Amsterdam: Elsevier Science Publishers).

Emmott, S. J. (1995) (ed.), Information Superhighways: Multimedia Users and Futures (London: Academic Press).

Eriksson, I. V., Kitchenham, B. A., and Tijdens, K. G. (1991) (eds.), *Women, Work and Computerization: Understanding and Overcoming Bias in Work and Education* (Amsterdam: North Holland).

Ernest, P. (1994) (ed.), *Mathematics, Education and Philosophy* (London: Falmer).

ESRC (1994), Economic and Social Research Council, *ESRC Corporate Plan 1994–99* (Swindon: ESRC).

ETL (1994), European Technology in Learning, *Proceedings of the European Technology in Learning Conference, ETL 94* (Blackburn: Business and Industrial Consultancy).

European Commission (1983), *Interim Report—Realities and Tendencies in European Television: Perspectives and Options.* COM(83) 229 (Brussels: Commission of the European Communities).

—— (1984a), *Towards a European Television Policy.* European File 19/84 (Brussels: Commission of the European Communities).

—— (1984b), *Television without Frontiers: Green Paper on the Establishment of the Common Market for Broadcasting, especially by Satellite and Cable.* COM (84) 300 final (Luxembourg: Office for Official Publications of the European Communities).

—— (1986), *Television and the Audiovisual Sector: Towards a European Policy.* European File 14/86 (Luxembourg: Office for Official Publications of the European Communities).

—— (1991), *STAR: Programme Report* (Brussels: Commission of the European Communities).

—— (1992), *1992 Review of the Situation in the Telecommunication Services Sector.* IV/A/3/GL/cd; XIII/D/2/HU/mrd (Brussels: Commission of the European Communities).

—— (1993), *New Location Factors for Mobile Investment in Europe.* Study carried out by Netherlands Economic Institute and Ernst & Young. Regional Development Studies 6 (Brussels: Commission of the European Communities).

—— (1994a), *Growth, Competitiveness, Employment: The Challenges and Ways Forward into the 21st Century.* A White Paper (Luxembourg: Office for Official Publications of the European Communities).

—— (1994b), *Competitiveness and Cohesion: Trends in the Regions.* Fifth Periodic Report on the Social and Economic Situation and Development of the Regions in the Community (Brussels: Commission of the European Communities).

—— (1994c), *Strategy Options to Strengthen the European Programme Industry in the Context of the Audiovisual Policy of the European Union* (Luxembourg: Office of Official Publications of the European Communities).

—— (1994d), *Europe's Way to the Information Society. An Action Plan*. COM(94) 347 (Brussels: European Commission).

—— (1995), 'Theme Paper on Universal Service Issues'. Draft, 7 Sept. (Brussels: Commission of the European Communities DG XIII).

European Parliament (1982a), *Report on Radio and Television Broadcasting in the European Community on behalf of the Committee on Youth, Culture, Education, Information and Sport*. PE Document 1-1013/81 (Strasbourg: European Parliament).

—— (1982b), *Resolution on Radio and Television Broadcasting in the European Community*. OJ 87/82 (Strasbourg: European Parliament).

Eurostat (1994), *Panorama of EU Industry* (Brussels: European Statistics, Commission of the European Communities).

Evenson, R. E., and Ranis, G. (1990) (eds.), *Science and Technology: Lessons for Development Policy* (Boulder, Colo.: Westview Press).

Ewbank Preece (1993), *STAR—Special Telecommunications Action for Regional Development: Community-level Evaluation, Executive Summary* (Brighton: Ewbank Preece Ltd.).

Executive Office of the President (1994), *High Performance Computing and Communications FY 1995 Implementation Plan* (Washington, DC: Office of Science and Technology Policy).

Fairclough, J. (1992), 'Sizzling Start for the White Heat', *The Times Higher Education Supplement*, 23 Oct.: 17.

Faulkner, W., and Arnold, E. (1985) (eds.), *Smothered by Invention: Technology in Women's Lives* (London: Pluto).

Ferguson, M. (1990) (ed.), *Public Communication: The New Imperatives—Future Directions for Media Research* (London: Sage).

Fincham, R. (1987), 'From "Post-Industrialism" to "Information Society": Comment on Lyon', *Sociology*, 21: 463–6.

—— Fleck, J., Procter, R., Scarbrough, H., Tierney, M., and Williams, R. (1995), *Expertise and Innovation: Information Technology Strategies in the Financial Services Sector* (Oxford: Oxford University Press).

Finnegan, R., Salaman, G., and Thompson, K. (1987) (eds.), *Information Technology: Social Issues* (London: Hodder & Stoughton).

Fish, S. E. (1980), *Is there a Text in this Class?: The Authority of Interpretive Communities* (Cambridge, Mass.: Harvard University Press).

FITLOG (1994), Foundation for Information Technology in Local Government, *Under New Management* (Tonbridge, Kent: LGC Communications).

Flaherty, D. (1989), *Protecting Privacy in Surveillance Societies* (Chapel Hill, NC: University of North Carolina Press).

Flamm, K. (1987), *Targeting the Computer: Government Support and International Competition* (Washington, DC: Brookings Institution).

Fleck, J. (1988), *Innofusion or Diffusation*. Edinburgh PICT Working Paper No. 7 (Edinburgh: Edinburgh University).

Bibliography

Fleck, J., Webster, J., and Williams, R. (1990), 'The Dynamics of IT Implementation: A Reassessment of Paradigms and Trajectories of Development', *Futures*, 22: 618–40.

Flowers, S. (1996), *Mega Mistakes: Lessons from Information System Failures* (Chichester: John Wiley).

Floyd, R. W. (1967), 'Assigning Meanings to Programs', in *Mathematical Aspects of Computer Science: Proceedings of Symposia in Applied Mathematics*, 19: 19–32.

Forester, T. (1980), The Microelectronics Revolution (Oxford: Basil Blackwell).

—— (1989) (ed.), *Computers in the Human Context* (Oxford: Basil Blackwell; Cambridge, Mass.: MIT Press).

—— and Morrison, P. (1993), *Computer Ethics: Cautionary Tales and Ethical Dilemmas in Computing* (Cambridge, Mass.: MIT Press).

Fothergill, A. (1994), 'Telework: Women's Experiences and Utilisation of Information Technology in the Home', in Adam *et al.* (1994), 175–89.

Fransman, M. (1992), 'Japanese Failure in a High-Tech Industry? The Case of Central Office Communication Switches', *Telecommunications Policy*, 16: 259–76.

—— (1995), *NTT and the Evolution of the Japanese Information and Communications Industry* (Oxford: Oxford University Press).

Freeman, C. (1984), *The Economics of Innovation* (London: Penguin).

—— (1987), *Technology Policy and Economic Performance: Lessons from Japan* (London: Pinter).

—— (1988), *The Factory of the Future: The Productivity Paradox, Japanese Just-in-Time and Information Technology*. PICT Policy Research Paper No. 3 (Uxbridge: PICT, Brunel University).

—— (1995), *Unemployment and the Diffusion of Information Technologies: The Two-Edged Nature of Technical Change*. PICT Policy Research Paper No. 32 (Uxbridge: PICT, Brunel University).

—— and Perez, C. (1988), 'Structural Crises of Adjustment: Business Cycles and Investment Behaviour', in Freeman *et al.* (1988), 38–66.

—— and Soete, L. (1987) (eds), *Technical Change and Full Employment* (Oxford: Blackwell).

—— —— (1994), *Work for All or Mass Unemployment: Computerised Technical Change into the 21st Century* (London: Pinter).

—— Clark, J., and Soete, L. (1982), *Unemployment and Technical Innovation: A Study of Long Waves in Economic Development* (London: Pinter).

—— Dosi, G., Nelson, R. R., Silverberg, G., and Soete, L. L. G. (1988) (eds.), *Technical Change and Economic Theory* (London: Pinter).

Friedman, A., and Cornford, D. (1989), *Computer Systems Development: History, Organisation, and Implementation* (Chichester: John Wiley).

Gabel, R. (1969), 'The Early Competitive Era in Telephone Communication, 1893–1920', *Law and Contemporary Problems*, 34: 340–59.

Galal, A., Jones, L., Tandon, P., and Vogelsang, I. (1994), *Welfare Consequences of Selling Public Enterprises* (Oxford: Oxford University Press).

Galliers, R. D. (1992) (ed.), *Information Systems Research: Issues, Methods, and Practical Guidelines* (Oxford: Blackwell Scientific).

Gandy, O. (1993), *The Panoptic Sort: Towards a Political Economy of Information* (Boulder, Colo.: Westview Press).

Garnham, N. (1990), *Capitalism and Communication* (London: Sage).

—— (1993), 'The Mass Media, Cultural Identity, and the Public Sphere in the Modern World', *Public Culture*, 5, 251–65.

—— (1994), 'Whatever Happened to the Information Society?', in Mansell (1994a), 42–51.

—— and Mulgan, G. (1991), 'Broadband and the Barriers to Convergence in the European Community', *Telecommunications Policy*, 15: 182–94.

Gates, B. (1995), *The Road Ahead* (London: Viking).

GATT (1990), General Agreement on Tariffs and Trade, *International Trade* (Geneva: GATT).

Gell, M., and Cochrane, P. (1994), 'Education and the Birth of the Experience Industry', in ETL (1994), 54–67.

Gershuny, J. (1987), *After Industrial Society?* (London: Macmillan).

—— and Miles, I. (1983), *The New Service Economy* (London: Pinter).

Giddens, A. (1990), *The Consequences of Modernity* (Oxford: Polity Press).

Gillespie, A., and Cornford, J. (1995), 'Network Diversity or Network Fragmentation? The Evolution of European Telecommunications in Competitive Environments', in Banister *et al.* (1995), 319–32.

—— Goddard, J. B., Robinson, J. F., Smith, I. J., and Thwaites, A. T. (1984), *The Effects of New Information Technology on the Less-Favoured Regions of the Community*. Regional Policy Series No. 23 (Brussels: Commission of the European Communities).

Glanz, J. (1995), 'Mathematical Logic Flushes out the Bugs in Chip Designs', *Science*, 267 (20 Jan.): 332–3.

Gleckman, H. (1993), 'The Technology Payoff', *Business Week*, 14 June: 57–68.

Glenn, E. N., and Feldberg, R. L. (1979), 'Proletarianising Clerical Work: Technology and Organizational Control in the Office', in Zimbalist (1979), 51–72.

Goddard, J. B. (1992), 'New Technology and the Geography of the UK Information Economy', in Robins (1992), 178–201.

—— and Cornford, J. (1994), 'Superhighway Britain: Eliminating the Divide Between the Haves and Have-Nots', *Parliamentary Brief* (May/June), 48–50.

Gödel, K. (1931), 'Über Vollständigkeit und Widerspruchsfreiheit', *Ergebnisse eines mathematischen Kolloquiums*, 3: 12–13.

Golding, P. (1990), 'Political Communication and Citizenship: The Media and Democracy in an Egalitarian Social Order', in Ferguson (1990), 84–113.

Gore, A., Jr (1991), 'Infrastructure for the Global Village', *Scientific American*, 265 (Sept.): 108–11.

—— (1993a), *Reengineering Government through IT* (Washington, DC: US Government Printing Office).

—— (1993b), *Creating a Government that Works Better and Costs Less: Report of the National Performance Review* (Washington, DC: US Government Printing Office).

Grabiner, J. V. (1974), 'Is Mathematical Truth Time-Dependent?', *American Mathematical Monthly*, 81: 354–65.

Bibliography

Graham, C., Lewin, D., Milne, C., Moroney, J., and Skouby, E. (1996), *The Consumer in the Information Society*. Consultative Document for the Consumer Policy Directorate (DG XXIV) of the European Commission (London: Ovum Ltd.).

Graham, S. D. N. (1994), 'Planning for the Telecommunications-Based City: Experience and Prospects', *NETCOM*, 8, pt. 1: 39–65.

—— (1995), 'Cities, Nations and Communications in the Global Era: Urban Telecommunications Policies in France and Britain', *European Planning Studies*, 3: 357–80.

Gray, M., Hodson, N., and Gordon, G. (1993), *Teleworking Explained* (Chichester: John Wiley).

Green, E., Owen, J., and Pain, D. (1993) (eds.), *Gendered by Design: Information Technology and Office Systems* (London: Taylor & Francis).

Green, K. (1992), 'Creating Demand for Biotechnology: Shaping Technologies and Markets', in Coombs *et al.* (1992), 164–84.

Greenbaum, J., and King, M. (1991) (eds.), *Design at Work: Cooperative Design of Computer Systems* (Hillsdale, NJ: Erlbaum Associates).

Gregory, G. (1986), *Japanese Electronics Technology: Enterprise and Innovation* (New York: Wiley).

Grindley, K. (1991), *Managing IT at Board Level: The Hidden Agenda Explained* (London: Pitman).

Grint, K., and Willcocks, L. (1995), 'Business Process Re-engineering in Theory and Practice: Business Paradise Regained?', *New Technology, Work and Employment*, 10: 99–109.

—— and Woolgar, S. (1995), 'On Some Failures of Nerve in Constructivist and Feminist Analyses of Technology', *Science, Technology and Human Values*, 20: 286–310.

Grübler, A. (1990), *The Rise and Fall of Infrastructures: Dynamics of Evolution and Technological Change in Transport* (Heidelberg: Physica Verlag).

Gunter, B. (1982), *Audience Reactions to Eurikon: Evidence on UK Viewer Ratings of a New Pan-European TV Service* (London: IBA [Independent Broadcasting Authority]) .

Guthrie, K. K., and Dutton, W. H. (1992), 'The Politics of Citizen Access Technology', *Policy Studies Journal*, 20: 574–97.

—— Schmitz, J., Ryu, D., Harris, J., Rogers, E., and Dutton, W. (1990), 'Communication Technology and Democratic Participation: The PEN System in Santa Monica'. Paper presented at the Association for Computer Machinery (ACM) Conference on Computers and the Quality of Life (Washington, DC).

Haack, S. (1976), 'The Justification of Deduction', *Mind*, 80: 112–19.

Haddon, L., and Silverstone, R. (1993), *Teleworking in the 1990s: A View from the Home*. SPRU/CICT Report No. 10 (Brighton: University of Sussex).

Hague, D. (1991), *Beyond Universities: A New Republic of the Intellect* (London: Institute of Economic Affairs).

Hall, P. (1990), 'Urban Europe after 1992', in Swedish Commission on Urban Problems (1990), 117–34.

Hall, R. E. (1993), *Long Distance: Public Benefits from Increased Competition* (Menlo Park, Calif.: Applied Economics Partners).

Hamilton, J. M. (1992), 'Keeping up with Information: On-Line in the Philippines and London', in Kanter *et al.* (1992), 108–24.

Hamlin, C. (1992), 'Reflexivity in Technology Studies: Towards a Technology of Technology (and Science)?', *Social Studies of Science*, 22: 511–44.

Hammer, M. (1990), 'Reengineering Work: Don't Automate, Obliterate', *Harvard Business Review*, 90: 104–12.

—— and Champy, J. (1993), *Re-engineering the Corporation: A Manifesto for Business Revolution* (New York: Harper Business; London: Nicholas Brealey).

Handy, C. (1990), *The Age of Unreason* (London: Arrow).

Hardy, A. P. (1980), 'The Role of the Telephone in Economic Development', *Telecommunications Policy*, 4: 278–86.

Harrison, R. (1994), *Study of the International Competitiveness of the UK Telecommunications Infrastructure*. Report for the Department of Trade and Industry (London: PA Consulting Group).

Harvey, D. (1989), *The Conditions of Post-Modernity* (Oxford: Blackwell).

Harwood, J. (1993), *Styles of Scientific Thought: The German Genetics Community, 1900–1933* (Chicago: University of Chicago Press).

Hausman, J. T. T., and Belinfante, A. (1993), 'The Effects of the Breakup of AT&T on Telephone Penetration in the United States', *American Economic Review Papers and Proceedings*, May: 178–84.

Hawkins, R. (1995), 'Enhancing the User Role in the Development of Technical Standards for Telecommunication', *Technology Analysis and Strategic Management*, 7: 21–40.

Hayek, F. A. von (1945), 'The Use of Knowledge in Society', *American Economic Review*, 35: 519–30.

Healey and Baker (1992), *European Real Estate Monitor* (London: Healey and Baker).

Heap, N., Thomas, R., Einon, G., Mason, R., and Mackay, H. (1995) (eds.), *Information Technology and Society* (London: Sage).

Heldman, R. K. (1988), *ISDN in the Information Marketplace* (Blue Ridge Summit, Pa.: TAB Books).

Henwood, F. (1993), 'Establishing Gender Perspectives on Information Technology: Problems, Issues and Opportunities', in Green *et al.* (1993), 31–49.

Hepworth, M. E. (1989), *The Geography of the Information Economy* (London: Belhaven).

Hills, J. (1989), 'Universal Service: Liberalization and Privatization of Telecommunications', *Telecommunications Policy*, 13: 129–44.

—— (1993), 'Universal Service: A Social and Technological Construct', *Communications & Strategies*, 10: 61–86.

Hine, C. (1994), *Virtual Ethnography*. CRICT Discussion Paper No. 43 (Uxbridge: Brunel University).

Home Office (1995), *Identity Cards: A Consultative Document*. Cmnd. 2879 (London: HMSO).

Horrocks, I., and Webb, J. (1994), 'Electronic Democracy: A Policy Issue for UK Local Government', *Local Government Policy Making*, 21: 22–30.

House of Commons Trade and Industry Select Committee (1994), *Optical Fibre Networks* (London: HMSO).

Howells, J., and Hine, J. (1993) (eds.), *Innovative Banking: Competition and the Management of a New Networks Technology* (London: Routledge).

Hudson, H. (1995), 'Universal Service in an Information Age', *Telecommunications Policy*, 18: 658–67.

Hughes, T. (1983), *Networks of Power* (Baltimore: Johns Hopkins University Press).

Hull, R. (1994), 'The Governance of Computing: Computer Science and the Social Sciences'. Paper presented to the Economic and Social Research Council's Seminar on The Transformation of the Professions (Manchester: CROMTEC, Manchester School of Management).

Humphrey, W. S. (1991), 'Software and the Factory Paradigm', *Software Engineering Journal*, 6: 372–3.

Hutton, G. (1995), 'BPR: Overcoming Impediments to Change in the Public Sector', in *New Technology, Work and Employment*, 10: 147–50.

Huws, U. (1982), *Your Job in the Eighties: A Women's Guide to New Technology* (London: Pluto).

—— (1984), *The New Homeworkers: New Technology and the Changing Location of the White Collar Workers* (London: Low Pay Unit).

—— (1993), *Teleworking in Britain*. Research Series No. 18 (Sheffield: Department of Employment).

IBEX (1992), *Review of Possible Teleport Roles in Europe*. Stage 2 Final Report to the Commission of the European Communities (London: IBEX Consultants).

IITF (1993), Information Infrastructure Task Force, *National Information Infrastructure: Agenda for Action* (Washington, DC: National Telecommunications and Information Administration).

—— (1994), *Putting the Information Infrastructure to Work: Report of the Information Infrastructure Task Force Committee on Applications and Technology* (Washington, DC: US Government Printing Office).

ILO (1991), International Labour Office, *Yearbook of Labour Statistics* (Geneva: ILO).

IMD International (1990), *World Competitiveness Report* (Geneva: IMD International).

IMF (1991 and other years), International Monetary Fund, *International Financial Statistics* (Washington, DC: IMF).

—— (1994), *World Economic Outlook* (Washington, DC: IMF).

IMO (1994), International Market Observatory, 'The Internet and the European Information Industry'. IMO Working Paper 94/3, (Luxembourg: IMO).

Innis, H. (1951), *The Bias of Communication* (Toronto: University of Toronto Press).

Ireland, J. (1994), *The Importance of Telecommunications to London as an International Financial Centre*. The City Research Project, Subject Report No. 17 (London: London Business School and Corporation of London).

ITAP (1982), Information Technology Advisory Panel to the Cabinet Office, *Report on Cable Systems* (London: HMSO).

—— (1983), *Making a Business of Information* (London: HMSO).

ITU (1992), International Telecommunications Union, *Statistical Yearbook 1992* (Geneva: ITU).

—— (1995), *World Telecommunications Indicators* (Geneva: ITU).

Jefferson, A., and Robey, D. (1986), *Modern Literary Theory: A Comparative Introduction* (London: Batsford).

Jenkins, C., and Sherman, B. (1979), *The Collapse of Work* (London: Eyre Methuen).

Jones, B. (1988), 'Work and Flexible Automation in Britain: A Review of Developments and Possibilities', *Work, Employment and Society*, 2: 451–86.

Jones, C. B. (1990), *Systematic Software Development Using VDM* (New York: Prentice Hall).

Kanter, R. M. (1995), *Word Class: Thriving Locally in the Global Economy* (New York: Simon and Shuster).

—— Stein, B. A., and Dick, T. (1992) (eds.), *The Challenge of Organizational Change* (New York: Free Press).

Kapor, M. (1993), 'Where is the Digital Highway Really Heading? The Case for a Jeffersonian Information Policy', *Wired*, July–Aug.: 53–9, 94.

Kaserman, D. L., and Mayo, J. W. (1994), 'Long-Distance Telecommunications: Expectations and Realizations in the Post-Divestiture Period', in Crew (1994): 83–111.

Keen, P. G. W. (1991), *Shaping the Future: Business Design through Information Technology* (Cambridges Mass.: Harvard Business School Press).

Keirstead, B. G. (1948), *The Theory of Economic Change* (Toronto: Macmillan).

Kelly, K. (1994), *Out of Control: The New Biology of Machines* (London: Fourth Estate).

Kettle, J. (1993), 'Working in Canada', *Society for the Production of Human Labor Newsletter*, 3: 5–8.

Keynes, J. M. (1930), *Treatise on Money* (London: Macmillan).

Kirkup, G., and Keller, L. (1992) (eds.), *Inventing Women: Science, Technology and Gender* (Cambridge: Polity Press).

Kline, M. (1982), *Mathematics: The Loss of Certainty* (New York: Oxford University Press).

Knights, D., and Morgan, G. (1991), 'Corporate Strategy, Organisations, and Subjectivity: A Critique', *Organization Studies*, 12: 251–73.

—— and Murray, F. (1994), *Managers Divided: Organisational Politics and Information Technology Management* (London: Wiley).

—— —— Willmott, H. (1993), 'Networking as Knowledge Work: A Study of Strategic Interorganisational Development in the Financial Services Industry', *Journal of Management Studies*, 30: 975–95.

Knorr, K., Krohn, R., and Whitley, R. (1980) (eds.), *Sociology of the Sciences Yearbook. Vol. 4: The Social Process of Scientific Investigation* (Dordrecht, Netherlands: Reidel).

Kooiman, J. (1993) (ed.), *Modern Governance: New Government–Society Interactions* (London: Sage).

Bibliography

Kortteinen, M., Lehto, A-M., and Ylöstalo, P. (1987), *Information Technology and Work in Finland* (Helsinki: Tilastokeskus Statistikcentralen).

Kraemer, K. (1994), *IT and Economic Development: Lessons from the Asia-Pacific Region*. PICT Policy Research Paper No. 26 (Uxbridge: PICT, Brunel University).

—— and Dedrick, J. (1994), 'Payoffs from Investment in Information Technology: Lessons from the Asia-Pacific Region', *World Development*, 22: 1921–31.

—— —— (1995), 'From Nationalism to Pragmatism: IT Policy in China', *IEEE Computer*, 28: 64–73.

La Porte, T. R. (1991) (ed.), *Social Responses to Large Technical Systems* (Dordrecht: Kluwer Academic Publishers).

Lall, S. (1985), 'Trade in Technology by a Slowly Industrializing Country: India', in Rosenberg and Frischtak (1985), 45–76.

Lang, J. (1988), 'The Future of European Film and Television', *European Affairs*, 2: 12–20.

Latour, B. (1986), *Science in Action* (Milton Keynes: Open University Press).

—— (1988), 'How to Write *The Prince* for Machines as well as Machinations', in Elliott (1988), 20–43.

—— (1991), 'Technology is Society Made Durable', in Law (1991), 103–31.

Laudan, R. (1984), *The Nature of Technological Knowledge* (Dordrecht, Netherlands: Reidel).

Laudon, K. (1977), *Communication Technology and Democratic Participation* (New York: Praeger).

—— (1987), *Dossier Society* (New York: Columbia University Press).

Law, J. (1988), 'The Anatomy of a Socio-Technical Struggle: The Design of the TSR 2', in Elliott (1988), 44–69.

—— (1991) (ed.), *A Sociology of Monsters: Essays on Power, Technology and Domination* (London: Routledge).

Leonard, D. (1994), *Economist Guide to the European Community* (London: Economist Books).

Levidow, L., and Young, B. (1981) (eds.), *Science, Technology and the Labour Process* (London: CSE Books).

Levitan, K. (1987) (ed.), *Government Infrastructures* (Westport, Conn.: Greenwood Press).

Lockett, M. (1987), *The Factors behind Successful IT Innovation* (Oxford: Templeton College).

Loveman, G. W. (1988), *An Assessment of the Productivity Impact on Information Technologies*. MIT Management in the 1990s Working Paper No. 88-054 (Cambridge, Mass.: Massachusetts Institute of Technology).

Lyon, D. (1986), 'From "Post-Industrialism" to "Information Society": A New Social Transformation?', *Sociology*, 20: 577–88.

—— (1987), 'Information Technology and Information Society: Response to Fincham', *Sociology*, 21: 457–8.

—— (1994), *The Electronic Eye: The Rise of Surveillance Society* (Cambridge: Polity Press).

Lyons, M. J., and Gell, M. (1994), 'Companies and Communications in the Next Century', *British Telecommunications Engineering*, 13: 112–18.

Machlup, F. (1962), *The Production and Distribution of Knowledge* (Princeton, NJ: Princeton University Press).

—— (1980), *Knowledge: Its Creation, Distribution and Economic Significance* (Princeton, NJ: Princeton University Press).

McHoul, A. (1986), 'The Getting of Sexuality: Foucault, Garfinkel and the Analysis of Sexual Discourse', *Theory, Culture and Society*, 3: 65–79.

Mackay, H., and Gillespie, G. (1992), 'Extending the Social Shaping of Technology Approach: Ideology and Appropriation', *Social Studies of Science*, 22: 685–716.

MacKenzie, D. (1990), *Inventing Accuracy: A Historical Sociology of Nuclear Missile Guidance* (Cambridge, Mass.: MIT Press).

—— (1991), 'The Fangs of the VIPER', *Nature*, 352: 467–8.

—— (1992), 'Economic and Sociological Explanation of Technical Change', in Coombs *et al.* (1992), 25–48.

—— (1993), 'Negotiating Arithmetic, Constructing Proof: The Sociology of Mathematics and Information Technology', *Social Studies of Science*, 23: 37–65.

—— (1994), 'Computer-Related Accidental Death: An Empirical Exploration', *Science and Public Policy*, 21: 233–48.

—— (1995), 'The Automation of Proof: An Historical and Sociological Exploration', *IEEE Annals of the History of Computing*, 17: 7–29.

—— (forthcoming), 'The Certainty Trough', in Dutton (forthcoming).

—— and Wajcman, J. (1985) (eds.), *The Social Shaping of Technology: How the Refrigerator Got its Hum* (Milton Keynes: Open University Press).

Mackintosh, I. (1986), *Sunrise Europe* (Oxford: Basil Blackwell).

McLuhan, M. (1964, repr. 1994), *Understanding Media: The Extension of Man* (London: Routledge).

McNally, F. (1979), *Women for Hire: A Study of the Female Office Worker* (London: Macmillan).

Maddison, A. (1987), 'Growth and Slowdown in Advanced Capitalist Economies: Techniques of Quantitative Assessment', *Journal of Economic Literature*, 25: 649–98.

Maizels, A. (1962), *Industrial Growth and World Trade* (Cambridge: Cambridge University Press).

Mandel, M. J. (1994), 'This Investment Boom Gives the Economy Running Room', *Business Week*, 25 July: 68–70.

Mandon, N. (1988), *New Information Technologies and Office Employment: European Comparisons* (Berlin: CEDEFOP [European Centre for the Development of Vocational Training]).

Mansell, R. (1993*a*), *The New Telecommunications: A Political Economy of Network Evolution* (London: Sage).

—— (1993*b*), *From Telephony to Telematics Services: Equity, Efficiency and Regulatory Innovation*. PICT Policy Research Paper No. 24 (Uxbridge: PICT, Brunel University).

Mansell, R. (1994*a*) (ed.), *Management of Information and Communication Technologies: Emerging Patterns of Control* (London: Aslib).

Bibliography

—— (1994*b*) (ed.), *Information, Control and Technical Change* (London: Aslib).

—— and Credé, A. (1995), *Telecommunication Infrastructure Competition and 'Commodity' Supply. Research Report.* (Montpellier: ENCIP [European Network for Communication and Information Perspectives]).

—— and Jenkins, M. (1992), 'Networks, Industrial Restructuring and Policy: The Singapore Example', *Technovation*, 12: 397–406.

—— and Morgan, K. (1990), 'Perspectives on Advanced Communications for Europe', *PACE'90*, vol. 7 (Brussels: Commission of the European Communities).

Margetts, H., and Willcocks, L. (1993), 'Information Technology in Public Services: Disaster Faster?', *Public Money and Management*, Apr.–June: 49–56.

Marstrand, P. (1984) (ed.), *New Technology and the Future of Work and Skills* (London: Pinter).

Mazza, C., Fairclough, J., Melton, B., de Pablo, D., Scheffer, A., and Stevens, R. (1994), *Software Engineering Standards* (Hemel Hempstead: Prentice Hall).

Melody, W. H. (1985), 'The Information Society: Implications for Economic Institutions and Market Theory', *Journal of Economic Issues*, 19: 523–39.

—— (1988), *The Changing Role of Public Policy in the Information Economy*, PICT Policy Research Paper No. 0 (Uxbridge: PICT, Brunel University).

—— (1989), *Papers in Science, Technology and Public Policy No. 20* (London: Imperial College; Brighton: SPRU, University of Sussex).

—— (1990), 'Communication Policy in the Global Information Economy: Whither the Public Interest?', in Ferguson (1990), 16–39.

—— and Mansell, R. E. (1986), *Information and Communication Technologies: Social Science Research and Training. Vol. 1* (London: Economic and Social Research Council).

Miles, I. (1987), 'Information Technology and the Services Economy', in Zorkoczy (1987).

—— (1988*a*), *Information Technology and Information Society: Options for the Future.* PICT Policy Research Paper No. 2 (Uxbridge: PICT, Brunel University).

—— (1988*b*), *Home Informatics: Information Technology and the Transformation of Everyday Life* (London: Pinter).

—— (1988*c*), 'The Shaping of Technologies to Come', *Project Appraisal*, 3: 231–33.

—— (1990), *Home Telematics: Information Technology and the Transformation of Everyday Life* (London: Pinter).

—— (1993), 'Services in the New Industrial Economy', *Futures*, 25: 653–72.

—— and Thomas, G. (1995), 'User Resistance to New Interactive Media: Participants, Processes and Paradigms', in Bauer (1995), 255–75.

—— Rush, H., Bessant, J., and Turner, K. (1988), *Information Horizons* (London: Edward Elgar).

—— Brady, T., Davies, A., Haddon, L., Matthews, M., Rush, H., and Wyatt, S. (1990), *Mapping and Measuring the Information Economy*. Library and Information Research Report 77 (Boston Spa, Lincs.: British Library).

—— Cawson, M., and Haddon, L. (forthcoming), *The Shape of Things to Consume* (London: Sage).

Mills, M. H. (1990), 'Changing the Culture to Overcome Risks in Information System Procurement', *Proceedings of the EPIS '90 Symposium* (The Hague, Netherlands).

Ministry of Defence (1991), *Interim Defence Standard 00–55: The Procurement of Safety Critical Software in Defence Equipment* (Glasgow: Directorate of Standardization, Ministry of Defence).

Mitchell, B., and Tenzing, D. (1994), *Utilization of the U.S. Telephone Network.* 436–EAC/WIK (Santa Monica, Calif.: RAND European-American Centre for Policy Analysis).

Mody, A., and Dahlman, C. (1992), 'Performance and Potential of Information Technology: An International Perspective', *World Development*, 20: 1703–19.

Molina, A. (1989), *The Social Basis of the Microelectronics Revolution* (Edinburgh: Edinburgh University Press).

—— (1990), 'Transputers and Transputer-Based Parallel Computers: Socio-Technical Constituencies and the Build-up of British-European Capabilities in Information Technologies', *Research Policy*, 19: 309–33.

—— (1992), 'Competitive Strategies in the Microprocessor Industry: The Case of an Emerging versus an Established Technology', *International Journal of Technology Management*, 7: 589–614.

Monnet, J. (1978), *Memoirs* (London: Collins).

Moss, M. (1992), 'Telecommunications and Urban Economic Development', in OECD (1992), 147–58.

Mueller, M. (1993), 'Universal Service in Telephone History: A Reconstruction', *Telecommunications Policy*, 17: 352–70.

Mulgan, G. J. (1989), 'A Tale of Two Cities', *Marxism Today*, Mar.: 18–25.

Mumford, E. (1995), *Effective Systems Design and Requirements Analysis: The ETHICS Approach* (London: Macmillan).

—— and Beekman, G. J. (1994), *Tools for Change and Progress: A Socio-Technical Approach to Business Process Re-engineering* (Leiden: CSG Consulting Services).

Mumford, L. (1934), *Technics and Civilization* (London: Routledge & Kegan Paul).

Murdock, G. (1990), 'Redrawing the Map of the Communications Industries: Concentration and Ownership in the Era of Privatization', in Ferguson (1990), 1–15.

Murray, F. (1993), 'Science, Technology and Masculinity', in Green *et al.* (1993), 64–80.

Myers, G. J. (1979), *The Art of Software Testing* (New York: Wiley).

National Research Council (1991), *Computers at Risk: Safe Computing in the Information Age* (Washington, DC: National Academy Press).

NEDO (1987), National Economics Development Office, *IT Futures—It Can Work* (London: NEDO).

Negroponte, N. (1995), *Being Digital: The Road Map for Survival on the Information Superhighway* (London: Hodder & Stoughton).

Nelson, R., and Winter, S. (1982), *An Evolutionary Theory of Economic Change* (Cambridge, Mass.: Harvard University Press).

Bibliography

NERA (1993), National Economic Research Associates, *Regional Telecommunications Investment Requirements and Financing Perspectives (to the year 2000) for Objective 1 Regions*. Report to DG XIII (Brussels: Commission of the European Communities).

Neumann, P. G. (1995), *Computer-Related Risks* (New York: Addison-Wesley).

Newton, K. M. (1990), *Interpreting the Text: A Critical Introduction to the Theory and Practice of Literary Interpretation* (New York: Harvester Wheatsheaf).

Nexus Europe (1995), *Economic and Social Cohesion Aspects of the Emergence of an Information Society in Europe: Initial Results II*. Report DG XIII.A.7 and DG XVI (Brussels: Commission of the European Communities).

Nickell, S., and Bell, B. (1994), 'The Collapse in Demand for the Unskilled and Unemployment across the OECD', mimeo (Oxford: Institute of Economics and Statistics, University of Oxford).

Nidditch, P. H. (1957), *Introductory Formal Logic of Mathematics* (London: University Tutorial Press).

Noam, E. (1991), *Television in Europe* (Oxford: Oxford University Press).

—— (1992), *Telecommunications in Europe* (Oxford: Oxford University Press).

—— (1994), 'Beyond Liberalization III: Reforming Universal Service', *Telecommunications Policy*, 18: 687–704.

Noble, D. (1979), 'Social Choice in Machine Design: The Case of Automatically Controlled Machine Tools', in Zimbalist (1979), 18–50.

Noll, M. (1994), 'A Study of Long-Distance Rates', *Telecommunications Policy*, 18: 355–62.

—— (1996), *Highway of Dreams* (Hillsdale, NJ: Lawrence Erlbaum).

Norman, D. A. (1994), *Defending Human Attributes in the Age of the Machine* (Irvington, NY: Voyager).

—— and Draper, S. W. (1986) (eds.), *User Centred System Design: New Perspectives on Human–Computer Interaction* (Hillsdale, NJ: Erlbaum Associates).

NRC (1993), Network Reliability Council, *Network Reliability: A Report to the Nation —Compendium of Technical Papers* (Chicago: National Engineering Consortium).

NRENAISSANCE Committee (1994), National Research Council, *Realizing the Information Future: The Internet and Beyond* (Washington, DC: National Academy Press).

NTIA (1991), National Telecommunications and Information Administration, *The NTIA Infrastructure Report: Telecommunications in the Age of Information* (Washington, DC: US Department of Commerce).

Ó Siochrú, S., Gillespie, A., and Qvortrup, L. (1995), *Advanced Communications for Cohesion and Regional Development (ACCORDE)*. Final Report to the Commission of the European Communities (Dublin: Nexus).

OECD (1981), Organization for Economic Co-operation and Development, *Guidelines on the Protection of Privacy and Transborder Flows of Personal Data* (Paris: OECD).

—— (1986), *Trends in the Information Economy* (Paris: OECD).

—— (1988), *New Technologies in the 1990s: A Socio-Economic Strategy* (Paris: OECD).

—— (1991), *Synthesis Report on TEP* (Paris: OECD).

—— (1992), *Cities and New Technologies* (Paris: OECD).

—— (1993), *The OECD Response* (Paris: OECD).

—— (1994), *The Benefits of Telecommunication Infrastructure Competition*. Working Party on Telecommunication and Information Services Policies (Paris: OECD).

Oftel (1995), Office of Telecommunications, *Effective Competition: Framework for Action* (London: Oftel).

Ong, W. J. (1982), *Orality and Literacy: The Technologising of the Word* (London: Methuen).

OPSS (1993), Office of Public Service and Science, *Realising Our Potential: A Strategy for Science, Engineering and Technology*. White Paper, Cmnd. 2250 (London: HMSO).

—— (1994), *The Civil Service: Continuity and Change*. White Paper, Cmnd. 2627 (London: HMSO).

OST (1995*a*), Office of Science and Technology, *Technology Foresight Panels* (London: HMSO).

—— (1995*b*), *Technology Foresight Panel 6: Progress through Partnership—Communications* (London: HMSO).

—— (1995*c*), *Technology Foresight Panel 8: Progress through Partnership—IT and Electronics* (London: HMSO).

—— (1995*d*), *Technology Foresight Panel 14: Progress through Partnership—Leisure and Learning* (London: HMSO).

OTA (1993*a*), Office of Technology Assessment, US Congress, *Making Government Work: Electronic Delivery of Federal Services*. OTA-TCT-578 (Washington, DC: US Government Printing Office).

—— (1993*b*), 'Electronic Delivery of Federal Services Requires Congressional Attention'. Press Release, 4 Nov. (Washington, DC: US Government Printing Office).

—— (1993*c*), *US Telecommunications Services in European Markets*. OTA-TCT-548 (Washington, DC: US Government Printing Office).

—— (1993*d*), *Advanced Network Technology*. Background Paper OTA-BP-TCT-101 (Washington, DC: US Government Printing Office).

—— (1995), *The Technological Re-shaping of Metropolitan America* (Washington, DC: US Government Printing Office).

Parker, E., and Hudson, H. (1992), *Electronic Byways: State Policies for Rural Development through Telecommunications* (Boulder, Colo.: Westview Press).

—— —— Dillman, D. A., and Roscoe, A. D. (1989), *Rural America in the Information Age: Telecommunications Policy for Rural Development* (Lanham, Md.: The Aspen Institute and University Press of America).

PECC (1992), Pacific Economic Co-operation Conference, *Pacific Economic Outlook 1992–1993* (Washington, DC: PECC).

Pelaez, E., Fleck, J., and MacKenzie, D. (1987), *Social Research on Software*. Paper presented to PICT workshop in Manchester (Edinburgh: Research Centre for Social Sciences, University of Edinburgh).

Perez, C. (1983), 'Structural Change and the Assimilation of New Technologies in the Economic and Social System', *Futures*, 15: 357–75.

Bibliography

—— (1985), 'Micro-Electronics, Long Waves and World Structural Change: New Perspectives for Developing Countries', *World Development*, 17: 441–63.

Perrow, C. (1984), *Normal Accidents: Living with High-Risk Technologies* (New York: Basic Books).

Petit, P. (1986), *Slow Growth and the Service Economy* (London: Pinter).

Pickering, A. (1992) (ed.), *Science as Practice and Culture* (Chicago: University of Chicago Press).

PICT (1995*a*), Programme on Information and Communication Technologies, *1995 Charles Read Lecture: Policies for a European Information Society* (Uxbridge: PICT, Brunel University).

—— (1995*b*), *A Profile of Research and Publications 1995* (Uxbridge: PICT, Brunel University).

Pinch, T., and Bijker, W. (1984), 'The Social Construction of Facts and Artefacts: Or How the Sociology of Science and the Sociology of Technology Might Benefit Each Other', *Social Studies of Science*, 14: 399–441.

Porat, M. U. (1971), *The Information Economy* (Washington, DC: Office of Telecommunications, US Department of Commerce).

Porter, M. (1985), *Competitive Advantage: Creating and Sustaining Superior Performance* (New York: The Free Press).

—— (1992), 'On Thinking about Deregulation and Competition', in Sapolsky *et al.* (1992), 39–44.

—— (1993), *Competition in the Long Distance Market* (Cambridge, Mass.: Monitor Company).

—— (1995), *The Competitive Advantages of the Inner City* (New York: Free Press).

Pressman, J. L., and Wildavsky, A. B. (1973), *Implementation* (Berkeley: University of California Press).

Price Waterhouse (annual), *Managing Information Technology: International Survey* (London: Price Waterhouse).

Probert, B., and Wilson, B. (1993), *Pink Collar Blues: Work, Gender and Technology* (Melbourne: Melbourne University Press).

Quinn, J. (1992), *Intelligent Enterprise* (New York: The Free Press).

Quintas, P. (1993) (ed.), *The Social Dimensions of Systems Engineering: People, Processes, Policies and Software Developments* (Chichester: Ellis Horwood).

—— (forthcoming), *Rethinking Software: The Management of Innovation in Software Development* (Oxford: Oxford University Press).

Raab, C. (1993*a*), 'The Governance of Data Protection', in Kooiman (1993), 89–103.

—— (1993*b*), 'Data Protection in Britain: Governance and Learning', *Governance*, 6: 43–66.

—— (1995), 'Connecting Orwell to Athens? Information Superhighways and the Privacy Debate', in Van de Donk *et al.* (1995), 195–211.

Rachel, J., and Woolgar, S. (1995), 'The Discursive Structure of the Social–Technical Divide: The Example of Information Systems Development', *Sociological Review*, 43: 251–73.

Rahim, S. A., and Pennings, A. J. (1987), *Computerization and Development in*

Southeast Asia (Singapore: Asian Mass Communications Research and Information Centre).

RAI (1983) Radiotelevisione Italiana, *Research on Attitudes to Eurikon Television Programmes*. LCMIANUS Typescript (Rome: RAI).

Rand, R. (1992) (ed.), *Logomachia* (Lincoln, Nebr.: University of Nebraska Press).

Ranis, G. (1990), 'Science and Technology Policy: Lessons from Japan and the East Asian NICs', in Evenson and Ranis (1990), 157–78.

Ranney, A. (1983), *Channels of Power: The Impact of Television on American Politics* (New York: Basic Books).

Reich, R. B. (1991), *The Work of Nations* (London: Simon and Schuster).

Rheingold, H. (1994), *The Virtual Community in a Computerized World* (London: Secker and Warburg).

Ricardo, D. (1911, first pub. 1821), *The Principles of Political Economy and Taxation* (Dent Dutton), repr. in Sraffa (1981).

Richardson, R. (1994), 'Back Officing Front Office Functions: Organisational and Locational Implications of New Telemediated Services', in Mansell (1994*a*), 309–35.

—— (1995), 'Teleservices and Economic Development: A Case Study of Ireland'. Mimeo (Newcastle upon Tyne: CURDS, Newcastle University).

—— Gillespie, A., and Cornford, J. (1994), *Requiem for the Teleport? Teleports as Metropolitan Development and Planning Tools in Western Europe*. Working Paper No. 17 (Newcastle upon Tyne: CURDS, University of Newcastle).

Rip, A., Misa, T. J., and Schot, J. (1995) (eds.), *Managing Technology in Society: The Approach of Constructive Technology Assessment* (London: Pinter).

Roach, S. (1988), *White-Collar Productivity: A Glimmer of Hope?* (New York: Morgan Stanley).

Robins, K. (1992) (ed.), *Understanding Information: Business Technology and Geography* (London: Belhaven).

Rochlin, G. I. (1991), 'Iran Air Flight 655 and the USS *Vincennes*: Complex, Large-Scale Military Systems and the Failure of Control', in La Porte (1991), 99–125.

Rockart, J. F., and Short, J. E. (1991), 'The Networked Organization and the Management of Interdependence', in Scott Morton (1991), 189–219.

Roller, L.-H., and Waverman, L. (1994), *The Impact of Telecommunications Infrastructure on Economic Growth and Development*. Working Party on Telecommunication and Information Services Policies (Paris: OECD).

Rosenberg, N., and Frischtak, C. (1985) (eds.), *International Technology Transfer: Concepts, Measures and Comparisons* (New York: Praeger).

Rosenbrock, H. H. (1989) (ed.), *Designing Human Centred Technology: A Cross-Disciplinary Project in Computer Aided Manufacturing* (London: Springer-Verlag).

—— (1990) (ed.), *Machines with a Purpose* (Oxford: Oxford University Press).

Rothwell, R., Freeman, C., Horsley, A., Jervis, V. T. P., Robertson, A. B., and Townsend, J. F. (1984), 'SAPPHO Updated: Project SAPPHO Phase II', *Research Policy*, 3: 258–91.

Royal Society (1983), *Risk Assessment*. Report of a Royal Society Study Group (London: The Royal Society).

Bibliography

—— (1992), *Risk: Analysis, Perception and Management*. Report of a Royal Society Study Group (London: The Royal Society).

Rush, H., and Miles, I. (1989), 'Surveying the Social Implications of Information Technology', *Futures*, 21: 249–62.

Rushby, J. (1993), *Formal Methods and the Certification of Critical Systems* (Menlo Park, Calif.: SRI International).

Russell, S., and Williams, R. (1988), *Opening the Black Box and Closing it Behind You: On Micro-Sociology in the Social Analysis of Technology*. Edinburgh PICT Working Paper No. 3 (Edinburgh: Edinburgh University).

Sable, C., and Piore, M. J. (1984), *The Second Industrial Divide* (New York: Basic Books).

Sackman, H., and Boehm, B. (1972), *Planning Community Information Utilities* (Montvale, NJ: AFIPS Press).

—— and Nie, N. (1970) (eds.), *The Information Utility and Social Choice* (Montvale, NJ: AFIPS Press).

Sacks, H. (1972), 'An Initial Investigation of the Usability of Conversational Data for Doing Sociology', in Sudnow (1972), 31–74.

Sagan, S. D. (1993), *The Limits of Safety: Organizations, Accidents and Nuclear Weapons* (Princeton, NJ: Princeton University Press).

—— (1994), 'Toward a Political Theory of Organizational Reliability', *Journal of Contingencies and Crisis Management*, 2: 228–40.

Sapolsky, H. M., Crane, R. J., Neuman, W. R., and Noam, E. M. (1992) (eds.), *The Telecommunications Revolution* (London: Routledge).

Sauer, C. (1993), *Why Information Systems Fail: A Case Study Approach* (Henley-on-Thames Alfred Waller Ltd.).

Saviotti, P., and Metcalf, S. (1991) (eds.), *Evolutionary Theories of Economic and Technological Change: Present State and Future Prospects* (London: Harvard).

Scarbrough, H., and Corbett, M. (1992), *Technology and Organisation* (London: Routledge).

Schalken, C., and Tops, P. (1995), 'Democracy and Virtual Communities: An Empirical Exploration of the Amsterdam Digital City', in Van de Donk *et al.* (1995), 143–54.

Schiller, H. I. (1989), *Culture Inc.: The Corporate Takeover of Public Expression* (New York: Ablex).

—— (1995), 'The Global Information Highway: Project for an Ungovernable World', in Brook and Boal (1995), 17–33.

Schmandt, J., Williams, F., Wilson, R. H., and Strover, S. (1990) (eds.), *The New Urban Infrastructure: Cities and Telecommunications* (New York: Praeger).

Schumpeter, J. A. (1939), *Business Cycles: A Theoretical, Historical and Structural Analysis* (New York: McGraw-Hill).

Schware, R. (1992), 'Software Industry Entry Strategies for Developing Countries: A "Walking on Two Legs" Proposition', *World Development*, 20: 143–64.

Scott Morton, M. S. (1991) (ed.), *The Corporation of the 1990s: Information Technology and Organizational Transformation* (Oxford: Oxford University Press).

Sendall, B. (1982), *Independent Television in Britain* (London: Macmillan).

Senker, P. (1987), *Towards the Automatic Factory? The Need for Training* (Bedford: IFS).

Shapin, S. (1994), *A Social History of Truth: Civility and Science in Seventeenth-Century England* (Chicago: University of Chicago Press).

Shapiro, S. (1992), *Its Own Worst Enemy: How Software Engineering has Fallen Victim to Engineering Mythology.* CRICT Discussion Paper No. 25 (Uxbridge: CRICT, Brunel University).

—— (1994), *A Conceptual Framework for Understanding Software Development Standards.* CRICT Discussion Paper No. 51 (Uxbridge: Brunel University).

—— and Woolgar, S. (1995), *Understanding Software Development in Commercial Settings: A Project Report.* CRICT Discussion Paper No. 54 (Uxbridge: Brunel University).

Sharangpani, H. P., and Barton, M. L. (1994), *Statistical Analysis of Floating Point Flaw in the Pentium TM Processor* (Santa Clara, Calif.: Intel Corporation).

Shields, R. (1995), *Cultures of Internet* (Newbury Park, Calif.: Sage).

Siemens (1994), *Telecommunication Statistics* (Munich: Siemens).

Sievers, M. (1994), 'Should the InterLATA Restriction be Lifted? Analysis of the Significant Issues'. Paper presented at the Rutgers University Advanced Workshop on Regulation and Public Utility Economics, (New Brunswick, NJ).

Silj, A. (1988) (ed.), *East of Dallas: The European Challenge to American Television* (London: British Film Institute).

Silverstone, R. (1994a), *Future Imperfect: Media, Information and the Millennium.* PICT Policy Research Paper No. 27 (Uxbridge: PICT, Brunel University).

—— (1994b), *Television and Everyday Life* (London: Routledge).

—— (1994c), 'Domesticating the Revolution: Information and Communication Technologies and Everyday Life', in Mansell (1994a), 221–33.

—— and Hirsch, E. (1992) (eds.), *Consuming Technologies: Media and Information in Domestic Spaces* (London: Routledge).

Singapore Government (1994), *Yearbook of Statistics 1993* (Singapore: Department of Statistics).

Slouka, M. (1995), *War of the Worlds: Cyberspace and the High-Tech Assault on Reality* (New York: Basic Books).

Smith, D. E. (1978), 'K is Mentally Ill: The Anatomy of a Factual Account', *Sociology*, 12: 25–53.

Smith, P. L., and Staple, G. C. (1994), 'Telecommunications Sector Reform', *IEEE Communications Magazine*, Nov.: 50–2.

Soete, L. (1985), *Technological Trends and Employment. Vol. 5: Electronics and Communications* (Aldershot: Gower).

Solow, R. M. (1988), 'Growth Theory and After', *American Economic Review*, June: 307–17.

Sørensen, K., and Levold, N. (1992), 'Tacit Networks, Heterogeneous Engineers and Embodied Technology', *Science, Technology, and Human Values*, 17: 13–35.

South West Thames Regional Health Authority (1993), *Report of the Inquiry into the London Ambulance Service* (London: South West Thames Regional Health Authority).

Spoonley, N. (1994), 'Quaternary Learning', *Engineering Science and Education Journal*, 3: 99–103.

Sproull, L., and Kiesler, S. (1991), *Connections: New Ways of Working in the Networked Organization* (Cambridge, Mass.: MIT Press).

Sraffa, P. (1981) (ed.), *The Works and Correspondence of David Ricardo*. Vol. 1 (Cambridge: Cambridge University Press).

Stark, W. (1944), *The History of Economics in its Relation to Social Development* (New York: Oxford University Press).

Steuart, Sir J. (1966, 1st pub. 1767), *An Inquiry into the Principles of Political Oeconomy* (Edinburgh: Oliver & Boyd for the Scottish Economic Society).

Stoll, C. (1995), *Silicon Snake Oil* (New York: Macmillan).

Stoutemyer, D. R. (1991), 'Crimes and Misdemeanors in the Computer Algebra Trade', *Notices of the American Mathematical Society*, 38: 778–85.

Suchman, L. (1987), *Plans and Situated Actions: The Problem of Human–Machine Communication* (New York: Cambridge University Press).

—— and Jordan, B. (1989), 'Computerization and Women's Knowledge', in Tijdens *et al.* (1989), 153–60.

Sudnow, D. (1972) (ed.), *Studies in Social Interaction* (New York: Free Press).

Suleiman, S., and Crosman, I. (1980) (eds.), *The Reader in the Text: Essays on Audience and Interpretation* (Princeton, NJ: Princeton University Press).

Swann, P. (1990), 'Standards and the Growth of a Software Network', in Berg and Schumny (1990), 383–93.

Swedish Commission on Urban Problems (1990), *Urban Challenges* (Stockholm: Statens Offentiga Unterdningar).

Tang, P., and Mansell, R. (1993), *Telecommunication, Multinational Enterprises and Globalisation: Implications for Future Network Development.* Report for Rank Xerox Cambridge Europarc (Brighton: SPRU, Sussex University).

Taylor, J. A. (1995), 'Don't Obliterate, Informate! Business Process Re-engineering for the Information Age', *New Technology, Work and Employment*, 10: 82–8.

—— (forthcoming), 'The Information Polity', in Dutton (forthcoming).

—— and Williams, H. (1990), 'The Scottish Highlands & Islands Initiative: An Alternative Model for Development', *Telecommunications Policy*, 14: 189–92.

—— —— (1991), 'Public Administration and the Information Polity', *Public Administration*, 69: 171–90.

—— Bardzki, B., and Webster, W. (1995), 'Laying Down the Infrastructure for Teledemocracy: The Case of Scotland', in Van de Donk *et al.* (1995), 61–78.

Telecommunications Policy (1994), Special Issue on 'Competition and Convergence', vol. 18, no. 8.

Taylor, W. E., and Taylor, L. D. (1993), 'Post-Divestiture Long-Distance Competition in the United States', *American Economic Review Papers and Proceedings*, May: 185–90.

Temin, P., and Galambos, L. (1987), *The Fall of the Bell System: A Study in Prices and Politics* (Cambridge, Mass.: Cambridge University Press).

Thistlewaite, P., McRobbie, M. A., and Meyer, R. K. (1988), *Automated Theorem Proving in Non-Classical Logics* (London: Pitman).

Thomas, G., and Miles, I. (1990), *Telematics in Transition* (London: Longman).

Thomas, P. (1995) (ed.), *The Social and Interactional Dimensions of Human–Computer Interfaces* (Cambridge: Cambridge University Press).

Thompson, L. (1989), 'New Technology and the Changing Role of the Secretary'. Work Research Unit Occasional Paper No. 44 (London: ACAS [Advisory, Conciliation and Arbitration Service]).

Thouless, R. (1954), *Straight and Crooked Thinking* (London: Pan).

Tijdens, K., Jennings, M., Wagner, I., and Weggelaar, M. (1989) (eds.), *Women, Work and Computerization: Forming New Alliances* (Amsterdam: North-Holland).

Toffler, A. (1980), *The Third Wave* (London: Collins).

—— (1990), *Power Shift* (New York: Bantam).

Tompkins, J. (1980), *Reader-Response Criticism: From Formalism to Post-Structuralism* (Baltimore: Johns Hopkins University Press).

Trade and Industry Select Committee (1994), House of Commons, *Optical Fibre Networks* (London: HMSO).

Trebing, H. (1969), 'Common Carrier Regulation: The Silent Crisis', *Law and Contemporary Problems*, 34, 299–329.

Turner, B. A. (1994), 'The Future of Risk Research', *Journal of Contingencies and Crisis Management*, 2, 146–54.

Turner, L., and Hodges, M. (1992), *Global Shakeout: World Market Competition and the Challenge for Business and Government* (London: Century Press).

Tylecote, A. (1992), *The Long Wave in the World Economy* (London: Routledge).

UN (1994), United Nations, *World Investment Report* (New York: United Nations).

—— (annual), *Yearbook of Industrial Statistics* (New York: United Nations).

UNDP (1991), United Nations Development Programme, *Human Development Report 1991* (Oxford: Oxford University Press).

UN/ECE (1986), United Nations/Economic Commission for Europe, *Recent Trends in Flexible Manufacturing* (New York: United Nations).

USNCTAEP (1966), United States National Commission on Technology, Automation, and Economic Progress, *Technology and the American Economy*. Report to the US Congress in 6 vols. (Washington, DC: US Government Printing Office).

US Bureau of Labor Statistics (1992), *Outlook 1990–2005: Projections of US Labor Force Occupations*. Bulletin 2402 (Washington, DC: US Government Printing Office).

US Department of Defense (1988), *Report of the Formal Investigation into the Circumstances Surrounding the Downing of Iran Air Flight 655 on 3 July 1988* (Washington, DC: US Government Printing Office).

Vallance, I. (1995), 'Policies for a European Information Society', in PICT (1995*a*), 16–18.

Van de Donk, W., and Tops, P. (1992), 'Informatization and Democracy: Orwell in Athens', in *Informatization and the Public Sector*, 2: 169–96.

Van de Donk, W., Snellen, I., and Tops, P. (1995) (eds.), *Orwell in Athens: A Perspective on Information and Democracy* (Amsterdam: IOS Press).

Bibliography

Vaughan, D. (1996), *The Challenger Launch Decision: Risky Technology, Culture and Deviance at NASA* (Chicago: University of Chicago).

Vehvilaïnen, M. (1991), 'Gender in Information Systems Development', in Eriksson *et al.* (1991), 247–62.

Vernon, M. K., Lazowska, E. D., and Personick, S. D. (1994) (eds.), *R&D for the NII: The Technical Challenges* (Washington, DC: Interuniversity Communications Council Inc.).

Veronis, Suhler and Associates (1993), *Communications Industry Forecast 1993–1997* (New York: Veronis, Suhler and Associates).

Vickers, Sir G. (1965), *The Art of Judgement* (London: Chapman Hall).

Vogel, H. L. (1995), *Entertainment Industry Economics* (New York: Cambridge University Press).

Wajcman, J., and Probert, B. (1988), 'New Technology Outwork', in Willis (1988), 51–67.

Walsh, V. (1993), 'Demand, Public Markets and Innovation in Biotechnology', *Science and Public Policy*, 20: 138–56.

Waters, R., and Cane, A. (1993), 'Sudden Death of a Runaway Bull', *Financial Times*, 19 Mar.: 11.

Webb, J. (1992), 'The Mismanagement of Innovation', *Sociology*, 26: 471–92.

Webster, F., and Robins, K. (1985), *Information Technology: A Luddite Analysis* (Norwood, NJ: Ablex).

Webster, J. (1990), *Office Automation: The Labour Process and Women's Work in Britain* (Hemel Hempstead: Harvester Wheatsheaf).

—— (1991), *Revolution in the Office? Information Technology and Work Organisation*. PICT Policy Research Paper No. 14 (Uxbridge: PICT, Brunel University).

—— (1993), 'Sado-Monetarism or Social Science? Social Studies of Technology in the 1990s'. Paper presented to the 1993 National PICT Conference, Kenilworth, Warwickshire.

—— (1995), *Information Technology, Women and their Work: Research Findings and Policy Issues*. PICT Policy Research Paper No. 30 (Uxbridge: PICT, Brunel University).

—— (1996), *Gender, Employment and Technology* (London: Longman).

—— and Williams, R. (1993), 'Mismatch and Tension: Standard Packages and Non-Standard Users', in Quintas (1993), 179–96.

WEFA Group (1993), *Economic Impact of Eliminating the Line-of-Business Restrictions on the Bell Companies* (Bala Cynwyd, Pa.: The WEFA Group).

Weingart, Peter (1984), 'The Structure of Technological Change', in Laudan (1984), 115–42.

Weizenbaum, J. (1976), *Computer Power and Human Reason: From Judgement to Calculation* (San Francisco: W. H. Freeman).

Wernecke, D. (1983), 'Women: The Vulnerable Group—Microelectronics at Work in the Office', *Employment Gazette*, Sept.: 392–5.

Westin, A., and Baker, M. A. (1972), *Databanks in a Free Society* (New York: Quadrangle Books).

Wiener, N. (1949), *The Human Use of Human Beings: A Cybernetics Approach* (New York: Houghton Mifflin).

Williams, F., and Pavlik, J. (1994) (eds.), *The Citizen's Right to Know: Media, Democracy and Electronic Information Services* (Hillsdale, NJ: Lawrence Erlbaum Associates).

Williams, R. (1976), *Keywords* (London: Fontana).

Williams, R. (1980a), 'Advertising: The Magic System', in Williams (1980b), 170–95.

—— (1980b), *Problems in Materialism and Culture: Selected Essays* (London: Verso).

—— and Edge, D. (forthcoming), 'The Social Shaping of Technology', *Research Policy*.

Willis, E. (1988) (ed.), *Technology and the Labour Process: Australian Case Studies* (Sydney: Allen & Unwin).

Wimsatt, W., and Beardsley, M. (1954), *The Verbal Icon: Studies in the Meaning of Poetry* (Lexington, Ky.: University of Kentucky Press).

Winner, L. (1977), *Autonomous Technology: Technics-Out-of-Control as a Theme in Political Thought* (Cambridge, Mass.: MIT Press).

Winner, L. (1985), 'Do Artefacts have Politics?', *Dædalus*, 109: 121–36.

—— (1993), 'Upon Opening the Black Box and Finding it Empty: Social Constructivism and the Philosophy of Technology', *Science, Technology and Human Values*, 18: 362–78.

Womack, J. P., Jones, D. T., and Roos, D. (1990), *The Machine that Changed the World* (Oxford: Maxwell Macmillan International).

Wood, S. (1982) (ed.), *The Degradation of Work? Skill, Deskilling and the Labour Process* (London: Hutchinson).

Woolgar, S. (1980), 'Discovery, Logic and Sequence in a Scientific Text', in Knorr *et al.* (1980), 239–68.

—— (1991a), 'The Turn to Technology in Social Studies of Science', *Science, Technology and Human Values*, 16: 20–50.

—— (1991b), 'Configuring the User', in Law (1991), 57–102.

—— (1993a), 'What's at Stake in the Sociology of Technology? A Reply to Pinch and to Winner', *Science, Technology and Human Values*, 18: 523–9.

—— (1993b), *The User Talks Back*. CRICT Discussion Paper No. 40 (Uxbridge: Brunel University).

World Bank (1991), *Development Report* (Washington, DC: World Bank).

—— (1993), *The East Asian Miracle* (Washington, DC: World Bank).

—— (1994), *World Development Report* (New York: Oxford University Press).

WTA (1992), World Teleport Association, *Membership Guide* (New York: WTA).

Zimbalist, A. (1979) (ed.), *Case Studies on the Labour Process* (New York: Monthly Review Press).

Zorkoczy, P. (1987) (ed.), *Oxford Surveys in Information Technology 4* (Oxford: Oxford University Press).

Zuboff, S. (1988), *In the Age of the Smart Machine: The Future of Work and Power* (New York: Basic Books).

Index

Index

bugs 72, 82–3, 178
Burnham, D. 52 n
Burnstein, D. 11
Business Process Re-engineering (BPR) 61, 162, 170–4, 175, 206; Business Process paradigm 173–4; in public sector 271–3, 275; 'soft' BPR 172–3

Cabinet Office 272; *see also* ITAP
Cable and Satellite Europe 248 n
cable TV 242, 297; and competition 388, 397; and regulation 110, 345, 347–8; in US 237, 388
Callon, M. 64, 65
CAMNET 261
Cane, A. 195 n
Carson, W. G. 192
Castell, S. 193
Castells, M. 52 n
Cawson, A. 43, 48
CCTA 405 n
CEA (Council of Economic Advisors) (US) 361, 364, 365
Central Policy Review Staff 145
Challenger space shuttle 195 n
Chambliss, W. 52 n
Champy, J. 282 n
change *see* organizational change; social change; technological change
Charter Technologies Ltd. 74–5
Chaum, D. 278, 296
Checkland, P. 168
Chenevière, Guillaume 246–7
China 29, 30, 31, 133, 153
Churbuck, D. C. 362
Cleland, G. 85 n
Clinton, Bill 388; Clinton Administration 274, 284–5, 286, 390–1, 393, 405 n; *see also* information superhighway
Cochrane, P. 251, 261
Cohn, A. 74, 75
Cole, B. G. 370 n
Colleran, E. K. 362, 364
Collins, H. M. 65, 70, 102 n
Collins, R. 243, 248 n
Committee on Women in Science, Engineering and Technology 155
communications *see* broadcasting; telecommunications infrastructure
Communications Act (1934) (US) 338
competition 6, 9, 219–20, 388, 397; benefits and costs 354–67, 368–9; international 319–33; and multimedia convergence 106–17, 306; and regulation 341–2, 343, 344–6, 347, 371–86, 401; and telecommunications infrastructures 250–1, 336, 341–2, 343–4, 353–70, 372–86; *see also* markets; monopolies
computer-aided design/computer-aided manufacture (CAD/CAM) 124, 139

Computer-Aided Despatch System 184, 185
Computer-Aided Software Engineering (CASE) 164, 189
computer-integrated manufacturing (CIM) 62, 134
Computer Numerical Control (CNC) 56, 58, 124, 139
computer-related disasters 7, 69–70, 71, 72, 177–95, 414–15; deaths 75, 178, 180; case studies 181–6; policies to minimize 190–4
Computer Supported Co-operative Work (CSCW) 162
computer systems verification 70, 71–3, 74–85; *see also* mathematical proof
computing, frameworks of 162–3, 164, 172
Comstock, G. 48
concordism 38, 39
configurational technology 62–3
Conservative government 397
Constructive Technology Assessment (CTA) model 54
consumption *see* access; domestic consumption; markets; users
continuism 38, 39, 41, 44, 47, 50, 393
convergence *see* multimedia convergence
Cooley, M. 100, 144
Coombs, R. 57, 162, 165, 172, 173
Cooper, D. 165
Cooper, G. 89, 93, 96, 101, 101 n
Cooper, M. 262
Corbett, M. 271
Corey, K. E. 343
Corner, J. 236
Cornford, D. 90, 163, 175 n
Cornford, J. 342, 405 n
Council of Europe 238, 296
Credé, A. 378, 386 n
Cringley, R. X. 119 n, 155
CRITO (Centre for Research on Information Technology and Organizations) 332 n, 333 n
Cronin, F. J. 338, 362, 364
Crosman, I. 101 n
CSE Microelectronics Group 145
Cullen, B. 375
cultural artefacts, ICTS as 87–102; social dimensions 87–91; technology as text 92–101
cultural determinism 238, 239, 240, 247
cultural imperialism 296–7
culture: culture gap 161, 169, 171; impact of satellite TV on 234, 235–6, 244–5; variations in 8
Curran, S. 145
Curtis, B. 101

DAEs (Dynamic Asian Economies) 25–31, 35
Dahlman, C. 320
Daniels, W. 44
Danziger, J. N. 5

Index

Index

Index

Printed in the United Kingdom
by Lightning Source UK Ltd.
339